SOCIETY FOR NEW TESTAMENT STUDIES
MONOGRAPH SERIES

GENERAL EDITOR
MATTHEW BLACK, D.D., F.B.A.

11

THE GOSPEL OF SIGNS

THE GOSPEL OF SIGNS

A RECONSTRUCTION OF THE
NARRATIVE SOURCE UNDERLYING
THE FOURTH GOSPEL

BY

ROBERT TOMSON FORTNA

Associate Professor of Religion
Vassar College

CAMBRIDGE
AT THE UNIVERSITY PRESS
1970

Published by the Syndics of the Cambridge University Press
Bentley House, 200 Euston Road, London N.W.1
American Branch: 32 East 57th Street, New York, N.Y. 10022

Library of Congress Catalogue Card Number: 74-93708

Standard Book Number: 521 07624 2

Printed in Great Britain
at the University Printing House, Cambridge
(Brooke Crutchley, University Printer)

To Evelyn

CONTENTS

vii

PREFACE

This study is occasioned by the recent emergence of *Redaktions-geschichte* as a method of gospel research. If, as that discipline proposes, an evangelist's purpose and meaning are to be investigated by examining his redaction of the sources available to him, it is obviously necessary to identify as objectively and distinctly as possible the exact form of a *Vorlage*. This is relatively simple in the case of Mt and Lk, whose sources are accessible to us. For Jn, as for Mk, however, it is necessary to reconstruct a source, if at all, primarily on the basis of data within the gospel. What is called for, now with special importance, is a renewed attempt at such a reconstruction in the case of the fourth gospel, and that is undertaken here for the narrative material. In a later work I hope to apply to the source reconstructed below the redaction-critical method which called it forth.

The present work is a version, somewhat revised, of a doctoral dissertation presented to the faculty of Union Theological Seminary, New York. It owes a great deal, at every stage of its evolution, to Professor J. Louis Martyn, who has been not only a critical and demanding 'doctor-father' but also a generous and uncomplaining friend. This study had its beginnings in his seminar on the fourth gospel, and it was in great measure from him that I learned the *wissenschaftlich* study of the New Testament in general and of the Gospel of John in particular.

To Professors J. M. Robinson and R. McL. Wilson I owe a very great debt of thanks for reading the MS in close detail and making many helpful suggestions.

I am indebted also to Professors W. D. Davies, Ernst Haenchen, John Knox, and George M. Landes for their advice and knowing criticism at a number of points.

I must thank two Vassar students, Miss Donna Bergen and Miss Alison Hilton, who as research assistants gave me a great deal of painstaking and loyal help in preparing the MS; Mrs Barbara Caswell, of the Vassar College Library, for her unfailing efforts in making available any book I needed, however far afield it lay; and Mrs Mildred Tubby, for skilfully typing so demanding a text. I am grateful to the Faculty Committee on Research of Vassar College for several grants in support of this work.

Finally I would give special thanks to my wife, to whom this book is affectionately dedicated and without whose patient moral support it could scarcely have been written.

R. T. F.

November 1968

Unless otherwise indicated, the Greek text of Jn which forms the basis of the source analysis is that of the 25th edition of Nestle.

ABBREVIATIONS

In this book 'John' represents the evangelist, and 'Jn' the gospel. 'Johannine' may pertain to either, but usually to the evangelist as opposed to the author of a source ('pre-Johannine') or a later editor ('post-Johannine'). 'SQ' sometimes refers to Bultmann's *Semeia-Quelle*, but more often to our corrected and expanded version of the pre-Johannine narrative source. The abbreviations for MSS of the NT are those of Nestle, even when a variant is found only in Tischendorf or *TGNT*.

AUTHORS

The following works are normally referred to by author only. Works listed in the bibliography at the beginning of any section are cited *in that section* by author alone, except where confusion would result.

Barrett: C. K. Barrett, *The gospel according to St John: An introduction with commentary and notes on the Greek text* (London, 1955).

Bauer: W. Bauer, *Das Johannesevangelium* (3rd ed.; Handbuch zum Neuen Testament, 6; Tübingen, 1933).

Brown: R. E. Brown, *The gospel according to John (i–xii)* (Anchor Bible, 29; Garden City, 1966).

Bultmann: R. Bultmann, *Das Evangelium des Johannes* (16th ed. with Ergänzungsheft; Meyers Kommentar; Göttingen, 1959).

Dodd: C. H. Dodd, *Historical tradition in the fourth gospel* (Cambridge, 1963).

Fuller: R. H. Fuller, *Interpreting the miracles* (Philadelphia, 1963).

Goguel: M. Goguel, *Introduction au Nouveau Testament*, 11 (Paris, 1923).

Hirsch: E. Hirsch, *Studien zum vierten Evangelium* (Beiträge zur historischen Theologie, 4; Tübingen, 1936).

Hoskyns: E. Hoskyns, *The fourth gospel*, ed. F. N. Davey (2nd ed. rev.; London, 1947).

Mollat: D. Mollat, *L'évangile de Saint Jean* (2nd ed.; Bible de Jérusalem; Paris, 1960).

Ruckstuhl: E. Ruckstuhl, *Die literarische Einheit des Johannes-evangeliums: Der gegenwärtige Stand der einschlägigen Forschungen* (Studia Friburgensia, n.s. 3; Freiburg in der Schweiz, 1951).

Schnackenburg: R. Schnackenburg, *Das Johannesevangelium, I. Teil: Einleitung und Kommentar zu Kap. 1–4* (Herders Theologischer Kommentar zum NT, IV; Freiburg, 1965).

Schwartz: E. Schwartz, 'Aporien im vierten Evangelium', in *Nachrichten von der Königlichen Gesellschaft der Wissenschaften zu Göttingen: Philologisch-historische Klasse* (1907), 342–72; (1908), 115–88, 497–650.

Schweizer: E. Schweizer, *Ego eimi...: Die religionsgeschichtliche Herkunft und theologische Bedeutung der johanneischen Bildreden* (*FRLANT* n.s. 38; Göttingen, 1939; 2nd ed. 1965).

Spitta: F. Spitta, *Das Johannes-Evangelium als Quelle der Geschichte Jesu* (Göttingen, 1910).

Wellhausen: J. Wellhausen, *Das Evangelium Johannis* (Berlin, 1908).

Wendt: H. H. Wendt, *Die Schichten im vierten Evangelium* (Göttingen, 1911).

Wilkens: W. Wilkens, *Die Entstehungsgeschichte des vierten Evangeliums* (Zollikon, 1958).

REFERENCE WORKS

Bl–D: F. Blass and A. Debrunner, *A Greek grammar of the New Testament and other early Christian literature*, tr. R. W. Funk (Chicago, 1961).

Nestle: Eberhard Nestle, ed., *Novum Testamentum Graece*, 25th ed. by Erwin Nestle and K. Aland (Stuttgart, 1963).

RGG: *Die Religion in Geschichte und Gegenwart* (Tübingen, 1909–13; 2nd ed. 1927–31; 3rd ed. 1956–62).

Str–B: H. L. Strack and P. Billerbeck, *Kommentar zum Neuen Testament aus Talmud und Midrasch*, vol. II (München, 1924).

TGNT: K. Aland, M. Black, B. Metzger and A. Wikgren, eds., *The Greek New Testament* (Stuttgart, 1966).

Tischendorf: C. Tischendorf, ed., *Novum Testamentum Graece*, 8th major critical ed., vol. I (Leipzig, 1872).

TWBzNT: G. Kittel, ed., *Theologisches Wörterbuch zum Neuen Testament* (Stuttgart, 1932–).

JOURNALS AND SERIES

Bib: Biblica
BJRL: Bulletin of the John Rylands Library
BVC: Bible et Vie Chrétienne
BZ: Biblische Zeitschrift
CBQ: Catholic Biblical Quarterly
CW: Die Christliche Welt
ET: Expository Times
EvTh: Evangelische Theologie
Exp: The Expositor
FRLANT: Forschungen zur Religion und Literatur des Alten und Neuen Testaments
HeyJ: Heythrop Journal
HJ: Hibbert Journal
HTR: Harvard Theological Review
JBL: Journal of Biblical Literature
JTS: Journal of Theological Studies
NovT: Novum Testamentum
NTS: New Testament Studies
RB: Revue Biblique
RThPh: Revue de Théologie et de Philosophie
SJT: Scottish Journal of Theology
StudEv: Studia Evangelica: Papers presented to the International Congresses on New Testament Studies
TB: Theologische Blätter
TL: Theologische Literaturzeitung
TR: Theologische Rundschau
TZ: Theologische Zeitschrift
VF: Verkündigung und Forschung: Theologischer Jahresbericht
ZNW: Zeitschrift für die Neutestamentliche Wissenschaft
ZTK: Zeitschrift für Theologie und Kirche

METHODOLOGICAL INTRODUCTION

The source criticism of John is hardly a new discipline; it has had a complex history, covering over three-quarters of a century.[1] And a study of that history is discouraging to any fresh contribution. It had, accountably, a later start than synoptic source analysis, and while it flourished vigorously for a time during the first half of this century, it has generally failed to produce a consensus,[2] and many seem now to regard

---

[1] For the history of Johannine literary criticism in general, see the following surveys: W. F. Howard, *The fourth gospel in recent criticism and interpretation*, ed. C. K. Barrett (4th ed. rev.; London, 1955), pts. i–ii and 297–303; Ph.-H. Menoud, *L'évangile de Jean d'après les recherches récentes* (2nd ed., Neuchâtel–Paris, 1947), 12–26, and 'Les études Johanniques de Bultmann à Barrett', in Boismard *et al.*, *L'évangile de Jean: Études et problèmes* (Recherches Bibliques, 3; Bruges, 1958), 11–40; W. G. Kümmel, *Introduction to the New Testament*, tr. A. J. Mattill, jr. (14th rev. ed. 'Founded by Paul Feine and Johannes Behm'; Nashville–New York, 1966), 139–54.

The course of Johannine source analysis in particular can be sketched by listing the principal authors, whether 'partitionist' or 'revisionist', and the dates of their principal works (see the Bibliography for titles): Delff (1890), Wendt (1900, 1911), Schwartz (1907, 1908), Wellhausen (1907, 1908), Bousset (1909, 1912), Spitta (1910), Goguel (1910, 1923), Bacon (1910, 1926), Moffatt (1911), Thompson (1915–17), Soltau (1916), Faure (1922), Garvie (1922), Hirsch (1936), Schweizer (1939), Jeremias (1941). With the first appearance, in 1941, of Rudolf Bultmann's commentary a kind of climax was reached. So exhaustive was his source theory, but at the same time so unacceptable in parts, that a kind of tacit moratorium was declared, with the result that since the Second World War there has been on the whole only a discussion of the problems raised by his work, and (since Ruckstuhl's study in 1951), a dwindling one at that: Dibelius (1942), Käsemann (1946), Behm (1948), Hirsch (1951), Mendner (1952), Noack (1954), Haenchen (1955, 1959), Bultmann (*RGG*, 3rd ed., 1959), D. M. Smith (1965). As these lists show, English-speaking scholars have contributed very little to the discussion; the several major studies of John to come out of England in the last quarter-century—those of Hoskyns (1940–7), Dodd (1953, 1963), Barrett (1955), and Lightfoot (1954 *posth.*)—have all avoided the source-critical question. The chief work to renew the enterprise is that of Wilkens (1958). There have also been a few recent attempts to find a *Vorlage* behind this passage or that—*e.g.* the articles of van Iersel (1: 19–36), Schnackenburg (4: 46–54), and Hartmann (ch. 20).

[2] There is one point, however, on which a growing number of critics agree: the existence of something like the *Semeia-Quelle* of Bultmann. See below, sec. 3.

the enterprise as abortive.[1] It will be the contention of the present study that what doomed the older research was its failure to give explicit treatment to methodological issues.[2] Therefore the present attempt to submit at least the narrative parts of the gospel once more to source analysis cannot begin without a detailed consideration of method, made against the background of earlier research and its seeming failures. What follows is only a prolegomenon to the source-critical task proper, but essential to it.

I. THE PLACE OF SOURCE CRITICISM IN FOURTH GOSPEL RESEARCH AND THE PRESUPPOSITIONS ENTAILED

The interpreter of John's gospel is confronted from the outset by a fundamental literary phenomenon, and one which, in degree at least, distinguishes that gospel from the other three, namely the presence of the so-called *aporias*—the many inconsistencies, disjunctures and hard connections, even contradictions—which the text shows, notably in the narrative portions, and which cannot be accounted for by textual criticism.[3]

At times it has been suggested that these phenomena are to

[1] *Cf. e.g.* Kümmel, *Introduction*, 153: '...it is improbable that the evangelist used any connected written sources (apart from the Synoptics)'.

[2] So perceives Ruckstuhl, vii.–As his subtitle indicates, S. Schulz, *Untersuchungen zur Menschensohn-Christologie im Johannesevangelium: Zugleich ein Beitrag zur Methodengeschichte der Auslegung des 4. Evangeliums* (Göttingen, 1957), 39–95, gives an extended treatment of method in Johannine research, but his appraisal of literary criticism (62–7) is a largely negative one. A recent beginning at filling the gap was made by H. M. Teeple, 'Methodology in source analysis of the fourth gospel', *JBL* 81 (1962), 279–86. *Cf.* also D. M. Smith, 'The sources of the gospel of John: An assessment of the present state of the problem', *NTS* 10 (1963/4), 336–51.–The continuing disinterest in the source criticism of Jn is due, however, more to the exaggerated claims of Ruckstuhl (to have shown it to be an invalid, or at the least futile, enterprise) than to an awareness of the methodological inadequacy of earlier work.

[3] So far as I know Schwartz was the first to apply the term 'aporia' to the Johannine material. While not in common use in English, the word is useful in the present study as a general term for the various phenomena in question. (See further Schulz, 64 f.) Recently E. C. Freed, 'Variations in the language and thought of John', *ZNW* 55 (1964), 167–97, and Brown, xxiv–xxv, have extended the discussion of these data.

be attributed to some defect in the evangelist, such as carelessness, unconcern for consistency, or senility.[1] Alternatively, theories have been advanced to the effect that the gospel as we have it is unfinished[2] or accidentally defective.[3] Such explanations cannot be ruled out, but they are counsels of despair. A more promising view, and one which has a claim to priority over those just cited, as we shall see, is that the unevenness of the text of John is due rather to *redaction*,[4] so that the aporias are indications—direct or indirect—of *editorial seams*.

Some have held that these seams are the result of the evangelist's joining together previously independent pericopes, units of oral tradition.[5] The fact, however, that the aporias group themselves into recurring patterns[6] suggests that the gospel as we have it is the product of a development involving *more than one literary stage*, the seams being due for the most part to the transition not from oral to literary form, but from one literary form to another.[7]

One cannot know in advance *how many* such stages in the gospel's literary history it will be necessary to postulate in order to account for the aporias. In fact some have held that John is the work of a number of authors, making complex, if not impossible, the task of identifying the various strata.[8] But while

---

[1] See further J. Behm, 'Der gegenwärtige Stand der Erforschung des Johannesevangeliums', *TL* 73 (1948), 21.

[2] Ph.-H. Menoud, 'Études johanniques', 15; W. Grundmann, *Zeugnis und Gestalt des Johannesevangeliums: Eine Studie zur denkerischen und gestalterischen Leistung des vierten Evangelisten* (Stuttgart, 1961), 6–8.

[3] See below, p. 7 n. 1, on page displacements.

[4] This term is used in a general way, and does not necessarily side with what used to be called theories of 'revision' as opposed to 'partition' (see B. W. Bacon, *The fourth gospel in research and debate* [New York, 1910], 481). That distinction was too sharply drawn. The redaction the gospel has undergone is obviously more than mere interpolation (as the 'partitionists' held), yet it is not a thoroughgoing recasting of the material (as 'revision' has sometimes been taken to mean). It will appear that something like J. Wellhausen's title of 1907 ('Expansions and alterations in the fourth gospel') correctly combines the two points of view and describes what we mean by redaction.

[5] Notably B. Noack, *Zur Johanneischen Tradition: Beiträge zur Kritik an der literarkritischen Analyse des vierten Evangeliums* (København, 1954).

[6] First noted in Schwartz.

[7] On Noack's fallacy, see further below, p. 12.

[8] An extreme instance is W. Soltau, *Das vierte Evangelium in seiner*

allowing for the possibility of multiple authorship, one must beware of unnecessarily complicating the critical task; furthermore justice must be done to the coherence and unity which are so clearly characteristics of the gospel, despite its many inconsistencies. Thus at the outset, and so long as the data permit, it will be useful to regard the gospel's formation as involving only two principal stages: *basic document* and *redaction*.[1]

It will be convenient to speak of this fundamental distinction between the two literary stages in another, and quite formal, way: as a distinction between *Johannine* and *non-Johannine* phases in the gospel's development, assuming for the sake of simplicity that there was a single person ('John') who gave to the gospel its unity and coherence, its 'Johannine' genius. (In calling this otherwise unknown author by the traditional name John, we do not hold any prior conception as to either his identity or the material in the gospel actually to be attributed to him.)[2]

As soon as this nominal distinction (Johannine/non-Johannine) is made, the question arises which of the two stages, the earlier or the later, *Grundschrift* or *Redaktion*, is to be regarded as

Entstehungsgeschichte dargelegt (Heidelberg, 1916), who nevertheless confidently assigns specific passages to each of the six stages he postulates; *cf.* also W. Hartke, *Vier urchristliche Parteien und ihre Vereinigung zur apostolischen Kirche*, 1: *Johannes und die Synoptiker* (Berlin, 1961). A far soberer but perhaps equally unmanageable hypothesis is that John is the work of a school of writers: K. Stendahl, *The school of St Matthew and its uses of the Old Testament* (Uppsala, 1954), 31, citing W. Heitmüller, 'Zur Johannes-Tradition', *ZNW* 15 (1914), esp. 207. See also the recent multiple-stage hypotheses adopted by O. Merlier, *Le quatrième évangile*, II: *Généralités—La question johannique* (Athènes, 1961), 405–32, and Brown, esp. xxxiv–xxxix.

[1] J. Jeremias, 'Johanneische Literarkritik', *TB* 20 (1941), 33–46, esp. 39, recognized the distinction between *Grundschrift* and *Redaktion* as fundamental to Johannine research. – Some have held that the gospel has been subject to successive rewriting by the same hand—most recently M.-É. Boismard, review of Schnackenburg and Brown, *RB* 74 (1967), 581–5. Such a hypothesis may be demanded for the discourses, but in the narrative material there is little if any evidence for more than two strata.

[2] Furthermore, there is of course no question here of implying anything as to the historical reliability of the gospel. Much of the early literary criticism (and, in a subtle way, some of the more recent as well) is hampered by the intrusion of the historical question. Thus 'John' has often been assumed to stand at the start of the process which produced the gospel; it will be an object of this study to show that he came rather at the end of it, or very nearly so.

the principal—that is, by definition, the Johannine—one. And according as one or the other, basic writing or its redaction, is assigned to John, two quite different views of the gospel's formation result. In one case we have a *Johannine gospel* which has been subjected to such *post-Johannine redaction* as to give rise to the aporias. In the other case we have one or more *pre-Johannine sources* (or a proto-gospel) which *John* has redacted but at the same time respected sufficiently to leave the aporias.

Each of these views of the gospel's formation-history demands its own method of investigation, the two methods differing from each other as to focus and goal.

On the *first* view (a Johannine original subsequently redacted) it is the task of the literary critic to *recover* the original gospel, buried under later redaction; interpretation is properly carried out primarily on this hypothetically reconstructed and expurgated document.[1]

It is perhaps not surprising that the majority of critics who ascribe the aporias to redaction have followed this course, taking the *Grundschrift* to be Johannine and assigning the disturbing elements in the extant gospel to a later hand. To look for the aporias at that stage is, superficially at least, a more promising approach, for it concentrates on what is the latest, so to speak the uppermost, and thus the most accessible, stratum in the gospel. But this advantage is only an apparent one.[2]

It is of course true that any ancient document is susceptible of corruption in its transmission, and no critic dares assume that he knows the gospel just as John left it. Furthermore it is possible, no doubt, to waste critical energy and imagination in seeking to understand obscurities not belonging to the original document. But it is invalid to *begin* by treating an obscurity as secondary. If for the textual critic the harder reading is often the better one where two or more witnesses differ, the exegete ought not to balk at some hard readings where the MSS are unanimous. The obscurity he would be inclined to excise as a

---

[1] Scholarship can of course focus on the post-Johannine stage of the gospel as itself of interest (much as Bultmann can examine the handling of the gospel by his hypothetical 'ecclesiastical redactor'), but this is secondary to the study of the original gospel.

[2] The alternative view to be proposed here, by assuming that post-Johannine scribal alterations are minor, also of course deals with the uppermost stratum, in this case the work of the evangelist.

gloss may in fact be a valuable clue to the evangelist's meaning, as that can be perceived through *his* handling of *earlier* material —and this observation brings us to the alternative conception of the gospel's development as outlined above.

The *second* view, namely that the aporias stem from John's redaction of one or more earlier sources, leads, like the first, to an attempt to uncover buried material. But here the intent is not to lay aside one of the two layers when they have been distinguished; on the contrary the analysis is made so as to allow detailed *comparison* of the two strata as a means of interpreting the gospel as a whole. This view may seem to disparage the work of the evangelist by assigning to him not the gospel itself but—to put it at its baldest—only the redaction of an earlier gospel. But with the emergence of the discipline of redaction criticism it is no longer possible to dismiss the redaction of a source, even of a gospel, as being less than gospel writing, authorship, in its own right, for then Matthew and Luke would not be evangelists any more than John.[1]

The contrast between these two views of the gospel's development involves, in a word, John's temporal relation to the non-Johannine material in the gospel: Is that material primarily *post*-Johannine, so that a comparison of the two strata tells us nothing about John's method or purpose? Or is it primarily *pre*-Johannine, so that John's reworking of it is directly relevant to our investigation of his gospel?

John can have been at the same time a redactor of earlier sources and the author of a work which was later re-edited.[2] But it may be of some methodological importance which alter-

---

[1] Brown, lxxxvii ff., distinguishes between the *author* ('whose ideas the book expresses' or, at least, 'the *authority* behind it') and the *writer*, so as to be true to ancient views of authorship. I prefer to use the terms interchangeably, as equivalent to *evangelist*; whatever labour of authorship preceded John's writing, in redacting his sources he himself was an author in the true sense.

[2] Thus Schnackenburg, 48 (as also Bultmann) holds that John should be thought of as occupying the middle point between earlier tradition or sources and later redaction. Of course it is as unlikely that John's work was not to some degree altered by later hands (if only those of scribes) as that he created his material *ex nihilo*; yet for the reasons given the transition from the pre-Johannine stage to the Johannine ought to be considered as the possible cause of aporias before opting for the Johannine/post-Johannine interval.

6

native is taken up first in trying to explain any particular aporia. If the explanation is sought in post-Johannine revision, the problem seems to solve itself—the obtrusive element is somehow identified and then ignored—possibly quite prematurely. On the other hand, if we seek the aporia's resolution in the Johannine revision of a source, while confronted by all the problems inherent in postulating a hypothetical document, we do not assume that the gospel has acquired major late accretions which must be eliminated. Nothing then is irrelevant to the interpretation of the gospel; even that which is non-Johannine has come to us only as the result of John's selection and so is significant for an understanding of his meaning. And the aporias are not corruptions of the Johannine original, but themselves Johannine—the very products (or rather by-products) of his work: in considering them we are dealing still with his authorship.[1]

---

[1] An illustration of the premature recourse to post-Johannine revision to explain the aporias is to be found in the theories of *accidental displacement* of the text (that is, page rearrangement) that are widely held in one form or another. While the aporias on which such theories are based could be expected to be considerably more glaring than those attributed to intentional redaction, in fact that is not the case. For example, the inconsistencies in itinerary at 5: 1 (Jesus' abrupt journey to Jerusalem) and 6: 1 (his unaccountable departure 'across the Sea of Galilee')—the aporias most often ascribed to accidental dislocation—are no more serious than that presented by 4: 54 ('This was the second sign that Jesus did...') after the signs mentioned at 2: 11, 23, and 3: 2. Similarly, the sudden departure at 5: 1 is no more abrupt than that at 2: 13, nor the geographical inconsistency of 6: 1 different from that at 3: 22. So long as possible, then, the state of the gospel as we have it should be treated as possibly intentional on the evangelist's part, the attempt being made to view the aporias as unavoidable difficulties arising from his redaction of a source and, at the same time, as valuable clues to his intention. This can be asserted solely on considerations of method, apart from the fact that 'while the proposed alterations generally improve some connections, they often worsen others' (Barrett, 20).

The importance of this methodological principle can be further illustrated in the case of the *twenty-first chapter* of Jn, a chapter widely held to be post-Johannine or at the earliest a postscript by John himself. Ideological differences between the chapter and the rest of the gospel are undoubtedly the chief basis for the usual view, and these in the end may be decisive. The only literary basis for the view is the apparent redundancy of the last two verses of ch. 20 and 21: 25. There is no question that the end of ch. 20, in its present location, poses an exegetical problem; but to solve it by holding that the whole of ch. 21 is not original (rather than simply its last verse, missing

Theoretically, then, source criticism as a means of explaining the gospel's aporias would appear to have a place in Johannine studies, and a place which from a procedural standpoint ought to be prior to hypotheses of post-Johannine redaction. And, as we have seen, the source-critical enterprise is itself a hypothetical one, entailing certain assumptions—ones which it is appropriate, by way of summary, to enumerate at this point. A source analysis of the narratives in Jn presupposes, so long as it is feasible to do so, that (*a*) *the gospel is the work of one principal author* ('John'), (*b*) *whose work substantially we have, and* (*c*) *who in the course of editing earlier material produced some or all of the aporias which the present text displays.*[1]

The would-be source critic of John may be confronted with either of two objections to his project which are so fundamental as to demand consideration before we go further—namely that the source analysis of John is either *unnecessary* or *impossible.*

The former objection can be put very simply: there is no need to try to reconstruct John's sources; we already possess them in the form of the synoptic gospels, at least one, and possibly all, of which John knew and used.

If it is true that John is dependent only on the other gospels known to us—as came to be widely assumed once belief in the apostolic authorship of the gospel was relinquished—the source-critical enterprise is not only simplified but virtually obviated. Beyond seeking to determine which of the synoptics John knew, it has lost all usefulness for the interpretation of the gospel. For if John knew the synoptics, he certainly did not use them as sources in any extended sense; and a comparison of his gospel with them leads to only the most tentative suppositions as to

in ℵ*) is possibly too drastic. It may be that an important segment of the evangelist's work is thereby overlooked (*cf.* Hoskyns, 561 f.) and that the anomaly of 20: 30 f. can better be explained by a theory of source redaction. (The present study does not necessarily presuppose the authenticity of ch. 21, but the methodological questions here under investigation at least raise doubt about the confidence with which the chapter's inauthenticity is sometimes taken for granted.)

[1] The synoptic gospels show a few aporias (*e.g.* Mk 2: 10, 14: 2, 12; Mt 22: 7; Lk 17: 11), but they are less numerous and in most cases less prominent than John's. This only means that his relation to the source material and his procedure in dealing with it are different from those of the other evangelists.

why he both varied so radically from, and yet at times reproduced so carefully, what he found in them—as the inconclusive
debate earlier in this century over the question of his purpose
with respect to them shows: Was it to interpret (Baur), to
supplement (Zahn, Goguel), to supplant (Windisch), or to
correct them (Bacon, Colwell)?[1]

That debate was all but cut off in 1938 by the attack of
Gardner-Smith on theories of dependence. Since then there has
grown up a new and much more lively debate (Was John in fact
dependent on the synoptics?), carried on largely in terms of
a single criterion, that of verbal parallels.[2] But the results of this

[1] F. C. Baur, *Kritische Untersuchungen über die kanonischen Evangelien, ihr
Verhältniss zu einander, ihren Charakter und Ursprung* (Tübingen, 1847), 239–80;
T. Zahn, *Einleitung in das Neue Testament*, II (2nd ed.; Leipzig, 1900), 500, 529;
Goguel, 215–26; H. Windisch, *Johannes und die Synoptiker: Wollte der vierte
Evangelist die älteren Evangelien ergänzen oder ersetzen?* (Untersuchungen zum
NT, 12; Leipzig, 1926); B. W. Bacon, 'Sources and method of the fourth
evangelist', *HJ* 25 (1926/7), 115–30; E. C. Colwell, *John defends the gospel*
(Chicago, 1936).

[2] The principal literature (arranged chronologically): P. Gardner-
Smith, *Saint John and the synoptic gospels* (Cambridge, 1938); Hoskyns, 58–85
(first published in 1940); E. R. Goodenough, 'John a primitive gospel', *JBL*
64 (1945), 145–82; R. P. Casey, 'Professor Goodenough and the fourth
gospel', *ibid.* 535–42; Menoud, *L'évangile*, 2nd ed., 27–9; E. Osty, 'Les
points de contact entre le récit de la passion dans saint Luc et dans saint
Jean', *Mélanges Jules Lebreton*, I (Recherches de science religieuse, 39;
Paris, 1951), 146–54; H. F. D. Sparks, 'St John's knowledge of Matthew:
The evidence of John 13: 16 and 15: 20', *JTS* n.s. 3 (1952), 58–61;
Gardner-Smith, 'St John's knowledge of Matthew', *JTS* n.s. 4 (1953),
31–5; C. H. Dodd, *The interpretation of the fourth gospel* (Cambridge, 1953),
449; W. Michaelis, *Einleitung in das Neue Testament* (2nd ed.; Bern, 1954),
101–5; Noack, *Tradition*, 89–125; I. Buse, 'John v. 8 and Johannine-
Marcan relationships', *NTS* 1 (1954/5), 134–6; Barrett, 14–16, 34–45;
Bultmann, review of Noack's *Tradition*, *TL* 80 (1955), 524; R. H. Lightfoot,
St John's gospel: A commentary (ed. C. F. Evans; Oxford, 1956), 26–42;
E. K. Lee, 'St Mark and the fourth gospel', *NTS* 3 (1956/7), 50–8; Buse,
'St John and the Marcan passion narrative', *NTS* 4 (1957/8), 215–19;
S. Mendner, 'Zum Problem "Johannes und die Synoptiker"', *ibid.* 282–307;
P. Borgen, 'John and the synoptics in the passion narrative', *NTS* 5
(1958/9), 246–59; E. Haenchen, 'Johanneische Probleme', *ZTK* 56 (1959),
19–54; Buse, 'St John and "The first synoptic pericope"', *NovT* 3 (1959),
57–61; also 'St John and the passion narratives of St Matthew and St
Luke', *NTS* 7 (1960/1), 65–76; W. Wilkens, 'Evangelist und Tradition im
Johannesevangelium', *TZ* 16 (1960), 81–90; S. Temple, 'The two traditions of the last supper, betrayal, and arrest', *NTS* 7 (1960/1), 77–85; E. D.

intricate exchange are somewhat unclear: do the parallels prove the dependence of John on the synoptics themselves[1] or only on synoptic tradition? Does Johannine divergence necessarily mean independence?[2] The bulk of opinion seems now to favour John's independence (but not necessarily ignorance) of the synoptics, though several recent and important works reaffirm dependence.[3] In any case, it is no longer possible simply to assume dependence, and if that is so the mere possibility that John used one or more of the synoptics cannot be held as an objection to Johannine source criticism.[4] On the

Freed, 'The entry into Jerusalem in the gospel of John', *JBL* 80 (1961), 329–38; E. Johnston, 'The Johannine version of the feeding of the five thousand: An independent tradition?', *NTS* 8 (1961/2), 151–4; M.-É. Boismard, 'Saint Luc et la rédaction du quatrième évangile (Jn 4: 46–54)', *RB* 69 (1962), 185–211; D. M. Smith, 'John 12: 12 ff. and the question of John's use of the synoptics', *JBL* 82 (1963), 58–64; J. A. Bailey, *The traditions common to the gospels of Luke and John* (Supplements to *NovT*, 7; Leiden, 1963); Dodd, *Tradition*, 1–30; H. Balmforth, 'The structure of the fourth gospel', *StudEv* II (1964), 25–33; L. Morris, 'Synoptic themes illuminated by the fourth gospel', *ibid.* 73–84; R. E. Brown, *New Testament essays* (Milwaukee, 1965), 143–213; Schnackenburg, 15–32; W. G. Kümmel, *Introduction*, 142–5; Brown, xliv–xlvii.

[1] Or *vice versa*: *cf.* F. C. Grant, 'Was the author of John dependent upon the gospel of Luke?', *JBL* 56 (1937), 285–307; Osty, 'Points de contact'. Boismard, 'Rédaction', holds that the evangelist Luke redacted John's gospel.

[2] Some consider it foolish to resort to a hypothetical tradition or source, when John's dependence on the gospels which we know would account for the similarities and his *Tendenz* for the differences; on the other hand Gardner-Smith argues that in the face of all the divergences, literary dependence as an explanation of a few parallels is a 'superfluous hypothesis' ('Matthew', 35).–The situation is analogous to the question of the early Fathers' knowledge and/or use of the individual gospels—see H. Köster, *Synoptische Überlieferung bei den apostolischen Vätern* (Berlin, 1957), and the review by R. McL. Wilson in *NTS* 5 (1958/9), 144–6.

[3] Notably the commentaries of Barrett and Lightfoot. Kümmel, *Introduction*, holds that John was acquainted with Mark and Luke but not in any strict sense dependent on them. At the same time some hold that John could *not* have known the synoptics since in several units of material (especially in the passion narrative) he seems to have known only the sources used by the synoptists (as they can be reconstructed independently) and not the redactional elements added by the evangelists—see Buse, 'Marcan passion narrative' and 'Matthew and Luke'; Temple, 'Two traditions'; Haenchen, 'Probleme'; and D. Daube, *The New Testament and Rabbinic Judaism* (Jordan Lectures 1952; London, 1956), 313–20.

[4] The questions of John's use of the synoptics, on one hand, and of non-extant sources, on the other, ought to be kept distinct. C. Goodwin, 'How

contrary, if the source-critical question can be answered, it then solves the question of John's relation to the synoptics. For if it is possible to identify a pre-Johannine form of John's synoptic pericopes which has significant differences from the synoptic gospels themselves, it is then possible to explain the peculiar combination of similarities and dissimilarities which a comparison of his version of the material with theirs shows: 'the similarities would be conveniently explained by the supposition that the [source] appealed to the same tradition as the synoptic gospels [and] the differences would be ascribed to the special transmission-history of this source...'[1]

The *second* objection likely to be raised to a resumption of Johannine source analysis—that it is an impossible undertaking—takes two forms, arguing from John's use of the Old Testament and from the stylistic unity of the gospel, respectively.

did John treat his sources?', *JBL* 73 (1954), 61–75, rightly points out (74) that it is invalid to deny John's knowledge of the synoptics *in order to* be able to carry out a source- or form-critical analysis; but he is incorrect in holding (61) that 'consistency requires' those who postulate lost sources to make such a denial and in conversely concluding (74 n. 33), from what he considers the likelihood that John used the synoptics, that he probably did not depend on other sources—a *non sequitur*.

[1] As Noack, *Tradition*, 113, demands of a source theory. There are of course other ways of accounting for the presence of synoptic material in Jn:

1. Post-Johannine assimilation to the synoptics. It is inherently likely that some harmonization has taken place in the transmission of the text of Jn, as of the texts of the other gospels (*cf.* Hoskyns, 71, who cites the whole of 12: 8 and a variant in 6: 19). But it is impossible to account for all the synoptic material, or even a major part of it, in this way. S. Mendner, the chief exponent of this view, is forced to postulate a very complex interaction between the continuing synoptic and Johannine *traditions* after the appearance of the written gospels and before the harmonizers set to work. And he cannot explain why a harmonizer would work to increase disharmony, for example by placing the cleansing of the temple episode in an utterly non-synoptic position in Jn. (See the Bibliography for Mendner's articles; also those of Osty and Boismard.)

2. Intermingling of synoptic and Johannine traditions in the pre-literary stage (*cf.* Borgen, 'Passion narrative', and especially Dodd). That this also has occurred is entirely likely; but recourse simply to oral tradition will not account for all the data, in particular for the presence of both non-synoptic *and* non-Johannine elements in the synoptic passages within the fourth gospel—elements which seem to require the existence of a third, intermediary, stage in the development of the material, such as a pre-Johannine source (so Jeremias, 'Literarkritik', 46).

John may not have used the synoptic gospels, but he certainly made use of the Old Testament. From that use can we deduce anything about how he might have used a source now lost to us? Charles Goodwin has maintained, in a much-cited article,[1] that since John's quotation of Old Testament passages is so inexact, and for no apparent reason, it is unlikely that he would have treated other sources with greater respect. Therefore 'we must despair', he held, 'of any attempt to reconstruct them from his text' (73); there is doubt even that 'John was constitutionally capable of holding a source before him and copying it *verbatim*' (61), and John's use of the synoptic gospels—which Goodwin considers likely—confirms this (74 f.). Bent Noack has taken much the same position, going on to deny the likelihood that John used any written sources, and holding instead that he worked only from oral materials, even for his Old Testament quotations.[2]

There is a fallacy in both these positions, namely that the Old Testament can be called a source, in any sense analogous to a lost document which John might have followed, so that John's 'respect' for the two kinds of material can be compared.[3] Undoubtedly the Old Testament had a considerable influence on John's—as on all of the evangelists'—thought, and provided an important authority which he could refer to, however allusively.[4] But unlike a gospel source in the strict sense it is a vast body of material, mostly irrelevant to an evangelist's purpose; even a collection of Christian *testimonia* could hardly be called a source which an author might follow.

The question whether John's use of the Old Testament might aid in the search for a lost source needed to be raised; but the negative answer which it must receive in no way argues against the possibility of making that search. And Goodwin is not justified in calling in John's alleged treatment of the synoptic gospels to support his argument, in view of the present uncertainty as to the evangelist's relation to them.

---

[1] 'Sources.'   [2] *Tradition*, 71–89.

[3] *Cf.* Goodwin's only partly whimsical dictum that 'any critic who undertakes to reconstruct the lost sources of the Fourth Gospel should first prove his competence for the task by showing how, if the OT were lost, he could reconstruct it from John's quotations from it' (74).

[4] *Cf.* C. K. Barrett, 'The Old Testament in the fourth gospel', *JTS* 48 (1947/8), 155–69; see also Stendahl, *School*, 162 f.

The other basis for holding a source reconstruction impossible
—namely the stylistic unity of John—is a more serious objection
and has probably served more than anything to bring about the
decline in Johannine source criticism since the time of Bultmann.
On the basis of a statistical examination of linguistic style in the
gospel, made first by Schweizer, supplemented with suggestions
from Jeremias and Menoud, and then thoroughly revised and
extended by Ruckstuhl,[1] it has come to seem hopeless to most
critics to pursue any longer the source question in Johannine
studies. For each of the various source theories tested (namely
those of Spitta, Wendt, Hirsch, and Bultmann)[2] is shown by
such an examination to be inexact at best and at worst quite
fanciful; in every case there is not sufficient difference between
the style of the putative source and that of the rest of the gospel
to support the theory that the source as reconstructed in fact
existed. While a certain amount of blurring of style between
source and its redaction is probably to be expected, due to the
redactor's imitation of the source's style,[3] the style characteristics selected by Schweizer and his successors are for the
most part just those which are not easily imitated but rather
represent unconscious linguistic habits.

Thus have the major attempts at Johannine source analysis
during the first half of this century foundered on the basis of an
objective test; and with their failure there has grown up the
belief that Johannine source analysis is pointless, so unified is the
present style of John.[4] Ruckstuhl in fact maintained that *no*
sources underlie the gospel. But this goes beyond the evidence
which the statistical data provide. Schweizer, in his recently
revised edition, corrects the excessive claims of his successor,
noting that only a source analysis *carried out on the basis of style
characteristics* is ruled out by the gospel's stylistic unity.[5] As a
matter of fact, it should be noted that 'stylistic unity' has no

---

[1] Schweizer, pt. III; Jeremias, 'Literarkritik'; Menoud, *L'évangile*, 12 f.;
Ruckstuhl, pt. II.　　　　　　　　　　[2] See above, p. 1 n. 1.

[3] So Hirsch, 'Stilkritik und Literaranalyse im vierten Evangelium',
ZNW 43 (1950/1), 129, answering Schweizer; *cf.* S. Mendner, 'Johanneische
Literarkritik', *TZ* 8 (1952), 418–34.

[4] *Cf.* Freed, 'Variations', 196.

[5] *Ego eimi*, 2nd ed., vi. While this is strictly true, and is taken into account
in the present study, it does not rule out the use of stylistic criteria altogether.
See below, sec. 2 (*b*).

meaning in any absolute sense. That the gospel is not made up of blocks of material, which on stylistic grounds can be assigned to different strata, is clear; in that sense its style is unified. But if, as is demonstrable, John has redacted his source material internally, and not in a crude scissors-and-paste fashion, *some* of the style characteristics which appear to pervade the gospel and give it its unity may in fact turn out to stem from John's detailed redaction, but *others* from a source underlying the gospel, once it has been properly reconstructed and separated from the rest of the gospel.[1] The stylistic tests, then, can serve to confirm or cast doubt upon a particular source theory—subsequent to its appearance. The failure of earlier theories shows the potential source critic today that his task is not an easy one; it does not show it to be impossible. In fact, as the present study hopes to demonstrate, ordinarily John's redaction, while pervasive, in that it may appear at any point in a story, is not in any sense a rewriting; it may have the effect of radically changing a passage's meaning, but it usually consists in what can be called 'slight retouching'.[2]

The recent promising attempts to investigate form-critically the *tradition* behind the fourth gospel,[3] which stem from a desire to find a new and more fruitful direction for Johannine studies, are not invalidated by a renewed source criticism, for they deal with the material which lies behind any sources that John might have used, as well as with any pre-literary tradition directly available to him. It is, on the other hand, improper to go directly to that material without raising the question of sources.[4] And a project such as that undertaken here can

---

[1] Thus a judgment (by no means uncommon) such as that of H. N. Ridderbos, 'The structure and scope of the prologue to the gospel of John', *NovT* 8 (1966), 188 f., that the style characteristics 'are scattered over the whole Gospel with such frequency and evenness that in general the literary unity can no longer be called into question', is quite invalid.

[2] R. Schnackenburg, '*Zur Traditionsgeschichte von Joh 4, 46–54*', *BZ* n.s. 8 (1964), 63.

[3] Notably those of Noack and Dodd; also S. Schulz, *Untersuchungen. Cf.* Schnackenburg, 1, 46–60.

[4] Dodd's failure to do so is puzzling and disappointing. Noack's exclusive preoccupation with the oral stage of John's tradition is due to a rigid (and invalid) principle of breaking every pericope into the smallest possible units (*Tradition*, 18); *cf.* Bultmann's review in *TL* 80 (1955), 521, and E. Haenchen, 'Probleme', 22 n. 2.

perhaps hope to close the gap at certain points between the gospel of John, in all its concreteness, and 'Johannine tradition' as it is somewhat amorphously reconstructed.

If we have now sufficiently defined the place of source analysis in Johannine research, we may proceed to a consideration of the chief methodological stumbling block in earlier source analyses, the question of criteria.

2. CRITERIA FOR THE SOURCE ANALYSIS OF JOHANNINE NARRATIVE[1]

Source criticism of the New Testament grew out of Pentateuchal literary analysis, and that discipline used a variety of criteria for distinguishing the strata, criteria which for our purposes may be classified into three types: (1) *ideological*[2] (for example, attitude toward sacrifice or the covenant, genealogical interest, northern or southern loyalty), (2) *stylistic* (for example, use of the divine names, novelistic [JE] or formal style [P]), and (3) *contextual* (for example, parallel stories of creation, contradictions in the flood story). In Old Testament research these types were hardly defined or distinguished from one another,[3] but all of them played a part, and it is not surprising that the same three kinds of criteria are those with which we have to do in analysing the narratives of John's gospel.[4]

[1] For the exclusion of the discourse material, see below, p. 22, esp. n. 4.

[2] I use this term, as a rough equivalent for the somewhat more general German *sachlich*, to indicate criteria which have to do with the material content, and very often the theological substance, of a passage.

[3] But *cf.* now in retrospect O. Eissfeldt, *The Old Testament: An introduction...*, tr. P. R. Ackroyd (New York and Evanston, 1965), 182–8. His four 'arguments for analysis'—*viz.* changes in the divine names, linguistic usage, diversity of ideas, 'literary phenomena'—are readily identified with the criteria we discuss here: his first two with our stylistic, the third and fourth with our ideological and contextual, respectively.

[4] B. H. Streeter, *The four gospels: A study of origins...* (New York, 1925), 378, maintains that no analogy between Old Testament and Johannine literary criticism can obtain since the Pentateuch combines strands widely different from each other in origin, date, and point of view, whereas the Johannine sources (*sc.* the synoptics) are interrelated. But we cannot thus assume what John's sources were. And in any case the task with respect to the fourth gospel is one of separating the pre-Johannine and Johannine

(a) Ideological

The readiest criterion, and the earliest to have been applied to the Johannine literary question, is that which deals with the content of the text: ideas and themes, terminology (where it is not a purely stylistic matter), theological points of view, *Tendenzen*.[1]

Bultmann has maintained that it is both possible and necessary to define the theological tendency of the evangelist, though perhaps not of the source, before source analysis begins.[2] And he is probably more capable than most of an almost intuitive perception of what is distinctively Johannine. Nevertheless, such an approach unavoidably involves a logical circle. The source analysis of John is undertaken precisely so as to enable us to perceive John's own theology more sharply, by observing his way of redacting earlier material; but to the extent that prior assumptions as to his theological slant have affected the isolation of that material the definition of his theology is deprived of objectivity.

It is a safe working principle that no two authors have precisely the same point of view, so that anyone who adapts an earlier work, however careful he may be to reproduce or even

strata, so that no analogy between the *character* of John's sources and those of the compiler of the Pentateuch need hold; if merely the present literary disjunctures in John are in any way analogous to those in the Pentateuch (as of course they are), the methods for distinguishing literary layers in the latter can be applied to the former. – Teeple, 'Methodology', 283–5, lists four criteria for the gospel as a whole (syntax, vocabulary, ideas or points of view, poetic rhythm); the last of these does not apply to the narrative material, and the rest can be subsumed under our stylistic or ideological criteria. – I am to some extent dependent on D. M. Smith, *The composition and order of the fourth gospel: Bultmann's literary theory* (New Haven and London, 1965), 7–12, for the classification of criteria used here.

1 A considerable list of such elements which have provided the basis for earlier source reconstructions could be drawn up. It would include the following: the beloved disciple; Jesus' sonship, pre-existence, and heavenly origin; 'works' *vs.* 'signs'; messianism; ways of citing the Old Testament; eschatology; the nature of faith.

2 'Das Johannesevangelium in der neuesten Forschung', *CW* 41 (1927), 502–11; 'Hirsch's Auslegung des Johannesevangeliums', *EvTh* 4 (1937), 115–42 (in which he criticizes Hirsch's analysis just because it proceeds on an incorrect prior understanding of John's theology—*cf.* especially sec. 3); most recently 'Johannesevangelium', *RGG*, 3rd ed. III (1959), 842.

imitate it, will nevertheless at times exhibit disagreement with it, if only implicitly or unwittingly. In so far as this disagreement is *discernible*, it will offer clues to the separation of the various conceptual elements;[1] but it is just here that two difficulties arise.

On the one hand, our basis for discerning real ideological stratification, prior to an actual separation of the strata, is inadequate. For an author's thought, especially in the case of a subtle theologian such as John seems to have been, may itself contain inner tensions which only appear to be contradictions. And on the other hand, even a tension correctly singled out as due to redaction is not always resolved so readily that its constituent poles can confidently be ascribed, in isolation from other data, one to the pre-Johannine and one to the Johannine layer: it is sometimes not clear which idea is the uppermost from a literary standpoint, for to assign the less 'primitive' one to John, even when it can be determined without subjectivity, is not always valid.

It is thus clear that ideological data are not very exact criteria for source reconstruction. The fact that so many critics, while arriving at differing conclusions, find the same *sachlich* tensions to exist in John suggests that these are not to be rejected as imaginary, but somehow correspond to a real compositional complexity in the gospel. But these data will at best emerge as the analysis is carried out, and come to have a kind of cumulative force in the argument; sometimes they will only pose questions to be answered after the analysis is complete. In either case they do not provide an exclusive tool for carrying out the analysis.

(b) Stylistic

Because the use of tests involving style characteristics has brought about the downfall of the major source reconstructions of the past half-century, it would seem on the face of it that such characteristics can hardly serve as criteria for a new source analysis. And such, as we have seen, is the relatively modest claim made by Schweizer (as over against Ruckstuhl) for the stylistic tests of the sort he devised.[2] It is certainly true that

---

[1] See further below, (c), on contextual criteria.
[2] See above, p. 13.

stylistic data, by themselves, cannot serve as the basis for a reconstruction since, as in the case of ideological ones, we cannot know in advance which characteristics are Johannine and which pre-Johannine.[1] And the elaborate attempts by both Schweizer (100–2) and Ruckstuhl (205–12) to find clusters of style characteristics in the text of Jn as it stands quite clearly have failed: the various elements of style which distinguish the gospel from the other New Testament writings do not naturally sort themselves into two or more lists which might be labelled Johannine and pre-Johannine respectively.

It is nevertheless possible that as the source analysis unfolds certain usages will appear to be characteristic of the source, appearing only rarely, if ever, in the material assigned on other grounds to the evangelist, and then only in imitation of the source; and other (perhaps more numerous) usages will appear characteristic of the evangelist's redaction of earlier material.[2] If this proves to be the case, then we shall be able to draw more and more on stylistic criteria, being careful, however, never to depend on them primarily, or to such an extent that later stylistic tests of our reconstruction will be vitiated by circularity.

A general verdict on the validity of stylistic criteria is that while somewhat less subjective than ideological ones, they too are inconclusive by themselves. A clear result of Schweizer's work would seem to be that if sources have been used by John they have been so re-edited as to contain his own style charac-

[1] From the start ('Forschung', 503), Bultmann has maintained that a stylistic, just as a theological, foundation for Johannine source criticism is necessary, and throughout his commentary he draws on a considerable list of usages which he ascribes to the evangelist (Smith, *Composition*, 9–11, lists thirty-two). In his recent encyclopaedia article, he explains how these are to be discovered: by observing the style of the transitional passages and editorial comments in the gospel (*RGG*, 842); it is evident, however, that only a fraction of the stylistic criteria he uses can be so based.

[2] It is undoubtedly in this way that Bultmann arrives at his catalogue of Johannine style characteristics; but Ruckstuhl's suspicion (105) that Bultmann has assigned the stylistically distinctive (*geprägt*) material to John and divided the 'neutral, colourless remainder' among the sources is sometimes justified; it is noteworthy that he is unable to define the style of the narrative sources with anything like the same clarity and detail as emerges from his treatment of John's style. For this reason, and because our analysis of particular passages will often differ substantially from his, we cannot lean on Bultmann's list, but must build up our own as we go along.

teristics; in this sense the gospel has stylistic unity. Due to this detailed intermingling of Johannine and pre-Johannine elements within the blocks of material which as units stem from the source, and due also to the possibility, already mentioned, of Johannine imitations of the source's style, the procedure of source analysis will often be an intricate and difficult one. It must be reiterated, however, that the discouraging results of the stylistic tests as applied to earlier source reconstructions do not *per se* argue against a new attempt: even a few mistakenly assigned words or phrases scattered through a hypothetical source would considerably blur its stylistic purity as that is defined statistically.[1] And it must be remembered that the 'Johannine' *Stileigentümlichkeiten* which Schweizer and Ruckstuhl use are not necessarily Johannine in the strict sense. They are called Johannine only in the sense that they are characteristic of the gospel as a whole, compared to the rest of the New Testament; some may turn out in fact to be pre-Johannine.

Ideological and stylistic criteria can often complement and correct each other;[2] but there is a third kind of criterion which presupposes the other two, yet is somewhat more objective and does not depend on prior decisions as to what is Johannine, and to this we now turn our attention.

(c) Contextual

The contextual evidence for John's use of sources, that is, the presence of the many aporias, which pose a major aspect of the 'Johannine problem'—such data are the best, and the least adequately exploited, criteria for the source analysis. It has always been clear that difficulties present themselves in the

---

[1] It is this kind of detailed correction of Bultmann's analysis which is proposed at a number of points in the present study.

[2] *Cf.* P. W. Meyer, 'The eschatology of the fourth gospel: A study in early Christian reinterpretation' (unpublished ThD dissertation, Union Theological Seminary; New York, 1955), 230: 'Criticism based on style alone has a tendency to make artificial divisions and to conjecture literary forms without parallel; conversely, theological criticism by itself tends to produce subjective results and to depend too much on a preconceived or arbitrary notion of the theological nature of a given author's prototype or source.' *Cf.* also G. von Rad, *Genesis: A commentary*, tr. J. H. Marks (London, 1961), 73: 'Literary criticism must go hand in hand with criticism of the subject matter.'

2-2

narrative portions of Jn, but it is not recognized that they themselves contain the means to their own solution. Critics have too often seized on one or more ideological or stylistic elements in the gospel as the key to the whole.[1] Bultmann, following Schwartz, gives the aporias their proper emphasis; yet he too, like Schwartz, improperly brings preconceived theological and stylistic judgments into the discussion, as we have seen. More recently Wilkens has virtually limited himself to contextual evidence and thus neatly demonstrated that strata can be made to emerge by letting the many aporias play against each other without specific *sachlich* or stylistic presuppositions.[2] The details of his reconstruction are not always acceptable, due to the other presuppositions he holds, but he exploits better than any other the possibilities of this method.

The technique is of course no automatic one; imagination and experimentation are required in applying it. Nor can the other criteria be ignored; but these are always made secondary to contextual criteria. In many cases an aporia is simply the collision of two ideological or stylistic elements; but instead of jumping to a conclusion, on the basis of a prior assumption, as to which is Johannine, the critic should examine the seam to see if it suggests a primary and a secondary stratum, that is, a *Vorlage* on which redaction has evidently taken place. Contextual evidence is strongest just because it is relative: the *relation* of conflicting data, rather than the mere presence of an absolute datum, is taken as a clue to the passage's composition. And when several data coincide, as is often true, the case is all the clearer.

We may note three special kinds of contextual evidence:

(1) A peculiarity of the fourth gospel is the frequent parenthetical comments (*Anmerkungen*) and explanations (*Erläuterungen*) which interrupt its narrative (e.g. 1: 41; 2: 9). Bultmann takes these to be John's additions to a source, providing a clear-

---

[1] This is true, for example, of the work of both Wendt and Thompson: they rightly understand the signs to be crucial, but instead of dealing with as many as possible of the aporias scattered through the signs stories, each narrows his view to a single issue—in the case of Wendt, the lexical contrast σημεῖον/ἔργον; in that of Thompson, the ideological significance of the signs.

[2] A careful reading of his book bears this out; he nowhere expresses it as a methodological principle. See the review by J. M. Robinson, 'Recent research in the fourth gospel', *JBL* 78 (1959), 242–6.

cut contextual criterion.[1] Ruckstuhl insists that they can as well
be John's comments on his own work.[2] This possibility should
be kept in mind, but very often the flow of narrative is so
disrupted by the comment, and the meaning of the context so
altered, that only redaction of a source will account for it.[3]

(2) Hirsch held that the repetition of a *catch-word* or *phrase*
is often the clue to an editorial insertion.[4] While the instances of
this phenomenon are perhaps not always so simple as he
suggests, this hint as to the mechanics of John's redaction of
sources can be a useful criterion, the redactional material beginning either *after* the first instance of the *Schlagwort*, and running
through the second,[5] or *with* the first and running *to* the second.[6]

(3) *Textual criticism* can sometimes point to aporias. Just as
some scribal alterations in the text are made in order to
'correct' earlier emendations felt to be unsatisfactory, so any
place at which variant readings are conspicuously attested may
be one where an aporia, due to *Johannine* redaction of a *source*,
has been eased in one way or another by later copyists. The
harder reading (unless it has arisen unintentionally and makes
no sense whatever) is then the original one and may be
susceptible of source analysis.[7]

The criteria we have considered are all internal ones; but it
may be that seams, where they in fact occur, are invisible, due
to the evangelist's having so deftly reworked his sources as to
leave no internal evidence. In that case the *synoptic gospels* can
sometimes provide us with external criteria. Even if, as is
possible, John did not know any of the gospels, he certainly
was dependent, *via* his source, on synoptic *tradition*. If so, in
reconstructing a source we can work not only backward from
Jn but also forward, as it were,[8] from the synoptics as witnesses

---

[1] P. 4, and *RGG*, 842; *cf.* Barrett, 102 ff. M. C. Tenney, 'The footnotes
of John's gospel', *Bibliotheca Sacra* 117 (1960), 350–65, gives a convenient list
of every possible instance.

[2] Pp. 54–6, citing Bultmann's own observation that ancient authors did not
employ footnotes.   [3] *Cf.*, for example, on 2: 6, below.

[4] 'Stilkritik', sec. 1.

[5] *Cf.* 11: 33, 38 (ἐμβριμᾶσθαι), 20: 14, 16 (στρέφειν).

[6] *Cf.* 2: 3, 5 (λέγει ἡ μήτηρ), 4: 47, 49 (ἀποθνήσκειν).

[7] *Cf.* below on 2: 3, for example.

[8] 'Sideways' is perhaps more accurate. We cannot assume that the source
was directly descended from our synoptics; whatever its temporal relation

of that tradition. At this point the form- and source-critical methods meet.[1]

Our investigation of criteria cannot claim to have resulted in a self-applying technique for source analysis. We may have succeeded in avoiding some of the pitfalls of earlier research, less conscious of methodological issues as it was; but just the wealth of data which the fourth gospel presents for the source critic's analysis makes acute the problem how they are to be approached. Shall he simply read through the gospel, noting every aporia, and hope that a pattern will somehow suggest itself? Or can he find a starting point, a clue as to which data are the most important and where the outlines of a source can most readily be discerned? To an examination of the latter possibility we must now finally turn.

3. A STARTING POINT: THE MIRACLE STORIES[2]

An obvious literary distinction to be made in John is that between narrative and discourse,[3] but it will be of no use here as a starting point. Such a crude differentiation can hardly be the basis for separating Johannine and non-Johannine parts of the gospel,[4] for both classes of material are probably composite;

to them, it is more apt to have had contact only with the common tradition.

[1] Cf. the method proposed and illustrated by Haenchen, 'Probleme'. A *strictly* form-critical approach is not appropriate; while an oral tradition undoubtedly lies behind whatever sources John used, a literary method must be used to deal with that tradition once it becomes literary. Dodd, as his title (*Historical tradition...*) implies, is concerned finally with historicity, and it can be argued that his eagerness to go directly to oral tradition, without raising the possibility of an intervening literary *Vorlage*, is attributable to this concern. But this partly vitiates the value of his work: neither concern with historicity nor the related hope that John's source will be closer in touch with primitive tradition must be allowed to prejudice the source-critical undertaking.

[2] The phrase 'miracle story' is used loosely in this study, without raising philosophical or hermeneutical questions as to the nature of a miracle, or form-critical ones as to the precise definition of the *Gattung*.

[3] J. M. Thompson, 'The structure of the fourth gospel', *Exp* 10 (1915), 514 f.; Jeremias, 'Literarkritik', 35; Bultmann, *RGG*, 841.

[4] As it was for Wendt. – The present study is in fact almost wholly limited to the narrative material in the gospel. This limitation has been made arbitrarily in the sense that it recognizes the probability that the source

Schweizer regarded it as demonstrable that at least in the case of some of the narratives more than one stratum is present.[1]

The relation of ch. 21 to the rest of the gospel is often held to provide the key to a literary analysis of Jn,[2] but the stylistic data warn us against treating that chapter as wholly non-Johannine,[3] as also do methodological considerations.[4] But in any case, if it is the appendix it is usually held to be, it can give us clues only to post-Johannine (or late Johannine) work on the gospel, not to a pre-Johannine source. If, instead, ch. 21 is tentatively taken to be the intended conclusion to John's gospel, it becomes relevant to the source-analytic problem, providing a test of the hypothesis that aporias in the gospel are best explained as due to John's redaction of a source. The chapter can at least be shown to submit to source analysis and to contain a structure (miracle with ensuing dialogue as commentary) common to the gospel. But it provides no starting point for the analysis: the difficulty presented by ch. 21 depends for its solution on the 'signs' of the gospel's first half.

Faure was the first to treat at length the question of the proper *Ausgangspunkt* for Johannine source criticism.[5] His claim to have discovered it in the Old Testament citations in the gospel was discredited by Smend,[6] but the existence of a source underlying the first twelve chapters of John, the skeleton of which Faure stumbled upon in the course of his analysis of the

analysis of the discourses is an exceedingly difficult, not to say impossible, task. But that the narratives and discourses demand separate treatment is widely held. And in any case it is only a working limitation that is made: the possibility that the narrative source to be reconstructed included some discourse material (or at least sayings) is not excluded. See further below, pp. 199 f.

[1] P. 100; *cf.* Kümmel, *Introduction*, 152.

[2] Jeremias, 'Literarkritik', 43: 'Opinion as to chapter 21 is the basis and point of departure (*Ausgangspunkt*) of all literary-critical work on the fourth gospel.'

[3] *Cf.* Schweizer, 108 n. 158; see further below, p. 88.

[4] See above, p. 7 n. 1.

[5] A. Faure, 'Die alttestamentlichen Zitate im vierten Evangelium und die Quellenscheidungshypothese', *ZNW* 21 (1922), 99–121; but *cf.* Wendt, *Schichten*, who raises the question.

[6] F. Smend, 'Die Behandlung alttestamentlicher Zitate als Ausgangspunkt der Quellenscheidung im 4. Evangelium', *ZNW* 24 (1925), 147–50. In the course of his commentary Bultmann, who is initially uncritical of Faure, recognizes the latter's failure.

citations,[1] is not so easily dismissed. Indeed the fact of some such source is corroborated, as a whole or in part, by a surprisingly full and diverse series of largely independent studies of Jn stretching over the past fifty years.[2]

As is well known, it was Bultmann who gave the fullest expression to Faure's suggestion by attempting a detailed reconstruction of the source and giving it a name.[3] It is in most respects impossible to recover Bultmann's procedure in arriving at his result,[4] but the success of his investigation of the source would seem to be due to two factors: (1) the use of contextual evidence and (2) *Gattungkritik*.

(1) Faure thought he could discern the pre-Johannine stratum in the narratives of Jn by means of stylistic criteria.[5] Bultmann instead set out primarily to explain the aporias presented by the narratives and so arrived at a similar but more exact result. A chief difficulty that impressed him was that presented by the two Cana signs (2: 1–11; 4: 46–54) and the other references to miraculous deeds of Jesus (2: 23; 4: 45); there seemed to be a tension between the actual accounts of the

---

[1] Faure assigned to it the 'signs' in chs. 2, 4, 5, 9 and 11, but not those in ch. 6.

[2] J. M. Thompson, 'Structure' (1915); also 'The Composition of the fourth gospel', *Exp* 11 (1916), 34–46; Faure, 'Zitate' (1922); Windisch, *Synoptiker* (1926), 55; E. Hirsch (1936), 131–3; Bultmann (1941); Jeremias, 'Literarkritik' (1941), 46; E. Käsemann, review of Bultmann, *VF* 3 (1942), 186; E. Haenchen, 'Aus der Literatur zum Johannesevangelium 1929–56', *TR* n.s. 23 (1955), 303; also 'Probleme' (1959), 28 ff.; Wilkens (1958); G. Ziener, 'Johannesevangelium und urchristliche Passafeier', *BZ* n.s. 2 (1958), 263–74; O. Michel, 'Der Anfang der Zeichen Jesu', in *Die Leibhaftigkeit des Wortes* (Festgabe für Adolf Köberle), ed. O. Michel and U. Mann (Hamburg, 1958), 15–22; B. Lindars, 'The composition of John xx', *NTS* 7 (1960/1), 142–7, esp. 147; Hartke, *Parteien* (1961); S. Temple, 'The two signs in the fourth gospel', *JBL* 81 (1962), 169–74; Fuller (1963), ch. 5; Schweizer (2nd ed., 1965), vi; Schnackenburg, 'Traditionsgeschichte' (1964), esp. 63–5, 77–88; also *Johannesevangelium* (1965), I, 50–4; D. M. Smith, *Composition* (1965), 113. See also J. M. Robinson, 'Kerygma and history in the New Testament', in *The Bible in modern scholarship: Papers read at the 100th meeting of the Society of Biblical Literature—December 28–30, 1964*, ed. J. P. Hyatt (Nashville, 1965), 136–41.

[3] But for the latter *cf.* Faure, *ibid.* 109, and Windisch, *ibid.* 55.

[4] *Cf.* however Smith, *Composition*, ch. 1.

[5] Thompson worked in a similar way but only concluded that such a stratum existed, without trying to identify it.

signs, with their accompanying summaries, on the one hand and the passing editorial comments about them on the other, and so a clue to source analysis was suggested.

(2) Two recent studies[1] stop with the first two signs in looking for a source—and it is true that the formula found in 2: 11 and 4: 54 does not appear again (except in a different form in 21: 14) and that the structural relation of these two stories to their contexts is unique. But there are other stories in the gospel (namely the rest of the miracles) which are of an apparently similar type and should be considered in conjunction with the Cana stories, on the possibility that the source consisted of a collection of just such accounts. This use of *Gattungkritik* led Bultmann to fill out his source with the miracles Faure included, and those of ch. 6 as well.[2]

We shall find reason to argue with some of Bultmann's results, but the consistency of his *Semeia-Quelle* suggests that he has partially uncovered a real source used by John. We can proceed, therefore, by looking in turn at each of the miracle stories in the gospel, distinguishing them from their context and analysing them internally, primarily on the basis of contextual evidence but also with the help of synoptic comparison where that is possible.

[1] Those of Michel and Temple.

[2] At the same time, form-critical method in the narrower sense occasionally helped him in the finer analysis of the individual passages themselves. It is therefore all the more surprising, in one of the fathers of synoptic form criticism, that Bultmann never adequately discusses the issues involved in the form criticism of John, or perhaps even fully recognizes its possibilities. *Cf.* now Schnackenburg, 47.—It is noteworthy that form criticism of the synoptics uses primarily contextual criteria to distinguish forms.

PART ONE
THE 'SIGNS SOURCE'

A. THE MIRACLE STORIES
IN JOHN

I. WATER CHANGED INTO WINE (2: 1–11)[1]

Although the story of the wedding feast at Cana is in itself so distinctive that many analysts have been content to assign the whole pericope to a single stratum,[2] in fact it is composite and betrays aporias,[3] which can best be explained as Johannine additions to a pre-Johannine source.

2: 1a. The temporal note here, while creating no aporia, serves only to connect the miracle with the events of ch. 1 as they now stand and is probably Johannine.[4] That is, unless the editorial

---

[1] M.-É. Boismard, *Du baptême à Cana (Jean 1: 19–2: 11)* (Lectio Divina, 18; Paris, 1956); J. D. M. Derrett, 'Water into wine', *BZ* n.s. 7 (1963), 80–97; R. J. Dillon, 'Wisdom tradition and sacramental retrospect in the Cana account (Jn 2, 1–11)', *CBQ* 24 (1962), 286–95; E. Dinkler, 'Das Kana-Wunder (Joh. 2, 1–12)', in *Fragen der wissenschaftlichen Erforschung der Heiligen Schrift: Sonderdruck aus dem Protokoll der Landessynode der evg. Kirche im Rheinland Jan. 1962*, 47–61; A. Feuillet, 'L'heure de Jésus et le signe de Cana: Contribution à l'étude de la structure du quatrième évangile', *Études johanniques* (Museum Lessianum, Section biblique, 4; Paris/Bruges, 1962), 11–33; O. Michel, 'Anfang'; K. L. Schmidt, 'Der johanneische Charakter der Erzählung vom Hochzeitswunder in Kana', *Harnack-Ehrung: Beiträge zur Kirchengeschichte...* (Leipzig, 1921), 32–43; R. Schnackenburg, *Das erste Wunder Jesu (Joh 2, 1–11)* (Freiburg, 1951); A. Schulz, 'Das Wunder zu Kana im Lichte des Alten Testaments', *BZ* 16 (1924), 93–6; Temple, 'Two signs'. See further Schnackenburg, I, 330 n. 1; A. Smitmans, *Das Weinwunder von Kana: Die Auslegung von Jo 2, 1–11 bei den Vätern und heute* (Beiträge zur Geschichte der biblischen Exegese, 6; Tübingen, 1966), esp. 6–8.

[2] So Wendt, Hirsch, Wilkens: Schweizer, 100, notes that not a single Johannine style-characteristic occurs, and even Bultmann finds very little Johannine editing. Derrett, on historical grounds, tries to show it as a coherent whole.

[3] Schmidt, 36, puts very strongly the case for the passage's unevenness. *Cf.* Dodd, 226 f.

[4] Dodd, 226, holds this kind of 'precise measurement of time' (and quantity, as in *v.* 6) to be a Johannine trait. We shall have reason to hold, on the contrary, that in general this is a characteristic of the source; but while the note of time here is precise, it clearly is related to John's repeated (and somewhat indefinite) use of τῇ ἐπαύριον in ch. 1.

matrix, as well as the substance, of 1: 19–51 proves to belong to the source (see below, pp. 188 f.), we may take τῇ ἡμέρᾳ τῇ τρίτῃ to be John's addition. The rest is pre-Johannine, except possibly τῆς Γαλιλαίας (see below on *v.* 11 *a*).

2 : 1 b. A minor uncertainty in analysing this story is that of the part 'the mother of Jesus' played in the source. As we shall see, John has heightened the prominence of Mary (to use a name he does not give to her) in the story, and her premature appearance on the scene at this point is possibly his insertion to that end: 1 *b* interrupts 1 *a* and 2, introduces an ambiguity (does ἐκεῖ refer to Cana or more specifically to the wedding?), and makes the full phrase *the mother of Jesus* in *v.* 3 (*cf. his mother* in *v.* 5) redundant.

2 : 2. Bultmann (79; cf. Wellhausen, 13) regards *his disciples* as possibly a Johannine replacement of an original *his brothers*— not impossible, but unlikely (see below, pp. 102 f. on 2: 12). The verse as it stands appears to come from the source.

2 : 3. The correct reading of 3 *a* is disputed. Bauer (44) considers the longer reading (οἶνον οὐκ εἶχον, ὅτι συνετελέσθη ὁ οἶνος τοῦ γάμου· εἶτα – ℵ* it sy^hmg) an explanatory gloss on the shorter genitive absolute (ὑστερήσαντος οἴνου), while Bultmann (80) sees the latter as a scribal attempt to smooth out the clumsiness of the original longer reading. The infrequency of genitive absolute in Jn would lend slight support to Bultmann's view, but a more basic argument for the longer reading involves the correct assignment of the end of the verse either to John or to the source.

According to Bultmann (*ibid.*), the miracle story *Gattung* ordinarily requires that someone in the story request the miracle, and so he regards the whole of 3 (and even 4) as pre-Johannine.[1] But although many synoptic miracles do contain a formal request for Jesus' intervention, this element is lacking in a number of them (e.g. Mk 2: 5, 3: 3; Lk 7: 13, 13: 12, 14: 3 f.) and even in three of the miracle stories in Jn (5: 6, 6: 5, 9: 1

---

[1] *Cf.* also Dodd, 226: 'The colloquy between Jesus and his Mother has the same suggestion of a certain tension within the family [as in the synoptic tradition].'

[but cf. 9: 2]), and so is not essential here. It is more likely that in introducing *v.* 4 (see below), John has created 3*c* (πρὸς αὐτόν κτλ) to prepare for it. The repetition of λέγει ἡ μήτηρ in 5 suggests that originally 3*ab* was followed by 5*b* (τοῖς διακόνοις κτλ).

To return to 3*a*—if in the source John found the shorter reading and added 3*c*, containing the statement of Mary that the guests were without wine, it is hard to see why a scribe would have expanded 3*a* ('When the wine gave out') to say awkwardly what was about to be said in 3*b*. But if the source had the longer reading, *it* would seem redundant after John added 3*c* and so readily be abbreviated in transmission. The shorter reading provides a good connection with 3*c* but fails to explain the variant; the longer reading shows an aporia instead, but both suggests how that aporia was created and explains how the variant arose. This verse illustrates the principle that the presence of textual variants in a passage may reflect redactional aporias which the scribes have sought to ease; the harder reading is the better one if it can be explained by source criticism.[1]

2: 4. All attempts to dismiss the inconsistency in 3*b*–4[2] are futile; Jesus clearly rejects (*v.* 4) what is at least an implicit request for a miracle (*v.* 3*bc*)—and yet proceeds in what follows to accomplish one. This basic contextual consideration for excising *v.* 4 (and with it 3*c*) is supported by the *sachlich* elements of 4*b*: the theme of Jesus' hour, and to a lesser extent also that of a rebuke to members of his family (cf. 7: 6, and note there the phrase 'my time'), is apparently Johannine, i.e. belongs not merely to certain passages which might or might not

---

[1] Mollat, 75, who usually follows Boismard's suggested short readings, prefers the longer reading here, regarding the shorter as a 'correction for stylistic elegance'. Schnackenburg, I, 332 n. 3, argues, in favour of the shorter reading, that a scribe has paraphrased the somewhat uncommon use of ὑστερεῖν, which has the meaning *give out* only in late Greek; but it is inherently more likely that the late usage is due not to the earlier writer but to a late scribe, neatly abbreviating a somewhat clumsy and (in view of John's redaction) redundant clause.

[2] *E.g.* by suggesting that Mary did not request a miracle but only expressed the hosts' embarrassment and was rebuked for her faithless anxiety (Boismard, 143 f., 155; *cf.* Feuillet, 25); or that the word of Jesus about his 'hour' is to be taken as a question, not a statement (Boismard, 156).

prove to be Johannine but to the editorial parts of the gospel which almost certainly are not from the source.[1]

2 : 5. Schwartz finds it psychologically impossible that Mary, as a wedding guest, should act so peremptorily toward the servants as she does here; but this treats the verse too realistically.[2] There may be a parallel here (and in the other miracles—e.g. 6: 10, 12, 9: 7, 11: 39, 21: 6) to the claim Elijah and Elisha make on those at hand to assist in a miracle.[3] With the repetition of λέγει ἡ μήτηρ (αὐτοῦ) John resumes the source where he left it in *v.* 3. Mary's words are a direct quotation from Gen. 41: 55.[4]

2: 6–8. The phrase *according to the purification of the Jews* in *v.* 6 appears to be Johannine since (1) it isolates the periphrastic κείμεναι from ἦσαν and the subject, a situation resulting in the various scribal tendencies either to omit the participle (אּ* *pc ae*) or to change the word order (𝔎 Θ *pm 69*); (2) it makes the fact of the pots' being empty (*v.* 7) inexplicable;[5] and (3) it contains the phrase *of the Jews* which we may suspect of being Johannine on the same grounds as those just adduced in the case of the *hour* of Jesus.[6] – Verses 7–8 continue the source's narrative quite naturally.

[1] So Schmidt, 36–8; *cf.* 7: 30, 8: 20, 13: 1.–Bultmann, 80 f., followed by Fuller, 92, 97, and Dinkler, 51, holds that Jesus' word about his 'hour' has the role, typical of elaborated miracle stories, of 'heightening the tension', but that phrase understates the problem posed by Jesus' reply, and in any case does not necessarily apply to the pre-Johannine form of the story.

[2] Dinkler, 51 f., on the other hand gives an overly spiritual (and Johannine) interpretation: Mary's words are not servant instructions but an admonition to Christians, in the light of Jesus' revelation about his 'hour', to be ready to do whatever the Lord commands! His insistence that the story cannot have to do with household servants is not borne out by W. Bauer, *A Greek–English lexicon of the New Testament and other early Christian literature,* tr. and ed. W. F. Arndt and F. W. Gingrich (Chicago, 1957), sub διάκονος, 1, *a.*

[3] So Schulz, 93 f., who also notes the parallels to ὑδρίαι (*v.* 6) in 1 Kings 18: 34 LXX and to the command of *v.* 8 in 2 Kings 4: 41.

[4] On the possible implication of this fact see below, p. 230.

[5] Brown, 100, implies that the pots themselves, and not their eventual contents, were awaiting (re-)purification, but this is unlikely; John, by his insertion, seeks to supply the symbolism of the Christian supplanting of Judaism, without noticing the slight incongruity he thereby produces.

[6] οἱ ᾽Ιουδαῖοι is found in the synoptics almost always in the mouth of a

2: 9. On both contextual and ideological grounds Bultmann (82 n. 9, following Faure and Schmidt) rightly takes 9*b* (καὶ οὐκ ᾔδει πόθεν ἐστίν, οἱ δὲ διάκονοι ᾔδεισαν οἱ ἠντληκότες τὸ ὕδωρ) to be Johannine: (1) both the sense and the syntax[1] of 9*ac* are broken by these two clauses which themselves form a unit; (2) the elements of secrecy and eye-witness are extraneous to the story; (3) the contrast between knowing and not knowing,[2] and especially when it involves origin (πόθεν),[3] is probably a Johannine theme. The redundant ὁ ἀρχιτρίκλινος at the end of the verse is necessary only after the change of subject in 9*b*, and so it also may be editorial (Spitta, 69).[4] Hirsch (5), noting how anomalous it is that the chief event of the story, the actual miracle, should be buried in an appositional phrase,[5] suggests that originally τὸ ὕδωρ κτλ (9*a*) was not the subject of ἐγεύσατο but an independent clause: 'When the master of the feast tasted [it], the water [was] made wine.'[6] This is quite possible.

2: 10. The connection between this verse and 11 is not entirely smooth. Wellhausen (14) believes that 10 cannot have ended a miracle story and that there must have been some more natural statement of the guests' acknowledgment of and reaction to the miracle than is now found in 11. On the other hand Schmidt (35 f.), who thinks the pre-Johannine version of the story was secular, humorous, and popular, finds *v.* 10 an appropriate conclusion to it and 11 extraneous.

Gentile and is very rarely editorial. Jn, on the other hand, contains the phrase much more frequently and almost always as an expression of the writer; it is frequently found in contexts which on any other grounds are not to be considered pre-Johannine.–*Cf.* Dodd, 226 n. 1, where, although generally forswearing source analysis, he makes the distinction between the traditional material at John's disposal and his redactional framework for, and changes in, that material.–The interest in καθαρισμός in 3: 25 seems also to be editorial, *i.e.* Johannine.

[1] Is ὡς (9*a*) to be taken causally with οὐκ ᾔδει after being used temporally with ἐγεύσατο?   [2] *Cf.* 6: 6 f., 12: 16, 20: 9, 21: 4*b*, etc.

[3] *Cf.* 3: 8, 4: 11, 7: 27 f., 8: 14, 9: 29 f., 19: 9—all outside the miracle stories. See further below on 6: 5.

[4] The alternative—taking this phrase as original and excising the whole of 9*a* as Johannine—is too drastic and ignores the disjuncture between 9*a* and *b* which we have just noted.

[5] *Cf.* the similar, though less blatant, circumstance in 6: 12.

[6] He must conjecturally emend οἶνον to οἶνος but can readily explain how an early scribe (or possibly John?) would have created the present reading.

Both the story's uniqueness, noted by many, and its abrupt ending, are perhaps best explained by regarding it not as a typical *Wunder* told about Jesus but as derived from a paradigmatic saying[1] or parable[2] of Jesus. The saying in 10, which on this conjecture is the kernel of the story,[3] has an obvious relation to Mk 2: 22 and parallels ('No one puts new wine into old wineskins...'), and even more to the independent saying in Lk 5: 39 ('No one after drinking old wine desires new...').[4] And even the elements which provide a kind of plot, and thus make the saying into a story, have parallels in the tradition of Jesus' sayings: bridegroom (Mk 2: 19!), wedding feast, ?steward. At some earlier stage the story was regarded as one told *by* Jesus; the puzzling command of Jesus to fill the waterpots (*v.* 6) may reflect the first attempt to introduce a thaumaturgic action (Schmidt, 35) and so transform the story into a miraculous narrative *about* Jesus, out of which the present form could develop.

All this is conjectural; however it suggests that the Cana pericope is not a true tale, but even now retains as its climax the pronouncement in *v.* 10, so that any further rounding off, as by a statement of the miracle's effect on the witnesses (*v.* 11) necessarily appears secondary and abrupt.

2: 11. Whether the author of the source placed any importance on the parabolic meaning of *v.* 10 (good and inferior wine) is not known,[5] but since he certainly wished to emphasize the miraculous power of Jesus, he could not have let the story end there. But how much of the source can now be recovered?

Verse 11 *a* has been variously assigned. On the one hand Wellhausen (24) considers it, indeed the whole verse, re-

---

[1] A possibility Schmidt (43) leaves open.

[2] So Dodd, 227; *cf.* on 11: 1 ff. and 21: 1 ff., below.

[3] Having a certain tension with what precedes: it is no longer the quantity of wine that is emphasized, but its quality.

[4] Richardson, 121 f., thinks the story in Jn is perhaps a midrash on this Lukan saying, deliberately correcting a Judaizing misinterpretation of it. *Cf.* F. E. Williams, 'Fourth gospel and synoptic tradition: Two Johannine passages', *JBL* 86 (1967), 312–16.

[5] John, by his setting and the insertion in *v.* 6, revives (perhaps unwittingly) a traditional understanding of the saying (Judaism replaced by Christianity).

dactional (in our terms, Johannine) since, as he believes, an enumeration of the two Cana signs (2: 11, 4: 54) would be out of place in the *Grundschrift* where they stood next to each other. On the other hand, Bultmann (79, 83), holding the same view of the relation between 2: 1 ff. and 4: 46 ff., regards the whole of 11*a* as taken over from the source by John; he argues that otherwise it is impossible to explain why 4: 54 ignores the signs alluded to editorially in 2: 23, 3: 2, 4: 45.

Bultmann's point is undeniable, but it is not clear that the source had 11*a* as it stands; indeed the confusion of MS readings in connection with the word ἀρχήν suggests that John's redaction of the source has given rise to the various scribal emendations. The textual evidence is as follows:

1. ταύτην ἐποίησεν ἀρχὴν τῶν σημείων κτλ ($\mathfrak{P}^{66c.75}$ ℵ *A* Θ *al*)
2. ταύτην ἐποίησεν τὴν ἀρχὴν τῶν σημείων κτλ (ℵ ℜ *W pm*)
3. ταύτην ἀρχὴν ἐποίησεν τῶν σημείων κτλ (*1241*)
4. ταύτην πρώτην ἀρχὴν ἐποίησεν τῶν σημείων κτλ ($\mathfrak{P}^{66*}$)

By far the best attested reading is the first one. The addition of a definite article (2) and inversion of the verb and noun (3 and 4) are trivial. But the appearance of πρώτην in $\mathfrak{P}^{66*}$ is puzzling and cannot be dismissed as capricious, since ℵ* has the same word at the end of the clause, after Γαλιλαίας. It is hard to understand how the reading πρώτην arose unless it is original (*i.e.* goes back at least to John): the obvious explanations—that πρώτην ἀρχήν is a conflation or that a scribe unthinkingly substituted *first* for *beginning* and immediately corrected it[1]—are ruled out by the feminine ending of *first*. Furthermore all the other readings are most readily explained by taking $\mathfrak{P}^{66*}$ as the true text, the redundancy of πρώτην ἀρχήν having been solved by scribes in various ways.[2]

---

[1] Thus V. Martin, *Papyrus Bodmer II: Évangile de Jean, Chap 1–14* (Bibliotheca Bodmeriana, 5; Cologny–Genève, 1956), 45, apparently thinks that the original scribe himself excised πρώτην, but this can only be conjecture: it would hardly be possible to decide whose hand added the excision dots over the word. They seem to me more likely to have been added later along with the transposition marks over ἀρχὴν ἐποίησεν. The uncorrected reading is then πρώτην ἀρχήν, not simply πρώτην.

[2] *Viz.* (*a*) a shift of the adjective to the end of the clause (ℵ*) or (*b*) deletion of the adjective (*1241*); or, more elaborately, since (*b*) leaves the anarthrous noun next to the pronoun, either (*c*) transposition of the noun

But if ταύτην πρώτην ἀρχήν is the correct reading, how are we to explain this all but intolerable Greek? By supposing that John, in attempting to reinterpret the source, has created the difficulty. Assuming that the *source* read τοῦτο πρῶτον ἐποίησεν σημεῖον ὁ 'Ιησοῦς,[1] then *John*, wishing to emphasize the first sign as the chief one of all, added an appositive ἀρχήν, changing σημεῖον to a genitive plural with the noun, and the gender of the pronoun and adjective to feminine by attraction.[2] This is only conjectural, to be sure, but it is supported by two facts—first, the parallels with 4: 54 and 21: 14 (see above, n. 1), and secondly, the fact, apparent in other ways, that John gives the Cana pericope unique symbolic importance,[3] a consideration which is strengthened by his redaction of the source in 1 ('the third day') and 4 ('My hour has not yet come').

Since the evangelist uses σημεῖον so frequently and distinctively (Bultmann, 79 n. 1, 161) it may be asked whether he himself has not introduced the word into his source (and therefore whether the latter is literally a 'signs source' at all). The answer is a simple one: there are in Jn two distinct and all but incompatible uses of the term (*e.g.* in ch. 4, *cf. vv.* 48 and 53 f.), and the most natural explanation is that John has both reproduced the term from the source and himself used it in a new way.—On the proper translation of this word, see below, p. 231 n. 4.

The reiteration of *Cana* here is probably Johannine, especially if, as I believe, John has made conscious use in his gospel of geography as a theological device (see below on 4: 46 ff.). It is likely that the places he adopts as pivotal for this purpose (Cana, Bethany, Jerusalem) were simply taken by him in the first instance from the source—a consideration which vouches for

and verb as well as deletion (𝔓⁶⁶ *etc.*), or, failing to recognize the noun in (*c*) as an object complement, (*d*) further insertion of an article (א *etc.*).

[1] *Cf.* 4: 54: τοῦτο [πάλιν] δεύτερον ἐποίησεν σημεῖον ὁ 'Ι.; 21: 14: τοῦτο [ἤδη] τρίτον [ἐφανερώθη] ὁ 'Ι. See below, secs. 2 and 8.

[2] Not easily translated but perhaps 'Jesus did this first, the beginning of the signs...' For a similar case of attraction, *cf.* Lk 24: 21: τρίτην ταύτην ἡμέραν ἄγει; see Bl–D, secs. 129, 292.

[3] Bultmann, 78; Dodd, 233 (*cf. Interpretation*, 297–300); Barrett, 161; Feuillet, 32. It is not so clear to me as to Bultmann, 83, that the source attached a similar importance to this miracle, even if it contained, as he supposed, the word ἀρχήν.

Cana in *v.* 1 but not here. The repetition of τῆς Γαλιλαίας is undoubtedly John's emphasis, and the phrase is perhaps his even in *v.* 1 (*cf.* 1: 43 *a*), unless Cana-of-Galilee is meant to be distinguished from another Cana.

So much for 11 *a*; the second clause of the verse is probably John's addition. It is almost a paraphrase of 11 *a* and contains the apparently Johannine idea of Jesus' glory.[1] Although the characteristic Johannine use of φανεροῦν is in the passive, the active appears in the clearly Johannine passage 17: 6.

Verse 11 *c* is often ascribed to the evangelist. In fact, we might suspect the use of εἰς αὐτόν with πιστεύειν of being Johannine,[2] but it is by no means peculiar to Jn in the NT (see below, p. 211). And there are *sachlich* reasons for assigning the last third of the verse to the source. There is in Jn a widely recognized tension between two kinds of faith, signs-faith and faith-without-seeing. While John is entirely capable of creating tensions, this one seems to be the result of his seeking to correct an improper understanding of faith, one in short which he found current in his time, and more particularly in the source he re-edits; for signs-faith is just what a 'sign' seeks to produce. Verse 11 *c* can be taken naturally with 11 *b*, as it usually is; but it just as smoothly follows 11 *a*, as it seems to have done in the source. John's corrective here is not so explicit as in the next pericope (4: 46 ff.), but it is adequate enough: the disciples' faith is appropriate because Jesus had not merely performed a miracle, but (according to John's addition) 'manifested his glory'.[3] – Bultmann[4] believes that *his disciples* may be Johannine, as he supposes to be true at 2: 2, or even post-Johannine, as (according to him) at 2: 12; but his reason is based on the textual variants in 2: 12, so that our grounds for rejecting the suggestion must await consideration of that verse (below, pp. 102 f.).

[1] 1: 14, 5: 41, 44, 8: 50, 11: 4, 40, 12: 41, 17: 1, 5, 22, 24; *cf.* Dodd, 226 n. 2. – For the clause's meaning if it was contained in the source, see Bultmann, 83 n. 7, Fuller, 98.

[2] Ruckstuhl, 204.

[3] Thus, whereas in the source the disciples' belief *in* Jesus on this occasion meant only what the sign had shown (*that he was* the wonder-working Messiah), for John it means full *commitment to the Lord*.

[4] P. 79 nn. 6, 7 (*Ergänzungsheft*).

Our analysis, then, has produced the following reconstruction of the source:[1]

2: 1 καὶ |...| γάμος ἐγένετο ἐν Κανὰ (τῆς Γαλιλαίας καὶ ἦν ἡ μήτηρ τοῦ Ἰησοῦ ἐκεῖ).

2 ἐκλήθη δὲ καὶ ὁ Ἰησοῦς καὶ οἱ μαθηταὶ αὐτοῦ εἰς τὸν γάμον.

3 καὶ [οἶνον οὐκ εἶχον, ὅτι συνετελέσθη ὁ οἶνος τοῦ γάμου· εἶτα] λέγει ἡ μήτηρ τοῦ Ἰησοῦ |...|

5 |...| τοῖς διακόνοις· ὅ τι ἂν λέγῃ ὑμῖν, ποιήσατε.

6 ἦσαν δὲ ἐκεῖ λίθιναι ὑδρίαι ἓξ |...| κείμεναι, χωροῦσαι ἀνὰ μετρητὰς δύο ἢ τρεῖς.

7 λέγει αὐτοῖς ὁ Ἰησοῦς· γεμίσατε τὰς ὑδρίας ὕδατος. καὶ ἐγέμισαν αὐτὰς ἕως ἄνω.

8 καὶ λέγει αὐτοῖς· ἀντλήσατε νῦν καὶ φέρετε τῷ ἀρχιτρικλίνῳ. οἱ δὲ ἤνεγκαν.

9 ὡς δὲ ἐγεύσατο ὁ ἀρχιτρίκλινος, τὸ ὕδωρ οἶνο[ς] γεγενημένον. |...| φωνεῖ τὸν νυμφίον (ὁ ἀρχιτρίκλινος)

10 καὶ λέγει αὐτῷ· πᾶς ἄνθρωπος πρῶτον τὸν καλὸν οἶνον τίθησιν, καὶ ὅταν μεθυσθῶσιν τὸν ἐλάσσω· σὺ τετήρηκας τὸν καλὸν οἶνον ἕως ἄρτι.

11 [τοῦτο πρῶτον ἐποίησεν σημεῖον] ὁ Ἰησοῦς |...| καὶ ἐπίστευσαν εἰς αὐτὸν οἱ μαθηταὶ αὐτοῦ.

2. A NOBLEMAN'S SON HEALED (4: 46–54)[2]

This pericope (together with 21: 1 ff.) presents closer parallels to the synoptic gospels (*cf.* Mt 8: 5–13 = Lk 7: 2–10; also Mk 7: 25–30 = Mt 15: 22–8) than the other miracle stories in Jn, except that of the feeding of the multitude (6: 1 ff.). It might seem wise, then, to begin by examining those parallels in the chance of finding some literary connection.[3] As will

[1] Here and in succeeding résumés of the reconstruction, material whose assignment to the source is uncertain is put in parentheses ( ), uncertain or conjectural readings appear in square brackets [ ], and points at which John has made insertions are indicated thus: |...|.

[2] Boismard, 'Saint Luc'; Feuillet, 'La signification théologique du second miracle de Cana (Jn iv, 46–54)', *Études*, 34–46; Haenchen, 'Probleme', 23–31; Michel, 'Anfang'; Schnackenburg, 'Traditionsgechichte'; E. Schweizer, 'Die Heilung des Königlichen, Joh 4, 46–54', *EvTh* 11 (1951/2), 64–71; Temple, 'Two signs'.

[3] The majority of Catholic scholars have held that the account in Jn 4: 46 ff. is not of the same event as that of the centurion's παῖς in Mt

appear, such an examination shows that while there are some striking similarities, the differences are such that no literary explanation can be confidently given. But in any case, as a methodological working rule, we have decided to leave open the question of contact with the synoptics as long as possible, noting parallels only from a form-critical standpoint, and attempting to reconstruct a source on internal grounds.

Bultmann (151) thinks it impossible to complete a thorough-going source analysis of this passage with any certainty. Indeed, as we shall see, there are some problems peculiar to it; but his pessimism appears unfounded.

4: 46. In the source, the pericope was introduced by 2: 12a,[1] and the nobleman's encounter with Jesus took place not in Cana (as John provides by the addition of 46a) but either *in* Capernaum (Bultmann) or, more likely, *on the road* between Cana and Capernaum (Wilkens—see below on 47a). Thus, while 46a in itself creates no obvious difficulty,[2] in order to explain the now pointless character of 2: 12a it must be regarded as Johannine,[3] substituted for 2: 12a when the source is resumed after 2: 13—4: 45.–In 46b we should perhaps follow the adequately attested reading ἦν δὲ (א D it, *etc.*), which fits the beginning of a story better than the variant καὶ ἦν, substituted in transmission as smoother after 46a.

4: 47a. Schnackenburg ('Traditionsgeschichte', 64) holds that, among the several changes necessitated by John's addition of 46a, almost the entire half-verse here (ἀκούσας... Γαλιλαίαν) must be ascribed to John; but this is too drastic. For the element of the suppliant's acting on *hearing* of Jesus, *cf.* Lk 7: 3, Mk 7: 25.

Wilkens (41 f.) sees no problem in the phrase 'out of Judea into Galilee', taking it to come from the source (on his view a

and Lk; Schnackenburg, 'Traditionsgeschichte', 70–6, takes exception to this position at considerable length, however; also Brown, 192 f. But in any case, a form-critical comparison is possible.   [1] See below, pp. 102 f.

[2] Though the juxtaposition of the two place names seems to have occasioned some variant readings in 46b: (*a*) omission of ἐν Καφαρναούμ (*e* vg^cod Aug, *etc.*), apparently as extraneous, and (*b*) transposition of the same phrase to precede τις βασιλικός (sy^c, *etc.*), apparently so as to clear up the ambiguity whether the nobleman or only his son was in Capernaum.

[3] So Boismard and 'many other scholars' (Brown, 190).

Johannine *Grundschrift*) and to refer to 1 : 43 a. As we shall see (below, p. 184) the latter was not part of the source; but more likely the phrase refers to 4 : 3, 43, 45—in every case Johannine material—and thus appears to be the evangelist's addition (Bultmann, 151).

Bultmann (*ibid.*) retains ἥκει as appropriate to the Capernaum locale of the source: 'when he heard that Jesus had come [*sc.* from Cana to Capernaum]...' At first glance this seems natural, and the suggestion of Wilkens (41), that the locale was rather the road outside Capernaum, unnecessarily contrived: it requires, when ἐκ... Γαλιλαίαν is excised (see above), that we conjecturally read ἔρχεται for ἥκει, and possibly κατέβαινεν for κατέβη in 2 : 12 (but see below, p. 102). But Bultmann's alternative (Capernaum) is even more artificial since it requires (*a*) either omitting καταβῇ καί in 47 (Spitta, 67) or changing it to ἐλθών (Bultmann, 151; Boismard, 204), (*b*) omitting ἐχθές in *v.* 52 (Bultmann, 152)[1] and (*c*) as Bultmann fails to recognize, either omitting altogether the genitive absolute in 51 (Spitta, *ibid.*) or somehow excising the idea of descent. In deciding for Wilkens' reading it is not simply a matter of weighing one change (or at most two) against three; both of those possibly required for the setting outside Capernaum occur at points where John is known to have made editorial changes and are necessitated by those changes,[2] whereas the changes Bultmann must suppose John to have made are all gratuitous, since the healing-at-a-distance is already clear enough with John's addition of 46 a. Thus we may take it as probable that the source had a setting on the road outside Capernaum— apparently a heightened form of the traditional *Fernheilung* in Capernaum (*cf.* Q)—and that John simply increased still further the distance between Jesus and the sick boy by making the encounter with the father take place in Cana.[3]

[1] Unless, as below, this verse is taken to be Johannine; Bultmann deals with κατάβηθι in 49 in this way.

[2] At 2 : 12 a, which he separates from the healing pericope and transforms into an independent notice; and here, where he inserts 'out of Judea into Galilee'.

[3] The variants ἀπῆλθεν/ἦλθεν have no bearing on the question of the source's locale for the miracle, since the compound verb can be used not only of a journey outside a city but also of movement within it (*cf.* Mt 9 : 7) and so is synonymous with the simple form.

4: 47b. This and 49 comprise a doublet, and we shall see that in the present text the latter is occasioned by John's insertion of 48. Nevertheless, the direct address of 49*b* is perhaps original, John having simply summarized it here in an anticipatory way, thereby underlining the imminence of the boy's death, just as his new life is emphasized by the repetition in 53. The use of a ἵνα-clause for the complementary infinitive is probably characteristic of John[1] and perhaps also μέλλειν ἀποθνῄσκειν.[2] The source perhaps read ἀπῆλθεν πρὸς αὐτὸν καὶ λέγει· κύριε κτλ (continuing as in 49*b*).

4: 48. As is widely recognized (*cf.* esp. Schnackenburg, 'Traditionsgeschichte', 59–62), the most acute aporia in the passage is the reply of Jesus to the nobleman: *cf.* the shift to 2nd person plural, the apparent criticism of a request for healing which is nevertheless eventually granted (*cf.* 2: 4) and, most notable of all, the logically inappropriate introduction of the question of faith. The man was certainly not looking for a sign *in order to believe* in Jesus' miraculous power, for his coming to Jesus shows that he already believed. This is John's insertion[3] and amounts almost to a denial of the miracle as a basis for faith, quite impossible in a signs source. At the same time the saying is unique in Jn ('signs and wonders') and appears to have been taken up by the evangelist from an independent tradition.

4: 49. The reiteration here of the nobleman's request is occasioned, as we saw, by the insertion of 48. But that the man's words (49*b*) are pre-Johannine is suggested by their lack of any justification or disclaimer in the face of Jesus' challenge; they simply state the man's need without any reference to 48.

The use of κύριε, while common in Jn, is not unique to it and appears several times in SQ contexts (5: 7, 11: 21, *etc.*; *cf.* Mt 8: 8 par. and Mk 7: 28 par.).

4: 50. Whether 48 displaced an exchange in the source between Jesus and the father can only be conjectured (see below on

---

[1] Howard, *Fourth gospel*, 4th ed., 277; *cf.* 8: 56, 9: 22, 11: 37, 50, 53, 12: 10, 17: 15, 21, 24.   [2] Schnackenburg, I, 498.
[3] So, to a different end, 6: 26.

comparison with the synoptics), but 49*b*–50*a* follows smoothly after 47*a*; the man having made his request, Jesus dismisses him, with the promise of his son's recovery: 'Thy son lives' (*cf.* 1 Kings 17: 23).[1] This declaration, on which John places some emphasis (see below on 50*b*, 53), might seem to be, already in the source, the act which effects the miracle. In that case the rest of 50 would belong to the source as well and simply portray the trust which appropriately is given to Jesus by those whom he encounters. But there is reason to suppose that 50*b* is John's addition: it interrupts the connection between Jesus' command (50*a*) and its compliance (50*c*) (the resulting anticlimax of καὶ ἐπορεύετο apparently led to that phrase's omission in *e* sy^c) and makes 53*b* anticlimactic. As we shall see, nowhere else in the source is there any instance of preliminary faith in Jesus, whereas such an interest is clearly Johannine (*cf.* 11: 20–7), as is the idea of belief of Jesus' *word* (4: 41, 5: 24, *etc.*).[2] The source characteristically uses, if anything, a *command* of Jesus as the thaumaturgic act (2: 6*a*, 7*a*, 5: 8, 9: 7*a*, 11: 43, 21: 6), so that in the pre-Johannine stage it was what precedes ὁ υἱός σου ζῇ, namely πορεύου, which was emphasized, and the man's obedience to the command (50*c*) was the appropriate sequel to Jesus' word. Verse 50*b*, suggested by the faith implied in the man's compliance, has been added by John after 48, apparently to show him as not belonging to those whose signs-faith is criticized by Jesus. For the possibility that 50*c* was originally followed by some such statement as *and at that hour the boy was healed*, see below.

4: 51. In the source, where the element of the man's belief was less prominent, this verse and the following one provided the story's *dénouement*. The reading καὶ [ἀπ/ἀν-]ἤγγειλαν (widely attested), with or without λέγοντες, may then be original, stemming from the source and expressing a solemn proclamation of the miracle.[3] It would appear premature with the addi-

---

[1] That this healing by Elijah was remembered in the tradition about Jesus is also evident from Lk 4: 26.

[2] The request for Jesus' *word* in the synoptic parallels (εἰπὲ λόγῳ—Mt 8: 8 = Lk 7: 7) would appear to be coincidental, for there is no suggestion that it becomes the object of belief.

[3] Schniewind, *TWBzNT* I, 60, lines 28–37.

tion of 52–3 *a* and so tend to disappear in transmission, as the MS evidence shows.

4: 52. Two locutions, reasonably frequent in the synoptics and occurring only here in Jn (*viz.* πυνθάνομαι[1] and ἔχειν in expressions of health) suggest that this verse is pre-Johannine; also the expression ἀφῆκεν αὐτὸν ὁ πυρετός (*cf.* Mt 8: 15, the next pericope after the healing of the centurion's servant). Detailed expressions of time will be seen to be characteristic of the source. The two instances of οὖν may be due to Johannine retouching; but the former is not necessarily the 'historical' use characteristic of John,[2] and the latter is textually quite uncertain. – Schnackenburg ('Traditionsgeschichte', 64) holds that ἐχθές is John's insertion, consequent to 46*a*. Possibly so, but it may be overly literal to ask why (even with the source's locale between Cana and Capernaum) the man took so long to get home; and in any case, the reckoning may be a Jewish one, *yesterday* then meaning *this afternoon* (Brown, 191).

4: 53a. The various reasons for taking 53*a* to be a Johannine insertion would be inadequate in isolation from each other but they are sufficiently numerous that they cannot be overlooked: (*a*) emphatic repetition of a word of Jesus (*cf.* 5: 11 f., 7: 33–6, 16: 16–19, 18: 6–8*a*, etc.); (*b*) the theme of *knowing* (*cf.* above on 2: 9); (*c*) πατήρ (*cf.* ἄνθρωπος in 50*b*) rather than βασιλικός; (*d*) οὖν-*historicum*. The explicit recognition of the miracle as instantaneous is thus probably Johannine. That the source contained the same idea is evident from *v.* 52; John's addition here may have been occasioned by his having omitted an explicit statement in the source after 50*c* (see further below).

4: 53b. The fitting conclusion to the story in the source is the faithful response of those who have witnessed the sign; that this is not Johannine is attested by its unusual missionary terminology (πιστεύειν = *become a Christian*,[3] οἰκία = *household*; *cf.* Acts 10: 2, 11: 14, 16: 15, 31, 18: 8).

[1] But *cf.* the variant reading in 13: 24.
[2] Schweizer, *Ego eimi*, 89 f.; Ruckstuhl, 193 f. – Here it perhaps is intended as consecutive: *So he inquired...*
[3] This is to be distinguished from the typically Johannine use of the absolute verb to mean *come to have faith*—Dodd, *Interpretation*, 185.

4: 54. Despite the second half of the verse which makes a 'brave attempt' (Schweizer, 'Heilung') to justify it, 54*a* is in fundamental conflict with the signs referred to by John in 2: 23, 3: 2, 4: 45 (as the omission of δεύτερον by *e* shows) and must therefore be assigned to SQ. Perhaps the pleonastic πάλιν is Johannine (*cf.* 21: 16[1] and the redundancy in what we have taken to be the original Johannine reading at 2: 11: 'this first beginning'); the word order ἐποίησεν σημεῖον (א *W* Chr; *cf.* also $\mathfrak{P}^{75}$), being the harder reading, is probably original. The result is structurally identical with the source of 2: 11:

$$\text{τοῦτο} \begin{Bmatrix} \text{δεύτερον} \\ \text{πρῶτον} \end{Bmatrix} \text{ἐποίησεν σημεῖον ὁ Ἰησοῦς.}$$

Wellhausen (23 f.) held that such an enumeration of the signs would have been pointless in the source, where they followed one another without intervening narrative; but it would not be pointless if the source sought to schematize the signs (*cf.* Gen. 1)[2] and to call attention to their number (see below, pp. 100 f.).

The Johannine additions to the verse (πάλιν and ἐλθὼν... Γαλιλαίαν—*cf.* the insertion in 47) serve both to overcome, at least formally, the contextual aporia of 54*a* and to relate the story to that which had immediately preceded it in the source (Michel, 17): 'Again' this, the second sign (taking place like the first in Cana), Jesus did 'after coming from Judea to Galilee'. The source seems simply to have asserted that 'this [was the] second sign [that] Jesus did'.

Having now differentiated the Johannine and pre-Johannine strata in the story, primarily on internal grounds, we may proceed to a comparison with the two synoptic accounts of the centurion's servant and the question whether thereby we can recover certain details which John has suppressed, as Bultmann holds. First, he sees (151) verification of a Capernaum setting in the connection with that city of both parallel accounts. But we have found reason to suppose that even if the author of the source has received the story as taking place in Capernaum, he himself (at the latest) has transferred it to the road from Cana in order to heighten the miraculous element. While the story in

---

[1] But see also Mt 26: 42, Acts 10: 15.
[2] Bultmann, 78 n. 4, cites a Rabbinic enumeration of OT miracles.

Jn undoubtedly is somehow related to synoptic tradition, we cannot rule out the possibility of some variation from that tradition already in John's source.

Secondly, Bultmann (*ibid.*) implies that the source, like Q, told the story of a Gentile (ἑκατόνταρχος), John having made him into a Jew by using βασιλικός instead. This is not impossible, of course—the other *Fernheilungen* in the gospels involve Gentiles—but since, as Dibelius[1] has observed, the Q story is a composite of dialogue (reflecting the Gentile question in the church) and straightforward healing story, we may suspect that SQ's tradition, which lacks the dialogue (see below), represents a simpler version than Q's, *i.e.* a healing only, without the Gentile element. It is then Q which has changed *nobleman* to *centurion*.[2]

Lastly, Bultmann (152) thinks that in 48 f., which he sees as an initial demurrer on Jesus' part, overcome by a further word from the petitioner, John has *replaced* an original, formally identical, dialogue rather than simply interrupt the source with his insertion. He cites Mt 8: 7 as a parallel, but his interpretation of that verse (indignant question—*Synoptic tradition*, 38) is dubious and finds no support in Lk; nor is 49 a skilful saying, winning Jesus' approval, such as is found in the dialogue in Q. A better illustration would have been that in the story of the Syro-Phoenician/Canaanite woman (Mk 7: 24–30 = Mt 15: 22–8), a story shown by Dodd (189 f.) to be formally nearer to Jn 4: 46 ff. than the Q story of the centurion. Bultmann's suggestion that something has been dropped from the source is not impossible, though the question is probably contingent on whether the petitioner in SQ was a Gentile, which as we have seen is unlikely. It seems to be due to a similar tendency in John and the author of Q that both have inserted into what was originally a healing story pure and simple a dialogue, on the subject of faith, between Jesus and a petitioner. But the substance of the Johannine dialogue is so

---

[1] Cited by R. Bultmann, *The history of the synoptic tradition*, tr. J. Marsh (Oxford, 1963), 389 (supplement to 38).

[2] Goguel, 397, points out that a Gentile officer would have been out of place in Capernaum, part of Herod's domain—an observation which has little validity for a late stage of the tradition but *may* apply to the stage of which we are speaking.

different from that in Q that no connection between them is possible. If John has displaced anything from the source, then, it cannot be reconstructed, and it is more likely that 48 is simply an insertion.[1]

In these three instances the use of synoptic parallels adds very little to our analysis. However, the appearance of the phrase *in that hour* in 53 a (assigned above to John), while not sufficient grounds for positing Johannine dependence on Mt 8: 13, suggests that the source may have contained this phrase.[2] The awkward syntax of 53 a is perhaps a result of John's having retained the dative phrase (ἐκείνῃ τῇ ὥρᾳ) where the nominative case would have been better before ἐν ᾗ κτλ. If the phrase appeared at this point in the source, it is hard to guess exactly how it was used; it is perhaps more plausible that it occurred after 50 c and was postponed by John so as to occasion the man's second (and deeper) act of faith— provided for by the addition of 50 b—an act based on *knowing* the hour. In that position it may have read (rather like the present conclusion of the parallel in Mt): καὶ ἰάθη ὁ παῖς ἐκείνῃ τῇ ὥρᾳ.

So far we have examined mainly the points of contact between Jn and Mt. In his arresting article, Boismard points out a number of verbal parallels (some of which we have already noted) between the present passage and Lk's story: in Jn 4: 47 and Lk 7: 2 f., ἀκούσας, πρὸς αὐτόν (missing in some MSS of Lk), ἐρωτᾶν and ἤμελλεν with verb of dying; in Jn 4: 50 f. and Lk 7: 6, πορεύεσθαι and ἤδη δέ with genitive absolute; also the *sachlich* parallels of an encounter *en route* and faith without seeing (*cf.* Lk 7: 9). He holds (198) that 'literary contact between the two texts is absolutely certain' and explains them as *Luke's* insertions in the gospel of Jn, which he edited! This radical, and at the same time conservative, theory, which Boismard thinks he can demonstrate at other places in the gospel, must await further statement before it can be fully assessed,[3] though it seems to me highly unlikely. Meanwhile,

---

[1] The fact that 49 is only a restatement of 47 suggests this.

[2] Professor W. D. Davies reminds me that the phrase is very common in Rabbinic miracle stories and so may very well be traditional here; *cf.* also Mt 15: 28 (Canaanite woman).

[3] But see Schnackenburg, 'Traditionsgeschichte', 67–88; also Brown, 196.

our analysis suggests an alternative and less spectacular explanation for the widely attested similarities between the third and fourth gospels:[1] that Lk, or his source, knew either SQ or the tradition behind it. It is noteworthy that almost all of the parallels Boismard points out are to be found in the pre-Johannine, not the Johannine, stratum on our reconstruction.[2] We may take these points of contact, then, as an indirect confirmation of our analysis.

While we have not ruled out the possibility that John used one or more of the synoptics, the obvious parallels between this story and that of the centurion's servant in Mt and Lk, *together with the many differences*, are better explained as the result of developing oral tradition. John's story has some fundamental differences from that in Q,[3] despite what must have been a common origin at some point in the tradition; and the differences cannot be ascribed to John's redaction, since the pre-Johannine stage shows them also. In fact, as we saw, comparison with Q gives only slight help in getting behind John to the version on which he based his story. The assumption of a non-synoptic (yet nevertheless synoptic-like) *Vorlage* behind John is at least not challenged by the evidence of Q, and in fact is strengthened.

Our analysis of this pericope produces the following reconstruction of the source:

4: 46 *b* [ἦν δέ] τις βασιλικὸς οὗ ὁ υἱὸς ἠσθένει ἐν Καφαρναούμ·
    47 οὗτος ἀκούσας ὅτι Ἰησοῦς [ἔρχεται] |...| ἀπῆλθεν πρὸς αὐτὸν καὶ |...|

[1] *Cf.* Bailey, *Traditions*, who discusses the present passage in a long footnote (17 n.1); although he believes that John used Lk elsewhere, he holds that here he drew on a related but distinct tradition, the elements of which, as he outlines them, are all to be found in the source as we have analysed it.

[2] The only important exception is the loose *sachlich* parallel he finds between 4: 50 *b* and Lk's story in general; there is no reason to suppose that this element (belief without evidence) is drawn from Lk, since it appears also in Mt and is so closely akin to John's own thought as well. – The parallels of ἐρωτᾶν and μέλλειν are hardly anything but coincidence (so Bailey, *ibid.*).

[3] And, as Dodd shows (188 ff.), has closer similarities to other synoptic stories where there can be no thought of direct borrowing. – Even the differences between Mt and Lk are now being attributed to different versions of the tradition (so Haenchen).

49 λέγει |...|· κύριε, κατάβηθι πρὶν ἀποθανεῖν τὸ παιδίον μου.

50 λέγει αὐτῷ ὁ Ἰησοῦς· πορεύου, ὁ υἱός σου ζῇ. |...| καὶ ἐπορεύετο, [καὶ ἰάθη ὁ παῖς ἐκείνη τῇ ὥρᾳ].

51 ἤδη δὲ αὐτοῦ καταβαίνοντος οἱ δοῦλοι ὑπήντησαν αὐτῷ (καὶ [ἀπ/ἀν-]ἤγγειλαν) λέγοντες ὅτι ὁ παῖς αὐτοῦ ζῇ.

52 ἐπύθετο οὖν τὴν ὥραν παρ' αὐτῶν ἐν ᾗ κομψότερον ἔσχεν· εἶπαν οὖν αὐτῷ ὅτι ἐχθὲς ὥραν ἑβδόμην ἀφῆκεν αὐτὸν ὁ πυρετός.

53 |...| καὶ ἐπίστευσεν αὐτὸς καὶ ἡ οἰκία αὐτοῦ ὅλη.

54 τοῦτο (πάλιν) δεύτερον [ἐποίησεν σημεῖον] ὁ Ἰησοῦς |...|.

3. A THIRTY-EIGHT-YEAR ILLNESS HEALED
(5: 1–9)[1]

As they stand in the gospel, the two Cana miracles are unique in that each (a) is *self-contained*, having no explicit connection with its respective context,[2] and (b) has for its *conclusion* an identification of the miracle as one in a numbered series of σημεῖα.[3] Both these elements are missing in the stories to which we now turn, the miracles of chs. 5, 6, 9, and 11, and apparently for a single reason: these stories now serve to introduce extended dialogues and discourses and so, if they once had individual conclusions, have lost them in being incorporated into the present gospel. The purpose to which they have been put—as points of departure rather than episodes significant in themselves—may lead us to expect rather less editorial change on John's part within the stories themselves than we found in the Cana stories, and such is the case at least in the present pericope.[4]

[1] J. Bligh, 'Jesus in Jerusalem', *HeyJ* 4 (1963), 121–4; Goodenough, 'Primitive gospel', 155 f.; Haenchen, 'Probleme', 46–50.

[2] They are not so self-contained as to be 'situationless' in the gospel's structure, however; in subtle and profound ways John has integrated them into his *schema*; see Fuller, 97.

[3] With these two pericopes must also be included 21: 1 ff., though its connection with what precedes it is more explicit—see below, sec. 8.

[4] Also in ch. 9 and, to a lesser degree, ch. 6. John has laid such theological importance on the story in ch. 11 that it is a conspicuous exception to the rule.

5: 1. The present occasion for the episode (an unspecified feast in Jerusalem) plays no role in the story itself and is clearly John's editorial addition (*cf.* 2: 13).[1] This judgment is supported by the presence of the phrases μετὰ ταῦτα (see below on 6: 1) and τῶν 'Ιουδαίων (see above on 2: 6). A seam is also indicated by the shift from anarthrous 'Ιεροσόλυμα to τοῖς 'Ι. in *v.* 2. On the original introduction of the story and its place in the source see below, pp. 107 f.

5: 2. This verse properly begins the pericope; with ἔστιν δέ *cf.* the opening of the preceding pericope (46*b*).–The numerous variant readings might suggest an original (*i.e.* Johannine) aporia which later scribes tried to smooth over; but, as it happens, in no case can a *lectio difficilior* be explained as the result of Johannine redaction of the source. Rather the text adopted by Aland (ἐπὶ τῇ προβατικῇ κολυμβήθρα ἡ [ἐπι-] λεγομένη: 𝔓⁶⁶.⁷⁵ *B C* 𝕽 *W pm*) appears to be original (both in Jn and SQ), and the variety of readings is to be explained entirely by the failure of scribes unfamiliar with the Sheep Gate in Jerusalem (Neh. 3: 1) to understand an implied πύλη after ἐπὶ τῇ προβατικῇ.–'Εβραϊστί will appear to be from the source.[2]– We need come to no final decision about the correct name of the pool, still less about its historical or topographical identification.[3] None of the variants appears to be the result of Johannine redaction; the multiplication of readings is the result of later historical misinformation, as in the case of προβατικῇ.

---

[1] Bultmann; so also Spitta, Wendt, Wilkens.

[2] *Cf.* 19: 13, 17, 20, 20: 16. On the other hand, the use of (μεθ)ἑρμηνεύειν is Johannine: 1: 38, 41 f., 9: 7; probably also the similar use of λέγειν: 1: 38, 20: 16 (but *cf.* 4: 25, 19: 13, 17, 21: 2—all probably SQ, imitated by John in 11: 16, 20: 24).

[3] Haenchen rejects Jeremias' 'rediscovery' of Bethesda (*Die Wiederentdeckung von Bethesda, Johannes 5, 2* [*FRLANT* n.s. 41; Göttingen, 1949]; *cf.* also 'The copper scroll from Qumran', *ET* 71 [1959/60], 227 f.), in favour of *Be[l]zetha*—*cf.* Hirsch, 10. If *Bethesda* is correct, it is strange that John makes nothing of the Aramaic meaning (contrast 9: 7); but on the other hand, why would Bethesda be introduced by later scribes? See further Brown, 206 f.; D. J. Wieand, 'John v. 2 and the pool of Bethesda', *NTS* 12 (1965/6), 392–404.

5: 3. There is nothing in 3*ab* to suggest that it has been added to the context and so, while not absolutely essential to the story (it only anticipates what is implied in 5–7), it may be assigned to the source. The case is different with 3*c* (ἐκδεχομένων κτλ); it also anticipates a later element in the story (*v.* 7) but on textual grounds (it is wholly lacking in 𝔓⁶⁶.⁷⁵ 𝕭 *A** *q* syᶜ sa) is to be assigned to post-Johannine redaction (*pace* Brown), apparently added only to prepare for the interpolation of *v.* 4: its deletion is far harder to explain.

5: 4. This is clearly spurious; it is found in roughly the same witnesses as 3*c* but with almost innumerable textual variations. It contains seven non-Johannine words and probably represents various scribal attempts (perhaps based on an old legendary tradition) to explain the cryptic details of *v.* 7 (see below).

5: 5. Here the central plot of the story begins (ἦν δέ), *vv.* 2–3*a* having only set the stage. With τις ἄνθρωπος *cf.* 4: 46*b*, Lk 14: 2.–Bultmann (180 n. 6) thinks the wording here (τριάκοντα καὶ ὀκτὼ ἔτη ἔχων ἐν τῇ ἀσθενείᾳ αὐτοῦ) is *un-griechisch*, but it is not clear whether he ascribes this to a seam or merely to literary ineptness. The fact that the use of ἔχειν with accusative phrases of time is confined almost entirely to Jn in the NT (5: 5 f., 8: 57, 9: 21, 23, 11: 17; *cf.* 4: 52) might suggest Johannine redaction here.[1] But it is equally likely that the usage is characteristic of the source (see below, pt. IV)— the construction, while rare in the NT outside Jn, is not uncommon in Koine (Bauer, *Lexicon*, 333); in any case it does not appear quite so barbarous as Bultmann holds (it is to be noted that there has been very little scribal attempt to correct it).[2]–An exact statement of the illness' duration is a common element in synoptic tradition (Mk 5: 25, Lk 13: 16, *etc.*).

5: 6. The theme of Jesus' *knowing* in the second clause is probably not Johannine,[3] paralleling ἰδών[4] as it does (contrast

---

[1] Barrett (211): 'a mark of John's style'.

[2] Only the omission of αὐτοῦ, which does not really meet Bultmann's objection.

[3] *Versus* Brown, 207, whose illustration (2: 25) is hardly parallel.

[4] *Cf.* Lk 7: 13, 13: 12.

6: 6, 15); it either reflects the typical miracle story's ascription of supernatural knowledge to the thaumaturge (Mk 2: 8, 5: 30, *etc.*) or means simply 'having learned, discovering' (so Bauer, *Lexicon, ad rem,* 2*b*).–Schwartz excises Jesus' question to the sick man as pointless, but Dodd (177) shows that it only makes explicit the question, implicit in a number of the synoptic healing stories, of the suppliant's will to be healed. That Jesus takes the initiative rather than the sick man or a third party is not unique (*vs.* Bultmann, 177 n. 3)—*cf.* Mk 3: 3, Lk 7: 13 f., 13: 12 f., 14: 4.

5: 7. This verse has given rise to considerable misunderstanding, both ancient[1] and modern.[2] It is possible that originally no legend was connected with the water, which was simply an intermittent spring thought to have a healing effect on the bather. There was no question, then, of a *troubling* of the water by an angel (*v.* 4) or of healing granted only to the first to step into the pool (as the glosses in the present verse assume). The man was simply prevented by his infirmity and by the crowd from reaching the pool while the water was flowing.

5: 8. Several critics (Wellhausen, Spitta, Wendt, Goguel) see an inconsistency in the possession of a pallet by a man who could make his way, however slowly, and so was not paralysed. But whatever the man's illness (see below) his need of a pallet is implied by κατακείμενον in *v.* 6!–Nothing indicates unequivocally whether for the source the man was crippled or blind—the two categories broadly included in *v.* 3—though the former is usually assumed from the nature of Jesus' command, taken to mean 'Get up and show that you can walk'.[3] This probably is correct, since (*a*) ὑγιής (*vv.* 6, 9, 14) is never used in the NT of one whose sight has been restored and (*b*) it is unlikely that the source would have two stories of blind men and none of a cripple in its carefully selected list of miracles (*cf.* 20: 30 f.).

---

[1] See above on *vv.* 3*c*–4.

[2] Schwartz (1908), 152 ff., arbitrarily maintains that the miraculous (*sic*) effect of the water is redundant to the story of Jesus' healing and has been added along with *v.* 6 and mention of the pool in *v.* 2!

[3] It could mean simply 'Get up and go [home]—you have no need to remain lying here'; *cf.* Mk 2: 9 with 11.

5: 9ab. Hirsch (10) unnecessarily takes εὐθέως (lacking in
ℵ* *D W*) as a post-Johannine addition imitating Mark's style.
The variant can as well be explained as due to a later omission
seeking to ease the inconsistency with *v.* 14, which might seem
to imply that the man recovered only during an interval
(Bultmann, 181 n. 1). And it is likely that John found the word
in his source, since this form occurs only in SQ contexts (6: 21,
18: 27); elsewhere in Jn always εὐθύς (13: 30, 32, 19: 34,
?21: 3 [missing in most MSS]).

5: 9c. Thus far, except for *v.* 1, we have found no evidence of
Johannine redaction. It appears again at this point. Bultmann
(177) thinks the source continued intact through *v.* 16, but he
does not appear to have analysed the passage closely enough.[1]
Goguel (399 f.) was the first to point out that the mention of
the Sabbath in 9*c* is a postscript,[2] as is not the case in the
comparable Sabbath conflict stories in the synoptic gospels
(Mk 2: 23 ff., 3: 1 ff. pars., Lk 13: 10 ff., 14: 1 ff.); it plays no
part whatever in the preceding healing but is a recurring theme
in the discussion which follows (*vv.* 10, 16, 18).

H. Windisch has demonstrated that a number of passages in
Jn can be analysed into a succession of dramatic scenes, each
involving two parties.[3] Most, if not all, of these passages begin
with SQ pericopes, but the dramatic *Erzählungsstil* does not stem
from the source; it is rather due to John's redaction of it. This
is clear in the present passage, which with its sequel Windisch
(189) analyses into five scenes, each except the first (1–9*b*) brief

[1] As witnessed by his contention that 7: 19–24 (*sic*) was the continuation
of this pericope in the source, which can hardly be the case as those verses
stand. Fuller (89) thinks 16 was followed by 18*a*, but this is no smoother.

[2] Bultmann (177 n. 3, 178 n. 4) recognizes the secondary character of
9*c* ff. but attributes it to redaction on the part of the author of SQ, an
unnecessary complication. – Against the recognition of a seam after 9*b*,
Brown (210) protests that the story has no point without the Sabbath
motif; this is perhaps true, from John's standpoint, but not from that of the
source, which is interested in the miracle *per se*. His finding (209) a consistently obtuse characterization of the man throughout *vv.* 1–15, if exegetic-
ally valid, only reflects John's use of a gratuitous detail in the source.

[3] 'Der johanneische Erzählungsstil', in ΕΥΧΑΡΙΣΤΗΡΙΟΝ (Gunkel
Festschrift), ed. H. Schmidt (*FRLANT* n.s. 19 [1923], pt. 2), 174–213.
Cf. the similar but somewhat contrived study of E. Lohmeyer, 'Über
Aufbau und Gliederung des vierten Evangeliums', *ZNW* 27 (1928), 11–36.

and consisting solely of dialogue. Evidently John has taken the self-contained miracle story and added to it a series of scened conversations. This elaboration begins with 9 c.[1]

5: 14 b. Did the SQ episode end with 9 b, or has anything in the following verses been taken up by John from the *Vorlage*? Haenchen (48 f.) suggests that the substance of 14 b—'Sin no more that nothing worse befall you'—concluded the story in the source. His basis for this judgment, the analogy of Mk 2: 10 f.,[2] by itself is insufficient, but we have already noted the difficulty presented by *v.* 14 in its present position (was the healing only gradual?); it could be that the inconsistency was caused by John's artificially postponing the final sentence of the source.[3] Further it is noteworthy that the subject of Jesus' saying (*viz.* sin and its consequences) is not reflected in the story's Johannine elaboration. (*Judgment* in 22 ff. is hardly an exception.) On the other hand, the possibility of illness as the consequence of sin does reappear in another SQ passage (9: 2—see below). It is possible, then, that something like the following originally completed the story in the source: καὶ [ὁ Ἰησοῦς] εἶπεν αὐτῷ· μηκέτι ἁμάρτανε, ἵνα μὴ χεῖρόν σοί τι γένηται.[4]–If the source added a concluding enumeration of the sign at this point, it was necessarily lost in John's addition to the story and his rearrangement of the signs (see below, p. 105).

While there is no extended synoptic parallel to this story, we have already seen a possible contact with Mk's story of the paralytic borne by four (Mk 2: 2–12); as a matter of fact the verbal identity of Jesus' command in *v.* 8 to that in Mk 2: 9, 11[5]

---

[1] Note how the first Johannine scene (9 b–13) contains repetition (twice!) of Jesus' word in the source, a Johannine trait (as in 4: 52–3 a).

[2] With 'Sin no more' *cf.* also [Jn] 8: 11, and with 'that nothing worse befall you' Mt 12: 45.

[3] The scene (the third in Windisch's analysis), which *v.* 14 now comprises, is contrived and serves only to provide for a delayed recognition of Jesus' identity by the man healed (*cf.* 9: 35).

[4] The phrase ἴδε ὑγιὴς γέγονας is probably a Johannine duplication of the source (9 a), bridging the gap caused by the insertion of 9 c–14 a.

[5] But περιπάτει, found only in the former verse, may not be original even there, but assimilated either from Jn or from Mt or Lk (*cf.* Dodd, 176 n. 2).

—in particular the use of the vulgar κράβατος which both Mt and Lk replace—has led many to affirm literary dependence. But it is just this kind of brief, vivid saying which (like *Sin no more*...) does not need a literary vehicle to be preserved. Even Barrett (212) admits that the use of κράβατος proves nothing about dependence. In view of the wholly different shape of the stories in Jn 5: 1–9 and Mk 2: 1–12, it is likely that we have to do with dependence only on a synoptic-like tradition.[1] That tradition, as conveyed in this case by SQ, represents a unique combination of various synoptic elements, whose family tree it would be impossible to reconstruct.[2]

Our analysis of 5: 1 ff. results in the following text of the source:

5: 2   ἔστιν δὲ ἐν τοῖς Ἱεροσολύμοις ἐπὶ τῇ προβατικῇ κολυμβήθρα, ἡ ἐπιλεγομένη Ἑβραϊστὶ Βηθζαθά, πέντε στοὰς ἔχουσα.

3   ἐν ταύταις κατέκειτο πλῆθος τῶν ἀσθενούντων, τυφλῶν, χωλῶν, ξηρῶν.

5   ἦν δέ τις ἄνθρωπος ἐκεῖ τριάκοντα καὶ ὀκτὼ ἔτη ἔχων ἐν τῇ ἀσθενείᾳ αὐτοῦ·

6   τοῦτον ἰδὼν ὁ Ἰησοῦς κατακείμενον, καὶ γνοὺς ὅτι πολὺν ἤδη χρόνον ἔχει, λέγει αὐτῷ· θέλεις ὑγιὴς γενέσθαι;

7   ἀπεκρίθη αὐτῷ ὁ ἀσθενῶν· κύριε, ἄνθρωπον οὐκ ἔχω, ἵνα ὅταν ταραχθῇ τὸ ὕδωρ βάλῃ με εἰς τὴν κολυμβήθραν· ἐν ᾧ δὲ ἔρχομαι ἐγώ, ἄλλος πρὸ ἐμοῦ καταβαίνει.

8   λέγει αὐτῷ ὁ Ἰησοῦς· ἔγειρε ἆρον τὸν κράβατόν σου καὶ περιπάτει.

9   καὶ εὐθέως ἐγένετο ὑγιὴς ὁ ἄνθρωπος, καὶ ἦρεν τὸν κράβατον αὐτοῦ καὶ περιεπάτει. |...|

14   (καὶ [ὁ Ἰησοῦς] εἶπεν αὐτῷ· |...| μηκέτι ἁμάρτανε, ἵνα μὴ χεῖρόν σοί τι γένηται.)

[1] So Goodenough; Bultmann, 181 n. 2; Dodd, 176 f., who notes (Table 4, p. 175) much closer structural similarities with other synoptic stories, where there is no question of verbal dependence.

[2] *E.g.* the story has obvious affinities to that about the *pool* of Siloam in ch. 9, which in turn is akin to Mk 8: 22 ff. (the blind man of *Bethsaida* [*sic*]).

4. THE MULTITUDE FED (6: 1–14)[1]

This pericope, together with the following one, presents the closest parallels to the synoptic gospels in Jn and is taken, by those who maintain Johannine dependence on the synoptics, to provide indisputable proof of such dependence. Presently we shall find reason to question this judgment, but for the time being the question may be put aside while we undertake a source analysis of the passage chiefly on internal grounds. It is interesting to note that even in the synoptics this miracle (together with the feeding of the 4,000) is less eschatological, more a pure *Wunder*, a sign, than the other miracles.[2] Thus the unusual similarities in the Johannine account are understandable without positing dependence on the synoptics.

6: 1. The miracle story proper begins only in *v.* 5; but since the evangelist has not detached the original introduction—as he did in the case of 4: 46 ff.—we may examine it at this point, rather than with other transitional passages (pp. 102 ff. below). – The geographical and chronological circumstances of 4: 46 ff. and 5: 1 ff. were somewhat artificially introduced into the source by the evangelist; they are abrupt—but plausible. Here, however, the connection with what precedes is intolerable, so much so that the weight of critical opinion favours some sort of theory of post-Johannine rearrangement here, if at no other place in the gospel. But before resorting to such a correction of the canonical gospel,[3] we must ask if the aporia does not result rather from John's rearrangement of the *source*.

This possibility is supported by the likelihood that 6: 1, unlike 5: 1, belongs to the source: although a setting *across the lake* is not strictly necessary to the story of the feeding, it is germane to the episode which inseparably follows it.[4] The

---

[1] J. Bligh, 'Jesus in Galilee', *HeyJ* 5 (1964), 3–17; B. Gärtner, *John 6 and the Jewish Passover* (*Coniectanea Neotestamentica*, 17; Lund/Copenhagen, 1959); Goodenough, 'Primitive gospel', 156–8; Haenchen, 'Probleme', 31–4; E. D. Johnston, 'Feeding'; J. Knackstedt, 'Die beiden Brotvermehrungen im Evangelium', *NTS* 10 (1963/4), 309–35; Wilkens, 'Evangelist'.

[2] Brown, 247.

[3] The order resulting from the transposition of chs. 5 and 6, the usual solution, is itself not without difficulties—*cf.* Barrett, *ad loc.*

[4] Bultmann, 156. It is true that the movements of Jesus and the crowd in 16 ff. are not entirely clear, but the suggestion of Hirsch (58 f.) to attribute

geographical note is appropriate if, in the source, the present story followed an episode at or on the sea of Galilee (either 4: 46 ff. or 21: 1 ff.—see below, pp. 103–5). μετὰ ταῦτα here appears to be a Johannine connective phrase¹ and represents John's only attempt to ease the aporia his rearrangement has caused.—The redundant τῆς Γαλιλαίας τῆς Τιβεριάδος is undoubtedly the original Johannine reading—so Barrett (227) and *TGNT*—and the scribal attempts to improve it (by either omission or addition) only support the probability that John has added one of the genitive phrases as an explanatory gloss.²

6: 2 f. On internal grounds there is very little in these verses to indicate whether they belong to SQ or John. With the preceding verse they contain elements common in the synoptic tradition—sea, following crowd seeking cures, (?retreat to) mountain, sitting (?*there*—lacking in some MSS): cf. Mk 3: 7 ff., Mt 5: 1, 14: 13 f., 15: 29 f., *etc.*³ Thus, if in general John is dependent on the source for his synoptic-like material, it contained the material in these verses, and that more or less as it stands, as a prologue to the feeding miracle just as in Mt 14 and 15. But the explanation (2 b) for the continuing throng of followers is now Johannine in form—cf. 2: 23, 4: 45 (Bultmann, 156 n. 3).⁴

πέραν τῆς θαλάσσης in *vv.* 1, 17, 22, 25 to a stratum (R) later than the story proper (E) is unnecessarily drastic.

¹ And, with μετὰ τοῦτο, one which John uses especially when joining a source to other material—3: 22, 5: 1, 14, 7: 1, 11: 7, 11, 19: 28, 21: 1. However, neither form is unique to Jn. See further Barrett, 227 (and *cf.* 162).

² *Tiberias*, found in Jn three times, does not occur in the rest of the NT. According to Dodd (244 n. 1), 'the name [Tiberias] is more likely to be due to the evangelist, writing for [a Hellenistic] public, than to any tradition'. It is thus slightly more probable that John's insertion is τῆς Τιβεριάδος. (See further on 21: 1, also 6: 23.)

³ No one of these synoptic parallels can account for John's text, and so, while the similarities are striking, it does not seem likely that John is working from one of the synoptic texts, certainly not (as Bligh, 6–8, thinks) deliberately substituting the eucharistic sign for Mt's Sermon on the Mount.

⁴ Since the crowd, described as witnessing more than one healing, is Galilean, it might be held (as Schnackenburg suggests) that 2 b is pre-Johannine and that the source contained other healings in Galilee besides 4: 46 ff. But this takes the notice too literally.

6: 4. Most readers[1] have felt this verse to be intrusive: it has no relevance to the story and as it stands clearly interrupts the narrative. Both Dodd (210 f.) and Bultmann (156 n. 6) think a Passover reference at this point incongruous for John and assign it to a pre- and a post-Johannine stratum respectively. But the verse has what appear to be Johannine characteristics: ἦν δὲ ἐγγὺς [τὸ πάσχα] (*cf.* 2: 13, 7: 2, 11: 55) and τῶν Ἰουδαίων (*passim*). It clearly is not SQ.

6: 5. Here the miracle story begins. The use of οὖν-*historicum* here and throughout the story (11, 14, 15)[2] may suggest some slight Johannine retouching, though this form of connective is not unknown outside the gospel. The same can be said of the phrase 'lifted up [his] eyes' (*cf.* 4: 35, 11: 41, 17: 1, but also Mt 17: 8, Lk 6: 20, 16: 23, 18: 13). Goguel (401 f.) finds it strange that in 2 f. Jesus leaves behind the crowd and then here is again met by a crowd. He concludes, rightly, that the latter is not the same (at least not precisely) as that in *v.* 2 (note the imperfect ἠκολούθει there) but, wrongly, that one of the crowds is necessarily redundant. The earlier mention serves to explain in a general way the appearance of the specific crowd here. While the question πόθεν is frequently Johannine (usually with a verb of knowing—see above on 2: 9), it is not so here, where it probably originally suggested perplexity just as in Mk 8: 4, Mt 15: 33 (*cf.* Lk 1: 43).[3]–If Barrett (288; *cf.* Schnackenburg, 'Traditionsgeschichte', 81 f.) is right that both (*a*) Jesus' taking the initiative and (*b*) the mention of disciples by name represent a late form of tradition, this can apply either to SQ or to John.[4] It is possible, nevertheless, that although Philip is known to the source (see below on 1: 43), John has introduced him here, in connection with *v.* 6, thereby creating the anomaly at *v.* 8, where the source already mentioned a particular disciple; πρός with verb of saying is perhaps a mark of Johannine

[1] Including at least one scribe—Minuscules *472* and *850* lack the verse.

[2] The use of οὖν in 10*b* and 13 is not historical but consecutive.

[3] Bauer, *Lexicon, ad rem*, 3. Brown, 233, cites Moses' question to Yahweh in Num. 11: 13, and notes (244) that the evangelist would hardly create a difficulty (Jesus' apparent ignorance) which he must solve in the next verse (*q.v.*).

[4] For the former detail, *cf.* Mk 8: 2 par. and Lk 7: 13, also Jn 5: 6; for the latter see below on 1: 40 ff. and 21: 2—further, Brown, 246.

(and Lukan) style.[1] The source, then, will have read τοῖς μαθηταῖς αὐτοῦ (*cf.* Mk 8: 1).

6: 6. Despite the presence of πειράζειν, only here in Jn, this verse is shown to be Johannine on every kind of criterion: (1) ideological (Jesus as foreknowing and in command of the situation—*cf.* 12: 32 f., 18: 4*a, etc.*), (2) stylistic (τοῦτο δὲ ἔλεγεν—7: 39, 11: 51, 12: 33, 21: 19; αὐτὸς γάρ—2: 25, 4: 44 f., 6: 34, 13: 11, 16: 27; *cf.* Bultmann, 157 n. 1), and (3) contextual (explanatory interruption—2: 9*b*, 21, 4: 2, *etc.*).

6: 7. Philip's reply shows both such similarities and such differences to Mk 6: 37 pars. as are to be expected in the oral tradition: *e.g.* the same amount of money, now however held to be inadequate to feed the crowd. There is no reason to attribute this to Johannine editing, but only a possible shift in subject from an original 'they' to 'Philip' (see above on *v.* 5).

6: 8f. Wellhausen (25) noted that 'one of his disciples' is strange immediately after the mention of Philip in 7, and although Wilkens (43) maintains that εἷς can mean simply *a certain one* or even *another*, it is less strained to suppose that John has caused the unevenness by introducing Philip in 5–7. That the phrase should be followed by a proper name (but *cf.* 11: 49), and that of a person already known to the reader (1: 40), is perhaps odd; Spitta (138 f.) and Hirsch (60) consequently take 'Andrew, the brother of Simon Peter' to be redactional. So it could be, but the present wording could as well be pre-Johannine, intentionally parallel to 1: 35, 40, where Andrew is identified as 'one of [John's] disciples'.[2]–In the synoptics the information about the loaves and fish is given in answer to a word of Jesus; that here it is volunteered by a disciple—with the ironic 'But what are they among so many?'—is best attributed to the distinct character of the source's tradition, especially since the vocabulary differs from that of the synoptists,[3] and is closer to that of the story of

---

[1] Boismard, 'Saint Luc', 195 f.; *cf.* 4: 48 f.

[2] In the only other appearance of Andrew, 12: 22, which is probably Johannine, he is not identified.

[3] παιδάριον and κρίθινος only here in NT; ὀψάριον only here and 21: 9 f., 13.

Elisha[1] which underlies all gospel versions of this miracle (Barrett, 229).

6: 10. As before, a regrouping and rewording of various synoptic elements (command to sit, grass, five thousand men), betraying not conscious editing by John but the vagaries of tradition as reproduced by SQ.–The explicit shift from ἀνθρώπους (10*a*, *cf.* 14*a*) to ἄνδρες (10*c*) signifies no seam but only a terse version of Mt's 'apart from women and children'[2]—10*c* should perhaps be translated, 'So they sat down, the men in number about five thousand'.–On this use of ὡς, see below on 11: 18.

6: 11. Wilkens ('Evangelist', 86) suggests that the presence of historical οὖν and partitive ἐκ shows this verse as a whole to be Johannine. That is unlikely.[3]

6: 12f. On *sachlich* grounds Dodd (207) holds that *v.* 12 is Johannine, for at least the clause ἵνα μή τι ἀπόληται, to which there is no parallel in the synoptic accounts, seems to anticipate the Johannine discourse in 27 ff. on ἡ βρῶσις ἡ ἀπολλυμένη.[4] He suggests that John has replaced a verse in the source similar to that found in all the synoptic accounts (καὶ ἔφαγον [πάντες] καὶ ἐχορτάσθησαν), since John indicates knowledge of this wording in *v.* 26.[5] If this is true, it helps to explain the redundancy created by 13 (κλασμάτων...ἃ ἐπερίσσευσαν) after 12 (τὰ περισσεύσαντα κλάσματα), John having necessarily anticipated 13 in adding 12. The first two words of 13 are then

---

[1] 2 Kings 4: 42—κρίθινος; 4: 38, 41 (LXX)—παιδάριον.

[2] Either heightening Mk or only making explicit what may be implied in Mk 6: 44 ('Those who ate...were five thousand ἄνδρες'), the crowd being referred to only as 'they' otherwise.

[3] For the former, see above on *v.* 5; and οὖν may not be original here: numerous MSS read δέ or καί. The latter (*cf. v.* 8) is frequent in Jn but also in the rest of the NT; the only uses unique to Jn are τις ἐκ (but *cf.* Lk 11: 15), πολλοὶ ἐκ, and οὐδεὶς ἐκ. See further below, pp. 209 f.–Most of the numerous variants in this verse, only some of which are shown in Nestle, represent assimilation to the synoptics.

[4] *Cf.* F.-M. Braun, 'Quatre "signes" johanniques de l'unité chrétienne', *NTS* 9 (1962/3), 147–55, and Hoskyns, 289, who also find something distinctively Johannine (*cf.* 6: 39 and 17: 11 f.) in the ἵνα-clause.

[5] He has then replaced this with the paraphrase ὡς δὲ ἐνεπλήσθησαν (imitating 2: 9*a*?).

Johannine along with 12, the remaining (καὶ ἐγέμισαν κτλ) following smoothly after Dodd's reconstruction of 12 (cf. Mk 6: 42 f., 8: 8, pars.). His suggestion is plausible, but perhaps only ἵνα μή κτλ is Johannine.

6: 14 f. These verses are very difficult to assign. The critics are divided here and illustrate the inconclusiveness of arguing from purely *sachlich* grounds. For while Wilkens ('Evangelist', 84), following Bultmann (157), finds in them the Johannine theme of misunderstanding and so assigns them to the evangelist, Haenchen denies this by a comparison with *v.* 26 and, with Dodd (212–16, who uses slightly different grounds), assigns them to the source. In fact, however, they cannot be treated as a unit.

Whatever the correct interpretation of 26 (is it a rebuke or a word of encouragement?), at least 15*a* seems to contain a typically Johannine portrayal of the inappropriate response (cf. ἁρπάζειν) to Jesus on the part of many who encounter him. This is supported to some degree by the presence also of two other Johannine themes: Jesus' (supernatural?) knowledge of danger (cf. 2: 24 f., 4: 1, 8: 59, 10: 39) and, by implication, the true (non-worldly) nature of his kingship (cf. 18: 33 ff.). It is probably safe to conclude that this much at least is contributed by the evangelist.

On the criterion of the theme of misunderstanding, *v.* 14, however, is ambiguous. On the one hand, while the next verse implies that the crowd's response here is inappropriate, 14 might by itself be quite appropriate in a gospel of signs (cf. 1: 49, 4: 19). On the other hand, in 14*b* as it stands the phrases οὗτός ἐστιν ἀληθῶς[1] ὁ προφήτης (cf. 7: 40) and ὁ ἐρχόμενος εἰς τὸν κόσμον (cf. ?1: 9, 11: 27), and the relevance of this acclamation to the Johannine dialogue about the Mosaic prophet in 31 ff., suggest the evangelist's hand.

At first the phrase ἰδόντες ὃ ἐποίησεν σημεῖον in 14*a* appears to be Johannine also, like 2: 23, 4: 45, 6: 2*b*. But in two ways (number and word order) it is different from those stereotyped editorial notes: (1) it speaks not of a general response to a number of signs (only alluded to) but of a particular reaction

---

[1] This word is lacking in *D 579 pc* and could be an assimilation to 7: 40.

(direct discourse) to a specific sign (that just depicted)[1] and (2) only here (but *cf.* 6: 30) does the word σημεῖον follow the verb, separated by it from its modifier.[2] This rather unusual word order would not be significant if it were not found also in the source as we have uncovered it at 2: 11 and 4: 54. On these grounds we may suspect that at least this phrase is derived from the source, a possibility which is strengthened by the fact that in both the other pre-Johannine uses of the phrase it is associated with an account of witnesses' positive response to a sign (2: 11 *c*, 4: 53 *b*), just as here. The latter is true of 2: 23, 4: 45, 6: 2 *b*, but they seem to be John's summary notices presumably patterned on this specific pre-Johannine model. It is a good guess that 14 is John's revision of the original conclusion to the pericope, which contained an enumeration of the sign and an acclamation, by οἱ ἄνθρωποι (*cf. v.* 10 *a*), of Jesus as *prophet*; an implicit pre-Johannine identification of this miracle with that of Moses in the wilderness is not impossible.[3] John rewrote it when he both altered the order of the signs and chose to treat the crowd's reaction as a misunderstanding. See further below, pp. 103–5.

In 15 *b* the withdrawal εἰς τὸ ὄρος (just as in *v.* 3) and the phrase αὐτὸς μόνος conform to the synoptic data (Mk 6: 46 f. = Mt 14: 23). This fragment, then, probably derives from the source and there, as in the synoptics, undoubtedly belonged to the introduction to the next pericope (see below), not to the conclusion of the loaves episode as now. John, with the addition of 15 *a*, has transformed it into a second (πάλιν is probably his

---

[1] The variant reading ἃ σημεῖα ($\mathfrak{P}$[75] *B pc a*) is probably an assimilation to the other passages, esp. *v.* 2. See also 11: 45 (*vs. v.* 46).

[2] And, if ὁ Ἰησοῦς ($\mathfrak{K}$ *A L* Γ Δ Θ λ φ *pl f q* vg[s.cl]) is original, interrupting verb and subject; the longer reading may have been abbreviated in transmission as redundant with Ἰησοῦς in 15.

[3] So Schnackenburg, 'Traditionsgeschichte', 84; *cf.* Lk 7: 16. That *John* accepts προφήτης as a title for Jesus is clear from purely Johannine contexts in which it appears (7: 40, 9: 17); but there is considerable evidence for the early use of this title in an eschatological and probably messianic way (O. Cullmann, *The christology of the New Testament*, tr. S. C. Guthrie and C. A. M. Hale [Philadelphia, 1959], 23, 36 f.), so that the source very possibly provided John with it (see below on 1: 21, 4: 19). Cullmann, *ibid.*, thinks ὁ ἐρχόμενος κτλ is traditionally part of the title (= Elijah) as well, but this is less certain. – On Mosaic typology in the source see pp. 232 f.

addition)[1] and more spectacular retreat from the now in-appropriate enthusiasm of the crowd in 14. In the next section we shall consider how it related to 16 ff. in the source; here we should note that the reading φεύγει (א* lat syᶜ) is undoubtedly genuine, being softened in transmission to ἀνεχώρησεν (no-where used in Jn), and perhaps represents John's alteration of an original ἀπῆλθεν (Mk) in the source. – The double notice of Jesus' going εἰς τὸ ὄρος (vv. 3, 15), with no intervening report of his movements, is due perhaps to the narrator's carelessness (Bultmann, 156 n. 4), the same unconcern for geographical consistency being found occasionally in Mk. Or the incon-sistency may be only apparent: the second withdrawal to the mountain is not described as an ascent (if indeed the first one was such—cf. variant ἀπῆλθεν) and may only mean a further retreat into the hill country (cf. Bauer, Lexicon, 586).

The impression gained above, that v. 14 was based on the original conclusion of the miracle, is thus reinforced by our judgment that 15b originally belonged with what follows; it is 15a, a clearly Johannine clause, which makes a unit of two originally distinct notices.[2]

We have already noted a number of the many similarities between Jn 6: 1–14 and Mk 6: 30–44, 8: 1–9 pars. Barrett (226–32) gives an exhaustive analysis of such verbal relation-ships, and even he, who maintains John's literary dependence on Mk and Mt, qualifies his conclusion at several points (e.g. on vv. 1, 6, 10) by admitting that John may have used a source 'similar to if not identical with Mark's'. That is just the point: the many close parallels must be explained, but so must the differences, and many of the latter are not explicable as the result of intentional changes on John's part.[3] As Dodd (196–222) has shown at great length, we find here just that combina-tion of (a) identity of word and detail, (b) heightened miracle, (c) streamlined narrative,[4] and (d) gratuitous difference, as is to be expected in the development of tradition. Where Johan-

[1] So Spitta, 140; or possibly a later gloss—lacking in a number of MSS.
[2] If so, the attempts of Dodd (216 f.) and Brown (249 f.) to find in 14 f. a historical reminiscence of a κρίσις in Jesus' ministry are not supported by the literary data.   [3] See further Brown, 236–50.
[4] E.g. Wilkens (Entstehungsgeschichte, 44 n. 151) shows how the preparation for the miracle in the synoptics has disappeared in Jn.

nine redaction is evident, it is usually distinguishable from a pre-Johannine *literary* stratum, and it is just this hypothetical *Vorlage* which provides the best explanation for the relation of Jn to the synoptics.

The argument against literary dependence can best be illustrated as follows: the verbal relationship between the two feeding stories in Mk 6 and 8 is in every way analogous to that between Jn's story and any one of the synoptic versions, yet obviously no one suggests that Mk 6 is literarily dependent on Mk 8, or *vice versa*; rather the relationship between them is held to lie somewhere behind the extant texts.[1] It is just this kind of relation which the present study urges in the case of Jn *vis-à-vis* the synoptics. The recent emphasis on the Johannine *tradition* (Noack, Wilkens, Dodd, Schnackenburg, Brown), with the application to it of form-critical method, is valid, confused though it is at times with considerations of historical reliability; nevertheless, the foregoing analysis suggests that between such a (more or less fluid) tradition and the extant gospel lies a literary stage which only source criticism can uncover.

The following self-contained stratum appears to underlie this passage:

6: 1 |...| ἀπῆλθεν ὁ Ἰησοῦς πέραν τῆς θαλάσσης τῆς Γαλιλαίας |...|.

2 ἠκολούθει δὲ αὐτῷ ὄχλος πολύς |...|.

3 ἀνῆλθεν δὲ εἰς τὸ ὄρος Ἰησοῦς, καὶ ἐκεῖ ἐκάθητο μετὰ τῶν μαθητῶν αὐτοῦ.

5 ἐπάρας οὖν τοὺς ὀφθαλμοὺς ὁ Ἰησοῦς καὶ θεασάμενος ὅτι πολὺς ὄχλος ἔρχεται πρὸς αὐτόν, λέγει [τοῖς μαθηταῖς αὐτοῦ] · πόθεν ἀγοράσωμεν ἄρτους ἵνα φάγωσιν οὗτοι;

7 ἀπεκρίθη[σαν] αὐτῷ |...| διακοσίων δηναρίων ἄρτοι οὐκ ἀρκοῦσιν αὐτοῖς, ἵνα ἕκαστος βραχύ τι λάβῃ.

8 λέγει αὐτῷ εἷς ἐκ τῶν μαθητῶν αὐτοῦ, Ἀνδρέας ὁ ἀδελφὸς Σίμωνος Πέτρου ·

9 ἔστιν παιδάριον ὧδε ὃς ἔχει πέντε ἄρτους κριθίνους καὶ δύο ὀψάρια· ἀλλὰ ταῦτα τί ἐστιν εἰς τοσούτους;

10 εἶπεν ὁ Ἰησοῦς· ποιήσατε τοὺς ἀνθρώπους ἀναπεσεῖν.

---

[1] Knackstedt argues that the two stories in Mt (*sic*) are not a doublet but derive from distinct historical events. Even if this were so, as seems to me quite unlikely, the problem of explaining the verbal relationships between the two accounts (as distinct from the event[s] they describe) remains.

ἦν δὲ χόρτος πολὺς ἐν τῷ τόπῳ. ἀνέπεσαν οὖν οἱ ἄνδρες τὸν ἀριθμὸν ὡς πεντακισχίλιοι.

11 ἔλαβεν οὖν τοὺς ἄρτους ὁ Ἰησοῦς καὶ εὐχαριστήσας διέδωκεν τοῖς ἀνακειμένοις, ὁμοίως καὶ ἐκ τῶν ὀψαρίων ὅσον ἤθελον.

12 **Either** ὡς δὲ ἐνεπλήσθησαν, λέγει τοῖς μαθηταῖς αὐτοῦ· συναγάγετε τὰ περισσεύσαντα κλάσματα |...| · 13 a συνήγαγον οὖν, **or** [καὶ ἔφαγον (πάντες) καὶ ἐχορτάσθησαν,] 13 b καὶ ἐγέμισαν δώδεκα κοφίνους κλασμάτων ἐκ τῶν πέντε ἄρτων τῶν κριθίνων ἃ ἐπερίσσευσαν τοῖς βεβρωκόσιν.

14 οἱ οὖν ἄνθρωποι |...| ἔλεγον ὅτι οὗτός ἐστιν |...| ὁ προφήτης |...|.

5. WALKING ON WATER AND A MIRACULOUS LANDING (6: 15–25)[1]

This pericope, especially at its conclusion, is not so clearly identifiable as a sign story. But that it was found by John in his source is evident: (a) one of the two synoptic versions of the feeding is followed immediately by a story parallel to this one (Mk 6: 45–52 par.); (b) the Johannine dialogue which follows this story has no relation to it whatever, and John apparently preserves it only out of respect for his source and perhaps because it brings Jesus and the crowd together again for that dialogue (Bultmann, 159).

6: 15–17. I suggested in the previous section that 15 b originally introduced the present story and that in adding 15 a John detached it, making of it a separate episode, as a completion of 1–14. It is perhaps impossible to reconstruct the source exactly at this point, due to John's redaction, but we can be guided by the Markan story. Mk's introduction is not entirely coherent: (a) Jesus compels the disciples to set off in a boat 'while he dismisses the crowd'; then, after (b) taking leave of 'them' (which at least Mt understood to mean the crowd, not the disciples), he (c) goes 'into the mountain' (instead of joining the disciples); when (d) evening comes he is alone there and (e) the

---

[1] See bibliography for sec. 4, above; also Boismard, 'Problèmes de critique textuelle concernant le quatrième évangile', *RB* 60 (1953), 359–71. References to Wilkens in this section are to *Entstehungsgeschichte*.

boat in mid-lake. Item (*a*) either collides with or duplicates (*b*) and (*c*), and one may ask whether Mk has not added it to a traditional introduction. This is given some support when we compare the present introduction in Jn: Jesus, (*b'*) fleeing the crowd, (*c'*) goes 'into the mountain'; when (*d'*) evening comes, (*e'*) the disciples set out across the lake. The parallels are not exact but close enough to suggest that the sequence may be pre-Johannine. Furthermore, because the Johannine version is told consistently from the standpoint of the disciples (whereas in Mk, predominantly from Jesus' standpoint), it is unlikely that in the source Jesus unnaturally forced the disciples' departure before sundown, as in Mk (*a*). On this basis, precarious as it may be, we can attempt the following reconstruction:

15b. In place of φεύγει πάλιν (see above, sec. 4) read, with Mk, καὶ ?(ἀποταξάμενος αὐτοῖς) ἀπῆλθεν, adding ὁ 'Ιησοῦς and continuing, with Jn, εἰς τὸ ὄρος αὐτὸς μόνος.

16–17a. The disciples make for Capernaum, from which they had come with Jesus before the feeding (see pp. 55 f. above).–κατέβησαν may refer to the mountain locale of *v.* 3, but perhaps instead only to the inevitable descent to a shore (Bultmann, 158 n. 6).

17b. Bultmann (158 n. 9) and others suggest that the reading of א *D* (κατέλαβεν δὲ αὐτοὺς ἡ σκοτία) has been influenced in transmission by 12: 35 (*cf.* 1: 5*b*), but it is hard to see just how. Hirsch (12) is probably right that this reading is the correct one and that dogmatic considerations (*i.e.* respect for the disciples) have produced the dominant reading. But on either reading the half-verse probably contains, as Wilkens (47) holds, Johannine symbolism for the death of Jesus (darkness, desolation of disciples). A similar interpretation is advanced by Richardson (117 f., 106): this miracle, which is ignored by its context, is developed by John in the Farewell Discourses (chs. 13–17) instead, in the themes of Jesus' going away from and returning to the disciples. Such theories may be forced, but they have the advantage of explaining an otherwise puzzling passage: why would either the disciples or the reader expect Jesus to 'come to them'? how is he to be seen walking on the water if it is dark?

It is likely, then, that 17 *b*—redundant as it is with the time reference in 16 *a*[1]—is John's insertion, whether for symbolic reasons (more likely if our text criticism is correct) or simply to provide an expectancy for a miraculous event which is otherwise ignored.

6: 18. Since this verse is superfluous to the plot of the miracle, Wellhausen (29) considers it a gloss, pointing out that the element of danger is absent from the rest of the story and so may be due to assimilation to Mk. But more likely it is *pre*-Johannine and represents an early stage of a development more apparent in Mk: the encroaching of the stilling-of-the-storm tradition upon this episode (Mk 6: 48 *a*, 51 *a*; Bultmann, *Synoptic tradition*, 216).

6: 19 f. Here we find the usual combination of similarities and dissimilarities to the synoptic parallels: identical phrases (ἐλαύνειν, περιπατεῖν, ἐπὶ τῆς θαλάσσης, ἐγώ εἰμι· μὴ φοβεῖσθε —but the last two words are lacking in sy[c]), often used quite differently, and some paraphrases (ἰδ-/θεωρε-, ταρασσ-/φοβε-). Dodd (198) subtly notes that even the delay of Jesus' appearance is expressed from the standpoint of those in the boat (the distance travelled) rather than of Jesus (the lapse of time—*cf.* Mk 6: 48 *b* = Mt 14: 25, but see Mt 14: 24). We may then take these verses to be distinctive of John's tradition and to stem from SQ.–It seems to me unlikely that in the source ἐπὶ τῆς θαλάσσης means 'by the sea' (as probably in 21: 1), so that no miracle is thereby intended (so Dodd, 198); if it does, it means only that the episode is not emphasized as a sign (see below, p. 101)—there is a miracle, in any case, in *v.* 21.

6: 21. The occurrence of θέλειν here is undoubtedly due to contact with synoptic tradition (Mk 6: 48 *b*), but characteristically it is used of the *disciples'* wish to take Jesus into the boat (*cf.* Mk 6: 51 *a*). εὐθέως (*vs.* εὐθύς) is probably SQ (see above on 5: 9 *b*). The verse is the succinct but unmistakable account of still a further wonder—a miraculous landing.

[1] If, as Wikenhauser (cited by Brown, 251) holds, 17 *b* is instead a parenthesis explaining 16–17 *a*, it is all the more clearly Johannine.–The mention of darkness here is not parallel to either of the time references in Mk: evening (*v.* 47 = 16 here), fourth watch of the night (*v.* 48 = 19 *a* here).

Here the miracle story itself ends, and a number of interpreters (*e.g.* Lohmeyer, Barrett, Brown) see a new section beginning with 22. Indeed for the evangelist this is true (*cf.* τῇ ἐπαύριον); here he begins to guide the narrative toward the dialogue which starts in 26. But *vv.* 22–5 are a literary crux: the verbosity and triviality of these verses suggest that they are the product of repeated redaction, as also the complexity of textual variation shows. We should consider the possibility, then, that SQ contained a part of these lines and that it was John's adaptation of them that began the process of 'correction'. It is plausible, on the analogy of other pericopes, that in the source the story did not end with *v.* 21 but went on to verify the miracle and show its effect on the crowd of the previous pericope (see below on 25). The synoptic parallels (Mk 6: 53 ff. = Mt 14: 34 ff.) also have crowds flocking to Jesus when he lands.

In 22–5, two inconsistencies seem to me to be fundamental:[1] (*a*) the redundancy of 24 after 22 (the two verses are substantially a doublet)[2] and (*b*) the awkward connection between 24 and 25 ('...they went to *Capernaum*, seeking Jesus. When they found him *across the lake*...'). The obvious solution is that 22 and 25 belong to one stratum and 23 f. to another.[3] With Bultmann (160), I take the bulk of 22, 25 to be pre-Johannine and 23 f. to be Johannine or later. The *sachlich* and stylistic character of 24 (on which see below) supports this, as does the fact that 23 f. can more readily be seen as a gloss on 22, 25 than the reverse.

On the basis of this rough analysis, we proceed to a more detailed (and, because of the passage's complexity, necessarily intricate) examination.

6: 22. Bultmann assumes that πέραν τῆς θαλάσσης is used from the standpoint of the feeding and so refers to the western shore. But πέραν is consistently used in Jn (1: 28, 3: 26, 6: 1, 17, 25, 10: 40) in a relative way, from the standpoint of the context; if, then, the verse follows 21 in the source, *across the lake* must

---

[1] Similarly Hirsch, *ad loc.*

[2] *Cf.* Schnackenburg, 45, who however considers the bulk of 22 to be later than 24, not earlier as we hold.

[3] Verse 23, which is structurally parenthetical, leads up to 24 and consequently belongs with it (*vs.* Schnackenburg, *ibid.*, who takes it with 22 as post-Johannine). On its authenticity, see below.

mean across from Capernaum (*cf.* 17*a*), *i.e.* on the eastern shore.[1] This interpretation is supported by the likelihood that τῇ ἐπαύριον is Johannine (*cf.* below on 1: 29 ff., 12: 12), so that in the source there is no clear-cut change of scene between 21 and 22.–The most important variants in this verse involve the principal verb (εἶδον in Nestle). ἰδών (*cf.* εἰδώς, ἰδόντες) is considered by Bultmann to be only a scribal conjecture, but in fact it is the harder reading, leaving the sentence incomplete. If it is original, both in Jn and SQ, it accounts for the way 24 is framed—to resume and complete the anacoluthon of 22. Verses 22, 25 were then originally one sentence in the source, which John broke up, but otherwise left unchanged, by the addition of ?23 and 24; only later was the verb corrected to εἶδον(-εν).–εἰ μὴ ἕν is probably a postscript, added by John to mean what the later interpolation in ℵ* *D, etc.* makes explicit ('that in which the disciples of Jesus embarked'). ἀλλὰ μόνοι κτλ, making the sentence pleonastic, is either Johannine or a later gloss.–The unanimous reading πλοιάριον here (variants in 23 f.) means either the same as πλοῖον (Barrett, 237) or emphasizes ἄλλο οὐκ: 'no other boat, not even a dinghy'.

6: 23. This, together with the following verse, was added simply to explain how the crowd found Jesus across the lake. It is not our present concern to distinguish Johannine from post-Johannine strata, but it is possible that the verse is a late gloss: it awkwardly provides a *deus ex machina* unlike anything in the gospel, contains the only NT reference to the city (as opposed to the sea—6: 1, 21: 1) of *Tiberias*, and refers to the loaves of 6: 9, 11, 13 as *bread* (singular). In any case, the last phrase of the verse (εὐχαριστήσαντος τοῦ κυρίου) is certainly late; it is lacking in *D 69 pc a e* sy^sc.

6: 24. This verse is more akin to *v.* 15*a* (Johannine) than to 22, 25. It speaks of the people *seeking* Jesus (*cf.* 26)—to make him king?—whereas 22, 25 shows the crowd *wondering* how he got to Capernaum.

---

[1] This consideration does not fundamentally affect Bultmann's argument, yet removes from it the chief basis for Wilkens' considering it contrived.

6: 25. Here the sentence begun in 22 is completed. The double instance of πέραν τῆς θαλάσσης is not a redundancy since in each case a different place is meant: (22) 'The crowd which was standing[1] on the opposite side of the lake [from the last event, the miraculous landing in 21], having seen that there had been no other boat there and that Jesus had not embarked in the boat with his disciples, (25) and having found[2] him across the lake [from where they had been standing], said to him, "Rabbi,[3] when did you come here?"' The question of the people has the same effect as the remark of the unsuspecting steward in 2: 9 f. and that of the uninformed servants in 4: 51: it provides a witness to the miracle of Jesus' walking on the water (Bultmann, 160).

6: 26. Wilkens (47) treats the earliest stratum as continuing through *v.* 27, but this is certainly wrong. Verse 26 is distinct from what precedes, introducing a wholly new dimension into the context (*cf.* 4: 48). Nevertheless it probably takes some of its wording from an earlier part of the source (see above on *v.* 12).—Bultmann is perhaps right that the pericope in the source cannot have ended with a question (but *cf.* Mk 4: 41, *etc.*) and that *vv.* 26 ff. have replaced the original ending. For the possibility that another episode followed in the source see below, pp. 195 f.

From the above analysis it will be evident that in some ways Jn's version of the story of the *Seewandeln* is more developed than that in Mk (*cf.* on 21), while in other ways less so (*cf.* on 18).[4] This suggests, once again, that we have to do not with a literary relationship but with contact between oral traditions. In this

---

[1] *I.e.* after the feeding; RSV overtranslates ('remained') because of τῇ ἐπαύριον. This does not necessarily include all the 5,000!

[2] The question how the crowds 'found' Jesus did not concern the author of the source, apparently, but perhaps a journey around the shore of the lake is presupposed (*cf.* the opening of the feeding episode, Mk 6: 33).—Strict consistency would require a singular participle (εὑρών) here, unless ἰδόντες is correct in 22. Either John has changed to the plural because of 24 (ζητοῦν-τες), or, more likely, in the source the plural verb (εἶπον) has influenced the participle nearer to it.

[3] On this form of address see below, pt. III, on 1: 38.

[4] See, in detail, Brown, 252–4.

case it is likely that Jn's tradition goes back to a pre-Markan version of the story.[1]

The source, then, appears to have consisted of the following:

6: 15b [καὶ ἀποταξάμενος αὐτοῖς ἀπῆλθεν ὁ Ἰησοῦς] εἰς τὸ ὄρος αὐτὸς μόνος.

16 ὡς δὲ ὀψία ἐγένετο, κατέβησαν οἱ μαθηταὶ αὐτοῦ ἐπὶ τὴν θάλασσαν,

17 καὶ ἐμβάντες εἰς πλοῖον ἤρχοντο πέραν τῆς θαλάσσης εἰς Καφαρναούμ. |...|

18 ἥ τε θάλασσα ἀνέμου μεγάλου πνέοντος διηγείρετο.

19 ἐληλακότες οὖν ὡς σταδίους εἴκοσι πέντε ἢ τριάκοντα θεωροῦσιν τὸν Ἰησοῦν περιπατοῦντα ἐπὶ τῆς θαλάσσης καὶ ἐγγὺς τοῦ πλοίου γινόμενον, καὶ ἐφοβήθησαν.

20 ὁ δὲ λέγει αὐτοῖς· ἐγώ εἰμι· μὴ φοβεῖσθε.

21 ἤθελον οὖν λαβεῖν αὐτὸν εἰς τὸ πλοῖον, καὶ εὐθέως ἐγένετο τὸ πλοῖον ἐπὶ τῆς γῆς εἰς ἣν ὑπῆγον.

22 (|...| ὁ ὄχλος ὁ ἑστηκὼς πέραν τῆς θαλάσσης [ἰδὼν] ὅτι πλοιάριον ἄλλο οὐκ ἦν ἐκεῖ |...| καὶ ὅτι οὐ συνεισῆλθεν τοῖς μαθηταῖς αὐτοῦ ὁ Ἰησοῦς εἰς τὸ πλοῖον |...|

25 καὶ εὑρόντες αὐτὸν πέραν τῆς θαλάσσης εἶπον αὐτῷ· ῥαββί, πότε ὧδε γέγονας;)

If this passage, as we have analysed it, lacks the integrity of the other signs, that is due partly to its having lost its original ending, partly to the fact that even in the source it probably was not a separate sign but only a traditional sequel to the feeding of the multitude. (See further below, p. 101.)

6. A MAN BLIND FROM BIRTH HEALED
(9: 1-8)[2]

9: 1. The episode is tersely introduced by this verse. παράγων is an editorial connective but not therefore Johannine[3]—*cf.* Mk 1: 16, 2: 14, *etc.*, where the same participle seems to be pre-Markan.[4]

[1] *Cf.* Goguel, 404; Dodd, 197f.; Schnackenburg, 'Traditionsgeschichte', 81.

[2] D. Mollat, 'La guérison de l'aveugle-né', *BVC* 23 (1958), 22–31; J. M. Thompson, 'An experiment in translation', *Exp* 16 (1918), 117–25.

[3] παράγειν only here in canonical Jn, but *cf.* the gloss on 8: 59.

[4] So Bultmann, 250 n. 6; Dodd, 181. *Cf.* also Mt 9: 27, 20: 30 (both healings of blind men!).

9: 2. At first glance, this verse (and the following one) seems extraneous to the *Wunder*. But the issue of the man's sin has no importance in the dramatic scenes which follow (only incidentally at *v.* 34), where the principal issue is whether *Jesus* is a sinner (16, 25, 31), and therefore is probably not John's addition. The story as John received it appears to have been a conflation of a healing episode (*cf. e.g.* Mk 8: 22–6) and a pronouncement story (*cf.* Lk 13: 4 f.—question of sin as cause of misfortune, Siloam!).–Various *religionsgeschichtlich* attempts have been made to resolve the apparent illogicality of the question whether a man's congenital blindness is the result of his own sin: pre-natal sin, pre-existence of souls, *etc.* (Bauer, 133). Spitta (201) and Bauer (*loc. cit.*) think, rather, that the source read not γεννηθῇ but γενηθῇ (*A al*)—'Who sinned... that this man *became* blind?'—John changing it to *born*. This reading would seem, however, to be a post-Johannine attempt at correction, for the mention in the question of the man's parents is explainable only if he had been blind from birth;[1] furthermore it would still be necessary to account for John's creating the difficulty due to γεννηθῇ. Bultmann (251) suggests that the disciples' question is intentionally absurd, but it seems more likely to be simply an anomaly created by the combination of two distinct stories.

9: 3. Dodd (107 f.) ascribes the whole of this verse to the source. He admits some Johannine editing in the second half, but by comparison with Mk 2: 1–12, *etc.* he finds even there 'nothing alien to the tradition'. This overstates the case—3 *b* is Johannine, both in style (elliptic ἀλλ' ἵνα—*cf.* 1: 8, 31, 11: 52, 13: 18, 14: 31, 15: 25, 1 John 2: 19) and thought (*manifest God's works*—3: 21, 10: 32, *etc.*). Bultmann is probably right that this clause has suppressed the original continuation of Jesus' reply; we can only guess whether it had any similarity to Lk 13: 5*b*: 'But unless you repent you will all likewise perish.' It is even possible that 3 *a* is Johannine as well, but if a pronouncement

---

[1] While the parents play a part in the Johannine sequel to the miracle (18–23), it is only a minor one and does not involve the question of their responsibility for the man's condition; there is no reason to believe that John added them to the story here to prepare for their appearance later.

story has influenced this story, it would appear to be reflected in the first part of Jesus' reply.

9: 4 f. The overwhelming opinion of critics is that these verses are redactional (Wellhausen, Wendt, Bultmann, Wilkens, Hartke, Schnackenburg). Some however (Spitta, Dodd; *cf.* Wilkens, 52) point out a seam between 4 and 5 and attribute only the latter to John. In fact both verses, along with 3 *b*, are from an ideological point of view thoroughly Johannine (*works, him who sent me, night/day, in the world, light of the world*) and are not to be assigned to SQ.[1] Any aporia found within them is due to a Johannine redaction of one or more traditional sayings.[2] The textual variation in 4 is no index of John's redaction but probably the result of dogmatic correction by scribes.[3]

9: 6 f. The phrase ταῦτα εἰπών could be pre-Johannine, especially if an original saying has been replaced by 3 *b*–5; but more likely it is the evangelist's way of resuming the source (*cf.* 11: 11, *etc.*).–The details of the healing (use of spittle,[4] application to the affected part, command to wash) are typical of stories of this kind,[5] hardly intentionally elaborate so as to emphasize Jesus' breaking the Sabbath (so Bultmann, 252).– The (mistaken) etymology in *v.* 7 is Johannine on all counts: use of ἑρμηνεύειν (see above on 5: 2), Jesus as sent,[6] parenthesis irrelevant to the context. Two witnesses (sy[sch] pers[p]) omit these three words but probably only because they are cryptic.–For

---

[1] Except for the pool of Siloam, which is apparently traditional (see above on *v.* 2), all of the elements which lead Mollat ('Guérison', 26) to find a Succoth background here are contained in these verses and so point only to John's intention.

[2] In this study, the term *Johannine* does not, of course, necessarily mean *stemming entirely from the evangelist.* It is my impression that he must have been dependent on some sort of tradition of Jesus' sayings—and dependent in such a way as to have borrowed not only a vocabulary but a rhetoric as well. In any case, it is just these linguistic features which are absent from our source and can for our purposes be called Johannine.

[3] Hirsch, 20; whether his reconstruction of the true text is correct is beside the point.

[4] *Cf.* esp. Mk 8: 23 (blind man of Bethsaida).

[5] Yet also unique—πτύσμα appears only here in NT, χαμαί only here and 18: 6.

[6] *Cf. v.* 4; also 3: 17, 34, 4: 34, 5: 24, 30, *etc.*

the command, 'Go, wash' *cf.* 2 Kings 5: 10 (Elisha); for
Siloam, see above on *v.* 2.–οὖν (7*b*) is not historical (*cf.* 6: 10).
Thus the bulk of *vv.* 6–7 is from the source.

9: 8. As the chapter now stands, a new scene begins here, and
most if not all of what follows is Johannine:[1] οὖν-*historicum*,
ἐκεῖνος (= *he*), argument over one's identity (ἄλλοι ἔλεγον),
mystery surrounding Jesus; a seam is also indicated by the new
vocabulary (ἀνοίγειν, ἀναβλέπειν, ἐπιχρίειν). We may wonder,
however, if the story in the source ended with *v.* 7. The effect
of the miracle on a group of people is perhaps to be expected;
v. 8 may then contain something of the original ending. The
blind and sitting προσαίτης[2] and the recognizing crowd are
logically afterthoughts, but the same elements are found in the
parallel stories (Mk 10: 46, Acts 3: 2, 10) and so possibly are
original. And the wondering question the neighbours ask might
be the unwitting authentication of the miracle which has
already appeared as a characteristic of the source (*cf.* above on
6: 25).[3] Verse 8 as a whole might, then, be pre-Johannine,
though this is less certain than the analysis of *vv.* 1–7.

While Dodd, as we have held, attributes too much of this
pericope to the source, he is right that, as in the other miracle
stories, we have here a novel version of various elements
(including, perhaps, a pronouncement story). That this is
mediated through a unique source rather than John's reworking of one or more of the synoptics is most clearly shown by
the close parallels with the story of Peter's healing the lame man
in Acts 3: 1 ff.,[4] which can hardly have been a source for John!
    The *Vorlage*, then, contained the following:

---

[1] *Versus* Spitta, Goguel, Bultmann, Hartke, who are misled by the
apparent homogeneity of ch. 9, a consequence of the restricted extent of
the source, which gives way so early to Johannine development. But on the
analogy of 5: 1 ff. it is clear that the source comprised little more than *vv.* 1–7.

[2] The noun is lacking in 𝕂 *al*, but this is hardly an assimilation to the
synoptics since the verb (8*b*) is unanimously attested.

[3] They do not have quite the same function as the knowing servants in
2: 9 (Johannine), *vs.* Schnackenburg, 337—rather they are analogous to the
ἀρχιτρίκλινος.

[4] Infirmity from birth, beggar, temple locale, amazed recognition of a
former invalid by the crowd.

9: 1 καὶ παράγων εἶδεν ἄνθρωπον τυφλὸν ἐκ γενετῆς.

2 καὶ ἠρώτησαν αὐτὸν οἱ μαθηταὶ αὐτοῦ λέγοντες·
ῥαββί, τίς ἥμαρτεν, οὗτος ἢ οἱ γονεῖς αὐτοῦ, ἵνα τυφλὸς γεννηθῇ;

3a (ἀπεκρίθη Ἰησοῦς· οὔτε οὗτος ἥμαρτεν οὔτε οἱ γονεῖς
αὐτοῦ.)

6 (ταῦτα εἰπών) ἔπτυσεν χαμαὶ καὶ ἐποίησεν πηλὸν ἐκ
τοῦ πτύσματος, καὶ ἐπέθηκεν αὐτοῦ τὸν πηλὸν ἐπὶ τοὺς ὀφθαλμούς,

7 καὶ εἶπεν αὐτῷ· ὕπαγε νίψαι εἰς τὴν κολυμβήθραν τοῦ
Σιλωάμ |...|. ἀπῆλθεν οὖν καὶ ἐνίψατο, καὶ ἦλθεν βλέπων.

8 (οἱ οὖν γείτονες καὶ οἱ θεωροῦντες αὐτὸν τὸ πρότερον,
ὅτι προσαίτης ἦν, ἔλεγον· οὐχ οὗτός ἐστιν ὁ καθήμενος καὶ
προσαιτῶν;)

7. A DEAD MAN RAISED (11: 1–45)[1]

This passage is a crux for the source criticism of Jn. Analysts
differ so radically in their reconstructions that Dodd can
maintain, 'Nowhere...in the gospel have attempts to analyse
out a written source, or sources, proved less convincing'. He
goes on to conclude that 'if the evangelist is following a traditional story of fixed pattern, he has covered his tracks',[2] an
assertion which is not altogether true since the passage abounds
in aporias. It is more its complexity and length than the
thoroughness of the evangelist's revision which provide the chief
obstacles to source analysis. In this passage alone, of the
Johannine miracle stories, John has chosen to intersperse the
source with major interpretive additions, rather than append
them to it;[3] and those additions are much more extensive and
intricate than in other passages. It is the peculiar importance he
gives this story as he finds it—an importance he can bring out

[1] R. Dunkerley, 'Lazarus', *NTS* 5 (1958/9), 321–7; J. P. Martin,
'History and eschatology in the Lazarus narrative, John 11: 1–44', *SJT* 17
(1964), 332–43; J. N. Sanders, '"Those whom Jesus loved" (John xi. 5)',
NTS 1 (1954/5), 29–41; R. H. Strachan, 'Is the fourth gospel a literary
unity?', *ET* 27 (1916), 280–2; Wilkens, 'Die Erweckung des Lazarus', *TZ*
15 (1959), 22–39. References to Wilkens in this section are to *Entstehungsgeschichte*.

[2] P. 230; *cf.* Hoskyns, 395: 'a complete literary unity'.

[3] An index of this is the fact that the analysis into scenes by Lohmeyer and
Windisch, which is so natural in other passages—because a purely Johannine
dramatic scheme has there been appended to the source—is here quite
artificial.

only by continually supplementing it—that occasions the difficulty of reconstructing it.

It is significant for our purpose that several critics—*e.g.* Bauer, Hirsch—who otherwise give no credence to the existence of a pre-Johannine stratum, resort to one in interpreting this passage. In the case of Hirsch this amounts to a third stratum in addition to the usual Johannine and post-Johannine ones. We shall see that in some places the story does in fact provide evidence of more than two stages in its development, but on methodological grounds we may ask whether the three are not rather pre-SQ, SQ, and Jn, respectively.

A number of earlier analyses of this passage are patently arbitrary (*cf.* esp. Spitta's): they do not produce strata which are internally consistent and coherent and they do not suggest reasons why the subsequent development took place as it did. Consequently in what follows we try to proceed on two presuppositions: (1) that the source has not been hopelessly fragmented by John but only greatly expanded, so that the original thread of continuity can still be traced, and (2) that the various changes John made were occasioned largely by the source.

11: 1. The opening words of the story (ἦν δέ τις...) are characteristic of the source (4: 46, 5: 5; *cf.* ...τις ἦν—Lk 7: 37, 16: 19, Acts 9: 36). The giving of a name to the human subject of a miracle is unique in the gospel, but not in synoptic tradition (*e.g.* Mk 10: 46; for the name Lazarus *cf.* Lk 16: 20 ff.), and there is no apparent reason why John should have introduced it here.[1]

The syntax of what follows (ἀπὸ Βηθανίας ἐκ τῆς κώμης κτλ) is awkward, as the scribal tendency to omit the second preposition (*28* sa sy[s] pers[p]; *cf.* also RSV) shows. Either *from Bethany* or *of the village of Mary and Martha* may then be Johannine. Wellhausen (52 f.) maintained that the sisters were unknown to the *Grundschrift*, and it is probably true that at an early point in the tradition this story concerned only Jesus and Lazarus. If *from Bethany* only was original, John has introduced the two sisters from the anointing episode in the next chapter.[2] But the

---

[1] He makes nothing of its potentially symbolic meaning.

[2] So E. Krafft, 'Die Personen des Johannesevangeliums', *EvTh* 16 (1956), 30 f.

relation between the pericopes in chs. 11 and 12 is more complex than that. We have here not simply a sharing of one or two details but an intricate combining of various separate traditions: the raising of a dead person (Mk 5, Lk 7, Acts 9, *etc.*), the parable of the rich man and Lazarus (Lk 16), Martha and Mary (Lk 10), the anointing by a weeping woman (Lk 7), the anointing at Bethany (Mk 14), and others—a coalescing such as can have taken place only in the pre-literary stage. On the one hand the sisters have a role in the story which cannot be attributed entirely to John (see below); on the other, while Bethany plays no essential part in the story proper, it seems to be the traditional setting for the story (see below on 18). We may conclude, then, that John found the whole of *v.* 1 already in the source.[1] With the construction here *cf.* 1: 44, Lk 2: 4.

Wilkens, following Wellhausen and Hirsch, points out that in this verse (as in 5 and 12: 2 f.) there is no suggestion of a family relationship between Lazarus and the two sisters (as in 2, 19, 21, 32, 39) and he holds that such a relationship belongs to the latest stratum of the gospel. But C. K. Barrett[2] convincingly denies that Lazarus is necessarily only the *neighbour* of Martha and Mary in these verses. As we shall see, the relationship seems to be pre-Johannine, and if the wording of 1 *b* is strange in the case of a brother and his sisters, it is perhaps due to the development of the tradition in stages somewhat as follows: (1) Lazarus alone, (2) Lazarus and *the sisters* (*cf. v.* 3), (3) Lazarus and *his* sisters.[3]

11: 2. The mention of Mary and Martha in *v.* 1 is startling— they appear there for the first time in the gospel and without introduction or identification—and the present verse is syntactically awkward. Consequently it is sometimes seen as a Johannine parenthesis seeking to ease the abruptness of the sisters' appearance by identifying Mary as the one who will soon be encountered again in ch. 12 (Bauer). But the instances of

---

[1] There are several variants for the phrase τῆς Μαρίας καὶ Μάρθας τῆς ἀδελφῆς αὐτῆς, one of them omitting reference to Martha altogether, but they all appear to be attempts to simplify the grammar of the verse.

[2] Review of Wilkens, in *TL* 84 (1959), 829.

[3] Or possibly: (1) Lazarus alone, (2) Lazarus and his (nameless) sister, (3) Lazarus and Mary (and Martha). See at the end of this section on the longer text of Mk.

past tense in forward reference usually cited in Jn (1: 15, 3: 13, 10: 18) are not syntactically parallel, and John is demonstrably capable of expressing a relative future with μέλλειν (twelve times in Jn, mostly Johannine; cf. esp. 6: 71, and contrast with Mk 3: 19). A better explanation would seem to be that this verse is pre-Johannine and originally served to identify Mary either as the person of that name well known to the reader[1] (Bl–D, sec. 339.1) or simply as one who would appear again later in the source. If so, it was probably an editorial addition of the author of SQ, where the story of Lazarus and that of the anointing come in contact for the first time. – The use of κύριος here is sometimes held to indicate that the whole verse is a *post*-Johannine gloss (Bultmann, 302; Wilkens, 56 n. 206; Schnackenburg, 45). It is true that nowhere else in Jn is Jesus certainly referred to as *the Lord* before the resurrection.[2] But this does not exclude the possibility of its being a *pre*-Johannine editorial usage.[3] If *v.* 2 is post-Johannine, αὐτόν in *v.* 3 is left without an antecedent.[4]

11: 3–6. In substance *vv.* 3–4 and 5–6 form a doublet (note the repetition of Jesus' love for Lazarus [3, 5] and of the phrase *when Jesus heard* [4a, 6]), and a choice between the two pairs of verses is impossible except on *sachlich* grounds. The phrase ὃν φιλεῖς (3) is akin to the obviously Johannine expression ' (the disciple) whom Jesus loved' (13: 23, 19: 26, 20: 2, 21: 7, 20), but there the relative clause is never used substantively and the verb is regularly ἀγαπᾶν, not φιλεῖν; *v.* 3 is thus probably pre-Johannine.[5] And on the other hand, the use of a synonym for φιλεῖν,[6] the inclusion of the sisters in Jesus' love for Lazarus, and

---

[1] *Cf.* Sanders, who also thinks that this account of the anointing is more original than 12: 3 because it lacks a description of the myrrh and a mention of anointing Jesus' feet; it is more likely, however, that 11: 2 lacks these elements only because it is a summary of 12: 3, to which otherwise it is almost identical verbally.

[2] In 4: 1 and 6: 23 the reading is dubious textually.

[3] *Cf.* Lk, *passim* but esp. 10: 39 (Mary at the feet of Jesus!), followed by κύριε in 10: 40; also the source's use of κύριε (see on *v.* 3).

[4] Unless τὸν Ἰησοῦν (*D* it sy^{s.p} aeth, *etc.*) is original, as seems unlikely.

[5] The vocative form κύριε is used frequently by the evangelist (4: 11, 15, 6: 34, 68, 9: 36, 38, *etc.*) but was found also in the source (*cf.* 4: 19, 49, 5: 7, and Lk 10: 40). – With ἀπέστειλαν...πρὸς αὐτόν *cf.* Acts 9: 38.

[6] *Cf.* Howard, *Recent criticism*, 278 f.

the retiring of Mary and Lazarus from centre stage (*Martha and her sister and Lazarus*)[1] in *v.* 5 suggest that it is Johannine. In *v.* 6 the same is true of the theme of deliberate delay on Jesus' part.[2] It appears, then, that in general the first pair of verses is SQ and the second Johannine.[3] But Jesus' words in 4*b* are Johannine also.[4] Their analogy with 9: 3 f. has often been noted; here, however, the original saying of Jesus has not been suppressed but only postponed (see below). Thus only 3 and the opening words of 4 (ἀκούσας δὲ ὁ Ἰησοῦς [εἶπεν]) stem from SQ.

11: 7–16. These verses, which hardly further the story, are apparently a radical expansion of Jesus' words which in the source followed 4*a*. Reconstruction of the text is precarious, but we are offered several clues to where the seams lie: the repetition of certain phrases and the quite unnecessary use of transitional formulas (*e.g. after this* and *having said this*). Each time John resumes the source after an interpolation he backtracks, repeating or paraphrasing a few words from before the interruption, and usually adds a temporal connective phrase. Thus, after the addition of the logion in 4, he repeats the gist of 3–4*a* in 5–6*a*, adds 6*b* (as both its strange logic after 5[5] and the superfluous particles[6] attest) and only then, with the verbose transition *then after this*,[7] takes up the source: λέγει τοῖς μαθηταῖς (7). But then once more, although he anticipates the source (ἄγωμεν), he goes off again in a new direction which has no relation to the context (Lazarus is not mentioned) but depends

---

[1] *Cf.* the prominence of both sisters, but especially Martha, in the Johannine additions below.

[2] See further below on *v.* 17; also n. 5, below.—The use of ὡς οὖν is perhaps Johannine (Schweizer, 90).

[3] The paradox raised by the juxtaposition of *vv.* 5 and 6 (Brown, 423) does not appear to be due to a literary seam, but to deliberate theological tension on John's part. See below, n. 5.

[4] *Cf.* πρὸς θάνατον (1 Jn 5: 16 f.); οὐκ...ἀλλά and double purpose clause (1: 7 f.); the idea that earthly events, even miracles, are but means of revealing the glory of God (9: 3*b*). See further Bultmann, 302 n. 7.

[5] The Markan story which most closely resembles this one (the raising of Jairus' daughter) also has an element of delay (the haemorrhaging woman) but there, unlike the present verse (and *cf.* 2: 4, 7: 10 [same construction]), the delay is hardly Jesus' intent. See further below, pp. 194 f., on 4: 4 ff.

[6] τότε after a temporal clause; uncompleted μέν.

[7] On μετὰ τοῦτο see above on 6: 1.

on earlier editorial passages (8: 59, 10: 31, 40) and in thought and structure parallels 9: 2–5.[1] This is brought to a close with the obviously editorial seam at the beginning of *v.* 11: ταῦτα εἶπεν, καὶ μετὰ τοῦτο λέγει αὐτοῖς—the last four words being a reiteration of the composite 7 *a*.

The first of Jesus' words in *v.* 11 are probably pre-Johannine, as the rough parallel in Mk 5: 39 (death as sleep) indicates. Some sort of foreknowledge is perhaps implicitly attributed to Jesus (*cf.* above on 5: 6). The original saying probably continued as here: *but*...; John, however, has added 11 *b*[2] to set the stage for the disciples' misunderstanding in 12–15.[3] Verse 14 is patterned on 11 and leads, after 15 *a*, to the resumption of the source in 15 *b*, illogical in its present context. – *Thomas called the Twin* (16)[4] as a distinct character seems to be Johannine (*cf.* 14: 5, 20: 24 ff.) though as a name probably known to the source (21: 2). The unexpressed antecedent of the personal pronoun in this verse is Jesus, whereas in 15 and 17 it is Lazarus (Wilkens, 57). The reference to Jesus' impending death takes up *v.* 8 (Johannine). ἄγωμεν is again borrowed from the source.

Thus the *Vorlage* in these verses probably consisted of a single saying of Jesus reading roughly as follows: (4) ἀκούσας δὲ ὁ Ἰησοῦς (7) λέγει τοῖς μαθηταῖς· (11) Λάζαρος ὁ φίλος ἡμῶν κεκοίμηται· ἀλλὰ (15) ἄγωμεν πρὸς αὐτόν.

11 : 17. Wilkens regards the latter part of this verse (*four days, etc.*) as secondary but for no very clear reason. The construction is not necessarily Johannine (see above on 5: 5).[5] Unlike *v.* 6, the element of delay here is entirely natural, as in synoptic tradition (*cf.* Mk 5: 35): by the time Jesus could get to Lazarus he was four days dead. The time elapsed since death has perhaps been heightened, a tendency already visible in synoptic tradition: Jairus' daughter had just died when Jesus arrived, whereas the young man of Nain was already being

[1] John's use of ῥαββί (*v.* 8) would seem to be an imitation of the source at 9: 2.

[2] With πορεύομαι ἵνα... *cf.* 10: 10, also 9: 39, 12: 46, 16: 28.

[3] *Cf.* 2: 21 f. With παρρησίᾳ (14) *cf.* 7: 4, 13, 26, 10: 24, 11: 54, 16: 25, 18: 20. With χαίρω κτλ (15) *cf. vv.* 41 f.

[4] Or however the phrase should be understood—see below, on 21: 2, and Brown, 424.

[5] Nor is the use of οὖν historical here: consecutive rather, after 15 *b*.

carried to his grave. *Four days* perhaps emphasizes the irreversibility of Lazarus' death (*cf.* Bauer, *ad loc.*, for the Jewish idea that the spirit hovered near the corpse for three days after death).[1] This heightening is probably not John's—*cf.* above on 4: 47*a.*–On the question whether in the source the gap of four days was empty or filled by another episode, see below, pp. 194f., on 4: 4 ff.–It is not clear at this point whether Jesus comes to the grave or only to the village. But the former is unlikely[2] in view of the question in *v.* 34 ('Where have you laid him?'); *found him...in the tomb* means only *found that he had been* etc. (*cf.* RSV). But in either case the information given here conflicts with *v.* 30 and, as it now stands, perhaps with 20 also.

11: 18f. Two stylistic details suggest that 18 is from the source: (1) the use of the article with Ἱεροσολύμων (see above on 5: 1 f.) and (2) the use of ὡς with a numeral.[3] If these are sufficient reasons for assigning the verse to the source, 19 (which occasions 18) must also be pre-Johannine, with the exception of ἐκ τῶν Ἰουδαίων.[4] Since they interrupt the basic plot of the story and contain relatively late elements (setting in Bethany, Lazarus as brother of the two sisters), these verses appear to have been added editorially by the author of the source, to provide the usual witnesses to the miracle.

11: 20–31. Jesus' encounter with the sisters has been greatly expanded by John but is based on something in the source, since a number of synoptic details and even terms reappear here:[5] the sisters' house (20), Martha the activist (20), Mary

---

[1] P. Trudinger, 'A "Lazarus motif" in primitive Christian preaching?', *Andover Newton Quarterly* 7 (1966/7), 29–32, thinks *four days* is in contrast to the shorter period Jesus was buried.

[2] As the insertion of εἰς Βηθανίαν in a number of MSS apparently seeks to make clear.

[3] The particle is lacking in D W* sy^s and may have been added to ease what according to Bultmann (305 n. 8) is geographically inexact, but that seems unlikely to me. This use of ὡς is found in Jn (1: 39, 4: 6, 6: 10, 19, 19: 4, 39, 21: 8) always in SQ contexts and is known to synoptic tradition (Mk 5: 13, 8: 9, Lk 1: 56, 8: 42, *etc.*).

[4] As partitive ἐκ with πολλοί suggests (see above on 6: 11)—unless the reading of D (Ἱεροσολύμων) is correct: 'many went out *from* Jerusalem'.

[5] *Cf.* Mk 5: 22 ff. (Jairus' daughter), Lk 7: 11 ff. (young man of Nain), 10: 38 ff. (Martha and Mary).

more sedentary (20) and reverent toward Jesus (32), Jesus addressed as κύριε (?21, 27, 34) and referred to as ὁ διδάσκαλος (28). These elements[1] fall entirely outside two blocks in this passage which appear to be Johannine, *viz.* 21-7[2] and 30 f. Some Johannine retouching is visible also in what remains (*viz.* 20 and 28 f.) after these blocks are excised.

If Martha's going out to Jesus upon hearing that he *was coming* (20 a) conflicts with 17 (*When Jesus came*),[3] John has perhaps changed an original ἥκει to ἔρχεται, the reverse of his change in 4: 47.

Verse 28 follows well enough after 20,[4] except that τοῦτο εἰποῦσα must be John's phrase for resuming the source (*cf.* above on *vv.* 7–16).[5]–The purpose of λάθρα is puzzling if it stems from the source; more likely it is John's insertion, related to the Johannine theme of danger in Judea (*cf. vv.* 8, 30—so Brown, 425).

Verse 29 probably stems from John also (*cf.* the non-demonstrative use of ἐκείνη); inceptive ἤρχετο prepares for the quite artificial interruption of 30 f.[6] and anticipates the source at 32 a.

11: 32. Mary's response (*When she saw him she fell at his feet*) is almost verbally identical to that of the father in Mk 5: 22 and appears to be pre-Johannine. (For Mary at the feet of Jesus *cf.* also Lk 10: 39.) The use of οὖν here may not be historical, but consecutive, typical of the source. The second half of the

---

[1] Except for κύριε in 27 (and 21?), easily imitated from the source.

[2] *The last day* (24) is Johannine—*cf.* 6: 39 f., 44, 54, 12: 48 (Barrett, 329); so also the themes of Jesus' relation to the Father (22) and of misunderstanding (23 f.).–For the Johannine parallels in 25-7, see Barrett, *ibid.*; Fuller, 105 f.–The first part of Martha's confession in 27 is apparently John's anticipation of the source at 20: 31 (see below, pp. 197 ff.); for the last phrase (ὁ εἰς τὸν κόσμον ἐρχόμενος) *cf.* above on 6: 14. Such quotation of titles from the source is understandable if it is John who has made this sign the last and most important one, and a prefiguring of Jesus' resurrection.

[3] Brown, 424, thinks not.

[4] For the identical sequence, involving pairs coming to Jesus, see 1: 39 b–41, 43-5 (SQ—see below, pt. III).

[5] The double instance of the same participle (esp. if one form is 2nd aorist and one 1st—so 𝔓[66] *B C** [*cf.* Barrett, 330 f.]) is clumsy.

[6] Verse 30 conflicts with 17, as we saw; 31 is highly contrived and is mainly a verbose paraphrase of 19 and 29 (note change of vocabulary).

verse (λέγουσα κτλ) is ignored in 33 (*When Jesus saw her weeping...*) and is Johannine (*cf.* 21).

11: 33. The grief (κλαίειν) of those present is common to the parallels in the synoptics: Mk 5: 38 (crowd), Lk 7: 13 (mother, with a crowd present), 7: 38 (Mary), Acts 9: 39 (widows). In view of these parallels and our analysis at 18 f., it is likely that the weeping of both Mary and the crowd[1] is original, John having added only 'Ιουδαίους. If, as Wilkens (59) believes, συνελθόντας αὐτῇ presupposes 31 and not merely 19, the participle may be a Johannine addition as well, the source having read simply τοὺς σὺν αὐτῇ κλαίοντας.[2]–ἐνεβριμήσατο (33*b*) is certainly traditional (*cf.* Mk 1: 43, 7: 34, 14: 5, Mt 9: 30, *Eg. Pap.* 2). ταράσσειν of a person is an important word for John (12: 27, 13: 21, 14: 1, 27), but except for the present verse[3] always appears in the passive. C. Bonner[4] thinks these two verbs are technical thaumaturgic terms meaning 'be frenzied' and 'tremble' respectively. This is undoubtedly true of an early stage of the tradition (see also below on 41 *a*), but already in the source this clause may have expressed Jesus' indignation, either at the display of grief (as in Mk 5: 39 f.) or at the power of evil.[5]

11: 34–7. Verse 34 carries forward the plot and leads directly to 38. Verse 35 ('Jesus wept') interrupts this connection and appears to paraphrase 33*b*; thus while in substance it might

[1] Wellhausen finds it inconsistent that those from Jerusalem came to console but here are shown mourning, but this is overly subtle: Jewish consolation probably included a visible show of grief. It is possible, however, that at an early stage this story was set in the midst of the burial procession (*cf.* Lk's story at Nain) and later grew into a miracle four days later; *cf.* above on *v.* 17.   [2] *Cf.* 𝔓66: τοὺς συνεληλυθότας σὺν αὐτῇ.

[3] The variant in 𝔓45.66 D, *etc.*—ἐταράχθη τῷ πνεύματι [*cf.* 13: 21] ὡς ἐμβριμώμενος—is undoubtedly a scribal attempt to ease either the redundancy of the two phrases or a christological difficulty felt to be present. There is evidence to suggest that 𝔓66 was itself so altered from an original reading like that adopted by Nestle; see H. M. Teeple and F. A. Walker, 'Notes on the plates in *Papyrus Bodmer II*', *JBL* 78 (1959), 148–52.

[4] 'Traces of thaumaturgic technique in the miracles', *HTR* 20 (1927), 176–8.

[5] And so paraphrased by John in *v.* 35 as 'Jesus wept'—*cf.* E. Bevan, 'Note on Mark i 41 and John xi 33, 38', *JTS* 33 (1932), 186–8.

have been found in SQ, it appears to have been added by John as an occasion for 36 f. (Wilkens, 58), another instance of the stereotyped Johannine reaction of *the Jews* to Jesus' words and deeds (*cf. e.g.* 7: 12, 10: 20 f.), as the reference to an earlier healing suggests (*cf.* 7: 23). For τινές ἐκ see above on 6: 11.

11: 38–40. οὖν here is typical of the source: (34) '"Come and see." (38) *So* Jesus...came.' πάλιν ἐμβριμώμενος ἐν ἑαυτῷ, which recapitulates the source in 33, apparently was added by John as Jesus' response to the lack of understanding of the Jews in 37. Verses 38 *b*–39 *a* move quickly toward the *dénouement*, but the command of Jesus in 39 *a* ('Take away the stone') and its compliance in 41 *a* are now interrupted by the Johannine insertion of 39 *b*–40. Martha's objection (39 *b*)[1] provides for the backward glance at Jesus' conversation with her (25 ff.; *cf.* 4) in 40. The suggestion of the decomposition of the corpse probably contradicts 44 which seems to imply it had been embalmed.

11: 41 f. The seam between 40 and 41 probably gave rise to the textual variants in 41.[2] The prayer which Jesus utters (41 *b*–42) is undoubtedly Johannine, but his lifting up his eyes (41 *a*) not necessarily so, despite 17: 1, since the phrase is common to all the gospels (*cf.* 6: 5 [SQ]). In the source, where it was followed by 43,[3] it was perhaps thaumaturgic (*cf.* Mk 7: 34, the healing of a deaf man: 'and looking up to heaven he groaned and said to him, "Ephphatha"'), and only to John does it suggest a prayer and so provide for his insertion.

11: 43 f. The cry to Lazarus is akin to the synoptic exorcisms (Mk 1: 25 f., 5: 7, Lk 4: 41, *etc.*: 'Come out', φωνῇ μεγάλῃ, κραυγάζειν). For τεθνηκώς *cf.* Lk 7: 12; with Jesus' command,

---

[1] Strachan (282) thinks this sentence is non-Johannine because it uses the synoptic verb for death (τελευτᾶν—only here in Jn), and ὄζειν and τεταρταῖος, both *hapax legomena* in the NT. The latter observation proves nothing— John is as apt to use rare words as the source; and the former usage may be a gloss (ἀδελφὴ τοῦ τετελευτηκότος is lacking in Θ it sy^s).

[2] D makes the first clause temporally dependent on what follows (ὅτε οὖν ἦραν...) and various MSS explicitly identify the stone, one way or another, as that of 38 f., necessary only with the insertion of 39 *b*–40.

[3] Note the Johannine ταῦτα εἰπών there, resuming the source after 41 *b*–42.

6-2

Mk 5: 43*b*. Here, as in 6: 21, there seems to be a miracle within a miracle. All of this suggests that the two verses are pre-Johannine.

11: 45. Bultmann (301, 313 n. 2) thinks that the original ending of the story in the source has been replaced by 45–54. If so, there is perhaps a remnant of it in 45. The clumsy syntax there (ἐκ τῶν ᾽Ιουδαίων οἱ ἐλθόντες, improved by *D*: . . . τῶν ἐλθόντων) may be due to John's prefixing πολλοὶ οὖν ἐκ τῶν ᾽Ιουδαίων[1] to a sentence (οἱ ἐλθόντες κτλ) from the source (*cf.* 2: 11, 6: 14). With ὃ ἐποίησεν here contrast ἃ ἐποίησεν in the following verses.

In the course of the foregoing analysis we have occasionally assumed Johannine independence of the synoptic gospels, so that synoptic parallels might be taken as indications of the pre-Johannine source. This is of course an unproved assumption, and it would be circular now to marshal an argument for such independence from the reconstructed *Vorlage*. Nevertheless, it can be pointed out that the same state of affairs obtains in this passage as in earlier ones we have examined: a loose combination of various synoptic elements suggesting the free development of oral tradition rather than a literary relationship with one or more of the other gospels. This typical conclusion is underscored for the present passage by the fact that although there is no single story in the synoptics to which this one is fundamentally parallel (unlike 4: 46 ff. or 6: 1 ff., *e.g.*), there is a much greater range of synoptic detail, coming from a wider list of stories, than we have found to be the case in any other section. A résumé of such a list speaks for itself: Mk 1 (unclean spirit), Mk 1 (leper), Mk 5 (Jairus' daughter), Mk 7 (deaf man), Mk 9 (epileptic boy), Mk 14 (anointing at Bethany), Lk 7 (young man of Nain), Lk 7 (weeping woman), Lk 10 (Martha and Mary), Lk 16 (rich man and Lazarus); to this list should be added also Peter's raising of Tabitha (Acts 9: 3*b* ff.) which shows an astonishing number of lexical parallels to the story of Lazarus.[2]

[1] With whom the τινές of *v.* 46 may be contrasted; on these uses of ἐκ, see above on 6: 11.

[2] Some of which we have already noted. The complete list follows (those parallel to Johannine elements in Jn 11 in parentheses): τις ἦν, ἀσθενήσασαν,

The uniqueness of this miracle and its similarity to the parable in Lk 16 (itself unique in giving a name to one of its characters) have led some to find in Jn 11 a tale derived from the parable. (We have already suggested something of this sort, behind SQ, in the case of 2: 1 ff.) Dodd (229) rejects such a view, holding instead that the parable has developed out of the miracle story. But if J. D. M. Derrett[1] is right that in the parable the name Lazarus is derived from that of Abraham's servant in Gen 15: 2 (*cf.* Lk 16: 23 f.), the parable would seem to be primary. The question makes little difference for the present study, however: if John's material (*via* SQ) was in any way related to synoptic tradition we have sufficient explanation for the Johannine–synoptic parallels.[2]

The following text of the source results from our analysis:

11: 1 ἦν δέ τις ἀσθενῶν, Λάζαρος ἀπὸ Βηθανίας, ἐκ τῆς κώμης Μαρίας καὶ Μάρθας τῆς ἀδελφῆς αὐτῆς.

2 ἦν δὲ Μαριὰμ ἡ ἀλείψασα τὸν κύριον μύρῳ καὶ ἐκμάξασα τοὺς πόδας αὐτοῦ ταῖς θριξὶν αὐτῆς, ἧς ὁ ἀδελφὸς Λάζαρος ἠσθένει.

3 ἀπέστειλαν οὖν αἱ ἀδελφαὶ πρὸς αὐτὸν λέγουσαι· κύριε, ἴδε ὃν φιλεῖς ἀσθενεῖ.

ἀποθανεῖν, ἔθηκαν, ἐγγύς, ἀκούσαντες, ἀπέστειλαν...πρὸς αὐτόν, (δύο), κλαίουσαι, ἔξω, ἐπίστευσαν (πολλοί).

[1] 'Fresh light on St Luke xvi: II. Dives and Lazarus and the preceding sayings', *NTS* 7 (1960/1), 371 f.

[2] Some who have felt the raising of Lazarus to be dependent on the parable in Lk have pointed out that the Johannine episode is a dramatic illustration of the pronouncement with which the parable now ends: 'If they do not hear Moses and the prophets, neither will they be convinced if some one should rise from the dead.' Then, since we have assigned the unbelieving response of the Jews in 46 ff. to John, it would seem to follow that John himself, and not simply his tradition, is dependent on the parable. But this parallel with Lk is more apparent than real—in Jn 'many' in fact believe, and the others ('some'), far from denying the miracle, seek to prevent a repetition of it (46 ff.). A miracle-story made out of a parable about a dead man will inevitably involve a return from the dead and, in a signs source, belief on the part of witnesses, so that the parallel with Lk's ending is coincidental. John, for his own purposes, has created the negative reaction to the miracle; and it is apparently Lk who has combined the parable (or tale) about the reversal of status after death with the saying about the nature of faith (J. Jeremias, *The parables of Jesus*, tr. S. H. Hooke [New York, 1955], 128).

4 ἀκούσας δὲ ὁ Ἰησοῦς |...|

7 λέγει τοῖς μαθηταῖς· |...|

11 Λάζαρος ὁ φίλος ἡμῶν κεκοίμηται· |...|

15 ἀλλὰ ἄγωμεν πρὸς αὐτόν. |...|

17 ἐλθὼν οὖν ὁ Ἰησοῦς εὗρεν αὐτὸν τέσσαρας ἤδη ἡμέρας ἔχοντα ἐν τῷ μνημείῳ.

18 ἦν δὲ Βηθανία ἐγγὺς τῶν Ἱεροσολύμων ὡς ἀπὸ σταδίων δεκαπέντε.

19 πολλοὶ δὲ (ἐκ τῶν Ἱεροσολύμων) ἐληλύθεισαν πρὸς τὴν Μάρθαν καὶ Μαριάμ, ἵνα παραμυθήσωνται αὐτὰς περὶ τοῦ ἀδελφοῦ.

20 ἡ οὖν Μάρθα ὡς ἤκουσεν ὅτι Ἰησοῦς [ἤκει], ὑπήντησεν αὐτῷ· Μαριὰμ δὲ ἐν τῷ οἴκῳ ἐκαθέζετο. |...|

28 καὶ |...| ἀπῆλθεν καὶ ἐφώνησεν Μαριὰμ τὴν ἀδελφὴν αὐτῆς |...| εἰποῦσα· ὁ διδάσκαλος πάρεστιν καὶ φωνεῖ σε. |...|

32 ἡ οὖν Μαριὰμ ὡς ἦλθεν ὅπου ἦν Ἰησοῦς, ἰδοῦσα αὐτὸν ἔπεσεν αὐτοῦ πρὸς τοὺς πόδας |...|.

33 Ἰησοῦς οὖν ὡς εἶδεν αὐτὴν κλαίουσαν καὶ τοὺς σὺν |...| αὐτῇ |...| κλαίοντας, ἐνεβριμήσατο τῷ πνεύματι καὶ ἐτάραξεν ἑαυτόν,

34 καὶ εἶπεν· ποῦ τεθείκατε αὐτόν; λέγουσιν αὐτῷ· κύριε, ἔρχου καὶ ἴδε. |...|

38 Ἰησοῦς οὖν |...| ἔρχεται εἰς τὸ μνημεῖον· ἦν δὲ σπήλαιον, καὶ λίθος ἐπέκειτο ἐπ' αὐτῷ.

39 λέγει ὁ Ἰησοῦς· ἄρατε τὸν λίθον. |...|

41 ἦραν οὖν τὸν λίθον. ὁ δὲ Ἰησοῦς ἦρεν τοὺς ὀφθαλμοὺς ἄνω |...|

43 καὶ |...| φωνῇ μεγάλῃ ἐκραύγασεν· Λάζαρε, δεῦρο ἔξω.

44 ἐξῆλθεν ὁ τεθνηκὼς δεδεμένος τοὺς πόδας καὶ τὰς χεῖρας κειρίαις, καὶ ἡ ὄψις αὐτοῦ σουδαρίῳ περιεδέδετο. λέγει αὐτοῖς ὁ Ἰησοῦς· λύσατε αὐτὸν καὶ ἄφετε αὐτὸν ὑπάγειν.

45 |...| οἱ ἐλθόντες πρὸς τὴν Μαριὰμ καὶ θεασάμενοι ὃ ἐποίησεν ἐπίστευσαν εἰς αὐτόν. |...|

This reconstruction is much less certain than in the case of other episodes, in view of the degree of Johannine redaction present in this passage. Some will insist we have erred on the side of assigning too much to the pre-Johannine stratum. In fact the source here is only slightly longer than, for example, that in 6: 1–14, and if it developed out of the Lukan parable, the length and detailed plot of the latter would account for its fullness. A kind of confirmation of the scope of our reconstruction is perhaps to be found in the parallel story contained in the longer text of Mk 10: 34, ascribed to the Carpocratians by a letter of ?Clement,[1] a story which is obviously independent of Jn 11 since it exhibits a more primitive form. Its basic elements are nevertheless in many points parallel to Jn, and it is noteworthy that every one of the parallels is to be found in our source, rather than in the Johannine portions of the story. While in our reconstruction we have not used this version of the tradition, uncertain as it is as to date and authenticity, and although it represents a somewhat different strain of tradition, it nevertheless suggests that in outline at least our analysis is correct—and in particular that the element of Lazarus' sister(s) is pre-Johannine.

We have now analysed all the miracle stories of the gospel, with one exception, that of the risen Jesus in ch. 21. If only on grounds of *Gattungkritik* we cannot leave it out of consideration.

8. A MIRACULOUS DRAUGHT OF FISH (21: 1–14)[2]

In what follows we provisionally take the bulk of Jn 21 to be part of the original gospel (whether 'appendix' or not) rather than a post-Johannine addition. This is done on methodological grounds (above, p. 7 n. 1) and not on the basis of the usual

---

[1] Ed. by Morton Smith and to be published by Harvard University Press. Exact title and date of publication have not yet been announced.

[2] M.-É. Boismard, 'Le Chapitre 21 de saint Jean: Essai de critique littéraire', *RB* 54 (1947), 473–501; F.-M. Braun, 'Quatre "signes"'; L. Brun, *Die Auferstehung Christi in der urchristlichen Überlieferung* (Oslo, 1925), 58; Bishop Cassian (S. Bésobrasoff), 'John xxi', *NTS* 3 (1956/7), 132–6; C. H. Dodd, 'The appearances of the risen Christ: An essay in form-criticism of the gospels', in *Studies in the Gospels: Essays in memory of R. H. Lightfoot*, ed. D. E. Nineham (Oxford, 1957), 9–35, esp. 14 f.; Goguel, 'Did Peter deny his lord? A conjecture', *HTR* 25 (1932), 18–25; Grant, 'John dependent', 301 ff.; W. Grundmann, 'Die Apostel zwischen Jerusalem und Antiochia', *ZNW* 39 (1940), 113 n. 5; R. H. Lightfoot, 'The narrative of St John 21', in *Locality and doctrine in the gospels* (New York–London [1937]), 101–5; Merlier, *Quatrième évangile*, 149 ff.; E. Schwartz, 'Johannes und Kerinthos', *ZNW* 15 (1914), 216 f.; R. H. Strachan, 'Spitta on John xxi', *Exp* 4 (1912), 363–9, 554–61.

lexical comparisons with the rest of the gospel. Yet such data, which are so ambiguous that by themselves they lead critics to quite opposite conclusions as to the chapter's authenticity,[1] are possibly more readily explained as the result of a Johannine redaction of pre-Johannine material than as due to a curious kind of post-Johannine imitation of the gospel. Thus, those stylistic data which are non-Johannine or, more important, anti-Johannine[2] are simply to be ascribed to the source, and those which are Johannine to John's redaction.[3]

In view, however, of the very widespread opinion that the chapter is post-Johannine, it should be pointed out that the source analysis in no way depends on positing the authenticity of ch. 21.[4] It could be maintained, as it is by Schnackenburg[5] and Grundmann,[6] that while John is not the author of the chapter, the skilful redactor who added it drew on John's source material for the miracle it contains. Certainly the story appears to bear the same relation to synoptic material as the other miracles: there is an extended parallel in Lk 5, and a number of elements are generally akin to synoptic tradition. If the story can be seen in the end to come from the same source as the rest of the miracle stories, it does not matter for our purposes who it was that included it in the extant gospel. (Whenever the terms *John* and *Johannine* appear below, then, they can be taken to mean *pseudo*-John and -Johannine, in either case distinguishing thereby the redactional stratum from the earlier, pre-Johannine one.)

---

[1] *E.g.* Wilkens, 158 f. (*pro*); Barrett, 479 f., and Merlier, 151 ff. (*con*).

[2] Boismard (484 f.) aptly distinguishes the expressions which appear nowhere else in Jn into four classes: 'neutral' (only here in Jn), of 'medium value' (sometimes a different but equivalent expression in Jn), of 'great value' (often an equivalent expression), 'unusual expressions' (rare outside Jn with very frequent equivalent in Jn).

[3] It is noteworthy that the expressions which according to Boismard's classification are of more than 'medium value' (see the previous note; pp. 489–95) are found entirely in the first fourteen verses of the chapter, where the underlying source is to be found.

[4] And certainly not that of *vv.* 15 ff. in any case. Many of the grounds for attributing the chapter to a later redactor concern either the ideology of the second half of the chapter (parousia, ecclesiology) or the collision of its ending with 20: 30 f.—issues which are irrelevant to a source analysis of *vv.* 1–14.   [5] Pp. 54, 60; also 'Traditionsgeschichte', 84–8.

[6] Cited in Kümmel, *Introduction*, 149.

The present passage is an intricate combination of elements (miraculous catch of fish, epiphany of Jesus, resurrection appearance, breakfast of fish, eucharist, Petrine legend), and there have been many attempts to trace the pedigree of the story as it stands, differing as to what element is taken as fundamental to it. In what follows, we try to make no such prior assumptions but simply to let a pre-Johannine *Vorlage* separate itself from John's redaction.

21: 1. Bultmann regards this verse, along with 14, as redactional.[1] Several details support a Johannine provenance: μετὰ ταῦτα (see above, *passim*), φανεροῦν (1: 31, 2: 11*b*, 3: 21, 7: 4, 9: 3, 17: 6; *cf.* 1 Jn 1: 2, 2: 19, *etc.*), πάλιν (apparently referring to 20: 19, 26), *Sea of Tiberias* (6: 1).

21: 2. Here the story begins. Several elements suggest a pre-Johannine origin. Elsewhere in Jn ὁμοῦ is temporal (4: 36, 20: 4), not spatial as here; for the present use, *cf.* Acts 2: 1. Thomas is of course known to all the evangelists; that the name is here translated ('which means Twin') is possibly a Johannine addition (*cf.* 20: 16), but since John repeats it almost every time he introduces Thomas, it probably is instead a traditional bilingual note: *who is* (also) *called Didymos*, Didymos treated as a second name and not an etymology (*cf.* Mt 10: 2, Col. 4: 11— Bauer, *Lexicon*).[2] Nathanael is known only to Jn but is not therefore the evangelist's invention; *cf.* below, pt. III, on 1: 45 ff. Similarly *Cana* is probably pre-Johannine, though τῆς Γαλιλαίας may be John's insertion, as at 2: 11, 4: 46. That *the sons of Zebedee* appear only here in Jn is not necessarily a sign of post-Johannine assimilation to the synoptic gospels, as is usually thought,[3] but traditional, stemming from the source (*cf.* their appearance at the end of the parallel story in Lk 5). Only speculation is possible as to the identity of the 'two others of his

---

[1] While he regards the whole chapter as post-Johannine, he distinguishes between a *Vorlage* and the changes of the redactor who appended it to the gospel.

[2] Merlier, 152, holds that since Thomas figured so prominently in the preceding episode (20: 24 ff.), the use of the full name here cannot be Johannine.—See above on 5: 2.

[3] In this phrase (οἱ τοῦ Ζεβεδαίου) the synoptics always add υἱοί (as do some MSS here, by assimilation).

disciples'—are they Andrew and Philip from the source's introduction?[1] or Andrew and Levi, as in a fragment of the Gospel of Peter?[2] or simply two faceless persons added to bring the number to seven?

21: 3. The situation here is quite different from that in the parallel story in Lk 5. At the same time, while in Lk's version Jesus is with Peter in the boat, a morning hour (*cf. v.* 4 here) and a previous night of fruitless work without him are probably presupposed by Peter's remark in Lk 5: 5*a*—just the kind of narrative similarity resulting from related traditions. – The lexical data support the supposition that this verse is pre-Johannine. Infinitive of purpose after a verb of motion (common in the synoptics) is rarer in Jn than a construction with ἵνα or καί. ἀλιεύειν only here in NT, but *cf.* ἁλιεύς in the synoptics. σύν, instead of μετά, is rare in Jn (only three times) but common in Lk–Acts (*cf. Gos. Pet.* above, on *v.* 2, and possibly the source at 11: 33). πιάʒειν is relatively common in Jn (though hardly a Johannine characteristic, *vs.* Ruckstuhl) but always of a person[3]—only here (and *v.* 10) literally. – The variant εὐθύς after πλοῖον might suggest John's hand here (*cf.* on 5: 9), but it is poorly attested and probably was added later, like οὖν, to ease (however clumsily) the asyndetic ἐξῆλθον κτλ.[4]

21: 4. The parallel with Lk 5: 1 suggests that the verb ἔστη here is from the source and has an everyday meaning.[5] For the time of day, *cf.* Lk 5: 5; the expression (*cf.* Mt 27: 1) is unique in Jn, but πρωΐ(α) is perhaps typical of the source.[6] On αἰγιαλός see below, *v.* 8. – Substantively, 4*b* might be from the source also (*cf.* the disciples' not recognizing Jesus in Mk 6: 49 par.), but

---

[1] The identical phrase in 1: 35 suggests this. See below, pp. 181 f.

[2] *Gos. Pet.* 60: 'I, Simon Peter, and my brother Andrew, taking our nets, went away to the sea, and Levi was with [σύν] us, the son of Alphaeus, whom the Lord...'

[3] Meaning 'arrest'; for this idea the source, like the synoptics, uses συλλαμβάνειν (18: 12).

[4] If σύν is original (א *G* Θ *L N X 33 al*), it has the consecutive meaning typical of the source.

[5] Probably only the fuller phrase 'came and stood in their midst' (20: 19, 26) is a *terminus technicus* for the resurrection.

[6] See below on 18: 28, 20: 1; also 1: 41. John would perhaps have written τῇ ἐπαύριον (1: 29, 35, 43, 6: 22, 12: 12).

it is strange that the disciples obey (in *v.* 6) an unknown person. The verse seems instead to have been added by John as necessary to a resurrection appearance and to prepare for 7*a* (Bultmann, 544; Wilkens, 160); the use of μέντοι[1] supports this, as does the similarity of this clause to 20: 14*c* (Johannine—see below, pp. 139 f.).

21: 5. This verse is hard to assign. The matter might seem to depend on whether the source had, as sequel to the catch of fish, a meal (see below on 10, 12 f.) for which Jesus' question here ('Have you any food?') might prepare. Decision on that point, however, will not necessarily solve the present issue, for προσφάγιον (only here in the NT) can mean simply *fish* (Bauer, *Lexicon, ad rem*), in which case Jesus asks rather about the fishermen's success, preparing simply for the miracle itself (as the expectation of a negative answer [μή] perhaps suggests). The close parallel to this verse in Lk's resurrection account (24: 41: ἔχετέ τι βρώσιμον ἐνθάδε;) might be taken to decide for a pre-Johannine origin and show that even in the source the story consisted of a resurrection appearance at a meal. But it is quite possible that that verse, among others in Lk 24, is a late interpolation dependent on Jn.[2] The present verse in Jn is substantially a doublet with the end of *v.* 3 ('they caught nothing'); its removal leaves a smooth enough linguistic connection between 4*a* and 6, but Jesus' command in the latter becomes a bit abrupt. The verse remains in doubt.[3]

21: 6. The content here is just that of Lk 5: 4, 6*a*, but in quite different words. The use of οὖν is typical of SQ. Causal ἀπό only here in Jn (instead of the usual διά [26 times]); similarly ἰσχύειν (for δύνασθαι [36 times]). There can be little question but that John here reproduces the source.

---

[1] Jn 4: 27, 7: 13, 12: 42, 20: 5—all apparently Johannine; elsewhere in NT only three times, in Jas, 2 Tim., Jude.

[2] So Grant, 'John dependent'; there is no textual support for his theory, but two factors give it plausibility: (*a*) the many longer readings in this chapter of Lk, most of them based on Jn, and (*b*) the fact that the verses he considers to be glosses (37, 39–43) all have a ring of being compressed from a longer story.

[3] For παιδία in the vocative (= 'friends'), *cf.* 1 Jn 2: 18, 3: 7.

21: 7. The first half-verse is undoubtedly Johannine: the *disciple whom Jesus loved* (see above on 11: 3) is not mentioned in *v.* 2 or again in the story. No doubt this sentence is meant to prepare for the Johannine discussion of the beloved disciple in *vv.* 20 ff. (*cf.* 20: 2 ff.). – Most critics attribute 7 *b* to John also, but that is unnecessary, except for ἀκούσας ὅτι ὁ κύριός ἐστιν. *Simon Peter* is pleonastic after 7 *a.* οὖν is consecutive: 'therefore [*i.e.* after *v.* 6] Simon Peter leapt into the sea' to help land the haul. Without 7 *a* there is probably no suggestion of anxiety on his part, either to avoid Jesus (*cf.* Lk 5: 8, an extraneous element there) or to go to him (most commentators). Barrett (483) is strictly correct that this is not a reminiscence of Peter's walking on the water (Mt 14: 28 ff.); but perhaps it represents instead an earlier stage of the tradition that gave rise to that legend (*cf.* Dodd, *Tradition,* 199). Originally Peter girds himself[1] not in order to greet Jesus (as now, apparently) but simply to wade ashore; ἦν γὰρ γυμνός may be John's insertion.

21: 8. Verse 8 *b* (οὐ γὰρ . . . διακοσίων) is a *non sequitur* after 8 *a*; it originally followed 7 *b,* explaining Peter's action there: they were so near to the shore that he could guide the net by wading. If 8 *a* is omitted, there is no need to change γάρ to δέ with Bultmann, Wilkens. The use of ἄλλος and πλοιάριον in 8 *a* parallels ?John's insertion at 6: 23 f. In 8 *b* ὡς with a numeral and ἀπό meaning *away* are characteristic of SQ (see above on 11: 18).[2] Verse 8 *c* (σύροντες κτλ) presumably was added by John, since it completes the verb in 8 *a* (*cf.* RSV).[3]

21: 9. This verse, which depends on 8 *a* for its subject, creates an aporia with 11: by bringing the boat to shore, it makes Peter's

---

[1] διαζώννυμι in NT only here and 13: 4 f. (SQ?).

[2] Merlier, 154, notes that whereas αἰγιαλός is used in 4 *a,* the more usual γῆ appears here (*cf.* 6: 21). But this does not necessarily mean a difference of authorship: the latter is used of a boat coming to *land* (in general), the former of the *beach* where someone stands (*cf.* Mt 13: 2, Acts 21: 5) or on to which something is hauled (Mt 13: 48, Acts 27: 39 f.).

[3] That John's insertion of 8 *ac* causes an aporia is evident from the re-arrangement of *vv.* 7 *b*–8 in sy[s]. – While there may be a connotative difference between ἑλκύειν (*haul in*) and σύρειν (*drag after*)—so Merlier, 156—they are roughly synonymous. But John uses the former in a figurative sense in 6: 44, 12: 32 (*vs.* 18: 10 and *vv.* 6, 11 here [all SQ]) and perhaps for that reason chooses the latter here.

action in 11 incomprehensible. It depicts Jesus providing a meal of fish (and bread!) and appears to be John's addition, preparing for 13 (see below).[1] Most critics see in *vv.* 9 ff. a separate tradition (akin to Lk's Emmaus story) which has been combined, either by John or his predecessor, with that of the catch of fish. In fact, however, 9 and 13 are only John's reminiscence of the miraculous feeding (Jn 6),[2] probably for eucharistic significance. This explains the introduction of bread (which in 13 becomes more important than the fish). The infrequent but not esoteric word ἀνθρακιά (only here and 18: 18 [SQ] in NT) was possibly suggested to John by the source's passion narrative. The parallel with Lk 24: 42 (*broiled fish*) is notable, but that verse is perhaps post-Lukan (*cf.* above on *v.* 5): it appears to be simply a gloss derived from the present more detailed scene.

21: 10. Whether the episode in the source ended with a meal of the fish miraculously caught (*v.* 12 a) or only with a landing of the catch on the shore (*v.* 11), Jesus' command here appears to be original; *cf.* 2: 8 (SQ), and partitive ἀπό only here in Jn (in place of ἐκ [51 times]), ἐνέγκατε (*vs.* φέρετε) only here in NT.

21: 11. If *v.* 10 is pre-Johannine, Peter here complies with Jesus' command, directed not just to the six ἄλλοι μαθηταί (on land according to John's additions—making *Peter*'s complying strange), but to all seven, still off-shore (8 b). οὖν (𝔅 W X Θ l al) may then be original. Peter's action is not to get into the boat (RSV) and from there haul the net—what had been impossible for seven men!—but to go ashore[3] before the others, pulling the net after him. Although the miracle had been hinted at in *v.* 6, its confirmation comes only here. The emphasis is on the catch, not on Peter's part in it; nevertheless, that he figures so

---

[1] If ἀνέβησαν (instead of ἀπ-) is original (א* *H W, etc.*), John has patterned his addition after 11.

[2] Note the difference in the use of ὀψάριον: in the source (6: 9, 11—also *v.* 10 here) it is used in the plural, but here in the singular, presumably collectively or generically (as in *v.* 13, despite the plural in 10).

[3] For this meaning of ἀναβαίνειν, Bultmann, 544 n. 5. That the term is ambiguous is shown by the variant ἐνέβη (א *L W l pc*), seeking to make unequivocal the sense *embark*. The misunderstanding is caused by the boat's landing in *v.* 9.

prominently is undoubtedly pre-Johannine (*cf.* Lk 5), for John seeks in chs. 20–1 to subordinate Peter's prestige to that of the beloved disciple.

According to Bultmann, the number of fish is pseudo-Johannine allegory, but this is unproved. The number seems to me instead to be traditional whatever its significance.[1] There is little likelihood that in the source at least it signified a complete church. Even if this story grew out of the logion about fishers of men (Mk 1: 17; also Lk 5, but there the juxtaposition seems editorial) or the parable of the net (Mt 13: 47 f.—see below), both ecclesiological, nevertheless in the source it is no longer an allegory but pure miracle, with only christological meaning. And perhaps the best guess as to the initial use of the number 153 (which, as is often noted, is a triangular, and so perfect, number) is that it represented the total number of kinds of fish (so Jerome, on Ezek. 47: 10)[2] and so the most complete (and miraculous) catch possible (*cf.* Mt 13: 47); it was then symbolic, but not allegorical. But in the source the number perhaps no longer has any more significance than, for example, the numbers in the stories of the sick man at the pool (5: 2, 5) or of the feeding (6: 10).

That the net is not broken, whatever its meaning for John, was originally not allegorical. Richardson[3] thinks it a less heightened (*i.e.* earlier) version of Lk's tearing nets and capsizing boats, but then why is the net mentioned? In fact it represents a minor miracle-within-a-miracle (as in 6: 21, 11: 44).

21: 12. This, like *v.* 5, is problematic. If there was a (quite rudimentary) meal in the original version of the story, 12 *a* is pre-Johannine; but just as likely it was added with 9 and 13.—Verse 12 *b* is undoubtedly Johannine (*cf.* 4: 27, 8: 25, 16: 23),[4] along with 4 *b*. The question of Jesus' identity is appropriate only to a resurrection appearance.

---

[1] R. M. Grant, '"One hundred fifty-three large fishes"', *HTR* 42 (1949), 273–5; J. A. Emerton, 'The hundred and fifty-three fishes in John xxi 11', *JTS* n.s. 9 (1958), 86–9.

[2] See M.-J. Lagrange, *Évangile selon saint Jean* (3rd ed.; Paris, 1927), 526 f.; Feuillet, *Études*, 20.

[3] A. Richardson, *The miracle-stories of the gospels* (2nd ed.; London, 1942), 109.   [4] However, ἐξετάζειν (*vs.* [ἐπ-]ἐρωτᾶν) appears only here in Jn.

21: 13. It is possible, of course, that the same source had two such similar verses as this one and 6: 11, as is the case in Mk (6: 41, 8: 6*b*); but in that gospel there are two clearly parallel stories, whereas here a single verse (with 9, perhaps) provides the only parallel to the feeding episode. It is more likely that John has added this verse, in imitation of 6: 11, to provide a liturgical (and so epiphanic?) note to the story. The parallel with Lk 24: 30 is less close[1] and is due apparently to Lk's redaction. In John's case, the eucharistic reference was suggested perhaps not by the Easter setting in which he has placed the story so much as by the reminder of Jn 6: 1 ff. in the mention of fish.–Bultmann (545) thinks the editor has suppressed the original ending of the story (the disciples' reaction), but none is strictly necessary; Jesus had already evoked the disciples' faith (2: 11*c*).

21: 14. The striking similarity of this verse to 2: 11 and 4: 54 suggests immediately that it either stems, like them, from the source or is an imitation. If the latter, why at this point in the gospel? Bultmann (546) believes the redactor has taken an independent tradition of an initial resurrection appearance to the disciples[2] and appended it to the two (actually three)[3] in ch. 20 and so adapted it in this way. But *v.* 1 more than adequately provides a connection ('after this...again', double use of φανεροῦν), and nothing is necessary after 13 before John continues with 15 ff. And none of the other resurrection appearances is numbered. Why then *v.* 14? The answer is simple: something like it appeared already in the source and was retained in the redaction (so Spitta, Schnackenburg).

Bultmann (546 n. 1) observes, probably rightly, that not only ἐγερθεὶς ἐκ νεκρῶν (analogous to 4: 54*b*: ἐλθών κτλ; *cf.* 2: 22)

---

[1] Here Jesus is made known only implicitly and in the miracle itself, before the meal, not 'in the breaking of the bread' (that action is missing here); in Lk, there is no suggestion that the meal involved fish (*cf.* Bailey, 13).

[2] It is often suspected of being a parallel to the lost ending of Mk, but it is not the appearance to Peter expected there.

[3] Mary Magdalene is not strictly a disciple, but there is no reason to distinguish so sharply between appearances to disciples and to others, as John apparently does; from the reader's standpoint, this is Jesus' *fourth* appearance. The word 'third' is hard to account for if created for the present context. *Cf.* Merlier, 159.

but also ἐφανερώθη Ἰησοῦς τοῖς μαθηταῖς must stem from the redaction. The use of φανεροῦν here is typical of John and understandably replaces something like ἐποίησεν σημεῖον (*cf.* 2: 11, 4: 54): the story is no longer a revelatory sign which Jesus *does* (as in the source) but a revelation, the content of which is *Jesus*; for the Johannine Jesus, to *do a sign* is to *be revealed*. John then here reiterates *v.* 1. He has retained the original τοῦτο ἤδη[1] τρίτον, appropriate in the source as adjectival, making it here a clumsy adverbial phrase.[2] How the sentence here and in 4: 54 ended is perhaps unanswerable—is the patently Johannine participial ending (4: 45*b*, 21: 14*b*) an addition or a replacement? No temporal or spatial predicate is necessary after the source's formula, since the anarthrous σημεῖον must, after the demonstrative pronoun, be taken as appositive: 'Jesus did this as a first [second, third] sign.'[3] It is possible, then, that the clause in both cases originally ended with ὁ Ἰησοῦς and that only in 2: 11 did another clause follow (11*c*).

We must postpone till the next chapter the related questions why John transposed a sign story, in the midst of the ministry, to a post-resurrection setting and why only three of the miracle stories are explicitly numbered.

We may summarize the results of our analysis as follows:

21: 2 ἦσαν ὁμοῦ Σίμων Πέτρος καὶ Θωμᾶς (ὁ λεγόμενος Δίδυμος) καὶ Ναθαναὴλ ὁ ἀπὸ Κανὰ (τῆς Γαλιλαίας) καὶ οἱ τοῦ Ζεβεδαίου καὶ ἄλλοι ἐκ τῶν μαθητῶν αὐτοῦ δύο.

3 λέγει αὐτοῖς Σίμων Πέτρος· ὑπάγω ἁλιεύειν. λέγουσιν αὐτῷ· ἐρχόμεθα καὶ ἡμεῖς σὺν σοί. ἐξῆλθον καὶ ἐνέβησαν εἰς τὸ πλοῖον, καὶ ἐν ἐκείνῃ τῇ νυκτὶ ἐπίασαν οὐδέν.

4 πρωΐας δὲ ἤδη γινομένης ἔστη Ἰησοῦς εἰς τὸν αἰγιαλόν. |...|

---

[1] But perhaps ἤδη is John's redundancy—see above on 4: 54.

[2] Can τοῦτο properly be used in this way? RSV improves with 'this *was* now the third *time* that...'; literally, 'this for the third time'. (But *cf.* the variant reading in 2 Cor. 12: 14—authentic or an assimilation to the present passage?)–The phrase τὸ τρίτον is, by contrast, not awkward in *v.* 17.

[3] So that the usual mistranslation is not far wrong: 'This was the first [*etc.*] sign that Jesus did.'

5 (λέγει οὖν αὐτοῖς Ἰησοῦς· παιδία, μή τι προσφάγιον ἔχετε; ἀπεκρίθησαν αὐτῷ· οὔ.)

6 ὁ δὲ εἶπεν αὐτοῖς· βάλετε εἰς τὰ δεξιὰ μέρη τοῦ πλοίου τὸ δίκτυον, καὶ εὑρήσετε. ἔβαλον οὖν, καὶ οὐκέτι αὐτὸ ἑλκύσαι ἴσχυον ἀπὸ τοῦ πλήθους τῶν ἰχθύων.

7 | ... | Σίμων οὖν Πέτρος | ... | τὸν ἐπενδύτην διεζώσατο, (ἦν γὰρ γυμνός,) καὶ ἔβαλεν ἑαυτὸν εἰς τὴν θάλασσαν·

8 | ... | οὐ γὰρ ἦσαν μακρὰν ἀπὸ τῆς γῆς ἀλλὰ ὡς ἀπὸ πηχῶν διακοσίων | ... |.

10 λέγει αὐτοῖς ὁ Ἰησοῦς· ἐνέγκατε ἀπὸ τῶν ὀψαρίων ὧν ἐπιάσατε νῦν.

11 ἀνέβη (οὖν) Σίμων Πέτρος καὶ εἵλκυσεν τὸ δίκτυον εἰς τὴν γῆν μεστὸν ἰχθύων μεγάλων ἑκατὸν πεντήκοντα τριῶν· καὶ τοσούτων ὄντων οὐκ ἐσχίσθη τὸ δίκτυον.

12 (λέγει αὐτοῖς ὁ Ἰησοῦς· δεῦτε ἀριστήσατε.) | ... |

14 τοῦτο (ἤδη) τρίτον [ἐποίησεν σημεῖον] Ἰησοῦς | ... |.

The chief uncertainty in this reconstruction concerns the inclusion of a meal (5, 10, 12 a), and to some extent it depends on the identity of the source's redactor (John or pseudo-John), the lexical data being in every case ambiguous. If the redactor is not John, the verses in doubt are perhaps to be ascribed to him, not the source; if on the other hand the chapter is authentically Johannine, the non-Johannine elements in those verses argue for a provenance in the source. We must leave the matter open, noting however that in either case we clearly have a pre-Johannine *Vorlage* with striking similarities to the other miracle stories.

At the start we chose to suspend the question of the fundamental character of this story until our analysis had been made. It is probably impossible to explain in detail the process by which the story evolved. Nevertheless it will have become clear that if our analysis is correct, a basic question (whether this story is essentially a resurrection appearance or a *Wunder*) is answerable. Bultmann[1] holds that in the tradition the Easter element was predominant and that it is Luke who has artificially inserted it into the Galilean ministry of Jesus (just as Mark allegedly did with the Caesarea Philippi and transfiguration

---

[1] Commentary, 545 f.; so also *Synoptic tradition*, 230, 218 n. 1 (supplement), but contrast 217 f.

97

stories).[1] From the foregoing, however, it appears that the story is basically a miracle like any other during Jesus' lifetime and that it is John who has made it into an Easter story. It has some similarity to Lk's Emmaus episode but no direct relation to it (which lacks a true miracle). By far the closest parallel is the story in Lk 5. I suspect that the parable of the net (Mt 13: 47 f.) may be involved also, may even have given rise to SQ's version:[2] cf. the net, cast (βάλλειν) into the sea, gathering a catch 'of every kind', and, when full, drawn up on the shore (αἰγιαλός).

B. THE STRUCTURE OF THE SOURCE

I. ITS INTEGRITY

No one supposes that all, or even a few, of the miracle stories in Mk, for example, stem from a single literary source; what justification is there, then, for speaking, as we have repeatedly done in the previous chapter, of a 'signs source' underlying such stories in Jn? The first two of the miracle stories are numbered and so clearly have a common origin, but Michel and Temple believe that these, the miracles in chs. 2 and 4, are distinct from all the rest.[3] What reason is there for supposing that all of the pericopes we have analysed, and not just those two, belonged to the same source?

Besides their enumeration, the first two miracles differ from all the rest in that they do not ensue in a Johannine dialogue[4] but stand self-contained in the present framework of the gospel. However, as we shall see, both of these differences between the earlier and later miracles are explicable in terms of John's

[1] Schnackenburg, 'Traditionsgeschichte', 87 f., thinks that there were two versions in the tradition (reflecting two events?), one of the earthly, one of the risen, Jesus, and that John's source had both accounts!

[2] For a sign derived from a parable, cf. above on 2: 1 ff. and 11: 1 ff. More distantly related is the logion about fishers of men (Mk 1: 17 = Mt 4: 19) with which Lk concludes his version of the story (5: 10).

[3] Temple, 'Two signs', 169 f., considers but lays aside the possibility that the miracle in ch. 21 is a third member of the same source (cf. 21: 14).

[4] The miraculous feeding (6: 1 ff.) does not lead directly to its Johannine development but only after the episode on the sea (6: 16 ff.); these two miracles are treated as one, however, the latter now serving primarily as a bridge between the former and its dialogue (6: 26 ff.).

redaction. Furthermore they are related to each other, that is, the purpose which led John to depart, after the first two signs, from what was apparently a consistent scheme of numbering for all the signs, is integral with that which caused him to let the first two stand alone, but to elaborate upon the others in a common way (below, sec. 3).

But more than that, the following indications of a *pre-Johannine editorial shaping* common to all the signs suggest that a single source lies immediately behind them, and not simply oral tradition (as with most of Mk's miracles): (1) As it stands each story is inseparably attached to a specific locale[1] and so seems to fit closely into a scheme of the travels of Jesus common to all. By contrast, many of the synoptic miracles have only the vaguest geographical reference or none at all beyond that implied by the larger editorial context in which they now stand. (2) We may defer till pt. IV a detailed analysis of the stylistic integrity of the source; but here it can be noted that in the broader sense of style all of the stories, while clearly stemming originally from quite disparate and independent traditions, have a similar shape. This is evident in (*a*) the repeated formula ἦν δέ (τις),[2] (*b*) the element, found in most of the stories, of the witnesses' response to the sign,[3] (*c*) the frequent sequence: Jesus' command, οὖν, compliance (in practically identical words),[4] and (*d*) the gratuitous 'novelistic' elaboration as to cast of characters,[5] situation,[6] and action,[7] which is found in every one of the stories and which makes them so different from terse Markan pericopes like that of Simon's mother-in-law (1: 30 f.) or the leper of ?Capernaum (1: 40 ff.).

---

[1] In their present order: Cana, (near) Capernaum, Jerusalem (Bethzatha/Bethesda), a mountain across the Sea of Galilee, near the opposite shore, Jerusalem (Siloam), Bethany, (Sea of Galilee). Note also the consciousness of location and distance displayed in the source: 'at the Sheep Gate' (5: 2), '25 or 30 stadia' (6: 19), '15 stadia' (11: 18), '200 cubits' (21: 8).

[2] 2: 6, 4: 46, (5: 2), 5: 5, 6: 10, 11: 1, (2), 18, 38, (21: 2).

[3] 2: 11 c, 4: 53 b, 6: 14, 25, ?9: 8, 11: 45.

[4] 2: 7, 8, (4: 51), 5: 9, 6: 10, 9: 7, 11: (32), 41, 21: 6, ?11.

[5] 'The disciples', ?Philip, Andrew, Lazarus, Martha, Mary, Simon Peter, Thomas, Nathanael, the sons of Zebedee.

[6] See above, n. 1; *cf.* also 2: 6, 4: 52, 5: 2 f., 7, 6: 22, 11: 17, 38, 21: 11.

[7] 2: 7 f., 6: 12, 9: 6, 11: 39, 41, 43 f., 21: 6.

This will perhaps suffice for the present to distinguish the nature of the pre-Johannine stock of material from that of the variegated and diffuse oral tradition lying behind most of the synoptic stories and so to suggest that in the miracles John had access to a single source.

2. THE NUMBER OF SIGNS

John reproduces eight miracle stories from the source,[1] and the question arises whether there were others now lost to us.[2]

He provides a good sampling of the various miracles associated with Jesus in the other gospel traditions, but with one notable exception: not a single exorcism appears. This lack can hardly be accidental, but whether it is due to conscious intent on the part of John cannot be known; it may be merely that the author of the source, or the tradition he relied on, took no interest in the demons and their overthrow. (See further below, p. 229.)

Thus the exact extent of the catena of signs which made up the core of the source is perhaps indeterminate; yet it is not likely to have been very long, for the author tells us (20: 30 f., on which see below, pt. III) that he has made a deliberate selection out of a larger stock of stories. And it is quite possible that the number of those selected by him was not random but either symbolic or at least fittingly complete, as evidenced by his numbering them (see below). It is a matter of speculation what that number was, but we may consider two possibilities.

[1] Jesus' unexplained knowledge of Nathanael (1: 47 ff.) and of the woman at the well (4: 16 ff.) is quasi-miraculous and probably stems from the source (pt. III, below), but these episodes have no standing as miracles in their own right (*cf.* perhaps the walking-on-the-sea episode).—Hartke finds twelve 'signs' in Jn, but includes (besides the first seven of our list) stories which are not true miracles and in some cases not even signs in a looser sense.

[2] Schnackenburg, 'Traditionsgeschichte', 64 f., suggests that John has omitted one or more Galilean healings and that their presence in the source is betrayed by the parallel to the healing of Peter's mother-in-law in 4: 52 (John having inserted the element of *fever* to compensate, as it were, for his omission) and by the mention of signs [*sic*] done on the sick in 6: 2*b* (the plural being appropriate in the source but not in its present context). Our analysis, however, does not bear this out: 4: 52 appears to be pre-Johannine, and 6: 2*b*, John's summary—see above, *ad loc.* For the suggestion that the source had two accounts of a draught of fish (*ibid.* 87), see above, p. 98 n. 1.

(1) If there was deliberate Moses typology in the author's mind (see below, pt. v), a parallel with the *ten* 'signs' in Exodus is perhaps to be expected.[1] In that case, we are lacking two (or three) of the original number.

(2) A more likely guess is the number *seven*, supported by the following considerations: (*a*) While we have analysed eight pericopes, two of them (those in ch. 6) were almost certainly regarded as a unit;[2] this is invariably true in the synoptic versions of these stories[3] and is borne out by John's treatment of them (see above, p. 98 n. 4). (*b*) The care with which John reproduces the source in detail (a respect which prevents him from smoothing over the seams his redaction creates—and so allows us to trace our way back over his steps) suggests that he may have reproduced all the miracle stories it contained.[4] (*c*) Many scholars have noticed a sevenfold structure, on various levels, in Jn.[5] If that is deliberate on John's part, as seems likely, it is nevertheless one which may have been suggested by the source.[6] (*d*) If it is true that the source is decidedly Jewish in character (see below, pp. 223 f.), the appropriateness of a sevenfold structure is immediately obvious.–All this suggests that while reorganizing and expanding it, John has reproduced the entire structural framework (*i.e.* the seven signs) of the source. We turn now to consider how in that case the elements in this core may originally have been arranged.

---

[1] As perhaps in Mt 8–9—*cf.* H. M. Teeple, *The Mosaic eschatological prophet* (*JBL* Monograph Series, 10; Philadelphia, 1957), 82, citing Schoeps.

[2] So Bultmann, 78 n. 1, who finds six signs, not counting 21: 1 ff.

[3] The connection is probably very early: even the feeding of the four thousand is followed by a sea crossing with a kind of epiphany.

[4] With one exception, if the draught of fish episode was added later (see above, A, sec. 8).

[5] Windisch, 'Erzählungsstil'; Lohmeyer, 'Aufbau'; Hirsch, *Das vierte Evangelium*; Dodd, *Interpretation*. Lohmeyer's study is the most thoroughgoing attempt at such an analysis and is probably overwrought (*cf.* Bultmann, 78 n. 2); Windisch's article is more scientific.

[6] Lohmeyer, *ibid.* 34, observes that the use of the number seven is intimately associated with the 'historical' element of the gospel, *i.e.* the narrative parts. These stem almost entirely from SQ.

3. THE ORDER AND INTERCONNECTION
OF THE SIGNS

In the course of analysing the individual miracles we left aside certain transitional verses at the beginning and/or end of some of the stories. We have now to consider them to find what pre-Johannine editorial links can be discovered and thus what of the original order can be reconstructed.

Because of the clues in 2: 11a and 4: 54a, we can be reasonably confident that the wedding at Cana and the healing on the road to Capernaum were respectively the first and second signs. That they originally came together is evident from the notice in 2: 12, which is pointless in its present context but becomes understandable as a transitional passage from the source: Jesus leaves Cana for Capernaum in preparation for the next miracle (4: 46 ff.).—The phrase μετὰ τοῦτο may be Johannine. If, as Wilkens holds (see above on 4: 47), the second sign took place outside Capernaum, on the road to Cana, it may be that the source read κατέβαινεν instead of κατέβη (cf. ἔρχεται for ἥκει in 4: 47); but the aorist may be ingressive ('he set out for Capernaum') and so original.—The phrase καὶ οἱ μαθηταὶ αὐτοῦ may be a gloss,[1] occasioned by what could be John's addition of αὐτὸς καὶ ἡ μήτηρ αὐτοῦ καὶ οἱ ἀδελφοί: in the source, a notice that Jesus alone departed from Capernaum would not exclude the disciples whose presence is sometimes simply assumed (e.g. 6: 1, 3, 9: 1 f.), but with the addition of his family explicit inclusion of the disciples becomes necessary after 2: 11c and before 2: 22. But a more likely explanation for the textual variation is that the original (Johannine) order was that of W (Jesus, disciples, Mary, brothers) and was rearranged out of reverence for Jesus' family, in the course of which the disciples were omitted in one strain of MSS.[2] In that case, the source probably read αὐτὸς καὶ οἱ μαθηταί (cf. 2: 2) and John has again brought Mary to the forefront (as in 2: 1b, 3b–4), and

---

[1] Lacking in ℵ a b e ff² al (cf. Epist. Apost. 5), and found before καὶ οἱ ἀδελφοί in some MSS, and before καὶ ἡ μήτηρ in W.

[2] Perhaps so that 'the brothers' (with or without the pronoun) could be taken as designating the band of disciples (cf. the variant at 20: 17) and so not contradicting the perpetual virginity of Mary—cf. Mollat, 77; Brown, 112 f.; similarly one MS omits 'the brothers'.

with her the brothers, who have no part whatever in the story and appear only at 7: 3 ff. (Johannine). The portraiture of Jesus' family in Jn appears to be Johannine.

The second half of 2: 12 is Johannine (*cf.* 3: 22, 4: 40*b*, 10: 40, 11: 6*b*, 54), preparing for the first visit to Jerusalem and the cleansing of the temple, which John moves forward from its traditional place in the ministry (see below, pt. II).

Presumably, then, the transition between the first and second signs read originally as follows:

2: 12*a* (μετὰ τοῦτο) κατέβη[-βαινεν] εἰς Καφαρναοὺμ αὐτὸς |...| καὶ οἱ μαθηταὶ αὐτοῦ.

Departing from the source at this point, John does not return to it till 4: 46*b*; there he brings Jesus, rather artificially, back to Cana,[1] whence the boy in Capernaum is now healed. Originally 46*b* followed 2: 12*a* immediately.

After the first two signs, one looks in vain in the next miracle story (the healing of the man at the pool, 5: 1 ff.) for an indication of its place in the source. What is certain, however, is that it did not originally follow the healing of the official's son as the third sign: the opening verse (just as abrupt as 2: 13, on which it is patterned) is clearly Johannine, yet the story presupposes Jesus' presence in Jerusalem, which only 5: 1 provides. Those who favour a transposition of Jn 5 and 6 point out that 4: 54 leads naturally into 6: 1 ff.[2] That pericope, with its own connective introduction (see above on 6: 1–4), may then have been the third sign in the source. But all that 6: 1 presupposes is that Jesus is still near the sea—that is, another episode on the sea may have intervened.

The only reason for supposing that the feeding of the five thousand is not the third sign but that another preceded it is the enumeration in 21: 14, which, as we noted, is inappropriate and

---

[1] *I.e.* to the place of the last real event in the source; to bring him to Capernaum would destroy the *Fernheilung* which he finds already in the source and heightens still more.

[2] In the former, Jesus is in, or on his way to, Capernaum; in the latter he goes away across the sea, presumably from Capernaum, and eventually returns there (6: 17, 21).–We must reject the hypothesis of post-Johannine redaction until we have considered whether the seam is not due to John's reworking of the source—see above, pp. 5 ff.

unnecessary, and concludes a pericope that jars with its context and in Lk stands within the ministry of Jesus. The obvious presumption, then, is that that pericope was the third sign in SQ (so Spitta, Schnackenburg).–Jesus, at 4: 54 on the road to Capernaum, or already there, now appears on the shore of the lake; but first his disciples, who in no way figured in the previous story but were last heard of in 2: 11c, 12a, come back into prominence. Thomas and the sons of Zebedee appear for the first time; Peter and Nathanael are already known to the reader (see below, on 1: 40 ff.) and possibly the two unnamed disciples are Andrew and Philip (*ibid.*).– We have already reconstructed the editorial conclusion to the third sign (above, pp. 95 f.).

It is not hard to guess why John transposed the third sign in the source to the end of his gospel, or—if its inclusion there is due to a later hand—at least failed to reproduce it in its original context. As we have already noted, the story lent itself (whether in Johannine or post-Johannine eyes) to a post-resurrection appearance, and it provided both for a Galilean ending and for the discussion of Peter's authority by which the author in question apparently wished to round out the gospel. In any case, however, the story could not remain in its pre-Johannine position because of the Johannine scheme of Jesus' ministry, one made up of periods in Judea (and especially Jerusalem) alternating with ones outside it (Galilee notably, but also Transjordan and 'the wilderness').[1] This plan is in fact already evident after the first sign (2: 13), where John forsakes the source in order to bring Jesus to Jerusalem, who returns to Galilee (and John to the source) only at 4: 46. Since there is no evidence of anything in the source which might have occasioned this quite artificial departure from its framework, it is evidently due entirely to John's over-all plan. In the same way, then, he introduces a Jerusalem sojourn at the end of the second sign by casting aside the third episode and bringing forward one found later in the source (in this case one of the actual signs, whereas at 2: 13 it was an episode which originally was part of the prelude to the passion).

[1] We need not consider in the present study what role this *Rahmen* plays in John's purpose. I propose to investigate that question in a future study.

John begins a new phase in his gospel with ch. 5.[1] Each of the first two Galilean signs stands alone, but just as the first Jerusalem episode (2: 13 ff.) was made by John to lead into a discourse between Jesus and a Jew (ch. 3), so here John creates another *Rede* with Jews in Jerusalem, occasioned by the episode from the source. And from this point on, as we have seen already, each of the signs is treated in the same way.[2] This means that if the stories originally had a stereotyped rounding off like that in 2: 11 and 4: 54, in each case it had to be discarded because the numerical scheme was now disrupted, that of the third sign alone capable of being salvaged (and then by a kind of *tour de force*). Only without their original endings are the stories capable of introducing the theological discussions which now follow them.

The fourth sign was presumably that of the loaves, 6: 1 providing the pre-Johannine editorial link. On the basis of our analysis above (A, sec. 4), we conjecturally reconstruct its conclusion:

6: 14 [τοῦτο τέταρτον ἐποίησεν σημεῖον ὁ Ἰησοῦς καὶ] οἱ οὖν ἄνθρωποι |...| ἔλεγον ὅτι οὗτός ἐστιν |...| ὁ προφήτης.

Since 6: 16 ff. (the walking on water) is inseparable from 1–14, it might have been expected that the rounding off would come at the end of that episode; but as we have seen, the actual sign is the miracle of the loaves and fish, and what follows was in the source apparently only a kind of coda for the Galilean half of the source.

There is no way of knowing what, if anything, followed 6: 25 in the source,[3] before Jesus goes up to Jerusalem—as he must before the next sign, since all the remaining signs take place in or near the capital. (Thus, while we cannot simply assume that Mk's twofold scheme for the ministry was fixed in the tradition, it appears in fact that the source, like Mk, consisted of a Galilean

---

[1] In this sense Lightfoot and Barrett, who see 2: 13—4: 54 as a unit, perceive something which Bultmann and Dodd (*Interpretation*) do not when they join 4: 46 ff. to 5: 1 ff., unmistakable as the links between these two passages are.

[2] Even those in Galilee—the miracle of the loaves for eucharistic reasons, apparently, that of the fish for ecclesiological.

[3] But see below, pt. III, on 6: 67 ff.

period followed by a Judean one.) Two of the Judean signs—the healings at pools—assume Jesus' presence in the city (*cf.* 5: 6, 9: 1*a*, 7), but the third, the raising of Lazarus, finds Jesus several days' journey from Bethany[1] and, what is more significant, tells of his coming there.[2] If the story is at all meant to be realistic (apart, of course, from its historicity), it seems likely that in the source this call to Bethany was the occasion of Jesus' leaving Galilee for Jerusalem.[3] If so the Lazarus story was, in a sevenfold scheme, the fifth sign in the series.[4] Because of its peculiar importance in John's interpretation,[5] he transposed it to a new context—as its present artificial introduction (10:40–2) shows—so as to be the last and greatest of the signs.[6]

If the Lazarus story is the fifth sign, the order of the two remaining episodes is problematic. It is perhaps the case that

[1] *Cf.* 11: 17—from the time the sisters sent word to Jesus, while Lazarus was still alive, until Jesus arrived, not less than four days had elapsed and possibly more. Even if allowance is made for the journey of a messenger to Jesus (or for some other delay—see below, p. 194), Jesus' distance from Bethany cannot be less than two days.

[2] And, implicitly, of the disciples' presence there too—unexplained at 9: 1 ff. as the gospel now stands (Brown, 371).

[3] Capernaum, where Jesus was last found in the source, is *c.* 90 miles from Bethany, more than two days' hard walk (see above, n. 1).–Is it more than accident that in Mk Jesus' journey to Jerusalem takes him first to Bethany (11: 1, 11, 14: 3)?

[4] An alternative to the above is the suggestion offered by Bultmann (85 n. 4, 217; *cf.* Wilkens, 48 f.), *viz.* that behind 7: 1–10 is a *Traditionsstück* which provided the transition to the Jerusalem ministry in the source. In that case the fifth sign was probably the healing at the pool, as they believe. But I find it impossible to isolate a pre-Johannine stratum in 7: 1 ff. and suspect that the passage is entirely John's creation (see further, pp. 196 f.).

[5] See above, A, sec. 7, where our analysis bore this out: John has embroidered this story in a way unlike any of the others and made it the occasion of the authorities' decision to put Jesus to death (11: 46 ff.), so that it now has a role analogous to that of the cleansing of the temple in Mk.

[6] So successfully has John adapted the pericope to his purposes that it is hard to conceive of its not being the climactic event in the source (so Schnackenburg, 'Traditionsgeschichte', 80). Dr Walter Wink puts the case clearly in a private communication: the Lazarus story must have been the last in the source for it is 'the greatest miracle of all, the chief sign, and the final one, since it deals with the final enemy and prefigures Jesus' glorification in his own death'. I would answer, tentatively (for my suggestion above is only hypothetical), that all of this is true, but of *John's* point of view, not the source's.

John simply reproduced the relative position of these two stories. That is, after 4: 46 ff., when he wished to introduce a Jerusalem episode in place of the draught of fish, having decided to defer the first Jerusalem story found in the source (Lazarus), he simply took the next one in line. The story of the healing at the pool (5: 1 ff.), then, was the sixth sign, and the healing of the blind man (9: 1 ff.) the seventh.[1]

But it is quite possible that for his own theological purposes John inverted the order of these two signs, saving for the context of ch. 9 the healing of the blind man, so symbolically appropriate to the discourse on light. Two considerations support this, suggesting that originally the episode of the lame man (ch. 5) was the seventh and last of the signs:

(1) If it had followed the fifth sign (Lazarus), set in Bethany, it would have required an introductory notice of Jesus' coming into Jerusalem, for he is shown actually in the city in 5: 6; but there is no evidence of such a passage, for John, who utilizes the source's transitions when they are available (*e.g.* 6: 1), must create 5: 1 out of whole cloth (see above, p. 49).

(2) The source elsewhere gives evidence of a very careful arrangement of the signs according to the logic of geography. While both of the signs in question here are associated with Jerusalem, only that in ch. 5 requires Jesus' presence in the city. In ch. 9, by contrast, we are not told where he meets the blind man, but only that he sends him to Siloam; thus merely the vicinity of Jerusalem is presupposed. And παράγων (9: 1),[2] which appears to be pre-Johannine, together with the spatial progression in the story it introduces, would neatly provide a transition from Bethany to Jerusalem. This is probably not the only instance in the source of a miracle *en route* (*cf.* on 4: 46 ff.).

We may thus take it as slightly more likely that the sixth and seventh signs were those in chs. 9 and 5, respectively, than the reverse.

The editorial framework connecting the last three signs must remain even more tentative than their order, since John has not merely rearranged them (as with those in Galilee) but in every

---

[1] It is then perhaps more than coincidence that the last of Mk's miracles, coming just before the passion events begin in Jerusalem, was the healing of blind Bartimaeus.   [2] Meaning perhaps *departing* (*sc.* from Bethany).

case replaced the original endings with his own dramatic elaboration (5: 9 ff., 9: 9 ff., 11: 46 ff.). But it is not unlikely that the stories followed one another with no more than the usual stereotyped summaries and the present opening verses (9: 1 and 5: 2) as transitions. Thus, conjecturally, at the end of the Lazarus story:

11: 45 [τοῦτο πέμπτον ἐποίησεν σημεῖον ὁ 'Ιησοῦς καὶ] |...| οἱ ἐλθόντες πρὸς τὴν Μαριὰμ καὶ θεασάμενοι ὃ ἐποίησεν ἐπίστευσαν εἰς αὐτόν.

followed by 9: 1 ff. And at the end of that pericope (*i.e.* after 9: 7):

[τοῦτο ἕκτον ἐποίησεν σημεῖον ὁ 'Ιησοῦς.]

possibly with 9: 8 preceding or following. Then 5: 2 ff., and after 5: 9*b* or 14*b*:

[τοῦτο ἕβδομον ἐποίησεν σημεῖον ὁ 'Ιησοῦς.][1]

Our reconstruction of the original arrangement of the signs is then as follows:

1. Wedding at Cana (Jn 2);
2. Official's son healed at Capernaum (Jn 4);
3. Draught of fish on the Sea of Galilee (Jn 21);
4. Feeding by the Sea of Galilee and sequel (Jn 6);
5. Lazarus raised at Bethany (Jn 11);
6. Blind man healed in Jerusalem (Jn 9);
7. Lame man healed in Jerusalem (Jn 5).

The first four appear to be an uninterrupted series, possibly also the last three.

While this arrangement is by no means certain, less so than the reconstruction of the individual stories, it is clear enough that they stood in a literary work with a far from haphazard structure.[2] They constitute, then, more than a 'collection of miracle stories' (Bultmann, *RGG*, 842); Fuller (88 ff.) speaks more appropriately of a 'Book of Signs', but in either case the question arises as to the *raison d'être* of a work which, while

---

[1] Or possibly, balancing 2: 11*a*, τοῦτο ἔσχατον ἐποίησεν κτλ.

[2] And one more coherent than much of Mk, for example; *cf.* that evangelist's repeated use of καί as the only connective between pericopes.

consisting solely of a series of self-contained stories, yet provides them with such a unity as their arrangement and common theme express. It is inherently likely that they constitute but the core (though certainly no less than that, for they appear to provide an organizing framework) for a larger work.

Haenchen[1] suggests that Bultmann has not gone far enough in looking for pre-Johannine sources of synoptic material in the gospel and suggests an extended SQ—'a kind of coarsened Mark'—to account for other parallels to the synoptics in the gospel. The most notable block of such parallels is of course to be found in the passion narrative, and so we turn now to the source analysis of that material.[2]

---

[1] 'Literatur', 303; also 'Probleme'.

[2] Schnackenburg, at the end of his programmatic article ('Traditions-geschichte'), calls for a closer investigation of the contacts between Jn and Lk in the passion narrative; such contacts in the *miracle stories* are rightly seen by him to be explained by the SQ hypothesis, so it will not be surprising if a similar hypothesis explains the contacts in the passion narrative.

PART TWO

THE PASSION AND RESURRECTION NARRATIVES

THE PASSION AND
RESURRECTION NARRATIVES

Many have investigated the passion and resurrection narratives of Jn, in part[1] or as a whole,[2] and all are agreed that the evangelist was dependent on some earlier literary narrative.[3] There is considerable evidence for supposing that this represents a tradition parallel to but essentially distinct from that underlying the synoptic passion narratives[4]—even some who elsewhere find direct Johannine dependence on one or more of the earlier gospels here argue for an independent source. Since we have reason to believe that in the miracle stories, where Jn is also parallel to the synoptics, the evangelist used a unique source, that hypothesis suggests itself here. There is no certainty, at this point, that the two sources are one; therefore, in the following analysis, we cannot take for granted the detailed stylistic criteria which were increasingly available to us in pt. I. (The integrity of the source uncovered here with SQ will be an important issue of the tests we shall apply in pt. IV.) It will become clear as we progress, however, that many of the same characteristics of style appear in the *Vorlage* here.

The introduction to John's passion source is harder to reconstruct than the bulk of the narrative, as is the case with Mk's gospel, since both evangelists, in quite different ways, have interwoven the opening episodes (the 'prelude to the

---

[1] See the bibliographies for the individual sections below.

[2] Borgen, 'Passion narrative'; Buse, 'Marcan passion narrative'; also 'St Matthew and St Luke'; M. Dibelius, 'Die alttestamentlichen Motive in der Leidensgeschichte des Petrus- und des Johannes-Evangeliums', in *Botschaft und Geschichte*, I (Tübingen, 1953), 221–47 (cited below as Dibelius); Dodd, 21–151; X. Léon-Dufour, 'Passion', II, 1: 'Le récit selon S. Jean', in *Dictionnaire de la Bible, Supplément*, VI (Paris, 1957–60), 1438–44; Osty, 'Points de contact'; A. M. Ramsey, 'The narratives of the passion', *StudEv* II, 122–34, esp. 131–3; Temple, 'Two traditions'; P. Winter, *On the trial of Jesus* (Studia Judaica, 1; Berlin, 1961 [cited below as Winter]).

[3] That John has not simply, for the first time, assembled various independent traditions into a continuous narrative needs hardly to be argued. See further, p. 134 n. 2 below.

[4] *Cf.* V. Taylor, *The formation of the gospel tradition* (London, 1933), 53 f.; Dibelius, 231 f.; Léon-Dufour, 'Passion', 1444.

passion', in Dodd's phrase) with other material, even in some cases transposing whole blocks of the source. But in both accounts, as they now stand, the source runs relatively un-interrupted after these preliminaries, and it is at this point in Jn (*viz.* the arrest, 18: 1 ff.)[1] that we can most confidently begin our analysis, to return to the introductory narratives at the end.

I. THE ARREST (18: 1–12)

A major division in the synoptic account of the passion, as Dodd analyses it, begins with the agony in Gethsemane, a place and scene unknown to John.[2] The next episode, however, the story of Judas' treachery and the resulting seizure of Jesus, appears here, with a number of parallels to the synoptics but also with major differences, some of which can hardly be due to anything but the vagaries of divergent traditions: *e.g.* the geographical note in *v.* 1, Judas' more active role in the arrest, the presence (and size) of the Roman military at the scene,[3] the identification of the disciple who struck the high priest's slave, the naming of the slave.

18: 1. The opening words here (ταῦτα εἰπών) are probably John's attempt to smooth the abrupt transition between the (Johannine) discourse that precedes and the source that is resumed here (*cf. e.g.* 11: 28). Otherwise the verse appears to be pre-Johannine.[4]

18: 2 f. The use of a stereotyped epithet (ὁ παραδιδοὺς αὐτόν) after Judas' name here is certainly pre-Johannine: the same

---

[1] The comparable place in Mk (14: 1) is at a point rather earlier in the story—the plot of the Jewish authorities, before the Last Supper.

[2] The garden across Kidron (18: 1) may of course describe the same place as Gethsemane on the Mount of Olives; but we are concerned here only with the wording of tradition, not its historical basis.—Dodd (68–72) finds hints that John was in contact with a tradition of Jesus' prayer on that occasion—12: 27 f., 14: 31 *b*, 18: 11 *b*; these passages are perhaps fragments from the source (see further below, p. 157), but it is no longer possible to reconstruct them.

[3] Winter, 44 ff., makes a strong case for the historicity of this detail, however exaggerated the number of soldiers may be.

[4] The use of σύν (for μετά) is relatively rare in Jn—see above on 21: 3; for αὐτός in a compound subject with singular verb, see also 2: 12, 4: 53 (and *cf.* 2: 2), all pre-Johannine.

usage (with slight variation in tense) is found in Mt 10: 4, 26: 25, 27: 3, and as a substantive clause at Mk 14: 42, 44 pars. – That Jesus and the disciples had a customary gathering place is found also in Lk 22: 39; Judas' knowledge of it, taken for granted in the other gospels, is remarked here, almost as if he were not a member of the disciple band. This, and the above-mentioned initiative taken by him in *v.* 3 (*cf.* Lk 22: 47), is probably a sign of developing tradition, rather than intentional alteration on John's part.[1] – The vocabulary used in *v.* 3 for the constituency of the posse and the implements carried represents the usual variation from that of the synoptics.[2]

18: 4–9. The dialogue of Jesus with his captors is certainly Johannine in its present form, though not necessarily John's invention *in toto*. Barrett (431) thinks the picture of Jesus here, entirely in command, is purely Johannine. The tendency to give Jesus the upper hand in the scene is already evident in Lk, however, and in the opening lines of the scene (4–5*a*) probably only the mention of Jesus' foreknowledge in *v.* 4 (εἰδὼς . . . αὐτόν) has been added to the source (*cf.* 13: 3, 19: 28). Dodd (75 f.) is right, I think, that the first instance of ἐγώ εἰμι (5*b*) is traditional (*cf.* 6: 20) and without theophanic significance, and that the double repetition (6, 8) is Johannine (*cf.* 4: 50–3). The notice about Judas in 5*c* is puzzling: Bultmann (493) holds it to be pre-Johannine, originally leading up to Judas' kiss as in Mk, and the mention of the betrayer in 2 f. John's invention. The opposite seems more likely to be the case, however, John having (redundantly) reintroduced Judas after the now highly theological *I am* so as specifically to include him in the devastating effect these words are made, dramatically and unrealistically, to have on Jesus' opponents (6–8*a*).[3] The rest of

---

[1] The use of μετά here (contrast σύν in *v.* 1) is not necessarily redactional —συνάγειν is never found with σύν in the NT. Likewise οὖν (3) is not historical, but logically connects the two verses.

[2] For σπεῖρα, *cf.* Mk 15: 16 par. (mocking of Jesus); for ὑπηρέτης, Mk 14: 54 par., 65 (Jesus before the Sanhedrin); ὅπλον (literally) and φανός only here in the NT. – Winter, 47–9, makes a case for the mention of both Roman and Jewish agents in the oldest tradition.

[3] Dodd, 76 f., thinks a traditional *testimonium* (derived from Pss. 27: 2 and 35: 4) underlies 6*b*, but if so it would seem to have been combined with the source only by John.

the section—Jesus' request of immunity for his followers and the consequent notice of the fulfilment of his own word (8b–9)—also derives from John's theological motives (see Dodd, 57). Originally Jesus simply came forward and hearing the posse's mission gave himself up (4–5b). Peter's impulsive action (10 f.) follows naturally enough.

18: 10 f. The episode of the sword, found in all the gospels, here shows no marks of John's editing. That it is Peter who strikes the slave and the right ear that he severs (*cf.* Lk 22: 50), and that the slave is named, is hardly due to Johannine *Tendenz.* Jesus' rebuke (11 a) resembles Mt 26: 52 (*cf.* Lk 22: 51); the word about the cup (11 b) is reminiscent of the synoptic saying in a slightly different context (Mk 14: 36 pars. [Gethsemane]).

18: 12. Winter (45) finds a conflict between the χιλίαρχος here and Judas' command of the cohort in *v.* 3, but this is probably an overly literal objection—Judas is certainly the instigator, but hardly the commander, in the earlier passage.[1] That the rank of the Roman officer here, like the size of his contingent, is unrealistic, is due to exaggeration, but not necessarily on John's part. The identification of the ὑπηρέται as being τῶν Ἰουδαίων is possibly Johannine (see above, on 2: 6, *etc.*), but in the present context might be original, distinguishing the Jewish guard from the Roman military.–On συλλαμβάνειν, see above, p. 90 n. 3.[2]

Our result is as follows:

18: 1 |...| Ἰησοῦς ἐξῆλθεν σὺν τοῖς μαθηταῖς αὐτοῦ πέραν τοῦ χειμάρρου τοῦ Κεδρών, ὅπου ἦν κῆπος, εἰς ὃν εἰσῆλθεν αὐτὸς καὶ οἱ μαθηταὶ αὐτοῦ.

2 ᾔδει δὲ καὶ Ἰούδας ὁ παραδιδοὺς αὐτὸν τὸν τόπον, ὅτι πολλάκις συνήχθη Ἰησοῦς ἐκεῖ μετὰ τῶν μαθητῶν αὐτοῦ.

3 ὁ οὖν Ἰούδας λαβὼν τὴν σπεῖραν καὶ ἐκ τῶν ἀρχιερέων καὶ ἐκ τῶν Φαρισαίων ὑπηρέτας ἔρχεται ἐκεῖ μετὰ φανῶν καὶ λαμπάδων καὶ ὅπλων.

4 Ἰησοῦς οὖν |...| ἐξῆλθεν καὶ λέγει αὐτοῖς· τίνα ζητεῖτε;

[1] So John understands, anyway—*cf.* 5 b.
[2] The same word is used in Lk 22: 54, and there also Jesus is not seized until the end of the scene.

5 ἀπεκρίθησαν αὐτῷ· Ἰησοῦν τὸν Ναζωραῖον. λέγει αὐτοῖς· ἐγώ εἰμι. |...|

10 Σίμων οὖν Πέτρος ἔχων μάχαιραν εἵλκυσεν αὐτὴν καὶ ἔπαισεν τὸν τοῦ ἀρχιερέως δοῦλον καὶ ἀπέκοψεν αὐτοῦ τὸ ὠτάριον τὸ δεξιόν· ἦν δὲ ὄνομα τῷ δούλῳ Μάλχος.

11 εἶπεν οὖν ὁ Ἰησοῦς τῷ Πέτρῳ· βάλε τὴν μάχαιραν εἰς τὴν θήκην· τὸ ποτήριον ὃ δέδωκέν μοι ὁ πατήρ, οὐ μὴ πίω αὐτό;

12 ἡ οὖν σπεῖρα καὶ χιλίαρχος καὶ οἱ ὑπηρέται (τῶν Ἰουδαίων) συνέλαβον τὸν Ἰησοῦν καὶ ἔδησαν αὐτόν.

2. JESUS IN THE HIGH PRIEST'S HOUSE
(18: 13–28a)[1]

The various evangelists put the story of Peter's denials at slightly differing points in the narrative. It is probable that, unlike most of the passion account, that story originally had an independent existence in the tradition. Nevertheless, all associate it somehow with the examination by the Jewish authorities, and therefore it is likely that John found both episodes in the source, though as we shall see he has probably somewhat rearranged them. The variations among the evangelists, and John's changes, apparently stem only from differing attempts to show the two episodes as simultaneous,[2] a relationship which (since by no means inevitable) must therefore have been fixed in tradition.

The whole passage in John presents serious aporias—notably the confusion as to the identity of the high priest making the examination and the almost literal repetition of 18b in 25a[3]—and these have led to various suggested rearrangements, both

---

[1] J. Schneider, 'Zur Komposition von Joh 18, 12–27', *ZNW* 48 (1957), 111–19.

[2] Only in Lk is this not so, for he has abbreviated Mk's night-long hearing to a brief meeting in the morning and so let Peter's denials fill the night of waiting.

[3] Also the awkward duplication of the phrase 'known to the high priest' in successive verses (15b, 16b), and the puzzling fact that although the disciple so described is known to Caiaphas (clearly identified as the high priest), it is to Annas' house that he gains admittance for himself and Peter. (Winter explains this by supposing that all references to Caiaphas are interpolations, Annas being the high priest in the original story; but this is arbitrary—both names appear to be imbedded in the tradition, whatever the historical actuality. See below, p. 119 n. 3.)

ancient[1] and modern,[2] all of which assume post-Johannine corruption of the text. The common denominator in these suggestions is that 24 (Jesus sent by Annas to Caiaphas) should be put after 13, or thereabouts, and 16*b*–18 (Peter's first denial) transferred to a place just before 25–7. All of them, even the textual variants, are undoubtedly no more than conjecture, but they point to the fact that rearrangement has certainly occurred—not, however, accidentally, after the gospel was completed, but intentionally on the part of John, as he redacted his source.[3] On this hypothesis, John found the two episodes—the hearing (*vv.* 13, 24, 15–16*a*, 19–23) and Peter's denials (16*b*–18, 25–7)—side by side in his source. In order to emphasize their simultaneity and perhaps heighten the dramatic suspense in Peter's case as well, he interwove them, joining the first of the three denials (16*b*–18) to 16*a*, before the hearing, and postponing 24, the original sequel of 13,[4] to its present position.[5] This created, out of what was originally only the suggestion (13 plus 24) of a hearing before Annas, a full-scale scene to that effect, followed by a second examination before Caiaphas,[6] during which the second and third denials (25–7) take place. If this is true, we have both solved the contextual problems of the passage and taken a major step toward the recovery of the source, to which we may now turn.

The hearing probably came before Peter's denials (as in Mk; see also Winter, 21 f.), since it follows naturally after the story of the arrest. The present wording is in the main simply reproduced from the source.

18: 13 f., 24. Jesus is taken 'first' to Annas, who is identified by reference to his more famous relative (13), then to Caiaphas

---

[1] *E.g.* sy[s], *225*, and Luther.

[2] Most recently Schneider.

[3] Dodd's attempt (82 n. 1, 94 n. 2) to justify the present order is correct in that it points to a certain logic underlying the text as it stands, and one which John must have used; but the difficulties remain and must be explained, particularly in the case of *v.* 24.

[4] The plainly Johannine *v.* 14 now fills the gap it left.

[5] The point at which John resumes the denial story.

[6] That the latter is now but a shadow of the former does not mean that Caiaphas is John's invention (so Bultmann)—*cf.* Mt 26: 57—rather only that for the evangelist he has already played his role (11: 49 ff.).

(24).[1] Whether or not the information in 13*bc* is inaccurate, it can as well stem from tradition as from John (*vs.* Winter), and there is nothing in 13 to suggest John's hand; we may attribute the whole verse, then, to the source. Verse 14, clumsy after the explanatory ἦν γάρ in the preceding verse, was evidently added by John (hence 'the Jews') to explain the mention of Caiaphas, made abrupt by the removal of 24.[2] It serves to recall 11: 50. Verse 24 is pre-Johannine, with the possible exception of τὸν ἀρχιερέα, unnecessary after 13 but helpful to the reader in the verse's present position.

18: 15–16a. This passage prepares for the episode of Peter's denials and so might appear out of place in the source's account of the hearing in Caiaphas' house.[3] But in fact it only sets the stage for the later scene outside the interrogation chamber, and while it can be made to lead directly into the first of the denials (as it is by John, when he detaches 16*b*–18 from 25*b* ff. and joins it to 16*a*), the connections with its present context are not altogether smooth.[4] It seems to have come between 24 and 19 ff. in the source—while strictly speaking parenthetical it gives, indirectly, the only notice of the actual entrance of Jesus into Caiaphas' house—and has the same function as Mk 14: 54.

18: 19–23. Though the actual interrogation has evidently been expanded by John, Dodd (95) is probably right that its essentially matter-of-fact, non-theological character (as compared with the synoptics) argues for a traditional origin.[5] It is not easy, however, to establish the exact contour of the source

[1] The structural parallel to the *Vorlage* in 1: 40 ff., as reconstructed below (pp. 183 f.), is striking; note also the element of a named disciple together with a nameless one (*v.* 15 here).

[2] *Cf.* 11: 2, the style of which John evidently imitates and improves on here.

[3] That at several points Caiaphas is referred to simply as *the high priest* does not necessarily mean (*vs.* Winter) that the name is a post-Johannine harmonization with Mt, but only that at an earlier stage in the tradition the high priest was anonymous.

[4] As the omission of the first *known to the high priest* by 𝔓[66]* and the need to recapitulate the end of *v.* 18 in 25*a* indicate.

[5] *Versus* Dibelius, 238, who sees the whole scene as Johannine 'in terminology and technique'.

in this passage. The imprecise summary of the high priest's questions (19) is possibly pre-Johannine, showing none of the signs of John's characteristic dialogues. Jesus' reply in 20 is undoubtedly partly Johannine, with its incongruous mention of *the Jews*, the use of the phrase *the world*, and the contrast between παρρησίᾳ and ἐν κρυπτῷ (see below on 7: 4); the second clause ('I have always taught in synagogue and in the temple') recalls Mk 14: 49, however, and may, with the opening words of the verse, be pre-Johannine. The rest of Jesus' reply (21) is uncertain. It is reminiscent of the blind man's parents' reply in 9: 21, 23, and so may be Johannine (as the theme of knowing in 21 c suggests); on the other hand, if 22 is pre-Johannine, some apparently impertinent reply on Jesus' part is presupposed, and 21 ab may be from the source. The assault by an officer (v. 22),[1] possibly together with Jesus' reply (23),[2] is undoubtedly traditional.

18: 16b–18. After the brief description of the hearing before Caiaphas the source went on to the story of Peter, the *other disciple* of v. 15 going out to get him (perhaps in Jesus' defence, seeing him unjustly treated). Peter makes the first denial just as he is coming into the courtyard (16b–17).[3] Verse 18, pointless in its present context, leads directly to the second and third denials (25 b ff.), which in the source immediately followed it.

18: 25–8a. That Peter is here still in the courtyard of (presumably) Annas' house, on the present reading, whereas Jesus has just been sent to Caiaphas (v. 24), is further evidence of the disorder of the canonical text. In the source both the interrogation and Peter's denials took place at Caiaphas' house. Verse 25 a is John's resumption of the source's denial narrative, now interrupted by 19–23; originally 25 b (εἶπον κτλ) followed 18, the indefinite *they* of the second question to Peter equivalent to the slaves and officers of 18 (*cf.* the *bystanders* of Mk's and Mt's third question). That the third questioner (26) is identified as related to the slave whose ear Peter had cut off is typical of the

---

[1] An early version, perhaps, of the fuller account in Mk 14: 65.

[2] For Jesus' posing of a dilemma (*if…if…*), *cf.* Lk 22: 67 f.

[3] It is instigated by a παιδίσκη (as in the synoptics for both the first and second denials); only here is she identified as θυρωρός.

tradition underlying the source. Peter's third denial (27*a*) leads directly[1] to the fateful climax of the episode (27*b*)—a detail which probably presupposes the prophecy in 13: 38 (see below, p. 157). The double scene in the high priest's house concludes with Jesus' being *led* (*cf.* Lk 23: 1) to Pilate (28*a*).[2]

The *Vorlage* gives a coherent narrative (and one in many ways similar to the synoptics but in as many others differing widely from them in just the way oral tradition might):

18: 13   καὶ ἤγαγον πρὸς Ἅνναν πρῶτον· ἦν γὰρ πενθερὸς τοῦ Καϊάφα, ὃς ἦν ἀρχιερεὺς τοῦ ἐνιαυτοῦ ἐκείνου.

24   ἀπέστειλεν οὖν αὐτὸν ὁ Ἅννας δεδεμένον πρὸς Καϊάφαν |...|.

15   ἠκολούθει δὲ τῷ Ἰησοῦ Σίμων Πέτρος καὶ ἄλλος μαθητής. ὁ δὲ μαθητὴς ἐκεῖνος ἦν γνωστὸς τῷ ἀρχιερεῖ, καὶ συνεισῆλθεν τῷ Ἰησοῦ εἰς τὴν αὐλὴν τοῦ ἀρχιερέως,

16*a*   ὁ δὲ Πέτρος εἱστήκει πρὸς τῇ θύρᾳ ἔξω.

19   (ὁ οὖν ἀρχιερεὺς ἠρώτησεν τὸν Ἰησοῦν περὶ τῶν μαθητῶν αὐτοῦ καὶ περὶ τῆς διδαχῆς αὐτοῦ.)

20   ἀπεκρίθη αὐτῷ Ἰησοῦς· |...| ἐγὼ πάντοτε ἐδίδαξα ἐν συναγωγῇ καὶ ἐν τῷ ἱερῷ |...|.

21   (τί με ἐρωτᾷς; ἐρώτησον τοὺς ἀκηκοότας τί ἐλάλησα αὐτοῖς·) |...|

22   ταῦτα δὲ αὐτοῦ εἰπόντος εἷς παρεστηκὼς τῶν ὑπηρετῶν ἔδωκεν ῥάπισμα τῷ Ἰησοῦ εἰπών· οὕτως ἀποκρίνῃ τῷ ἀρχιερεῖ;

23   ἀπεκρίθη αὐτῷ Ἰησοῦς· εἰ κακῶς ἐλάλησα, μαρτύρησον περὶ τοῦ κακοῦ· εἰ δὲ καλῶς, τί με δέρεις;

16*b*   ἐξῆλθεν οὖν ὁ μαθητὴς ὁ ἄλλος ὁ γνωστὸς τοῦ ἀρχιερέως καὶ εἶπεν τῇ θυρωρῷ, καὶ εἰσήγαγεν τὸν Πέτρον.

17   λέγει οὖν τῷ Πέτρῳ ἡ παιδίσκη ἡ θυρωρός· μὴ καὶ σὺ ἐκ τῶν μαθητῶν εἶ τοῦ ἀνθρώπου τούτου; λέγει ἐκεῖνος· οὐκ εἰμί.

18   εἱστήκεισαν δὲ οἱ δοῦλοι καὶ οἱ ὑπηρέται ἀνθρακιὰν πεποιηκότες, ὅτι ψῦχος ἦν, καὶ ἐθερμαίνοντο· ἦν δὲ καὶ ὁ Πέτρος μετ' αὐτῶν ἑστὼς καὶ θερμαινόμενος.

25*b*   εἶπον οὖν αὐτῷ· μὴ καὶ σὺ ἐκ τῶν μαθητῶν αὐτοῦ εἶ; ἠρνήσατο ἐκεῖνος καὶ εἶπεν· οὐκ εἰμί.

---

[1] Note εὐθέως, a spelling typical of SQ—see on 5: 9, above.

[2] With πραιτώριον here, *cf.* (in a slightly different context and sense) Mk 15: 16 par.

26 λέγει εἷς ἐκ τῶν δούλων τοῦ ἀρχιερέως, συγγενὴς ὢν
οὗ ἀπέκοψεν Πέτρος τὸ ὠτίον· οὐκ ἐγώ σε εἶδον ἐν τῷ κήπῳ μετ᾽
αὐτοῦ;

27 πάλιν οὖν ἠρνήσατο Πέτρος, καὶ εὐθέως ἀλέκτωρ
ἐφώνησεν.

28 ἄγουσιν οὖν τὸν Ἰησοῦν ἀπὸ τοῦ Καϊαφᾶ εἰς τὸ
πραιτώριον.

3. THE TRIAL BEFORE PILATE
(18: 28b—19: 16a)[1]

This is one of several major sections of the gospel which are
obviously the locus of considerable interest and emphasis on
John's part and in which, as a consequence, the source has been
so reworked by him as to leave it nearly unrecoverable at
points.[2] Discrepancies with the synoptics abound, but their
explanation is not always clear. They could be due, on the one
hand, to a unique (and possibly even accurate) tradition underlying the passage;[3] on the other, to the *Tendenz* of the evangelist.[4]
In view of the contrived character of the passage (so rightly
Winter, 89 f.) the latter possibility often will seem the more
favourable one.[5]

Very likely the present structure of the passage, in seven
scenes—four scenes showing Pilate with the Jews outside the
palace, interspersed by three with Jesus inside—is Johannine
invention (as at many points in the gospel);[6] the artificiality of
the scenes suggests an editorial origin. To this end John has
radically rearranged and expanded the source.

[1] J. Blank, 'Die Verhandlung vor Pilatus Joh 18, 28—19, 16 im Lichte
johanneischer Theologie', *BZ* n.s. 3 (1959), 60–81; E. Haenchen, 'Jesus vor
Pilatus (Joh 18, 23—19, 15): Zur Methode der Auslegung', *TL* 85 (1960),
93–102.

[2] *Cf.* the accounts of the baptist (1: 19–34), Lazarus (11: 1–45), the last
supper (ch. 13), the resurrection (ch. 20).

[3] So Dodd, who finds here a more consistent and legally accurate
account than in the synoptics; Winter, on the other hand, dismisses the
whole passage as late on historical grounds. Haenchen rightly criticizes the
use of historicity by itself as a criterion for the distinguishing of strata.

[4] Bultmann, in fact, finds very little of the source still visible in this
passage; similarly Haenchen.

[5] Some help is given toward identifying the Johannine motifs in the
excellent article of Blank.

[6] See above, p. 101.

18: 28b–32. The gratuitous note of time (28*b*) with which the episode opens, following what precedes without interruption, is probably traditional (*cf.* Mk 15: 1), as is very possibly the next sentence (28*c*);[1] only the last clause (ἀλλὰ φάγωσιν τὸ πάσχα) has clearly been added by John[2]—rather loosely, as the addition of ἵνα in some MSS shows.–Bultmann rightly, I think, remains undecided whether Pilate's highly contrived alternation between the interior of the palace and its courtyard is entirely Johannine or an elaboration of something in the source; 29*a* remains in doubt.[3] Dodd thinks that the substance of Pilate's words with those who bring Jesus to him (29*b*–31) is historically plausible and pre-Johannine,[4] including even the dubious assertion of the Jewish authorities' impotence to carry out the death sentence (31*b*).[5] But the shift from a religious charge (κακὸν ποιῶν, κατὰ τὸν νόμον ὑμῶν) in this scene to a political one (βασιλεὺς τῶν Ἰουδαίων) in the next is unaccountable and, together with the obvious tendency to exonerate Pilate, suggests that the scene is John's and has been inserted as a whole (with 29*a* and possibly 28*c*).[6]–Verse 32 is plainly John's footnote (*cf.* 13: 32 f.).

18: 33–8a. The bulk of this passage, Pilate's first interrogation of Jesus, is undoubtedly Johannine,[7] but Bultmann appears to be wrong in failing to see traditional material in both the first question to Jesus (33*c*: σὺ εἶ ὁ βασιλεὺς τῶν Ἰουδαίων;) and at least the opening words of his eventual answer (37*b*: σὺ λέγεις);[8]

[1] Note the absence of the phrase οἱ Ἰουδαῖοι, yet the implicit reference to Jewish practice.

[2] See below on 19: 14.–Barrett (444) notes that the ritual defilement, here rightly supposed to be sustained by Jews if they entered the praetorium, would nevertheless not prevent the eating of Passover the next day.

[3] That Pilate appears without introduction is no aporia, as Haenchen makes clear.

[4] The phrases *your law* (*cf.* 8: 17, 10: 34; also 7: 19, 51, 15: 25, 19: 7) and *the Jews* indicate Johannine reworking in any case.

[5] See Winter, 75–90.

[6] *Cf.* the lack of any formal accusation in Mk 15: 1 f.

[7] 'In contradistinction to the taciturnity of Jesus before Pilate in Mark ("inasmuch that Pilate marvelled"), the Johannine Jesus is inclined to be loquacious…[and] he does not, in fact, answer Pilate's questions; instead he treats Pilate to a course in Johannine theology' (Winter, 89).

[8] In both cases identical to Mk 15: 2 pars.

as in Mk the confrontation may originally have consisted primarily of this exchange, with the appropriate editorial introductions.[1]

18: 38b–40, 19: 15a. This scene (the second between Pilate and 'the Jews'), with the exception of the opening words (καὶ τοῦτο εἰπὼν πάλιν ἐξῆλθεν πρὸς τοὺς 'Ιουδαίους), is undoubtedly from the source: it parallels the synoptics with just the degree of dissimilarity we have repeatedly found.[2] But that the source's account has been rearranged by John is suggested by the incongruous πάλιν in *v.* 40.[3] The third and fourth scenes between Pilate and 'the Jews' (19: 4–7 and 12–16) are as evidently Johannine creations in their present form as the first one (18: 29–32), but contain pre-Johannine elements, originally, as in Mk, part of the present (*i.e.* Barabbas) episode. The fourth scene is especially artificial, for it combines two encounters on Pilate's part with the Jews (12, 14c–15), the second of which interrupts the formal act of condemnation (13–14b, 16):[4] even after he has *sat down on the judgment seat,* Pilate tries once more to dissuade the Jews in their determination to put Jesus to death ('Here is your king'). These words (14c), with the end of 15 ('We have no king but Caesar'), are John's addition, in line with his making Pilate an unwilling witness to the (true) kingship of Jesus (*cf.* 18: 37). But *v.* 15a is pre-Johannine: elsewhere in Jn κραυγάζειν is always from the source (11: 43, [12: 13], 18: 40, 19: 6, [12]);[5] with the crowd's cry *Away with him cf.* Lk 23: 18. The latter verse in Lk is preceded by a clearly Lukan insertion (23: 5–17—Jesus before Herod); when that

---

[1] Probably at least 33b (ὁ Πιλᾶτος ἐφώνησεν τὸν 'Ιησοῦν καὶ εἶπεν αὐτῷ) and 37b (ἀπεκρίθη ὁ 'Ιησοῦς).

[2] *E.g.* that the (probably spurious) *privilegium paschale* is ascribed to Jewish custom, not the wont of the governor, and that Pilate reminds the crowd of this privilege. In Mk, the initiative is taken by the crowd, but in Mt by Pilate.

[3] An incongruity that evidently gave rise to the alternative reading πάντες in some MSS, and then to the combined πάλιν πάντες in others.– Mk 15: 13 has a similarly anomalous πάλιν, not adequately explained as an Aramaism meaning *thereupon.*

[4] Originally—see below—the scourging of Jesus came here, as part of the act of judgment.

[5] The reading is uncertain at 12: 13, 19: 12.–The word is very rare in the rest of the NT (only three or four occurrences).

section is removed, it is clear that *v.* 18 quite naturally follows
v. 4, which is almost literally identical to Jn 18: 38*c*. It is
possible, then, that in John's source (at many points clearly very
similar to Lk's) 19: 15*a* (through Πιλᾶτος) came between
18: 38*c* and 39, John having postponed the first cry of the crowd
till his final scene. The resulting reconstruction gives a consistent episode (like Lk's and rather more orderly than Mk's,
which is patently uneven); Pilate declares Jesus innocent
(18: 38*c*), the accusers nevertheless cry for his death (19: 15*a*),
Pilate offers to release him (18: 39), they cry out ('again'):
Not this one but Barabbas (18: 40).[1] The following verse in Lk is
an editorial summary; in the comparable place in Mk and Mt
Pilate asks 'Then what shall I do with [Jesus]?' and we may
wonder whether the source did not have such a question—
cf. 19: 15*b*—continuing then with 19: 6 (see below).

19: 1–3. This scene is also pre-Johannine, paralleling fairly
closely the episodes of scourging and horseplay in the synoptics
but, on the analogy of the latter and on the basis of legal
procedure (Winter, 101 f.), it appears to have been taken by
John from a later part of the narrative and put here, probably to
set the stage for the next scene, which finds Jesus still clothed in
the mock regalia and thus becomes a kind of royal acclamation
(so Blank). The wording at points is very close to that of Mk
and Mt, at others takes its own course.[2] See further below, on
19: 13 ff.

19: 4–7. The scene of the *Ecce homo* is wholly John's creation,
imitating pre-Johannine elements in 4*c* and 5*a*.[3] Verses 5*b*
and 7 are Johannine,[4] but *v.* 6 appears to contain a fragment
from the source since it specifically identifies Jesus' accusers
(*cf.* 18: 3) rather than speaking of 'the Jews'. With the double

[1] *Cf.* Lk 23: 18 f. again.–The brief identification of Barabbas in 40*b* is
substantially equivalent to what is said, less economically, in Mk 15: 7—
see Bauer, *Lexicon*, on λῃστής (2). Its position in the account (as parenthesis)
is identical to that in Lk.

[2] *E.g.* ἐμαστίγωσεν, περιέβαλον, ῥαπίσματα.

[3] With the former, *cf.* 18: 38*c*. In the latter the dramatic emergence of
Jesus from the palace depends on the scourging scene (1–3) and imitates
the more casual and realistic notice of *v.* 13.

[4] *Cf.* resp. 14*c* (*Behold*) and 5: 18, 10: 33 (Jesus' crime).

cry *Crucify him! Crucify him!* and Pilate's repeated assertion of Jesus' innocence, *cf.* Lk 23: 21 f.[1] The mistaken idea that the Jews might themselves crucify Jesus is plainly a late bit of propaganda but may be pre-Johannine (see further below on 19: 16a). Only the verse's opening words ('When therefore they saw him') certainly stem from the evangelist, joining the verse to 5b.

19: 8–11. The artificiality of the second interrogation of Jesus appears from the fact that at its beginning it implies that Jesus is still in the praetorium, whereas in the previous scene he had been brought out, and at its end (*v.* 12) the unity of place is broken again in the dialogue between the Jews who are outside and Pilate who is still within (*cf. v.* 13). The fear of Pilate (8) is consonant with John's view of his role (as a near-convert). Jesus' silence in 9 is reminiscent of the synoptic account (Mk 14: 61, before the Sanhedrin; Lk 23: 9, before Herod), but there is little verbal similarity, and the question put to Jesus (πόθεν εἶ σύ;) is plainly Johannine (*cf.* above on 2: 9), leading to the following discussion of the nature of Pilate's authority (10 f.). Verse 11 is Johannine in vocabulary and reflects the typical tendency of the evangelist to shift blame from Pilate to the Jews.

19: 12. This verse, as we saw, stands apart both from what precedes and what follows. Several elements suggest its traditional character: Pilate's attempt to release Jesus (ἀπολῦσαι— *cf.* Lk 23: 20, 22); κραυγάζειν, if the true reading (see above on *v.* 15); even the reference to Caesar (*cf.* the striking parallel in Acts 17: 7).[2] Only the opening phrase is clearly Johannine (*cf.* 6: 66).

19: 13–16a, 1–3. In the concluding scene John is responsible for the insertion of 14c–15 (as we have already noted). The

---

[1] There are three such assertions also in Lk, but as in Jn (18: 38c, 19: 6) only two appear to be traditional (23: 4, 22), both evangelists having independently (and at different points—Jn 19: 4, Lk 23: 14 f.) contributed to the tendency to exonerate Pilate and heighten the story's dramatic effect (*cf.* Mt 27: 24).

[2] While φίλος is an important word for John, it has a quite ordinary (or possibly official) meaning here—Barrett, 452.

manifestation of Jesus as king is out of place here. The rest, namely 13–14*b*, 16, is pre-Johannine.[1] At the mention of Caesar,[2] Pilate brings Jesus out and takes his seat on the βῆμα in order to pass sentence.[3] This critical moment is dated by the source: ἦν δὲ παρασκευή...ὥρα ἦν ὡς ἕκτη,[4] into which notice John has apparently inserted τοῦ πάσχα.[5] It is likely that the scourging (19: 1) originally came here—as Mk indicates in passing (15: 15)—and that it was followed immediately, as it still is in its present artificial context, by the soldiers' mockery (2 f.): Mk (15: 16 ff.) portrays this latter scene as happening out of Pilate's sight;[6] but it is unlikely that John or a predecessor should have implicated Pilate in such a scene if earlier tradition had not. At the end of it Pilate delivers Jesus to the executioners (16*a*).[7]

The *Vorlage* as we have recovered it is by no means certain at a number of points. Still, the following arrangement of the pre-Johannine elements we have isolated gives a coherent text, and one which shows some signs of belonging to SQ:

18: 28   ἦν δὲ πρωΐ· (καὶ αὐτοὶ οὐκ εἰσῆλθον εἰς τὸ πραιτώ-
ριον, ἵνα μὴ μιανθῶσιν |...|.)

33 |...| ὁ Πιλᾶτος |...| ἐφώνησεν τὸν ᾽Ιησοῦν καὶ
εἶπεν αὐτῷ· σὺ εἶ ὁ βασιλεὺς τῶν ᾽Ιουδαίων;

[1] *Cf.* ῾Εβραϊστί, ἦν δέ, and ὡς with numeral, all typical of SQ.

[2] Pilate's implied fear contrasts with the (laudable) fear John attributes to him in *v.* 8 and is more in harmony with the traditional picture of him (Mk 15: 15, Mt 27: 24*a*).

[3] *Cf.* Mt 27: 19. If ἐκάθισεν is transitive for John (*cf. Gos. Pet.* 3: 7), it is surely intransitive for the source, which knows nothing of an enthronement of Jesus.   [4] *Cf.* Mk 15: 33.

[5] Whereas *the [day of] preparation* figures in one way or another in all four passion accounts (Mk 15: 42, Mt 27: 62, Lk 23: 54), only here within the NT is it taken to mean the day before Passover, rather than simply Friday. In 19: 31 it has the latter meaning quite clearly; the only other instance in Jn (19: 42) is ambiguous.

[6] As if *praetorium* (15: 16; *cf.* Jn 19: 16 in some MSS) were only a military guardroom; the source's use of the word (18: 28) is more accurate.

[7] αὐτοῖς here undoubtedly referred at some point in the tradition to the soldiers just mentioned (2 f.), but in the source it may have been ambiguous, as in Lk 23: 25 (*cf. v.* 6*b*). Only John, by his rearrangement, implies that it was the Jews who actually carried out the crucifixion; in the source it is Pilate, of course, who orders the inscription over the cross (*v.* 19) and gives permission to remove the body (38), and the Roman soldiers who carry out the execution (23). See Winter, 62–74.

37 |...| ἀπεκρίθη ὁ Ἰησοῦς· σὺ λέγεις |...|.

38c καὶ λέγει αὐτοῖς· ἐγὼ οὐδεμίαν εὑρίσκω ἐν αὐτῷ αἰτίαν.

19: 15 ἐκραύγασαν οὖν ἐκεῖνοι· ἆρον ἆρον, σταύρωσον αὐτόν. λέγει αὐτοῖς ὁ Πιλᾶτος·

18: 39 ἔστιν δὲ συνήθεια ὑμῖν ἵνα ἕνα ἀπολύσω ὑμῖν ἐν τῷ πάσχα· βούλεσθε οὖν ἀπολύσω ὑμῖν τὸν βασιλέα τῶν Ἰουδαίων;

40 ἐκραύγασαν οὖν πάλιν λέγοντες· μὴ τοῦτον, ἀλλὰ τὸν Βαραββᾶν. ἦν δὲ ὁ Βαραββᾶς λῃστής.

[ὁ δὲ Πιλᾶτος πάλιν εἶπεν αὐτοῖς· τί οὖν ποιήσω τὸν Ἰησοῦν;]

19: 6 |...| οἱ ἀρχιερεῖς καὶ οἱ ὑπηρέται ἐκραύγασαν λέγοντες· σταύρωσον σταύρωσον. λέγει αὐτοῖς ὁ Πιλᾶτος· λάβετε αὐτὸν ὑμεῖς καὶ σταυρώσατε· ἐγὼ γὰρ οὐχ εὑρίσκω ἐν αὐτῷ αἰτίαν.

12 (|...| ὁ Πιλᾶτος ἐζήτει ἀπολῦσαι αὐτόν· οἱ δὲ |...| ἐκραύγασαν λέγοντες· ἐὰν τοῦτον ἀπολύσῃς, οὐκ εἶ φίλος τοῦ Καίσαρος· πᾶς ὁ βασιλέα ἑαυτὸν ποιῶν ἀντιλέγει τῷ Καίσαρι.)

13 ὁ οὖν Πιλᾶτος ἀκούσας τῶν λόγων τούτων ἤγαγεν ἔξω τὸν Ἰησοῦν, καὶ ἐκάθισεν ἐπὶ βήματος εἰς τόπον λεγόμενον Λιθόστρωτον, Ἑβραϊστὶ δὲ Γαββαθά.

14a ἦν δὲ παρασκευή |...|, ὥρα ἦν ὡς ἕκτη.

1 τότε οὖν ἔλαβεν ὁ Πιλᾶτος τὸν Ἰησοῦν καὶ ἐμαστίγωσεν.

2 καὶ οἱ στρατιῶται πλέξαντες στέφανον ἐξ ἀκανθῶν ἐπέθηκαν αὐτοῦ τῇ κεφαλῇ, καὶ ἱμάτιον πορφυροῦν περιέβαλον αὐτόν,

3 καὶ ἤρχοντο πρὸς αὐτὸν καὶ ἔλεγον· χαῖρε ὁ βασιλεὺς τῶν Ἰουδαίων· καὶ ἐδίδοσαν αὐτῷ ῥαπίσματα.

16 τότε οὖν παρέδωκεν αὐτὸν αὐτοῖς ἵνα σταυρωθῇ.

4. THE CRUCIFIXION AND BURIAL
(19: 16b–42, 3: 1)

This narrative, which is largely pre-Johannine, with only occasional insertions by the evangelist, follows the preceding one without pause; only John's drastic expansion of the trial before Pilate makes of it a self-contained act in the drama.[1]

19: 16b–22. Some of the variant readings in 16b appear to be due to post-Johannine assimilation to Mk and Mt, who put the

---

[1] *Cf.* above on the connection at the beginning of the trial, 18: 28b.

mockery by the soldiers at this point; the rest are subsequent scribal attempts to rationalize the resulting anomaly of Jesus' return to the praetorium.[1] In the source 'they' simply take charge (παρέλαβον) of Jesus from Pilate. That Jesus explicitly is said to carry his own cross (17) is probably not due to Johannine correction of Mk, as often held, but only to a differing tradition (*cf.* Lk 14: 27). A 'Hebrew' (Aramaic) equivalent for the Greek name κρανίου τόπος is given, characteristically of SQ (5: 2, 19: 13).[2] Likewise the description of the multiple crucifixion (18)[3] and the wording of the *titulus* (19)[4] are parallel to, but also divergent from, synoptic tradition. The episode of the Jewish reaction to the superscription (20–2), which interrupts the flow of the story (as the need for the second clause in *v.* 23[5] shows), is undoubtedly John's creation; the detail of the title's being trilingual (20*b*) is probably pre-Johannine, however, since it in turn disrupts the connection of 20*a* and 21.

19: 23–7. The parting of the garments (23 f.) is told considerably more fully than in the synoptics, but without evidence of editorial expansion (apart from the second clause in 23—see above). Rather, this appears to be an independent version of the story and, in its explicit and literal use of scripture (*cf.* Mt 21: 2 ff.),[6] undoubtedly derives from a traditional *testimonium* (so Dodd). On 24*d*, see below.

Bultmann (585 f.) plausibly suggests that while the notice of

---

[1] By making it the occasion of Jesus' receiving the cross.

[2] The reverse of Mk 15: 22, where the Aramaic name is given, and then translated into Greek.

[3] The Greek is awkward, hardly a redaction of the smooth text of the synoptics. – This scene and that of the dividing of the garments (23 f.) are in reverse order in Mk and Mt, but as here in Lk.

[4] *I.e.* Ἰησοῦς ὁ Ναζωραῖος (*cf.* 18: 5), prefixed to the Markan wording ('the king of the Jews'); Mt prefixes only *Jesus*.

[5] Added by John, apparently—so Bultmann, 515.

[6] This, and not any ecclesiological symbolism, gave rise to the detail of the seamless robe; it is not even clear that John intends such a meaning. – Barrett, 'Old Testament', concludes (168) that the OT quotations in the passion narrative (19: 24, 28 f., 36 f.) are traditional: they are primitive, as compared with some of the quotations earlier in the gospel, and without the same 'range and freedom of knowledge and selection'. – The formula ἵνα...πληρωθῇ (here and *v.* 36; *cf.* 28), is undoubtedly a traditional apologetic formula, very common in Mt (*cf.* Mk 14: 49).

the women at the cross (25)[1] is from the source, it came there at the end of the crucifixion scene (see below) and has been moved forward by the evangelist in order to provide for his scene involving the beloved disciple (26 f.) ;[2] that there has been redaction at this point is the best explanation for the appearance of the prosaic and quite pointless summary with which 24 now ends ('So the soldiers did these things'), serving rather lamely to introduce v. 25 (cf. RSV).

19: 28–30, 25. The cry of dereliction is missing in Jn, and it could be that John, like Luke, has excised it for reverential reasons. But the fact that the episode with the sponge of vinegar (28 f.), which so cryptically accompanies the cry in Mk, is here quite clear and straightforward suggests that we have in Jn a more original form of the tradition,[3] based purely on the *testimonium* from Ps. 69: 21 (cf. Ps. 22: 53).[4] At any rate, there is no evidence of Johannine editing here, except for the insertion in 28 of εἰδὼς ὁ ᾽Ιησοῦς ὅτι ἤδη πάντα τετέλεσται[5] and possibly μετὰ τοῦτο at the beginning of the verse. In 30a the final word of Jesus (τετέλεσται) is undoubtedly Johannine (cf. 28), probably inserted, along with the rest of 30a, where the source had either nothing or simply the mention of a cry (cf. Mk). The account of the death (30b) is probably pre-Johannine and perhaps was followed by the mention of the women standing nearby (25) as in Mk,[6] a notice which somehow prepares for the empty tomb episode.

[1] Apparently not watching at a distance as in the synoptics. That they were *standing* is identical with Lk 23: 49.

[2] M. de Goedt, 'Un schème de révélation dans le quatrième évangile', *NTS* 8 (1961/2), 142–50, notes the structural similarity of 19: 26 f. to three passages in ch. 1. Two of these (1: 35 f., 47) will appear to be SQ on our analysis, but the present passage (like the third, 1: 29) is evidently an imitation of this *schème*.

[3] The reading ὑσσώπῳ in 29 is, however, not necessarily the source's divergence from the synoptics, but probably rather an early post-Johannine corruption of ὑσσῷ (cf. καλάμῳ in Mk) due to dittography (Dodd, 127 n. 2).

[4] See above, p. 129 n. 6.

[5] Cf. 13: 1, 3, 18: 4, ?4: 1. τελεῖν (only here and v. 30) is less common in Jn than τελειοῦν (cf. the following clause!), but the latter is not elsewhere used of the fulfilment of scripture and thus seems to be pre-Johannine here, equivalent to πληροῦν in v. 24.

[6] In Mk, of course, the rending of the temple veil and the centurion's confession intervene; it is quite unlikely that John found them in his source

19: 31–7. This scene is unique in Jn, and because it contains the significant assertion in 34*b* (on which John, or a later editor, puts so much weight in 35) and in a way parallels its sequel (38–42, in effect a second request to take the body down from the cross), it might be regarded as wholly John's invention, if it were not for the strong evidence it gives of containing two strata. It is probable that the basic story, centring around the two testimonies with which it ends, comes from the source. The *preparation day* (31*a*) is probably traditional (*cf.* Mk 15: 42) and originally referred merely to the Sabbath (*cf.* the next clause— also Lk 23: 56); John, however, takes it to mean the day before Passover, as in 14, and so adds the confusing γάρ clause. The subject (οἱ οὖν Ἰουδαῖοι) is apparently Johannine, and the original subject either has been lost or was indefinite. The parenthesis in 33 (ὡς... τεθνηκότα) also may be John's addition, since it perhaps detracts from the explanation given in *v.* 36. Verses 34*b*–35 clearly interrupt the connection between 34*a* and 36, and cannot be pre-Johannine.[1] For the rest, the section is from the source.[2]

19: 38–42, 3: 1. The burial by Joseph of Arimathea is certainly from the source, being known to all the evangelists.[3] That he was a disciple of Jesus (38) was probably found in the source (*cf.* Mt 27: 57), but the element of secrecy *for fear of the Jews* seems to be John's insertion (*cf.* 7: 13, 9: 22, 12: 42, 20: 19), as also perhaps the opening ligature μετὰ δὲ ταῦτα.[4]

and suppressed them.–The variation in the women's names (among the four gospels) can hardly be anything but an accident of tradition.

[1] With εὐθύς in 34*b*, *cf.* on 5: 9.

[2] Wilkens thinks that the *testimonium* in 36 is from the Pentateuchal laws regarding the Passover lamb and so represents John's *Tendenz*, but Dodd (42 n. 4) shows that the reference is clearer to Ps. 34: 20.–See also above, p. 129 n. 6.

[3] In an article on ch. 20 (see below, p. 134 n. 1), Benoit holds (147) that *v.* 38 (and hence all mention of Joseph) is a post-Johannine addition, harmonizing with the synoptics. He notes that it forms doublets with both *v.* 31 and *v.* 39. But the removal of 38 does not entirely solve the difficulty, since 39 (which Benoit retains) also overlaps with 31. Verse 39 may be the (Johannine) insertion, imitating 38 (see below); that the latter duplicates 31 is due, apparently, to the combination by the author of the source of originally distinct traditions of the removal from the cross.

[4] See above on 6: 1. Since here it does not serve to join pre-Johannine and Johannine material, however, it may have been found in the source (*cf.* Lk 5: 27, 10: 1).

The origin of 39 is unsure. On the one hand, the very specific (and exaggerated) account of the spices Nicodemus brings has a traditional ring.[1] And Nicodemus himself was evidently known to the source: the passage in ch. 3 where he first appears in the gospel is clearly Johannine, but there are indications of pre-Johannine style in 3: 1,[2] and while John occasionally introduces a character into his material—*e.g.* ?6: 5–7 (Philip; *cf.* 12: 21 f., 14: 8), 11: 16 (Thomas; *cf.* 14: 5, 20: 24 ff.)—he never wholly invents the figure, using rather a name known from the source.[3] This seems to be the case here. It is just possible that 3: 1 originally preceded 19: 39 in the present context, having then been removed by John to form the introduction to his dialogue in ch. 3 and replaced by the participial phrase in 39*b* (ὁ... πρῶτον).[4]

On the other hand, the appearance of Nicodemus on the scene here is redundant and may simply be John's invention (*cf.* 7: 50).[5] In the rest of the section, only the explanations for Gentile readers in 40*c* (καθώς κτλ) and 42*a* (τῶν Ἰουδαίων) are certainly Johannine.[6]

---

[1] According to Daube, *Rabbinic Judaism* (316), Nicodemus, a Pharisee, appears here to guarantee that Jesus was properly buried according to Jewish practice, perhaps a concern of the source.–The use of ὡς with numerals is typical of SQ.

[2] ἦν δὲ (*passim*), ἄνθρωπος...ὄνομα αὐτῷ (1: 6), ἐκ of origin (1: 44, 11: 1, 18: 3, *etc.*); only ἄρχων τῶν Ἰουδαίων is Johannine, added for Gentile readers (perhaps as equivalent to *man of the Pharisees*).

[3] The beloved disciple is a possible exception, but he differs from the others just in being nameless.–Attempts to identify Nicodemus with Naqdimon ben Gorion are apparently mistaken—S. Mendner, 'Nikodemus', *JBL* 77 (1958), 293–323; also Dodd, 304—but at least the Jewish use of the name is attested.

[4] Adverbial τὸ πρῶτον only here and 10: 40, 12: 16 (Johannine). Elsewhere without the article—1: 41, 2: 10, 18: 13 (pre-Johannine); πρῶτον in 15: 18 is probably adjectival.

[5] The removal of the verse would perhaps not require a change from plural to singular verbs in 40 and 42, since the verbs which would immediately precede it (in 38*c*) may be plural (ℵ* *N pc* it sa)—Joseph alone obtains permission, but he and others unidentified (*cf.* Acts 13: 29; possibly the women) carry out the burial. If this reading is correct, *v.* 39 is all the more unexpected, except as John's attempt to explain the plurals.–Verse 40*a* (through Ἰησοῦ), redundant without 39, and μετὰ τῶν ἀρωμάτων (in 40*b*) may also be Johannine if 39 is to be removed.

[6] For the assertion that the tomb was new and unused (no doubt intended by Mk), *cf.* Mt 27: 60 and Lk 23: 53 respectively.

We have assigned the following material to the source:

19: 16 παρέλαβον οὖν τὸν Ἰησοῦν·

17 καὶ βαστάζων ἑαυτῷ τὸν σταυρὸν ἐξῆλθεν εἰς τὸν λεγόμενον κρανίου τόπον, ὃ λέγεται Ἑβραϊστὶ Γολγοθά,

18 ὅπου αὐτὸν ἐσταύρωσαν, καὶ μετ' αὐτοῦ ἄλλους δύο ἐντεῦθεν καὶ ἐντεῦθεν, μέσον δὲ τὸν Ἰησοῦν.

19 ἔγραψεν δὲ καὶ τίτλον ὁ Πιλᾶτος καὶ ἔθηκεν ἐπὶ τοῦ σταυροῦ· ἦν δὲ γεγραμμένον· ΙΗΣΟΥΣ Ο ΝΑΖΩΡΑΙΟΣ Ο ΒΑΣΙΛΕΥΣ ΤΩΝ ΙΟΥΔΑΙΩΝ.

20b (καὶ ἦν γεγραμμένον Ἑβραϊστί, Ῥωμαϊστί, Ἑλληνιστί.)

23 οἱ οὖν στρατιῶται |...| ἔλαβον τὰ ἱμάτια αὐτοῦ καὶ ἐποίησαν τέσσερα μέρη, ἑκάστῳ στρατιώτῃ μέρος, καὶ τὸν χιτῶνα. ἦν δὲ ὁ χιτὼν ἄρραφος, ἐκ τῶν ἄνωθεν ὑφαντὸς δι' ὅλου.

24 εἶπαν οὖν πρὸς ἀλλήλους· μὴ σχίσωμεν αὐτόν, ἀλλὰ λάχωμεν περὶ αὐτοῦ τίνος ἔσται· ἵνα ἡ γραφὴ πληρωθῇ· διεμερίσαντο τὰ ἱμάτιά μου ἑαυτοῖς καὶ ἐπὶ τὸν ἱματισμόν μου ἔβαλον κλῆρον. |...|

28 (μετὰ τοῦτο) |...| ἵνα τελειωθῇ ἡ γραφή, λέγει· διψῶ.

29 σκεῦος ἔκειτο ὄξους μεστόν· σπόγγον οὖν μεστὸν τοῦ ὄξους [ὑσσῷ] περιθέντες προσήνεγκαν αὐτοῦ τῷ στόματι.

30b καὶ κλίνας τὴν κεφαλὴν παρέδωκεν τὸ πνεῦμα.

25 εἱστήκεισαν δὲ παρὰ τῷ σταυρῷ τοῦ Ἰησοῦ ἡ μήτηρ αὐτοῦ καὶ ἡ ἀδελφὴ τῆς μητρὸς αὐτοῦ, Μαρία ἡ τοῦ Κλωπᾶ καὶ Μαρία ἡ Μαγδαληνή.

31 |...| ἐπεὶ παρασκευὴ ἦν, ἵνα μὴ μείνῃ ἐπὶ τοῦ σταυροῦ τὰ σώματα ἐν τῷ σαββάτῳ, |...| ἠρώτησαν τὸν Πιλᾶτον ἵνα κατεαγῶσιν αὐτῶν τὰ σκέλη καὶ ἀρθῶσιν.

32 ἦλθον οὖν οἱ στρατιῶται, καὶ τοῦ μὲν πρώτου κατέαξαν τὰ σκέλη καὶ τοῦ ἄλλου τοῦ συσταυρωθέντος αὐτῷ.

33 ἐπὶ δὲ τὸν Ἰησοῦν ἐλθόντες (ὡς εἶδον ἤδη αὐτὸν τεθνηκότα) οὐ κατέαξαν αὐτοῦ τὰ σκέλη,

34a ἀλλ' εἷς τῶν στρατιωτῶν λόγχῃ αὐτοῦ τὴν πλευρὰν ἔνυξεν.

36 ἐγένετο γὰρ ταῦτα ἵνα ἡ γραφὴ πληρωθῇ· ὀστοῦν οὐ συντριβήσεται αὐτοῦ.

37 καὶ πάλιν ἑτέρα γραφὴ λέγει· ὄψονται εἰς ὃν ἐξεκέντησαν.

38 (μετὰ δὲ ταῦτα) ἠρώτησεν τὸν Πιλᾶτον Ἰωσὴφ ἀπὸ Ἀριμαθαίας, ὢν μαθητὴς τοῦ Ἰησοῦ |...|, ἵνα ἄρῃ τὸ σῶμα τοῦ Ἰησοῦ· καὶ ἐπέτρεψεν ὁ Πιλᾶτος. ἦλθ[ο]ν οὖν καὶ ἦρ[α]ν τὸ σῶμα αὐτοῦ.

3: 1 (ἦν δὲ ἄνθρωπος ἐκ τῶν Φαρισαίων, Νικόδημος ὄνομα αὐτῷ.)

19: 39 (ἦλθεν δὲ καὶ Νικόδημος |...| φέρων μίγμα σμύρνης καὶ ἀλόης ὡς λίτρας ἑκατόν.)

40 (ἔλαβον οὖν τὸ σῶμα τοῦ Ἰησοῦ) καὶ ἔδησαν αὐτὸ ὀθονίοις (μετὰ τῶν ἀρωμάτων) |...|.

41 ἦν δὲ ἐν τῷ τόπῳ ὅπου ἐσταυρώθη κῆπος, καὶ ἐν τῷ κήπῳ μνημεῖον καινόν, ἐν ᾧ οὐδέπω οὐδεὶς ἦν τεθειμένος·

42 ἐκεῖ οὖν διὰ τὴν παρασκευήν |...|, ὅτι ἐγγὺς ἦν τὸ μνημεῖον, ἔθηκαν τὸν Ἰησοῦν.

5. THE RESURRECTION (20: 1–20)[1]

The account of the resurrection of Jesus is more difficult to analyse source-critically than the passion narrative to which it is attached,[2] for two reasons (as will become apparent in the course of the analysis): the *Vorlage* itself (apparently a combination of traditions) is more complex here than elsewhere, and

[1] P. Benoit, 'Marie-Madeleine et les disciples au tombeau selon Joh 20, 1–18', in *Judentum, Urchristentum, Kirche* (Jeremias Festschrift), ed. W. Eltester (Beihefte zur *ZNW*, 26; Berlin, 1960), 141–52; Dibelius, 'Motive', 232–5; C. H. Dodd, 'The appearances of the risen Christ: An essay in form-criticism of the gospels', in *Studies in the gospels: Essays in memory of R. H. Lightfoot*, ed. D. E. Nineham (Oxford, 1957), 9–35; G. Hartmann, 'Die Vorlage der Osterberichte in Joh 20', *ZNW* 55 (1964), 197–220; B. Lindars, 'The composition of John xx', *NTS* 7 (1960/1), 142–7; O. Michel, 'Ein johanneischer Osterbericht', in *Studien zum Neuen Testament und zur Patristik* (Klostermann Festschrift; Texte und Untersuchungen, 77; Berlin, 1961), 35–42.

[2] The integrity of the resurrection source with that underlying the passion narrative cannot simply be assumed, though it is hard to imagine an account of the death of Jesus which failed to describe the resurrection. Hartmann (218 f.), while noting some contacts between ch. 20 and the account of the burial of Jesus (19: 31 ff.), holds that the source in ch. 20 is an independent unity with no original connection to ch. 19. Undoubtedly that is true of the tradition at some point in its development, but that John was the first to make a continuous narrative of these stories is very unlikely. We shall note a number of indications of a pre-Johannine unity as we progress.

John has redacted it in a more complex way.[1] The temptation is to solve the source-critical problems it presents by a simple recourse to partition on the basis of form-critical considerations (so Bultmann, for example, who assigns *vv.* 1, 11–18 and *vv.* 3–10 to different sources). But Hartmann has shown that the whole passage exhibits a pre-Johannine literary continuity. Our reconstruction follows his at many points, departing principally where our earlier analysis makes it possible to correct him.

20: 1. As Lindars shows, this verse is full of verbal parallels to the synoptics; practically every word is traditional, with the exception of the phrase σκοτίας ἔτι οὔσης;[2] John has apparently added it (for symbolic reasons? *cf.* 6: 17 *b*).—It is true that, just as in Lk, there was no mention of a *stone* in the account of the burial (19: 42), but if, as a number of indications suggest, the same author is responsible for the source in ch. 11 as here, the usual manner of sealing a tomb would simply have been taken for granted, having already been alluded to in the Lazarus episode (11: 38, 41), where the same verb for removing the stone is also found (11: 39, 41).

20: 2. On the whole this verse is pre-Johannine, corresponding to the synoptics in its essentials (Mary's running and the phrase *where they have laid him*); only the beloved disciple is added by John.[3] For αὐτοῖς, the source undoubtedly read αὐτῷ. That it is to Peter that Mary comes is true also in Lk 24: 12.[4]—If κύριος is

[1] The only passage in the passion narrative that John has treated with comparable intricacy is the trial before Pilate.

[2] Lacking in Lk 24: 1 and perhaps unnecessary here after πρωΐ, as the latter's omission in several MSS shows. A similar phrase is Johannine in 6: 17 *b*; πρωΐ is pre-Johannine at 18: 28, 21: 4.

[3] *Cf.* 13: 23, *etc.*; in the account of Jesus' trial the source mentions *another disciple* alongside Peter (18: 15), and that may have suggested John's addition here and in what follows.

[4] This verse, with its striking parallels to John 20, is of disputed authenticity (lacking in D it sy^pal Mcion Diatess). Despite the considerable evidence for its omission, there is a growing opinion that it may have been original—so A. R. C. Leaney, 'The resurrection narratives in Luke (xxiv. 12–53)', *NTS* 2 (1955/6), 110–14; also tentatively Benoit, Lindars, and Hartmann, and, on the basis of 𝔓^75, apparently Aland (in the forthcoming 26th ed. of Nestle). That the verse is not a post-Lukan harmonization to Jn

pre-Johannine in 11: 2 (see above, p. 77)—and in any case in the light of the source's use of κύριε—it is not surprising to find it used here of the risen Jesus.–The plural οἴδαμεν suggests that originally in this story Mary was not alone (*cf.* the other women in the various synoptic versions), and Hartmann leaves open the question whether it was John or the author of the source who eliminated Mary's companions. But there are two indications that John probably found only Mary in his source: (1) when he writes without a *Vorlage*, as he does in *v.* 13, paraphrasing this passage, he uses οἶδα, taking it for granted that Mary was alone; but if *he* had made the change from a group of women, he would probably have altered οἴδαμεν here. (2) The source's tendency to delineate individual characters in the story (*e.g.* Philip, Mary and Martha) suggests that it was its author who chose to single out Mary here.

20: 3 f. It is Hartmann's important contribution to the source analysis of 20: 1–18 to suggest that the *Vorlage* of *vv.* 1 f. underlies 3–10 also; if the mention of the beloved disciple (in 3), and consequently the foot-race with Peter (the whole of *v.* 4), is excised as Johannine, there remains a coherent account, the continuation of 1 f.: on hearing Mary's news, Peter comes out[1] and 'they' (*i.e.* he and *Mary*) go to the tomb. If the imperfect in 3 *b* implies more than that they merely *set out* for the tomb, 4 *a* creates an aporia after it[2]—one neatly explained by the source analysis proposed.–That Peter *runs* to the tomb in Lk 24: 12 does not argue for assigning *v.* 4 to the source; both Lk and John have made the disciple(s) imitate Mary's haste in the traditional account.

20: 5–8 a. Clearly the duplication in the actions of Peter and of the disciple is the product of John's redaction. Verse 6 seems to be entirely Johannine: together with Mary, Peter has already gone εἰς τὸ μνημεῖον (*v.* 3). Then 5 *a* originally applied to Peter;

is supported by the fact that it shows no knowledge of the Johannine elements in the present passage (as we identify them on other grounds) and exhibits the closest lexical parallels to words found here, and elsewhere in Jn, *only in the source*: ὀθόνια (19: 40), κείμενος (= *lie, stand*: 2: 6, 19: 29; 21: 9 [Johannine] is transitive: *laid*).

[1] *Cf.* ἀναστάς in Lk 24: 12.
[2] As the omission of 3 *b* in ℵ* shows.

but with the addition of *v.* 4, the beloved disciple is allowed to assume Peter's role, an audacity on John's part tempered by the reticence of 5*b* (οὐ μέντοι εἰσῆλθεν).¹ An explicit subject (ὁ Πέτρος) may have been omitted by John, but more likely the source simply intended that phrase in *v.* 3 to carry over, for there, despite the intervening plural in 3*b*, the emphasis has momentarily shifted to Peter.–After the duplication of 5*a* in 6*b*,² John resumes the source in *v.* 7. If the detailed description here is intended to counter anti-Christian polemic to the effect that Jesus' body had been stolen, that is a pre-Johannine concern (*cf.* Mary's words in *v.* 2), for it is not suggested in John's additions here.³ That the vocabulary in 7 is 'Johannine', as Lindars here (and at many other points) asserts, is true only in that it is unusual in the NT;⁴ in fact it is *pre*-Johannine: σουδάριον (as a burial cloth) is found only here and 11: 44 (SQ); χωρίς (as an adverb) is unique in the NT; the rare verb ἐντυλίσσειν is found, in a rather different sense, also in the burial accounts of Mt and Lk.–Verse 8*a* is Johannine, continuous with 4, 5*b*, 6.

20: 8b–10. The *non sequitur* of 9 after 8*b*⁵ suggests the collision of two strata, and 8*b* is undoubtedly the Johannine element (the beloved disciple's faith here contrasting with Thomas' doubt in 24–9). But that the singular verbs now exclude Peter, and for no apparent reason, is probably accidental: 8*b* is not entirely John's creation but his appropriation to the beloved disciple of Peter's reaction to the empty tomb in the source. Hartmann

¹ For μέντοι, *cf.* above on 21: 4.

² The catchword κείμενα follows τὰ ὀθόνια in ℵ, *etc.*, occasioning the haplography of ℵ* (omission of 5*b*–6).

³ So Hartmann, 200 n. 10. But that John at least understands the source in this way is suggested by the words he has Mary address to the (supposed) gardener in *v.* 15.–Rather than apologetic, Michel finds a distinct tradition as to Jewish burial customs, stemming from John's source.

⁴ This much is not always true of the data he gives. Apparently unaware of the valid dictum of Schweizer and Ruckstuhl that only words common in Jn *and* rare in the rest of the NT can be considered Johannine characteristics, he suggests, for example, that ἀκολουθεῖν in *v.* 6 is Johannine, whereas, while certainly 'frequent' in Jn, it is very common in all the gospels.

⁵ Even if 9 is taken to explain why the beloved disciple only *now* believed, it is anomalous, for then why did Peter not also believe when he saw?

argues that Peter's reaction was originally perplexity, much like Mary's, and this is probably correct: (1) it explains the otherwise enigmatic return home in *v.* 10, and (2) it corresponds to Lk 24: 12.[1] Hartmann reconstructs καὶ εἶδεν καὶ ἐθαύμασεν, but the former verb is redundant, when applied to Peter, after βλέπει in 5 and seems instead to be John's imitation of the source; after *v.* 7 we read, therefore, simply καὶ ἐθαύμασεν.[2]

Verse 9 is pre-Johannine, as the lexical details show.[3] The plural verb refers to Peter and Mary (as representing all the disciples) and explains their perplexity: they had not dreamed of a resurrection. It is probably impossible to say whether ἤδεισαν means *understand* or *come to be aware of*, though the former interpretation is probably more appropriate to John than his source; for the latter, *cf.* 5: 6 (SQ).

Verse 10, on the analogy of Lk 24: 12, is essentially pre-Johannine, involving only Peter originally, and reading probably as follows: ἀπῆλθεν οὖν πάλιν πρὸς αὐτὸν ὁ Πέτρος.

20: 11 f. In the source *v.* 11 *a* continued the account of Mary's second visit to the tomb, after Peter's departure. That she stands *at the tomb outside* is slightly pleonastic (*cf.* the scribal omission of ἔξω) and probably due to John's having added the adverb to indicate that unlike the disciples Mary did not enter the tomb; in the source neither Peter nor Mary did so, and thus the adverb would have been unnecessary. πρός with the dative is rare in the NT; besides *v.* 12 (below), the only other instance in John—*viz.* 18: 16, also at an entrance—is pre-Johannine.[4]

The temporal phrase ὡς οὖν (11 *b*) is one of Schweizer's Johannine style characteristics, but its use here (with the imperfect) is unique in Jn and probably derives from the source. That Mary stoops to look into the tomb (*cf. v.* 5) is not

---

[1] Once again this is shown not to be dependent on our Jn: otherwise why is faith on the beloved disciple's part reduced to perplexity on Peter's?

[2] As Benoit (143) shows, τὸ γεγονός is Lk's addition.

[3] When John uses γραφή in the singular it regularly refers to the OT in general and is equivalent to the plural (7: 38, 42, 10: 35, 17: 12, ?2: 22); on the other hand, the instances where a specific passage (or prophetic idea) is meant are pre-Johannine (19: 24, 28, 36, 37; ?13: 18).—δεῖ...ἐκ νεκρῶν ἀναστῆναι is unique in Jn, but quite characteristic of the synoptics; ἀναστῆναι, while frequently used by John, never refers to the resurrection.

[4] The (appropriate) use of ἔξω there perhaps suggested John's addition here.

John's imitation of the source (so Hartmann) but Mary's imitation of Peter.

Hartmann holds *v.* 12 (along with 13–14*a*) to be a post-Johannine addition, but in the absence of textual evidence for this (such as obtains for 5: 3*b*–4) it is more plausible that the contacts with synoptic tradition so evident here were provided by John's source; we find just that mixture of verbal parallels and discrepancies we have already encountered many times in the pre-Johannine material. That Peter saw no angels in the tomb, and Mary no burial clothes, is due to the combining (by the author of the source or at some earlier point) of two traditions, originally distinct, as form-critical analysis shows. That it was in fact the author of the source who joined the two accounts is suggested by the formal parallels between 5*a*, 7 and 12: in both cases the witness sees something, in the place of the body of Jesus and quite precisely described as to position, which attests, to the reader at least, the resurrection of Jesus.

20: 13. At first glance this verse now leads nowhere and on that account might be taken as the vestige of a fuller conversation in the source; but in form it appears to be a Johannine para-phrase[1] of *v.* 2, serving to heighten the tension which Jesus' appearance resolves. According to the synoptic accounts also, the angel[s] addressed the women, but there the latter were silent, and what they were told would be superfluous at this point in the source, for Jesus himself appears, and it is he who gives the command *Go tell*. . . (*v.* 17). It is likely, then, that the verse is wholly John's insertion, and that the source's account had already been compressed from a slightly more detailed form akin to the synoptics'.

20: 14–16. The clumsy duplication of Mary's *turning* to Jesus in *vv.* 14*a* and 16*b* is undoubtedly due to redaction; it is not entirely clear, however, which of the incidents is pre-Johannine, for either alternative presents difficulties. If 14 (with 13 and 15) is Johannine, Jesus' appearance on the scene (16) is left very

---

[1] *Cf.* '*my* lord', '*I* know'. – While the vocative γύναι (Johannine also in 2: 4, 19: 26) is found once each in Mt (15: 28) and Lk (22: 57), in both cases it appears to be the evangelists' addition, foreign to the older and more Semitic tradition (Schnackenburg, 333).

abrupt in the source, unless *vv.* 13–15 have displaced an older parallel to 14*ab*; on the other hand, if 14 (or the bulk of it) is pre-Johannine, John's addition of στραφεῖσα in 16*b* is strange, unless it means somehow either a mental turning (*recognizing*) or *starting* in surprise. A stylistic datum suggests that 14*a* is pre-Johannine: elsewhere in Jn the phrase εἰς τὰ ὀπίσω is used only with the verb ἀπέρχεσθαι and means *draw back* (6: 66, 18: 6—both Johannine); the present usage is like the synoptic *turning* (or *looking*) *around* (Mk 13: 16 = Lk 17: 31, Lk 9: 62; *cf.* Gen 19: 26). Just as Mary saw (θεωρεῖν) the angel sitting (12) so here she sees Jesus standing.–The opening words of the verse are Johannine (after 13), and probably the last clause: initially not knowing *that it was Jesus* is Johannine in 21: 4*b* (*cf.* Lk 24: 16).

The Johannine theme of misunderstanding is the occasion of *v.* 15, which parallels details in the Lazarus story: κύριε εἰ σύ... (11: 21, 32—Johannine), Martha's misunderstanding, Mary weeping.[1]

Verse 16 followed 14*ab* in the source; there Mary's expostulation was not an expression of her recognizing Jesus, as it now is (hence, apparently, John's addition of στραφεῖσα), but her worshipful response to the risen lord—*cf.* Mt 28: 9. The parenthesis is John's addition.

20: 17 f. Jesus' words of instruction to Mary are a combination of pre-Johannine and Johannine elements. The theme of ascension to the Father in 17*b* and *d* is clearly the evangelist's.[2] The warning μή μου ἅπτου is puzzling. It is the only instance of ἅπτεσθαι in Jn, and it corresponds (negatively) to Mt 28: 9; on the other hand it may have some relation to the Johannine episode of Thomas (24 ff.), who must touch in order to believe. Verse 17*c* (πορεύου... αὐτοῖς) appears to be the burden of Jesus' words in the source:[3] 'Go to my brothers and tell them (*sc.* what has happened)'.[4]

---

[1] *Cf.* also 2: 4—γύναι and a question, expressing a certain distance between Jesus and the woman so addressed.

[2] Both ἀναβαίνειν and οὔπω, very frequent in Jn, are never pre-Johannine.

[3] So Dibelius, 234, citing Ps. 22: 22.–*Cf.* Mt 28: 7 (*Go and tell*—same verbs), 10 (*my brothers*).

[4] Such an absolute use of λέγειν, while not very common, is well attested in all the gospels (*e.g.* Mk 7: 36, Mt 12: 48, Lk 5: 14).

The bulk of *v.* 18 is pre-Johannine,[1] Mary's announcement balancing her earlier words in *v.* 2. It is John who adds the last four words, to accommodate the verse to his additions in 17; the clumsiness of the result is evident in the various scribal corrections.

The reconstruction of the source's account of Jesus' appearance to the disciples is full of problems, as we shall see; but it is evident from the unevenness of the passage as it now stands (19–23) that the source continued beyond *v.* 18.

20: 19. For fear of the Jews is undoubtedly Johannine here (*cf.* on 19: 38), and probably *on that first day of the week*, which prepares for the Johannine sequel a week later (26), and without which *v.* 19 follows smoothly on 18; that the *evening* is that of the same day goes without saying.[2] The quasi-miraculous character of Jesus' appearance (through closed doors) is consonant with the minor miracles clustering around Jesus' signs (*e.g.* 6: 21 *b*), and serves to heighten the supreme sign, that of the resurrection. With *standing in the midst cf.* Lk 24: 36. The Jewish greeting is perhaps pre-Johannine (*cf.* Mt 28: 9, ?Lk 24: 36).[3]

20: 20. Jesus' display of hands and side, while it reappears in 24–9, is pre-Johannine here (*cf.* ?Lk 24: 39 [hands and feet], Jn 19: 34 [side—SQ]).[4] The second half of the verse (the disciples' joy) is not so easy to assign (*cf.* Lk 24: 41, but also Jn 16: 22), but for the likelihood that it is in fact from the source, see below on 24–9.

20: 21. Whether or not the *shalom* in 19 is pre-Johannine, its doublet here is certainly John's, leading to his introduction of 21 *b* (with which *cf.* 17: 18, etc.).

20: 22 f. The theme of receiving the Spirit (22 *b*) is important in John's thought (7: 39, 14: 16 *b*). The act of afflatus (22 *a*) is

[1] For -αγγελλ-, *cf.* Mt 28: 8, 10, [Mk] 16: 10, Lk 24: 9.
[2] For ὀψία, fairly common in Mk and Mt, *cf.* only 6: 16 (SQ) in Jn.
[3] It could also be John's addition: *cf.* 14: 27 and the following τοῦτο εἰπών here, frequently added by John at a seam.
[4] The verb δεικ- is especially common in Jn, but *cf.* 2: 18 (SQ).

141

unique in the NT (*cf.* Gen 2: 7, Wis 15: 11). It is quite likely that John borrowed it, if at all, from some independent tradition. – The commission of 23 is clearly parallel somehow to synoptic material, and the use of the verbs in question is unique in Jn.[1] It appears to be pre-Johannine but shows no signs of coming from our source.[2]

20: 24–9. Hartmann and Dodd concur (against Bultmann) that the pericope of faithless Thomas is John's creation and does not derive from any distinct tradition; it is inseparable from what precedes it[3] and to a great extent consists simply in the literal reiteration of earlier phrases and even whole sentences. But the question arises whether it was inspired by something in the source, which John has expanded. The element of initial disbelief on the part of the disciples in the face of the resurrection, and the subsequent resolution of that doubt, is found, in a variety of forms, in all the gospels (Mt 28: 17, Lk 24: 11, 41, [Mk] 16: 11–16). Undoubtedly this element is traditional; while it came to speak to the church's experience of failure in its preaching and even perhaps of incomplete faith within the church itself, it can hardly have been invented once respect for the original disciples had established itself.[4]

If then, as would seem likely, John's source also alluded to such a general disbelief, John has dealt with it by confining it to one disciple,[5] with whom consequently the others are contrasted. Hartmann notes that *v.* 20, particularly the display of hands and side, is superfluous in the present context, a scene of commissioning. He suggests that the verse derives from the source,

[1] ἀφιέναι elsewhere in Jn always means *leave* or *allow*; the present use, on the other hand, is common in the synoptics. κρατεῖν only here in Jn, and in this sense unique in the NT.

[2] *Cf.* Dodd, 144 n. 1, 347–9, who regards this as a bit of 'common oral tradition'.

[3] While, on the other hand, that passage is oblivious of it—see Dodd, *Tradition*, 148 n. 2.

[4] All of the gospels show embarrassment over this traditional detail. In Lk 24: 41 it is rationalized: 'they still disbelieved *for joy*'; in Mt it is reduced to an editorial aside: 'but *some doubted*' (ἐδίστασαν), *i.e.* not all the disciples, and not quite disbelief; in pseudo-Mk Jesus upbraids the disciples for their unbelief.

[5] One known to John from his source (21: 2) and twice before made to serve a dramatic purpose in John's work: 11: 16, 14: 5.

where it showed the dispelling of the disciples' disbelief. Their *joy* (20*b*, *cf*. Lk 24: 41) then expressed a contrast with their earlier attitude, a more natural explanation than that John invents it to contrast with the Thomas passage that follows.[1]

John has expunged all mention of the disciples' disbelief, on this hypothesis, and we can perhaps only guess at the form of the material omitted. It is clear, however, that the omission must have occurred at the end of *v*. 18, for it is to a scene made exactly parallel to this one (*viz*. *v*. 25*a*) that John transfers the expression of disbelief. Hartmann believes that originally the disciples spoke the words now ascribed to Thomas (25*b*), but this seems unlikely to me. These words do not express *disbelief* on Thomas' part so much as the unwillingness to believe except on the basis of tangible evidence, an imperfect kind of faith which is clearly a Johannine concern,[2] as John's additions to the story of the nobleman's son indicate (particularly 4: 48, syntactically identical to the present passage). After Mary's report in 18, it is likely that the source read simply that the disciples disbelieved (ἀπιστεῖν—Lk 24: 11, 41, [Mk] 16: 11, 16).

Thus 24–9 is entirely Johannine, perhaps suggested to John by a detail in the source, but nothing more; it is directed to a single end, the clearly Johannine saying with which it concludes.[3]

Hartmann rightly points out (211) that the source's account of the appearance to the disciples allows for no further episode in the Easter story; neither the Thomas pericope nor the christophany at the Sea of Galilee (ch. 21) followed in the source.

We can recapitulate the results of our analysis as follows:

20: 1 τῇ δὲ μιᾷ τῶν σαββάτων Μαρία ἡ Μαγδαληνὴ ἔρχεται πρωΐ |...| εἰς τὸ μνημεῖον, καὶ βλέπει τὸν λίθον ἠρμένον ἐκ τοῦ μνημείου.

[1] It is not after all the disciples' emotion that is contrasted with Thomas; he too could be described as rejoicing when he saw (*i.e.* recognized) the Lord. See further below on *v*. 25*b*.

[2] For John it is not real faith, so that Thomas can be described as ἄπιστος in *v*. 27; but this is not the same as the disciples' traditional disbelief.

[3] I am not convinced by Hartmann's elaborate attempt (213–16) to show that Thomas' confession (28) is pre-Johannine; *my lord* (with the pronoun) is Johannine (contrast *vv*. 2 and 13), and that John used θεός as a title for Jesus in 1: 18 is now quite likely (𝔓66.75; *TGNT*).

2 τρέχει οὖν καὶ ἔρχεται πρὸς Σίμωνα Πέτρον |...| καὶ λέγει αὐτ[ῷ] · ἦραν τὸν κύριον ἐκ τοῦ μνημείου, καὶ οὐκ οἴδαμεν ποῦ ἔθηκαν αὐτόν.

3 ἐξῆλθεν οὖν ὁ Πέτρος |...| καὶ ἤρχοντο εἰς τὸ μνημεῖον.

5 καὶ παρακύψας βλέπει κείμενα τὰ ὀθόνια |...|

7 καὶ τὸ σουδάριον, ὃ ἦν ἐπὶ τῆς κεφαλῆς αὐτοῦ, οὐ μετὰ τῶν ὀθονίων κείμενον ἀλλὰ χωρὶς ἐντετυλιγμένον εἰς ἕνα τόπον.

8 |...| καὶ [ἐθαύμασεν] |...| ·

9 οὐδέπω γὰρ ᾔδεισαν τὴν γραφήν, ὅτι δεῖ αὐτὸν ἐκ νεκρῶν ἀναστῆναι.

10 ἀπῆλθ[ε]ν οὖν πάλιν πρὸς αὐτ[ὸν ὁ Πέτρος].

11 Μαρία δὲ εἰστήκει πρὸς τῷ μνημείῳ |...| κλαίουσα. ὡς οὖν ἔκλαιεν, παρέκυψεν εἰς τὸ μνημεῖον,

12 καὶ θεωρεῖ δύο ἀγγέλους ἐν λευκοῖς καθεζομένους, ἕνα πρὸς τῇ κεφαλῇ καὶ ἕνα πρὸς τοῖς ποσίν, ὅπου ἔκειτο τὸ σῶμα τοῦ Ἰησοῦ.

14 ἐστράφη εἰς τὰ ὀπίσω, καὶ θεωρεῖ τὸν Ἰησοῦν ἑστῶτα |...|.

16 λέγει αὐτῇ Ἰησοῦς· Μαριάμ. |...| ἐκείνη λέγει αὐτῷ Ἑβραϊστί· ῥαββουνί |...|.

17 λέγει αὐτῇ Ἰησοῦς· (μή μου ἅπτου) |...|· πορεύου (δὲ) πρὸς τοὺς ἀδελφούς μου καὶ εἰπὲ αὐτοῖς. |...|

18 ἔρχεται Μαριὰμ ἡ Μαγδαληνὴ ἀγγέλλουσα τοῖς μαθηταῖς ὅτι ἑώρακα τὸν κύριον |...|, [ἀλλ' ἠπίστησαν].

19 οὔσης οὖν ὀψίας |...| καὶ τῶν θυρῶν κεκλεισμένων ὅπου ἦσαν οἱ μαθηταί |...|, ἦλθεν ὁ Ἰησοῦς καὶ ἔστη εἰς τὸ μέσον, καὶ (λέγει αὐτοῖς· εἰρήνη ὑμῖν.)

20 (καὶ τοῦτο εἰπὼν) ἔδειξεν καὶ τὰς χεῖρας καὶ τὴν πλευρὰν αὐτοῖς. ἐχάρησαν οὖν οἱ μαθηταὶ ἰδόντες τὸν κύριον.

6. THE PRELUDE TO THE PASSION

(a) The Cleansing of the Temple (2: 14–19) and Death Plot (11: 46 ff.)[1]

Because the episode of the temple cleansing has a fundamental connection to the events of the passion (even though now

---

[1] C. H. Dodd, 'The prophecy of Caiaphas', in *Neotestamentica et patristica* (Cullmann Festschrift, ed. W. C. van Unnik; Supplements to *NovT*, 6;

separated from them) in the synoptic gospels, it is possible that this connection is traditional and obtained also in John's source. The possibility is strengthened by the fact that the passage clearly is intrusive in its present Johannine setting.[1] Furthermore its place in the synoptic pattern (just before the death plot) is now held by a story (Lazarus) which appears to have occupied an earlier position in the original version of the signs;[2] in putting the Lazarus episode in its present place, John would have had to displace the present passage. (His reason for placing it where he does need not concern us here; on the setting in the source, see further below.)

The outlines, at least, of the pre-Johannine story are clear enough. Verse 13, one of a series of stereotyped editorial formulas punctuating the gospel, is undoubtedly John's;[3] the story proper begins at *v.* 14. There is nothing in 14–16 to suggest Johannine editing. Both the similarities and dissimilarities to the synoptic versions are those we have become accustomed to finding; the story is perhaps somewhat heightened by comparison with them, but it remains consistent (*cf.* Dodd, 158). Whereas the account in the synoptics culminates in Jesus' direct quotation of Isaiah, here the story only alludes (*v.* 16*b*) to Zechariah (an equally important source of Christian *testimonia*); but this is a kind of OT reference which is very common in the synoptics, more so in Mk than explicit citation (see Dodd, 31–6).

Leiden, 1962), 134–43; V. Eppstein, 'The historicity of the gospel account of the cleansing of the temple', *ZNW* 55 (1964), 42–58; Haenchen, 'Probleme', 34–46; R. H. Lightfoot, 'The cleansing of the temple in St John's gospel', in *The gospel message of St Mark* (Oxford, 1950), 70–9; S. Mendner, 'Die Tempelreinigung', *ZNW* 47 (1956), 93–112. See further the bibliography in Brown, 125.

[1] As we have already seen (p. 102), 2: 12*a* originally led directly into 4: 46*b*; in order to make the transition to the cleansing story John must artificially add 12*b* and the very abrupt notice in 13.–The suggestion of J. A. T. Robinson, 'Elijah, John, and Jesus: An essay in detection', *NTS* 4 (1957/8), 263–81, that John preserves the original date, relative to the ministry of Jesus, of the cleansing of the temple is thus contradicted by the literary data.　　[2] See p. 106; also Dodd (162), Brown (118).

[3] *Cf.* 5: 1, 6: 4, 11: 55. Despite what is loosely implied by their setting of the story, nowhere do the synoptics state that this episode took place at Passover time (Mk does not mention the feast until 14: 1). On the other hand, the *implied* date in the source probably suggested John's device here for introducing the story out of place.

Verse 17, which separates the account of Jesus' action from the witnesses' reaction to it and appears to be parallel to *v.* 22 and 12: 16 (both Johannine), has probably been added by John from a traditional stock of testimonies (so Dodd) in order to direct the reader's attention to the death of Jesus, a reference the story had, due to its position, much more clearly in the source.

Verse 18 represents the typical Jewish *Legitimationsfrage* so common in the synoptics. It is paralleled by 6: 30 (Johannine), but that it belongs to the source[1] is suggested by its parallels with the obviously pre-Markan continuation of the story in Mk 11: 27 f. ('By what authority ταῦτα ποιεῖς?'). The use of σημεῖον here differs from the special meaning given it elsewhere by the author of the source (2: 11, 4: 54, 20: 30) and is undoubtedly traditional (*cf.* Mk 8: 11, *etc.*).[2] Coming at the head of the passion narrative (see below), it may have served for the author of the signs source to identify the death and resurrection of Jesus (promised here in Jesus' response, *v.* 19) as another, and the chief, of the signs, and thus appropriately joined a cycle of miracle stories to a traditional passion narrative.

The cryptic saying in 19, which is well attested in synoptic tradition (Mk 14: 58, 15: 29, *etc.*), may well be the pre-Johannine ending of the story,[3] pointing, as proper for an episode in the prelude to the passion, to the death and resurrection. John, then, in his supplement (20 ff.) has correctly interpreted the saying.[4]

---

[1] Where the subject was almost certainly not *the Jews*. Perhaps it was indefinite, referring to the pigeon vendors of *v.* 16 and the others; or specific Jewish authorities (*cf.* Mk 11: 27) may have been named, perhaps the chief priests and Pharisees (as in 11: 47, the probable sequel in the source; *cf.* 18: 3).

[2] But the request for a sign is not necessarily inappropriate here, as it is in the synoptics. It is entirely understandable after Jesus' provocative action in the temple, and so the request is met by Jesus with at least the promise of a sign (19). The promise falls on deaf ears but is itself apparently not the basis for the officials' rejection of Jesus (contrast Mk 14: 58, 15: 29 pars.).

[3] The shift from ἱερόν to ναός does not indicate John's hand (*cf.* the parallels in Mk), but only that originally the saying circulated independently and had nothing to do with the Jerusalem temple.

[4] With the theme of misunderstanding (20) *cf.* 3: 3, *etc.*; for belief in Jesus' word (22) *cf.* 4: 41, 50 *b* (also 5: 24, *etc.*); and for its fulfilment, 18: 9, 32.

The probable pre-Johannine form of the story is as follows:

2: 14 καὶ εὗρεν ἐν τῷ ἱερῷ τοὺς πωλοῦντας βόας καὶ πρόβατα καὶ περιστερὰς καὶ τοὺς κερματιστὰς καθημένους,

15 καὶ ποιήσας φραγέλλιον ἐκ σχοινίων πάντας ἐξέβαλεν ἐκ τοῦ ἱεροῦ, τά τε πρόβατα καὶ τοὺς βόας, καὶ τῶν κολλυβιστῶν ἐξέχεεν τὰ κέρματα καὶ τὰς τραπέζας ἀνέτρεψεν,

16 καὶ τοῖς τὰς περιστερὰς πωλοῦσιν εἶπεν· ἄρατε ταῦτα ἐντεῦθεν, μὴ ποιεῖτε τὸν οἶκον τοῦ πατρός μου οἶκον ἐμπορίου.

18 ἀπεκρίθησαν οὖν [οἱ ἀρχιερεῖς καὶ οἱ Φαρισαῖοι] καὶ εἶπαν αὐτῷ· τί σημεῖον δεικνύεις ἡμῖν, ὅτι ταῦτα ποιεῖς;

19 ἀπεκρίθη Ἰησοῦς καὶ εἶπεν αὐτοῖς· λύσατε τὸν ναὸν τοῦτον, καὶ ἐν τρισὶν ἡμέραις ἐγερῶ αὐτόν.

On the analogy of Mk, the original setting of the story would be as sequel to the account of the triumphal entry (12: 12 ff.). But Mark's scheme in ch. 11 is artificial, and there is no real connection between the two stories involving the capital city: Mark assigns them to separate days and gives the fig-tree episode a place between them. It is more likely that in John's source (and possibly in Mark's)[1] the present passage came where the Lazarus pericope now does, at the beginning of the events leading up to the passion, *i.e. before* the anointing and the triumphal entry. For the author of the source, Jesus is already in Jerusalem, if, as we have held, the healing of the lame man (5: 2 ff.) precedes this passage,[2] so that the entry is not needed as the prelude to the temple cleansing it has become in Mk.

Several have suggested that the story of the Sanhedrin's plot against Jesus (11: 47–53) is based on a pre-Johannine account.[3] No clear-cut *Vorlage* suggests itself on internal grounds, however, and we can only infer what the shape of the source was by

The datum of the forty-six years in 20 is historically very difficult; it could represent an independent tradition available to John, but more likely is due to his calculation or conjecture (Barrett, 167).

[1] Mark's rearrangement then would be the result of his natural wish to make the entry the culmination of Jesus' journey from Galilee up to Jerusalem; the two episodes which on our theory originally preceded it (temple cleansing and anointing) are postponed, the one coming soon after the entry, the other inserted into the account of the passion proper (see below).   [2] See above, p. 107.

[3] Dodd, 'Caiaphas', and *Tradition*, 24; Fuller, 89; even Barrett, 337.

synoptic analogies. Mark gives no account of the actual decision to put Jesus to death, but presupposes it at several points (11: 18, 12: 17, 14: 1).[1] Mt 26: 3 f., however, an expansion of the third allusion to the plot in Mk, shows some clear parallels with the present passage: συνάγειν (47a), ἀρχιερεῖς (47a), Καϊαφᾶς (49),[2] -εβουλεύσαντο ἵνα... ἀποκτείνωσιν (53). On this basis 47a[3] and 53 appear to be pre-Johannine, and the notice in the source may have consisted of nothing else; if Caiaphas was mentioned, it is no longer possible to reconstruct his role in the story. Dodd ('Caiaphas') and Winter (37–43) find an important piece of tradition underlying 48–50, since John's interpretation (51 f.) of Caiaphas' words appears to have been added on to them somewhat artificially; this may be, but it does not seem very likely to me that the tradition stemmed from our source.[4]

We have, then, what may be only a fragmentary *Vorlage*:

11: 47a συνήγαγον οὖν οἱ ἀρχιερεῖς καὶ οἱ Φαρισαῖοι συνέδριον.

53 ἀπ' ἐκείνης οὖν τῆς ἡμέρας ἐβουλεύσαντο ἵνα ἀποκτείνωσιν αὐτόν.

The place of this brief but important notice in the source is not certain. Mt, following one of Mk's clues, puts it just before the story of the anointing and the last supper, but it has no inherent connection to either story, and the comparable context in Mk is clearly an artificial one, Mk having inserted the anointing story into the opening of the last supper account. The first of Mk's references to the plot (11: 18), while also falling in a composite section, may represent the traditional place of the story, *i.e.* after the episode of the temple cleansing. John, then, having substituted the Lazarus story for the cleansing, has retained the latter's original sequel.

[1] In every case the imperfect ἐζήτουν is used.

[2] *Cf.* 18: 13 ff.—SQ; Caiaphas is not mentioned in the passion narratives of Mk and Lk, but *cf.* Lk 3: 2.

[3] Containing also the only instance in Jn of συνέδριον, found several times in the synoptics.

[4] A number of elements make it quite unique among gospel materials: *e.g.* Ῥωμαῖος and this use of τόπος (whatever its exact reference).

(b) The Anointing at Bethany (12: 1–8)[1]

This passage gives strong evidence of Johannine independence of the synoptics. While it has an obvious linguistic relation to both Mk 14: 3 ff. = Mt 26: 6 and Lk 7: 36 ff., any hypothesis of dependence must go to extraordinary lengths to explain both the differences between John and the synoptic parallels and the curious combination of only certain elements from each of them which John on this theory must have made. This is rather a third version of the story, distinct from but parallel to those in Mk and Lk.[2]

The dating of the event in v. 1 (πρὸ ἓξ ἡμερῶν τοῦ πάσχα) might be Johannine, particularly if a six-day scheme were intended here, like that which John subtly works into 1: 19 ff.; but after this explicit assertion, no such scheme is sustained.[3] The parallel with the other Johannine Passover notices (2: 13, 6: 4, 11: 55) is not close, and in fact the similarity of the difficult construction here to the source's use of ἀπό with genitive of separation (11: 18, 21: 8), suggests that it is pre-Johannine.[4]

In the attempt to distinguish Johannine and pre-Johannine elements here, the same uncertainty arises as in the Lazarus pericope: how much of the interpenetration of the two stories is the evangelist's and how much his source's? I think it likely that although neither Lazarus nor Martha plays any major part in the story itself, they were mentioned in the account before it reached John. The unnecessary identification of Lazarus suggests that originally the two episodes were not contiguous, as they are now.[5] And, unless John depends on Lk, the role

---

[1] Daube, *Rabbinic Judaism*, 313–20; J. D. M. Derrett, 'The anointing at Bethany', StudEv II (1964), 174–82; Goodenough, 'Primitive gospel', 152–5; A. Legault, 'An application of the form-critique method to the anointings in Galilee (Lk 7, 36–50) and Bethany (Mt 26, 6–13; Mk 14, 3–9; Jn 12, 1–8)', CBQ 16 (1954), 131–45; Sanders, '"Those whom Jesus loved"'.

[2] So Dodd, 162–73, Goodenough, and Daube. *Cf.* Haenchen, 'Probleme', 50 n. 3.

[3] Only τῇ ἐπαύριον at 12: 12. We would certainly expect a more specific notice in 13: 1 if John had a scheme in mind; that passage, instead, is only a pale imitation of 12: 1.

[4] That Mk 14: 3 lacks a paschal date is not significant; Mark has just indicated one at 14: 1.

[5] The longer reading (with ὁ τεθνηκώς—𝔓⁶⁶ 𝕏 D Θ pl lat) may then be original. (Why would it have been added in the present context?) The same

given in *v.* 2 to Martha, in contrast to Mary, is surely traditional (*cf.* Lk 10: 38 ff.). We have noted already that such a coalescing of several originally distinct stories as we find here is more likely to have occurred in the tradition than as the result of John's redaction. – That the event takes place at a meal,[1] in a private home, and in Bethany, is traditional, but explicit mention of the host (Mk: Simon the leper; Lk: Simon the Pharisee) has dropped out with the appearance of the more familiar participants (who are probably implied as hosts in the indefinite *they*, as Martha's serving suggests).

In *v.* 3 there has perhaps been post-Johannine assimilation to Mk 14: 3 (or *vice versa*),[2] so it is not certain what description of the ointment the source (and Jn) contained; but even if the two texts were identical, there is no proof of literary contact: this kind of vivid (and in this case rare) phrase is readily retained by tradition (*cf.* also *v.* 5). Any incongruity in Mary's action here, as compared with Lk, is the result of developing tradition;[3] when the woman ceases to be a nameless repentant sinner and becomes Mary, the mention of tears is dropped, but the wiping with her hair remains, now following the anointing of the feet of Jesus. (There is no anointing of Jesus' head, as in Mk,[4] but some sort of messianic designation is probably intended.)

That it is Judas who objects (4 f.) to the anointing is probably not a Johannine innovation: the synoptics vary widely at this point.[5] The overloading of phrases identifying Judas (*cf.* 6: 71— less compressed) is perhaps due to expansion by John (or a later hand, as the chaotic state of the text may suggest), but if so there are no clues[6] as to what is Johannine, and all the quali-

substantive is used of Lazarus in 11: 44. It would seem especially redundant immediately after the Lazarus story, and so tend to be omitted. Similarly, while the second Ἰησοῦς is awkward (missing in some witnesses), it is less so in the source, which in any case apparently sought to emphasize the agency of Jesus.

[1] With ἀνακείμενος in *v.* 2 *cf.* Mk 14: 3; with this use of σύν, 18: 1, 21: 3 (SQ—nowhere else in Jn).

[2] *D* shows no similarity between Jn and Mk except *myrrh*.

[3] Goodenough is probably right that Lk's version of the story is the most primitive of the three.

[4] Does this derive somehow from the reference to the head of the *woman* in Lk 7: 38?   [5] Mk: *some*; Mt: *the disciples*; Lk: *the Pharisee*.

[6] With the possible exception of μέλλειν (4*c*), which may be Johannine (*cf. v.* 6); this construction (participial) is very rare in the synoptics. Perhaps the source had only 4*ab*.

fiers—Iscariot, disciple, betrayer—are used of him by the synoptics.–The substance of Judas' objection (5), while somewhat more terse than its parallel in Mk (here the story in Lk takes a quite different direction), is linguistically very close to it.

The explanatory and parenthetical v. 6 is Johannine (cf. 11: 51, 12: 33), a further step in the heightening of Judas' wickedness: he not only is the only one to cavil at the waste of oil (source), but also does so out of dishonesty and greed (John; cf. Mt 26: 15a). That Judas was treasurer (cf. 13: 29) is, if not John's invention, an independent bit of tradition (possibly derived by surmise from Iscariot).

The sense of Jesus' reply in v. 7 is notoriously uncertain; it can hardly be a derivative of the solemn declaration in Mk 14: 8, but rather appears to be an earlier version of that saying. The following verse is possibly pre-Johannine, but since it is lacking in D it^d sy^s, it is almost certainly a post-Johannine assimilation.

We can recapitulate our analysis as follows:

12: 1 ὁ οὖν Ἰησοῦς πρὸ ἓξ ἡμερῶν τοῦ πάσχα ἦλθεν εἰς Βηθανίαν, ὅπου ἦν Λάζαρος, (ὁ τεθνηκὼς) ὃν ἤγειρεν ἐκ νεκρῶν Ἰησοῦς.

2 ἐποίησαν οὖν αὐτῷ δεῖπνον ἐκεῖ, καὶ ἡ Μάρθα διηκόνει, ὁ δὲ Λάζαρος εἷς ἦν ἐκ τῶν ἀνακειμένων σὺν αὐτῷ·

3 ἡ οὖν Μαριὰμ λαβοῦσα λίτραν μύρου νάρδου πιστικῆς πολυτίμου ἤλειψεν τοὺς πόδας τοῦ Ἰησοῦ καὶ ἐξέμαξεν ταῖς θριξὶν αὐτῆς τοὺς πόδας αὐτοῦ· ἡ δὲ οἰκία ἐπληρώθη ἐκ τῆς ὀσμῆς τοῦ μύρου.

4 λέγει δὲ Ἰούδας ὁ Ἰσκαριώτης εἷς τῶν μαθητῶν αὐτοῦ (ὁ μέλλων αὐτὸν παραδιδόναι)·

5 διὰ τί τοῦτο τὸ μύρον οὐκ ἐπράθη τριακοσίων δηναρίων καὶ ἐδόθη πτωχοῖς;

7 εἶπεν οὖν ὁ Ἰησοῦς· ἄφες αὐτήν, ἵνα εἰς τὴν ἡμέραν τοῦ ἐνταφιασμοῦ μου τηρήσῃ αὐτό·

8 (τοὺς πτωχοὺς γὰρ πάντοτε ἔχετε μεθ' ἑαυτῶν, ἐμὲ δὲ οὐ πάντοτε ἔχετε.)

There is no reason to doubt that John retains the original setting of the story, that is as preceding the triumphal entry.[1]

---

[1] Barrett (341) implies that John has deliberately altered Mk's order, putting the anointing before the entry so that Jesus can then be acclaimed as the (already) anointed king; but in fact there is in Jn (and Lk), unlike Mk, no explicit messianic designation in this story (so Sanders).

Mk's present setting for it is contrived: it interrupts what precedes and follows it and shifts suddenly to Bethany without reason. In both Jn and Mk, Jesus makes his solemn entry into the city from Bethany, a detail all the more striking since Mk, although apparently rearranging the original sequence of events, goes to some length to retain this datum: Jesus stops his journey temporarily at Bethany to prepare for the entry (11: 1) and returns there afterwards (11: 11), returns again apparently after the cleansing of the temple (11: 19), and still again just before the arrest, when the anointing occurs (14: 3). It could be argued that John has merely simplified the awkward and unnecessary complexity of Mk's scheme for the last days of Jesus, but such simplification does not seem to have been a conscious intention, since John at other points provides his own quite artificial itinerary (11: 54; *cf.* 10: 40, 12: 36*b*); it is far more likely that at this point John simply leaves unchanged the order of the source: after the episode in the temple, which crowns a period of activity in Jerusalem, Jesus goes out to Bethany, where the anointing occurs, and then returns to Jerusalem, at which time he is acclaimed by the crowds.

Lk's setting for the story, as an isolated event during the ministry, is perhaps not due to his deliberately removing it from the passion context, but simply to the alternative form of the story in his special material. But while John's version bears, as we saw, some relation to Lk's, it is patently more developed and already had the form of an episode pointing to the death of Jesus, as Lk's, with its parable of the two creditors and the emphasis on the question of forgiveness, did not.

(c) The Triumphal Entry (12: 12–15)[1]

Dodd (152 f.) is in one sense right that this story does not now have the form of a self-contained pericope; at both beginning (12) and end (17 ff.) it is tied into the Johannine framework to be seen in 11: 55–7, 12: 9–11, so as to provide the conclusion for the Lazarus episode.[2] Nevertheless a pre-Johannine version,

---

[1] Freed, 'Entry'; D. M. Smith, 'John 12: 12 ff.'

[2] So rightly Freed. It does not follow, however, that John has taken it out of a context like Mk's in order to provide this complex of events stemming from the healing of Lazarus; see further below.

with both the likenesses to and differences from Mk's story that we might expect, is still visible.

It is no longer quite certain how the story originally opened. It was probably not parallel to Mk's introduction (Jesus providing in advance for the animal on which he will ride), since the text treats the fulfilment of Zech. 9: 9 as almost coincidental; if John had found in the source an instance of Jesus' foreknowledge and anticipation of the event, he would hardly have suppressed it, in view of his own interest in such themes (*cf.* 6: 6, *etc.*). If, as seems likely to me (see above on 12: 1 ff.), this passage originally followed without pause the episode in Bethany, its introduction undoubtedly in some way indicated Jesus' return to the capital city. But that notice was probably an indirect one, as it now is in Jn (and, in different form, in the synoptics too), and *v.* 12, despite some possibly Johannine elements,[1] probably contains the substance of the source, leading into *v.* 13 so directly as it does.[2] The source, then, may have read more or less as follows: (τῇ ἐπαύριον) ὄχλος πολύς, ἀκούσαντες ὅτι ἔρχεται Ἰησοῦς (εἰς Ἱεροσόλυμα)...[3]

Verses 13-15 appear to reproduce the pre-Johannine story without interruption. It does not seem to me valid to find, as does C. W. F. Smith,[4] an intentional reference on John's part to the *lulab* of Succoth (Lev. 23: 40) in the *palm branches* (13 *a*) any more than in the *tree branches* (also mentioned in the same verse in Lev.) of Mk and Mt. This difference from the synoptic

---

[1] The reference to those *who had come for the feast* (*cf.* 11: 55 f.; also 7: 11); possibly τῇ ἐπαύριον (*cf.* below on 1: 29) and anarthrous Ἱεροσόλυμα (*cf.* on 5: 1)—but see further below, n. 3.

[2] The Jerusalem crowd here, even without ὁ ἐλθὼν εἰς τὴν ἑορτήν, appears to conflict with the accompanying crowd in *v.* 17 (*cf.* 11: 55 f., 12: 9). For *hearing that Jesus was coming* and going out to meet him *cf.* 4: 47, 11: 20 (SQ).

[3] While the phrase τῇ ἐπαύριον is used elaborately by John in one passage (1: 29 ff.), it is found in Mk 11: 12 and Mt 27: 62 (both in the context of the passion), and may be original here.—The article is lacking before ὄχλος in most MSS; it seems more likely to have been added in unconscious identification with the crowd of 12: 9 than to have been omitted to solve the rather subtle aporia we have noted (see previous note).—While articular Ἱεροσόλυμα is probably characteristic of the source (pre-Johannine in 5: 2, 11: 18 f., of dubious textual basis in two Johannine contexts, nowhere else in the gospels), the anarthrous noun was not necessarily lacking in it, being frequent in the synoptics.

[4] 'Tabernacles in the fourth gospel and Mark', *NTS* 9 (1962/3), 130-46.

version is far rather a random variation in the tradition. That the quotation from Ps. 118 is not introduced by a formula of citation, as is usually the case in Jn, is not significant,[1] for such a formula is lacking in the parallels (even Mt), and would be out of place, since the passage is put on the lips of participants in the story. The addition of *and the king of Israel* (see below on 1: 49) to the Psalm verse in 13 *d* is probably not a sign of John's hand—the kingship the evangelist ascribes to Jesus is clearly not an Israelite one (6: 15, 18: 36); the phrase is as natural a paraphrase of the ensuing Zechariah prophecy (*v.* 15) as the various synoptic parallels.[2]

That 14 f. follows as something of an afterthought perhaps shows that this version of the story is less worked over than the synoptic one; the earliest form appears to have been a loose combination of the two OT passages (Ps. 118 and Zech.) which all versions exhibit (though the latter is not explicit in Mk and Lk). The citation formula is that which John uses throughout the first twelve chapters, but it is not unique to him (Mk 1: 2, 7: 6, 9: 12 f., *etc.*) and does not necessarily indicate his retouching. That the present account, unlike Mt's, omits the element of meekness from the Zechariah quotation is just possibly due to the source's author: in a signs source, a messianic emphasis without the theme of humility might be expected (*cf.* Lk).

Verse 16 is John's comment (*cf.* 2: 22); and 17–19 have nothing to do with the event of the entry but only serve to recall still again the effect of the raising of Lazarus. Thus the original ending of the story has been lost, unless, as in Mk, the story had no rounding off, the quotation (15) of the scripture which Jesus had re-enacted serving as a sufficient commentary on the episode.

The source, then, contained a brief but vivid passage which may have involved no more than the following:

12: 12 (τῇ ἐπαύριον) ὄχλος πολύς |...|, ἀκούσαντες ὅτι ἔρχεται Ἰησοῦς (εἰς Ἱεροσόλυμα),

13 ἔλαβον τὰ βαΐα τῶν φοινίκων καὶ ἐξῆλθον εἰς ὑπάντησιν αὐτῷ, καὶ ἐκραύγαζον· ὡσαννά, εὐλογημένος ὁ ἐρχόμενος ἐν ὀνόματι κυρίου (καὶ ὁ βασιλεὺς τοῦ Ἰσραήλ).

[1] As D. M. Smith, 61, points out, in answer to Freed.

[2] Mk: 'the kingdom of our father David'; Mt: 'son of David'; Lk: 'king'.

14 εὑρὼν δὲ ὁ Ἰησοῦς ὀνάριον ἐκάθισεν ἐπ' αὐτό, καθώς
ἐστιν γεγραμμένον·

15 μὴ φοβοῦ, θυγάτηρ Σιών· ἰδοῦ ὁ βασιλεύς σου ἔρχεται,
καθήμενος ἐπὶ πῶλον ὄνου.

While the following passage (12: 20–6) contains some material
paralleled in the synoptics and is very similar in structure to
another pre-Johannine passage (1: 35 ff.—see below, pp. 180
ff.), it has no analogue in the synoptic passion narratives and
appears to derive from Johannine aims, serving (with the rest of
ch. 12) to bring to a close the first half of the gospel.

(d) The Last Supper (ch. 13)[1]

John's narrative of the leave-taking (as Dodd calls the first part
of the passion narrative proper, common to all the gospels) is
notorious for its divergence from the synoptic accounts. The
question arises to what extent this divergence is due to the
peculiarity of John's source and to what extent to his own
tendency, a question tied to a larger one,[2] whether John
deliberately suppresses explicit reference to the eucharist in his
gospel. On the one hand, if it is John's conscious intent to avoid
any portrayal of the institution of the Lord's Supper, it may be
(to cite the extreme possibility) that he has taken a traditional
episode having no connection with the passion—simply a
parabolic act of Jesus 'at a dinner' (cf. δείπνου γινομένου
[13: 2])—and with it displaced a synoptic-like account of the
Last Supper found in the source at this point. On the other hand,
the uniqueness of John's portrayal of the final meal may be due
simply to the distinctiveness of the source. We cannot hope to
give a satisfactory answer to these issues here, and so our source
analysis of ch. 13 remains tentative.

But we can perhaps find the kernel of a *Vorlage* in 13: 4 f., the
simple narrative of the foot-washing, which has a fundamental

---

[1] M.-É. Boismard, 'Le lavement des pieds (Joh xiii, 1–17)', *RB* 71
(1964), 5–24; W. K. Grossouw, 'A note on John xiii 1–3', *NovT* 8 (1966),
124–31; J. A. T. Robinson, 'The significance of the foot-washing', in
Neotestamentica et Patristica (Cullmann Festschrift; ed. W. C. van Unnik;
Supplements to *NovT*, 6; Leiden, 1962), 144–7.

[2] And hinging on the much debated question of the authenticity of
6: 51–8.

connection to synoptic sayings of Jesus (*e.g.* Mk 10: 42 ff., the Lukan parallel to which is put in the present context).[1] The preceding verses are literarily very complex, as their overloaded syntax shows. Whether anything in these verses is pre-Johannine is hard to know. The date in 1*a* could be traditional; but being imprecise (unlike 12: 1 [SQ] and Mk 14: 1) it is more likely part of the evangelist's editing, perhaps related to his viewing the crucifixion, not the Last Supper, in paschal terms. The rest of *v.* 1 is now plainly Johannine in form (but, for the coming of 'the hour', *cf.* Mk 14: 41 par., Lk 22: 53). The opening clause of *v.* 2 is probably pre-Johannine, setting the stage for *v.* 4. Some might be tempted to ascribe the rest of the verse, which often is taken to conflict with 13: 27, to the source, but that conflict may be only an apparent one (depending on the correct reading of the text here), and in any case *v.* 27 may itself be pre-Johannine. Because of the unnatural way 2*b* (with a second genitive absolute) fits its context, I am inclined to see it as John's anticipation (*cf.* 6: 71) of the Judas episode still to come. Verse 3 is certainly John's (resuming *v.* 1), as may be also ἐκ τοῦ δείπνου in *v.* 4 (resuming 2*a*).

The dialogue with Peter which follows (6–11) is apparently Johannine (*cf.* Martha's objection and its rebuke in 11: 39*b*–40). But Jesus' explanation of his act in 12–15 is probably traditional[2] and in some form may have been found in the source.[3] The logia in 16, 17, and 20 have synoptic parallels,[4] but they seem to have been gathered together by John, as the repeated formula ἀμὴν ἀμὴν λέγω ὑμῖν indicates.

The source must have contained an account of Jesus' prediction of the betrayal, for despite the fundamentally different character of the account here, there are a number of striking details paralleling the synoptic accounts. It does not appear to

---

[1] So Bultmann, Boismard, and Grossouw, though otherwise they arrive at quite divergent conclusions. – We perhaps cannot decide what the significance of Jesus' act was in the source—*cf.* Robinson, especially the bibliography given there (p. 144)—but it seems likely to have been meant as more than merely an act of humility.

[2] So Boismard, pointing out the incompatibility of the sacramental interpretation in 6–11 with the moral one here.

[3] Both of the titles in 13 are found in other SQ passages. The summary in 15 is probably Johannine (*cf.* 13: 34).

[4] Mt 10: 24 par., Lk 11: 28, and Mt 10: 40 par., respectively.

be possible to reconstruct the source with any exactness, but elements of it are clearly now to be found in 18*b* (*cf.* Mk's variant translation of the same Psalm verse in 14: 18), 21*b* (*cf.* the same passage in Mk and its parallel in Mt 26: 21), 26 (*cf.* Mk 14: 20 par.), 27 (*cf.* Lk 22: 3, ?Mt 26: 50). Similarly there are indications of the tradition in the prediction of Peter's denials, *vv.* 37 f. (*cf.* Mk 14: 30 f. pars., especially Lk 22: 34). Dodd points out, further, hints of contact with a traditional account in 12: 27 (*cf.* Mk 14: 34), 14: 31*b* (*cf.* Mk 14: 42) and 16: 32*b* (*cf.* Mk 14: 27 par.).

So extensive has been John's redaction of his source that we can do no more, by way of summary, than to enumerate those verses where fragments of the source appear to be visible: 12: 27, 13: (1*b*), 2*a*, 4 f., 12–14, 18*b*, 21*b*, 26 f., 37 f., 14: 31*b*, 16: 32*b*.

If, as is possible, there was in the source an account of the eucharistic institution, alongside (and probably preceding) the foot-washing scene, it has perhaps left its influence on John at other points in the gospel,[1] but cannot now be reconstructed.

The farewell discourse (chs. 14–17), which rather loosely extends the Last Supper account, is the most purely Johannine section of the gospel (if we may use that term without ruling out the possibility that John has there drawn on a certain amount of earlier material). The conception, even much of the content, is undoubtedly the work of the evangelist. But Bailey (45), who thinks John dependent on Lk, holds it impossible that John did not borrow the *idea* for such a discourse from Lk 22: 21–38. The question arises, then, since we have been looking to a synoptic-like source rather than to the synoptics themselves for the origin of John's material in common with them, whether the source did not have at least the rudiments of a farewell discourse. This is possible but unlikely. Luke's so-called discourse is really only a collection of sayings, commenting on themes which appear as events in Jn 13; Jn 14–17, on the other hand, is a free creation without Lukan parallels. The two evangelists

---

[1] Dodd, 58 f.; also E. Schweizer, 'Das johanneische Zeugnis vom Herrenmahl', *EvTh* 12 (1952/3), 341–63. Wilkens, 75 f., thinks 6: 51*c* and 53 are based on traditional words of institution in the source (see further Brown, lxxiv); it seems equally likely, however, that they stem from an independent tradition and that John lacks an institution of the Lord's Supper because his source did.

have independently seen the Last Supper as an appropriate locus for a final dominical instruction, but they have carried this out in quite different ways. Evidently only the account of the foot-washing, with the attendant saying at table, comprised the source's Last Supper, and led directly to the scene of the arrest (18: 1 ff.).

It is not necessary to argue for the inner integrity of the passion source, whose reconstruction we have now completed. While its integrity with the signs source has appeared evident at a number of points, that question can remain open until we have surveyed the remainder of the gospel for further indications of a pre-Johannine narrative source.

PART THREE
OTHER PRE-JOHANNINE MATERIAL

OTHER PRE-JOHANNINE MATERIAL

Besides those we have examined, there are various other narratives in the gospel, some of them parallel to synoptic accounts, where evidence of an earlier source can be seen. These do not comprise a common *Gattung*, of the sort that provided the focus of our investigation in Parts One and Two, so that we shall have to deal with each of them on its own merits, for convenience following the order of their appearance in the extant gospel. In each case we shall ask what part, if any, the passage *might* have played in the larger blocks of source material already uncovered, but we shall leave till later the question whether it in fact did so.

I. JOHN THE BAPTIST AND THE FIRST DISCIPLES (CH. I, 3: 23 f.)

Bultmann holds convincingly that the first sign in the source was preceded by an account of the gathering of Jesus' disciples (1: 35–50): the stylistic parallels between that passage and 2: 1–11 are very striking. But no source could have begun precisely with 1: 35, for it presupposes a narrative introducing John the Baptist. Nor can mention of him be excised from 1: 35 ff., for he is inseparably part of the account of the winning of Jesus' first disciples, who are depicted as having previously been disciples of the Baptist;[1] the evangelist would hardly have invented that embarrassing fact. We must therefore look at the Baptist material earlier in ch. 1, and there is nothing to discourage our beginning with the Baptist's very first appearance, in *v*. 6.

(*a*) *The Exordium* (1: 6 f.)

The literature on the prologue of the gospel is apparently limitless; that on its literary analysis alone is extensive and, up

---

[1] Although 'the man whose name was John' is never designated in the gospel either as the Baptist or as the baptizing one, we shall consistently use this title to avoid confusion with the evangelist.

to the very present, controversial.[1] Nevertheless, there has emerged a consensus (not quite unanimous, to be sure) to the effect that in writing the prologue John made use of an earlier Logos-hymn which can be reconstructed, despite some uncertainties. No two of the reconstructions are quite identical, but on one point they are in agreement without exception: that *vv.* 6–8 are *not* part of the pre-Johannine hymn. Most of those who espouse such a source theory have held that these verses are to be ascribed to John, added by him as commentary on the otherwise self-contained hymn which he puts at the beginning of his gospel. But recently Haenchen has argued that they cannot be attributed to John, on two grounds: (*a*) their insertion by John at this point in the hymn is unthinkable since it means asserting that John misunderstood the hymn, and (*b*) they contain ideas and phrases foreign to John. On these counts Haenchen attributes the verses (along with others) instead to a post-Johannine redactor (probably the same as the editor who added, according to Haenchen, ch. 21).

While we have not altogether ruled out the possibility of post-Johannine redaction (see above, p. 88, in the case of ch. 21) we have operated on the assumption that such a hypothesis should be used only as a last resort in explaining an aporia in the extant gospel. We must therefore examine Haenchen's reasoning closely before accepting it.

[1] M.-É. Boismard, *St John's prologue*, tr. Carisbrooke Dominicans (London, 1957); W. Eltester, 'Der Logos und sein Prophet, Fragen zur heutigen Erklärung des johanneischen Prologs', in *Apophoreta* (Haenchen Festschrift), eds. W. Eltester and F. H. Kettler (Berlin, 1964), 109–34; H. C. Green, 'The composition of St John's prologue', *ET* 66 (1954/5), 291–4; E. Haenchen, 'Probleme des johanneischen "Prologs"', in *Gott und Mensch: Gesammelte Aufsätze* (Tübingen, 1965), 114–43 [= *ZTK* 60 (1963), 305–34]; J. Jeremias, 'The revealing word', in *The central message of the New Testament* (New York, 1965), 71–90; E. Käsemann, 'Aufbau und Anliegen des johanneischen Prologs', in *Libertas Christiana* (Delekat Festschrift), ed. W. Matthias (München, 1957), 75–99; C. Masson, 'Le prologue du quatrième évangile', *RThPh* 28 (1940), 297–311; Ridderbos, 'Prologue'; J. A. T. Robinson, 'The relation of the prologue to the gospel of St John', *NTS* 9 (1962/3), 120–9; H. Sahlin, 'Zwei Abschnitte aus Joh 1 rekonstruiert', *ZNW* 51 (1960), 64–9; R. Schnackenburg, 'Logos-Hymnus und johanneischer Prolog', *BZ* n.s. 1 (1957), 69–109; S. Schulz, 'Die Komposition des Johannesprologs und die Zusammensetzung des 4. Evangeliums', *StudEv* 1 (1959), 350–62. – See further the literature cited by Brown, 36 f.

In the case of the former of his arguments, can we hold that John was *incapable* of misunderstanding the hymn's original meaning or, if he understood it, *bound to adhere* to that meaning in the course of his reinterpretation? Since two writers (Eltester and Ridderbos) have recently maintained, with some cogency, the overall unity of the prologue, we ought not to insist on the intolerable connection, from John's standpoint at least, between *vv.* 1–5 and 6–8.

The other of Haenchen's arguments, the *sachlich* character of *vv.* 6 f.,[1] is far more persuasive, as we shall presently see in detail. But here we must be clear exactly what the non-Johannine character of these verses implies: it means that the substance of them is not Johannine in origin, but it does not mean that John did not add them to the hymn.

It has often been recognized that *v.* 6 would be quite suitable for the opening line of a gospel, as Lk 1 : 5 shows (*cf.* Mk 1 : 4),[2] and some (*e.g.* Robinson, Brown) have even held that *John's* gospel originally began in this way. I propose instead that John found *vv.* 6 f. as the opening words of his narrative *source* and, in adapting the Logos-hymn, inserted them into it.[3]

1: 6. Attempts have been made to dismiss the aporia so widely felt between *vv.* 5 and 6.[4] Thus Eltester (117 n. 24) points out that although ἐγένετο in 6*a* contrasts, as has frequently been pointed out, with the insistent ἦν of the hymn (seven times in *vv.* 1 f., 4, 10), the same word is also found in the hymn (four times, in *vv.* 3, 10, 14). But against this it must be noted that the sense of ἐγένετο in 6 is quite different from that in the other instances cited.[5]

---

[1] This point does not apply to *v.* 8.

[2] Also many OT parallels—see Schnackenburg, 1, 226 n. 1. See further below, p. 165 n. 2.

[3] For a qualification of this statement of the case, see below, p. 165.

[4] The most ingenious is that of Sahlin, who sees 6 f. as originally a continuation of 5, with the same subject: 'He (*i.e.* the Logos) *became man*, sent from God. He came for witness, *etc.*' The present text he attributes to a post-Johannine editor who misunderstood 6*ab* as applying to the Baptist and so added 6*c* (ὄνομα αὐτῷ 'Ιωάννης) and the whole of 8.

[5] So Schnackenburg, 1, 226. Even 17*b* (which in any case is ascribed to the hymn by very few critics) is not really parallel, for ἐγένετο there hardly speaks of the concrete appearance of a person on the stage of history.

Of 6*b* Haenchen (135) notes that *sent from God* (or *the Father*) is John's most characteristic designation of Jesus' status, and he doubts, therefore, that John would spontaneously have chosen that phrase to apply to the Baptist. He fails to note two further instances (1: 33, 3: 28), both probably Johannine, where the Baptist refers to his having been sent by God, but in each case John appears to be composing with 1: 6*b* in mind; and his uses of the idea, incidentally and as it were novelistically, contrast with the stark formula, almost title, of the source: ἀπεσταλμένος παρὰ θεοῦ.[1] – With the construction ὄνομα αὐτῷ 'Ιωάννης (6*c*) *cf.* 18: 10 (pre-Johannine).

1: 7. Eltester (117) finds a parallel between 2 (οὗτος ἦν κτλ) and 7*a* (οὗτος ἦλθεν κτλ), but it is merely superficial; there the pronoun introduces a summary of what has gone before (*cf.* οὗτος ἦν also in *v.* 15), whereas here it furthers the story. – That it is said of the Baptist here that he *came* is simply the earthly side of his having been *sent from God* (6).[2] – A great deal has been made of the marked emphasis in John's gospel on μαρτυρία (Schnackenburg, I, 222 n. 4, cites the statistics), but being an important OT idea it is not necessarily Johannine here. In fact, the role of witness ascribed to the Baptist is in conflict with Jesus' assertion (5: 34–7), made explicitly in the face of the Baptist's witness (5: 33), that no one (properly) bears witness to him except the Father. This inconsistency is probably best explained by the supposition that the Baptist's role as witness was a pre-Johannine one, found by John firmly imbedded in his source and only in this way corrected by him.

The double instance of ἵνα in 7*b* and *c*, particularly after the final use of εἰς in 7*a*, suggests that one of those clauses is not original. The substance of 7*b* (ἵνα μαρτυρήσῃ περὶ τοῦ φωτός) identifies it as John's addition to the source—μαρτυρεῖν περί is a locution peculiar to Jn[3]—inserted to tie in with the hymn (*the light* of *vv.* 4 f.). The effect of the insertion is that of a paraphrase: the Baptist came *for witness, to witness...*

The original sequel to εἰς μαρτυρίαν was 7*c*—the purpose

---

[1] For the idea, *cf.* Mk 1: 2 (= Mal. 3: 1).

[2] Schnackenburg, I, 227.

[3] It is one of the Johannine style characteristics added by Ruckstuhl (201) to Schweizer's original list.

of the testimony is, quite naturally, that men *might believe*. Schnackenburg, who like most critics sees *vv*. 6–8 as Johannine, holds (227 f.) that the unexpressed object of πιστεύσωσιν is Jesus, as it almost always is for John. This is true, in the passage's present context within the Logos-hymn. But in the source the absolute verb would have been used in a somewhat less exalted way, either(*a*) to denote belief in the content of the testimony (*i.e.* that Jesus was the Messiah—*cf*. on 20: 31, below),[1] or (*b*) with much the same sense but expressed in a more technical way, to mean 'become a Christian', as in 4: 53*b*; the latter is perhaps more consonant with the assertion that men believe *through* the Baptist, tautological if the object of belief is his testimony. – While the fact that the Baptist's testimony is made so that *all* might believe is suggestive of John's universalism (*e.g.* 3: 15–17), it is not stressed here, and may derive from the tradition (*cf*. Mk 1 : 5) that the whole of Judea and all (πάντες) the inhabitants of Jerusalem went out to the Baptist at Jordan.

Verse 8, which serves to explain the Baptist's relation to *the light* of the hymn, is Johannine, reiterating 7*b* word for word and prefixing to it what may be a note of anti-Baptist polemic. – It is disputed whether *v*. 9 is from the hymn or Johannine; it is certainly not from the prose source.

The much debated question why John interrupts the hymn at *v*. 5 to insert the account of the Baptist is fortunately irrelevant to our present concern: it belongs to the exegesis of the hymn in its Johannine redaction. But perhaps the question is eased somewhat once it is recognized that John has not so much interrupted the hymn with an extraneous reference to the Baptist as added the *hymn* to the prose source; for the Baptist fragment here is not an isolated piece of tradition but the opening of an extended account of the Baptist and indeed the beginning of the narrative source as a whole. The prose account, not the hymn, is the fundamental literary stratum, for it is nothing less than the opening of the proto-gospel with which John starts.[2] To the small piece of it which we have uncovered

---

[1] See also above, p. 37 n. 3, on 2: 11*c*.

[2] O. J. F. Seitz, 'Gospel prologues: A common pattern?', *JBL* 83 (1964), 262–8, points out the many parallels between what we here consider the opening of SQ and Mk 1 : 1–15 and draws a comparison between the

here (6, 7*ac*), John has added both the hymn (1–5, [9–]10 ff.) and his own comments (7*b*, 8[–9]).[1]

The unanimity of scholars who exclude 6–8 from the pre-Johannine hymn extends also to *v*. 15, and we must therefore consider whether it belonged to the prose source and there followed 7*c*. The latter, at least, is quite unlikely: the present force of the verbs (μαρτυρεῖ and κέκραγεν) in 15*a*, the need for an antecedent of αὐτοῦ there, and the device of the Baptist's self-quotation (15*b*) all argue against the verse as the original sequel to 6, 7*ac*. The fact that one element in the Baptist's self-quotation is in fact a forward reference to something in the source (27) does not alter the matter. And the implied polemic[2] in making the Baptist the witness of Jesus' *pre-existence* (only here in the gospels) is possibly a sign of John's hand. Or the verse was inserted by a post-Johannine redactor, possibly along with 19: 35, 21: 24, where the reference to a witness in the present (and perfect) tense is apparently, as here, addressed to the congregation (if this is a true, not historic, present).

The result, then, of our examination of the prologue for indications of an underlying prose source is as follows:

1: 6 ἐγένετο ἄνθρωπος, ἀπεσταλμένος παρὰ θεοῦ, ὄνομα αὐτῷ Ἰωάννης·

7 οὗτος ἦλθεν εἰς μαρτυρίαν, | . . . | ἵνα πάντες πιστεύσωσιν δι' αὐτοῦ.

While the connection in the source with *v*. 19 will appear clearly enough, it is also true that these two verses stood by themselves, as a kind of *exordium* to the source, bearing (as we shall see) a relation to *vv*. 30 f. of ch. 20, which brought it to a close.

addition of the birth narratives of Mt and Lk on the one hand and that of the 'poetic prologue-before-the-prologue' (Jn 1: 1–18) on the other.

[1] The recognition that there are three strata in *vv*. 1–18, far from complicating the analysis of the prologue, may ease some of the ambiguities felt on the assumption of only two levels.

[2] So both Eltester and Schnackenburg.

(b) The Baptist's Testimony (1: 19–34)[1]

The account of the Baptist's witness to Jesus and interpretation of his own role is so complex as it stands that there can be little doubt that redaction of some sort has brought about the present state of the text. The separation of strata is difficult, however, as the wide variation among critics shows (*cf.* Wellhausen, Goguel, Hirsch, Bultmann, Wilkens, Sahlin, Hartke, van Iersel, Boismard). The presence of *doublets* is especially noteworthy, but it is not always clear how they have arisen.

By its very complexity the passage raises its own methodological questions, which have not been adequately discussed.[2] Bultmann resorts entirely to post-Johannine addition (mostly of synoptic material)[3] and rearrangement to explain the aporias. So also do Sahlin and van Iersel, and together they illustrate the ambiguity involved in taking the synoptics as a standard for correcting the canonical text: van Iersel thinks that the present text resulted from an editor's seeking to harmonize, with the synoptics, a much more divergent original, while Sahlin holds that the original was very similar to the synoptics and the differences arose accidentally.[4] Rather than seek to correct the given text by assuming a certain view of its relation to the synoptics, it seems preferable to examine it for evidence of a pre-Johannine source having both similarities to and differences from the other gospels, such as we have found in other passages.

[1] T. Barrosse, 'The seven days of the new creation in St John's gospel', *CBQ* 21 (1959), 507–16; M.-É. Boismard, *Baptême*; also 'Les traditions johanniques concernant le Baptiste', *RB* 70 (1963), 5–42; Buse, 'Pericope'; T. F. Glasson, 'John the Baptist in the fourth gospel', *ET* 67 (1955/6), 245 f.; J. Howton, '"Son of God" in the fourth gospel', *NTS* 10 (1963/4), 227–37; B. M. F. van Iersel, 'Tradition und Redaktion in Joh 1 19–36', *NovT* 5 (1962/3), 245–67; Robinson, 'Elijah'; H. Sahlin, 'Abschnitte'; Williams, 'Fourth gospel', 317–19; W. Wink, *John the Baptist in the gospel tradition* (Society for New Testament Studies Monograph Series, 7; Cambridge, 1968).   [2] But see Brown, 70.

[3] It is inconsistent that Bultmann here assigns synoptic material to the ecclesiastical redactor, but elsewhere always (with very minor exceptions) to a pre-Johannine source (see Smith, *Composition*, 119–25, 219 f.). If harmonization was the occasion for the introduction of the synoptic material, it can be asked why the passage is still so divergent from the synoptics, in particular why no account of the baptism of Jesus is found in it.

[4] By 'vertical haplography' on the part of a scribe.

Boismard's hypothesis, while involving the same fallacy, is more intricate. Following Wellhausen he postulates the evidence of (at least) two parallel accounts of the Baptist's testimony, both employing some of the same verses but one much closer to the synoptics than the other. Each was written by John, one replacing the other. Eventually they were combined by another hand (that of Luke!). Apart from its over-confident identification of the authors involved, this theory goes a certain way toward explaining the passage's many doublets. But it would appear unlikely (*a*) that the evangelist discarded in their entirety whole blocks of an early version of the story (not itself the first, on Boismard's theory), virtually replacing them with another account, rather than rewrite or expand the story, and (*b*) that a later editor resurrected the discarded material and reinserted it. Such an involved and haphazard history of the passage does not do justice to what Brown (70) calls its 'considerable literary artistry',[1] for it betrays a very studied balance and structure, as we shall see. Doublets do not necessarily arise from the interweaving of two parallel accounts; they can be the result of one author's redaction of an earlier's work, expanding and imitating it.

The criterion of historicity is applied to the literary analysis of this passage by several scholars (Robinson, Dodd, Brown). Where a detail of the story (particularly one at variance with synoptic tradition) is on other grounds held to be historical (see below, *e.g.*, on the Baptist's denial that he is Elijah, *v.* 21), it is ascribed to a pre-Johannine source or tradition rather than to John's *Tendenz*. This procedure is valid in so far as the historicity of the detail can be established, but as that is rarely possible without some doubt it must be used only very tentatively as a criterion.[2]

Before leaving the methodological issues presented by 1: 19–34 we must consider a final question. If the passage's aporias are to be explained, for the most part at least, by John's redaction of a source, the question arises *why* John has treated this material so elaborately. The question is premature: only when the source has been reconstructed, so that it is clear just what John has done to it, can one say why he did so; and as such

---

[1] *Cf.* Howton, 231 f.
[2] See the following note.

it falls outside the present study. But an answer or two can be at least suggested here. It is not impossible, first of all, that John had access to Baptist traditions apart from his narrative source, especially if he was engaged apologetically or polemically with continuing disciples of the Baptist.[1] In that case the denseness of the passage is due, apart from John's tendency, to his having supplemented the source with other pre-Johannine material.[2] But, secondly, the chief reason for the present condition of this account is that John saw the Baptist as a theologically important and fertile figure and so gave to him a manifold part to play in the gospel.[3] Such elaborate redaction is not unique in Jn; whereas this passage stands at the start of the account of Jesus' ministry, another highly complex passage stands at its close, namely the episode of the raising of Lazarus, showing many of the same kind of doublets.[4]

1: 19–23. It has often been noted that the question put to the Baptist, *Who are you?* (19*c*), is not adequately answered until *v.* 23, and the suggestion is made that *vv.* 20–2 are therefore intrusive.[5] It is further noted that while the whole passage (through 28) has an official (*amtlich*) ring, the indications of a legal interrogation are the most concentrated in 20 f. (Brown [45] suggests that John in fact intended the Baptist's 'trial' scene as a foreshadowing of the trial of Jesus.) But against excising these verses it can be pointed out that the function of the Baptist in the source was already a quasi-juridical one, namely as *witness* (see below on 20*a*). And while *v.* 23 would follow smoothly enough after 19, the omission of the intervening verses robs the passage of its meaning: the Baptist, as witness, testifies not to himself (*v.* 23) but to *Jesus* (see below on 20*b*). Furthermore, there is no clear structural or linguistic parallel

[1] To the extent that he did have such access, it becomes more difficult to assign what are clearly traditional elements (for example, those thought to be historical) to the *source*, as opposed to Baptist tradition generally.

[2] So possibly in *v.* 23 (Isaiah *testimonium*), 28 (Jordan).

[3] Note the Baptist's importance in a number of primarily Johannine passages—3: 22–30, 4: 1–3, 5: 33–6, 10: 40 f.

[4] For a further indication that the Baptist is closely connected in John's mind with ch. 11, *cf.* 10: 40 and note its similarity to *v.* 28 (both Johannine).

[5] The catchword τίς εἶ; in 19*c* and 22*a* then defines the limits of the insertion, the latter instance preparing for the resumption of the source.

between the present scene and the Johannine redaction of Jesus' trials. There is no reason to assume, then, that the scene is Johannine.

Verse 19. If, as we have supposed, μαρτυρία in *v.* 7 is pre-Johannine, the source is resumed in *v.* 19.[1] After the exordium this is the *opening episode* of the source,[2] though it begins what is only the introduction to the main narrative (the signs of Jesus). The second part of the verse is suspect, however, with its Ἰουδαῖοι and anarthrous Ἱεροσολύμων.[3] Yet Dodd (263) suggests that even there the unique expression *priests and Levites* (*vs.* John's usual Pharisees or chief-priests) is a gratuitous element which only tradition could have supplied. If we may hazard a guess, perhaps the source in 19*b* read simply ὅτε ἀπέστειλαν πρὸς αὐτὸν [. . .] ἱερεῖς καὶ Λευῖται (*sic*) ἵνα κτλ.[4] In that case John has added his *Jews* at *Jerusalem*, making the priests and Levites only their agents, for theological or schematic reasons.[5] – The question σὺ τίς εἶ; is probably Johannine in 8: 25 and 21: 12 (in both cases, of Jesus), but not necessarily here (*cf.* Mk 8: 27); speculation about the Baptist is undoubtedly traditional (*cf.* Lk 3: 15, Acts 13: 25; further Mk 11: 30 f., Mt 11: 7–9).

Verse 20. The pleonasm in 20*a* ('And he confessed and did not deny and confessed. . .') is evidently the result of Johannine redaction. At the least one of the instances of ὁμολογεῖν is secondary, and it appears to be the former one, which presumably for John has the meaning 'admitted', as if the Baptist were

[1] Most analysts have noted the continuity between 6 f. and 19 (see Schnackenburg, 198 n. 2, 199). Some (*e.g.* Robinson, Brown) have even held that originally *John's* gospel began with 1: 6 f., 19.

[2] With καὶ αὕτη ἐστίν κτλ *cf.* Mt 2: 18.

[3] See above on 5: 1 f., but also on 12: 12.

[4] For such a use of absolute ἀποστέλλειν, quite rare, *cf.* 11: 3 (SQ), Mk 3: 31; the only other instance in Jn is 5: 33, obviously dependent on this passage and perhaps reflecting its pre-Johannine form. – Alternatively, the verb may have had an unexpressed subject—*cf.* Mk 12: 13: '*they* sent to him some of the Pharisees', *etc.*—Boismard suggests that Φαρισαῖοι (*cf. v.* 24) has been replaced by Ἰουδαῖοι, but this only aggravates the problem posed by *priests and Levites*.

[5] *Cf.* Wink, 90: *the Jews* are here ranged against the Baptist, as against Jesus.

on trial.[1] *Deny* is found only here and in 18: 25, 27 (pre-Johannine) in Jn, and appears to be from the source. This, with the following *and confessed*, originally meant the same as 'gave his testimony' (as a *witness*, that is, but not a defendant).[2] This is borne out by the likelihood that the Baptist's disclaimer of messiahship (20*b*)[3] is an implied testimony to Jesus ('*I* [emphatic ἐγώ] am not the Messiah', *i.e.* another is).[4]

Verse 21. Two factors, neither by itself decisive, together argue for the traditional character of *v.* 21. (1) Its substantive parallels (Elijah, Prophet) to the variant versions of false speculation about *Jesus* in the synoptic gospels: Mk 6: 15 par., 8: 28 pars. It is noteworthy that, in addition to the implication that Jesus is not Elijah or (one of) the prophet(s), in both versions an identification of Jesus as the Baptist is also excluded, just as here the Baptist is not the Messiah, which Jesus *is*. (2) The second factor is the probability that historically the Baptist did *not* claim to be Elijah—a later Christian identification.[5]

Verse 22. From the standpoint of the questioners, the Baptist's negative testimony is confusing, and so they repeat the question *Who are you?* (22*a*). We shall consider below (*vv.* 23, 25) whether this verse as a whole is John's addition. But at least the elliptical ἵνα-clause (22*b*) is Johannine (*cf.* 9: 36)—it contains a shift in vocabulary (πέμπειν for ἀποστέλλειν) and implies a distinction between the questioners and the Jerusalem authorities who delegated them, as in the Johannine additions to *v.* 19. The last clause of the verse, a paraphrase of the re-iterated question, could have been added by John along with 22*b*, but the latter appears to depend syntactically on what precedes it.[6]

---

[1] Bauer, *Lexicon, ad rem.* Or possibly 'professed' (*sc.* Christ)—*cf.* 12: 42, also 9: 22, 1 Jn 2: 23, 4: 2 f., 15. In either case, anti-Baptist polemic.

[2] Though of course the church's use of these terms probably grew out of official persecution of Christians.

[3] *Cf.* Acts 13: 25 (οὐκ εἰμὶ ἐγώ), Lk 3: 15.

[4] Schnackenburg, 277, 322.

[5] Robinson, followed by Brown.

[6] As in 9: 36; the punctuation in Nestle, then, is slightly incorrect (correctly: Bl–D, sec. 483; Brown, 42).

Verse 23. The Baptist's answer is hard to assign. Possibly it belongs to the same stratum as 22, but that verse is in doubt. When we look for internal evidence, it is ambiguous. Some see the verse as conflicting with the Baptist's denial that he is Elijah (21), but it is only synoptic tradition which clearly combines the voice in the wilderness of Isa. 40: 3 with the returning Elijah of Mal. 4: 5.[1] It is unique among the gospels that here the OT verse is on the lips of the Baptist, but that is not necessarily a sign of John's work, for it is consistent with the Baptist's role as witness in the source.[2] The OT citation formula (καθὼς εἶπεν Ἡσαΐας ὁ προφήτης) is not exactly parallel to any other instance in the gospel, but it is equally close to both pre-Johannine (12: 14, 19: 37) and Johannine (6: 45, 7: 38) examples. Finally, comparison of the text of the quotation is of no help. It almost certainly is not dependent on the synoptics (so that harmonization, whether by John or a post-Johannine redactor, is not in question).[3] It could derive either from the source or from independent Baptist tradition. Once again we must postpone decision on the question of the verse's provenance.

1: 24–8. Verse 24 is obtrusive, whether its subject is the original questioners (as the variant οἱ ἀπεστ. seeks to make clear) or new ones:[4] the interrogation following it is plainly a continuation of that which precedes. The Pharisees figure large in the Johannine parts of the gospel,[5] and the evangelist has possibly added them to explain the 'dogged persistence' of the interrogators (Bauer, 34) or, more likely, to emphasize the meaning of his additions to 19, *viz.* that the Baptist single-handedly defends the truth against the powers of this world (the Jewish

[1] See Smith, *Composition,* 122 f.

[2] P. Borgen, 'Observations on the midrashic character of John 6', *ZNW* 54 (1963), 232–40, holds (238) that the use of ἐγώ (εἰμι) to identify a figure with an OT counterpart is Johannine, citing 6: 35, 41, *etc.* as parallels; but these parallels are not really exact: the verb εἰμί is missing here, and in the passages in ch. 6 only allusions to an OT passage (quoted in 6: 31), not the cited text itself, are joined to the *I am*-formula.

[3] Dodd, Brown, *vs.* Freed.

[4] Translating perhaps: '[Some] of the Pharisees were sent also.'

[5] *Cf.* 7: 32, 45, 47, 48, 8: 13, 9: 13, 15, 16, 40. Dodd's distinction (264) between their usual role as an authoritative body and their acting only as agents here seems overly subtle.

authorities at Jerusalem). The verse is inserted at this point as part of the Johannine scheme which breaks the originally continuous account of the Baptist's testimony into two parts, of two scenes each (19-23, 24-8; 29-31, 32-4).[1]

Verse 25. Some (*e.g.* Bultmann, Wilkens) hold that *vv.* 22-4 interrupt the connection between 21 and 25, and so they excise them. But the summary of 20 f. here suggests more reiteration than continuation. In fact the present verse appears to be Johannine: the question it raises (*Why do you baptize?*)[2] is properly answered only in *v.* 31 (Johannine—see below), and only lamely introduces the pre-Johannine saying in *v.* 26 *b*.

On this basis we are at last in a position to decide the origin of *vv.* 22 f. If the persistence of the questioners is Johannine here, so it probably is in *v.* 22. But although the prolongation of the interrogation (22, 25) appears to be Johannine, both of the Baptist's replies (23, 26 *b*) could be pre-Johannine; in that case, after his third denial (21), he goes on, without interruption,[3] first to describe his role ('I am the voice of one crying...' [23]) and then to contrast it with that of Jesus ('I baptize with water...' [26]). But *v.* 23 may be John's insertion, from commonly available Baptist tradition, so that *v.* 21 was possibly followed directly by 26 *b*. In either case, the extended structure of the interrogation is Johannine. Only the questions of 19-21 are from the source, where the scene did not have the menacing character it does now, one involving an official and hostile delegation; rather it reflected only the interest of the priests and Levites and supplied an occasion for the Baptist's witness.

In *v. 26* the opening clause obviously belongs in the same stratum as 25, and so is Johannine. But the assertion *I baptize with water* (that is, not simply the mention of water baptism, but the direct quotation of the Baptist's words) is so constant in gospel tradition[4] that it undoubtedly appeared in the source.

---

[1] Each of the four scenes, in turn, is made up of two parts, though at that level the structure is not so explicit.

[2] Possibly added by the evangelist to distinguish the baptism of 'John' from that of Jesus (3: 22, 4: 1), who, as Messiah–?Elijah–Prophet, understandably baptizes.

[3] John has perhaps added ἔφη.

[4] Despite minor differences—aorist tense in Mk, no preposition in Mk and Lk, ὑμᾶς in all synoptics (but note textual variation).

That 'the man named John' baptized is indicated here for the first time in the source; his activity as a baptist is not depicted[1] any more than his preaching of repentance, but this is probably due merely to the concentration of interest on his act of witnessing to Jesus, and not to any conscious polemic.

The rest of 26 (μέσος ὑμῶν κτλ) appears to be Johannine: it (prematurely) asserts the presence of the worthier one, and it contains the Johannine theme of failing to know Jesus (*cf.* 8: 19, 20: 14, 21: 4).

The removal of 26*cd* robs *v. 27* of its principal verb, but on the basis of the close parallel here to Mt 3: 11 it appears that 27 was followed in the source by 33*e* (οὗτός ἐστιν ὁ βαπτίζων ἐν πνεύματι ἁγίῳ); thus, whereas in Mk 1: 7 f. the saying about the two kinds of baptism is preceded by that about the coming one's sandals, in the source, as in both Mt and Lk, the two sayings are combined chiastically, the common order being: water baptism (26*a*), the one coming 'after me' (27*a*), sandal(s) (27*b*), spirit baptism (33*e*). As usual the minor differences from the synoptic wording (see Brown, 52) are best explained as due to dependence, not on the synoptics, but on a source parallel to them (*cf.* Acts 13: 25). The only significant difference is the absence of the phrase ἰσχυρότερός μου, which is found in all the synoptics. This is perhaps not surprising in view of the phrase's absence from Acts 13: 25. For the possibility, nevertheless, that a comparable phrase in the source has been omitted here, see below on *v.* 30.

At this point (*i.e.* the end of *v.* 27) John begins an elaborate expansion of the traditional Baptist saying which finds its completion only at the end of *v.* 33.

The afterthought which constitutes *v. 28* is, like 24, intrusive and pointless in its present place, so much so that several critics (Bultmann, Wilkens, van Iersel) transpose it to a place later in the passage. Dodd (249; *cf.* Schnackenburg, 283) argues that the place-name here is traditional; this may be the case (*cf.* Aenon in 3: 23), but even so its present use remains puzzling, except as a purely Johannine note: it artificially divides in two the account of the Baptist's witness and in a typical way rounds off the episode thereby defined (*cf.* 6: 59, 8: 20). It can hardly stem from the source.

---

[1] But see on 3: 23, below.

174

1: 29–31.–Verse 29. That the scheme of days (expressed by the repeated τῇ ἐπαύριον) is secondary[1] to the continuous story of the source will appear below (on *v.* 43). It has been imposed on the material by John, and the phrase's insertion here is already made possible by the scene *v.* 28 creates. The Baptist's seeing *Jesus coming to him* is perhaps a vestige of the source (*cf.* the synoptic accounts of the baptism of Jesus);[2] as we shall see (on *vv.* 32, 34), already in the source the baptism of Jesus was presented only indirectly, through the report of the Baptist. – The Baptist's acclamation has been the subject of much discussion.[3] The title *Lamb of God* is probably pre-Johannine (see below on *v.* 36), but it appears here as John's anticipation of the source, made in order to create an explicit witness to Jesus on the Baptist's part in the presence of 'Israel' (*v.* 31). The artificiality of the scene is clear from the fact that the evangelist has not entirely finished with the testimony begun in 26 f., as the many doublets in *vv.* 30 f., 33 with *vv.* 26 f. show, even though the audience here is ostensibly changed. Jesus' atonement for sin is not prominent in John's thought, but the likelihood that the words ὁ αἴρων τὴν ἁμαρτίαν τοῦ κόσμου (*cf.* 1 Jn 3: 5) are his addition to the older title is strengthened by Eltester's observation ('Logos', 127) that just as the Baptist is made a witness to Jesus' pre-existence in 30*c* (Johannine—see below), so here he is a prophet of Jesus' destiny.

The artificiality of *v. 30* is shown by the fact that the Baptist here quotes an earlier proclamation, presumably that of *v.* 27. The verse as a whole is Johannine. But it may shed further light on the pre-Johannine state of that earlier verse. With the exception of the last clause (see below), the saying here does not appear to contain specifically Johannine *Tendenz*,[4] and is either a paraphrase or a traditional variant of the synoptic logion involving the antithesis ὀπίσω/ἰσχυρότερος. The form of the antithesis here (ὀπίσω/ἔμπροσθεν) is a good deal more balanced and may be a less derived version of the saying if, as

---

[1] As even Dodd (153 n. 3) acknowledges.

[2] See below on *v.* 36; *cf.* also *v.* 47.

[3] See especially C. K. Barrett, 'The lamb of God', *NTS* 1 (1954/5), 210–18; S. Virgulin, 'Recent discussion of the title, "Lamb of God"', *Scripture* 13 (1961), 74–80; Brown, 58–63.

[4] But *cf.* Wink, 89 f., who sees it as a polemical denial to the Baptist of the status of forerunner.

has been argued,[1] the prepositions are to be understood not temporally but as expressing rank: Under me (as my disciple) is a man who has become (is) over me. We noted that there was no equivalent in *v.* 27 to ἰσχυρότερος, but it may be that the evangelist omitted from the source such an element (in its ἔμπροσθεν form)[2] and only here gives evidence of it.[3]–It is generally agreed that the clause ὅτι πρῶτός μου ἦν is John's explanatory (and possibly polemical) addition, interpreting the traditional Baptist saying as an assertion of Jesus' pre-existence.[4] For the use of πρῶτος with genitive, *cf.* 15: 18 (the only NT instances).

Verse 31 as a whole appears to be Johannine on ideological and stylistic grounds: for ignorance of the greater one, *cf. v.* 26 *d*; the use here of ἀλλ᾽ ἵνα and διὰ τοῦτο is common in the discourses; on φανεροῦν, *cf.* above on 21: 1. The insertion, a premature resumption of the still incomplete saying of 26 f. (*I baptize with water...*), answers finally the question of *v.* 25.[5]

The entire scene (29–31), then, is a Johannine creation, imitating both pre-Johannine and Johannine elements.

1: 32–4. By the opening words of *v. 32* (...ὅτι), quite superfluous in the context, John once again creates a scene, the last of the four into which the Baptist's witness is now divided. But the rest of the verse is so close to the synoptic accounts of Jesus' baptism that it appears to have been taken bodily from the

---

[1] K. Grobel, '"He that cometh after me"', *JBL* 60 (1941), 397–401; Dodd, 272–4.

[2] That the phrase ἔμπροσθέν μου is not John's own is suggested by the fact that he can describe the Baptist as ἔμπροσθεν ἐκείνου (*sc.* Jesus) in 3: 28.

[3] It is even possible that John did *not* omit it at *v.* 27; the words ὃς ἔμπροσθέν μου γέγονεν are found after ἐρχόμενος in many MSS. They are usually taken to be an assimilation to *v.* 30, but it is equally possible that they were omitted by a scribe as too cumbersome, for with John's additions at the end of *v.* 26 the sentence would have four relative clauses.

[4] But *cf.* Brown's attempt (64) to argue the possible historicity of these words (as referring to Elijah, who appeared nine hundred years before the Baptist).

[5] That it is to *Israel* that Jesus is revealed does not suggest a more primitive perspective than John's. On the contrary, the source's πάντες (1: 7) probably refers only to Jews, the applicability of the gospel to non-Jews not being in question; *Israel* for John means the whole people of God (undoubtedly including Gentiles) in a positive light (*vs.* 'the Jews')—*cf.* Brown, 56.

source. Consistent with the Baptist's role in the source as witness, the account is seen through his eyes and becomes part of his testimony.[1] Whereas it was Jesus who *saw the spirit descending* in Mk 1: 10 = Mt 3: 16, in Lk 3: 22 a the descent is told objectively; that here it is seen, but by the Baptist, is quite possibly traditional. θεᾶσθαι is a word with special Johannine importance (1: 14, 1 Jn 1: 1, 4: 12, 14),[2] and its use in the perfect tense (see below on v. 34) may reflect John's hand here; but the verb is common enough in the synoptics and occurs in SQ (6: 5, ?11: 45). We are not told that the heavens opened, but the phrase ἐξ οὐρανοῦ is not significantly different.[3] Even the spirit's *remaining* on Jesus may be traditional; for John this detail is undoubtedly of great theological importance (3: 34),[4] but more traditionally it could mean simply that the spirit 'came to rest' on him (*cf.* Isa. 11: 2).–The conclusion of the account of Jesus' baptism is found only in v. 34, but John has not yet exhausted his expansion of the saying reported in 26 f., an expansion comprising vv. 28–31 and most of 33, and interrupted by the present verse, which he has apparently moved forward from its original place after 33 e so as to give content to the testimony artificially opening the fourth scene (32 a). Thus, before completing the pre-Johannine saying begun in 32 b, he returns to the interrupted chain of thought.

Verse 33 is clearly a Johannine construct whose sole function is to lead up to the original conclusion of 26 b and 27: *This is he who baptizes with holy spirit* (33 e). It does so with a reminiscence of 26 b[5] and a reiteration of 31 f.

It is possible that in *v. 34* the Baptist originally reported that he heard the heavenly voice,[6] a version of whose utterance now appears on his own lips.[7] But even in the synoptics it is not said

---

[1] The same tendency which leads, in both Mt 3: 14 f. and *Gos. Heb.*, to an apology for the fact that Jesus submitted to baptism may be responsible for the lack of an actual scene of the baptism. [2] See Bauer, *Lexicon, ad rem*, 2.

[3] *Cf.* Lk 3: 22 b (the *voice* ἐξ οὐρανοῦ); the present version is somewhat compressed by comparison with the synoptics. In Mk, Jesus *sees* the heavens opened; in Mt and Lk they are simply said to have been opened; it is thus not an essential part of the event viewed as vision.

[4] Further Brown, 510–12.

[5] For the substitution of πέμπειν for ἀποστέλλειν (*v.* 6), *cf.* 22 b.

[6] *Cf.* the form of 33: ἐκεῖνός μοι εἶπεν...οὗτός ἐστιν...

[7] This is true even if the true reading is ἐκλεκτός rather than υἱός— Isa. 42: 1 seems to be more basic to the episode in the tradition than Ps. 2: 7.

that Jesus *heard* the voice from heaven, only that it *came*, and in Mt it is not addressed to Jesus at all (*This is*..., as here). It is consistent with the source's conception of the Baptist's role that here he simply asserts, as culmination of his testimony, that the one to whom he is testifying (not yet identified) is *the Chosen One* (or *Son*) *of God*.[1] – The opening words of the verse (κἀγὼ ἑώρακα καὶ μεμαρτύρηκα) seem to be a Johannine reiteration of 32*a* (*cf.* also the perfect in *v*. 15) and answer to ἐφ' ὃν ἂν ἴδῃς of 33. Verse 34*b* (οὗτος κτλ) follows directly on 32.

Despite the many uncertainties involved, the following compact, logically coherent, text results from our reconstruction. All of the Johannine additions to it, producing its notorious doublets, are explicable as theologizing expansions, brought about by both imitation and supplementation.

1: 19 καὶ αὕτη ἐστὶν ἡ μαρτυρία τοῦ Ἰωάννου, ὅτε ἀπέστειλαν πρὸς αὐτὸν |...| ἱερεῖς καὶ Λευῖτα[ι] ἵνα ἐρωτήσωσιν αὐτόν· σὺ τίς εἶ;

20 |...| οὐκ ἠρνήσατο, καὶ ὡμολόγησεν ὅτι ἐγὼ οὐκ εἰμὶ ὁ χριστός.

21 καὶ ἠρώτησαν αὐτόν· τί οὖν; Ἠλίας εἶ σύ; καὶ λέγει· οὐκ εἰμί. ὁ προφήτης εἶ σύ; καὶ ἀπεκρίθη· οὔ.

23 (ἐγὼ φωνὴ βοῶντος ἐν τῇ ἐρήμῳ· εὐθύνατε τὴν ὁδὸν κυρίου, καθὼς εἶπεν Ἠσαΐας ὁ προφήτης.)

26 |...| ἐγὼ βαπτίζω ἐν ὕδατι· |...|

27 ὁ ὀπίσω μου ἐρχόμενος, (ὃς ἔμπροσθέν μου γέγονεν,) οὗ οὐκ εἰμὶ ἐγὼ ἄξιος ἵνα λύσω αὐτοῦ τὸν ἱμάντα τοῦ ὑποδήματος, |...|

33 |...| οὗτός ἐστιν ὁ βαπτίζων ἐν πνεύματι ἁγίῳ.

32 τεθέαμαι τὸ πνεῦμα καταβαῖνον ὡς περιστερὰν ἐξ οὐρανοῦ, καὶ ἔμεινεν ἐπ' αὐτόν.

34 |...| οὗτός ἐστιν ὁ [ἐκλεκτὸς] τοῦ θεοῦ.

---

[1] On the correct reading here, see below on *v*. 49. Both Schnackenburg (305) and Brown (57, 66 f.) opt for ἐκλεκτός, *vs. TGNT*.

(c) The Conversion of the First Disciples
(3: 23 f., 1: 35–50)[1]

In its content the testimony of the Baptist is complete, and *v.* 34, as we saw, brought the source's account of it to a close. But the Baptist's actual identification of Jesus as the subject of his testimony has still to be made; once that is done (*vv.* 35–7), he disappears from the stage, the purpose of his testimony (that men should believe) already in process of fulfilment.

It is possible that the source continued, without interruption, with the pre-Johannine parts of *v.* 35, but it is odd that the next episode, clearly a new scene already in the source, begins so casually, and it would be strange also if nowhere in the source (which elsewhere is very interested in place-names) were there a datum as to the Baptist's locale.[2] Its absence up to this point is not surprising: despite its occasion (1: 19), his testimony is universal, almost timeless, as it is presented; but his designation of Jesus in the presence of his disciples is necessarily concrete. It is possible, then, that John has omitted an earlier notice of place (and perhaps time) at this point. He might do so because he has substituted his own schemes of geography (28, 43) and sequence (29, 35, 43). The possibility arises, also, that John has preserved such a datum in another place. In general the references to the Baptist in the gospel after ch. 1 (*viz.* 3: 22–30, 4: 1 f., 5: 33–6, 10: 40 f.) are obvious Johannine constructs; but there is one gratuitous fragment—3: 23 f.—which is perhaps best explained not as a floating piece of tradition which John has included, but rather as a remnant of the source.

3: 23 f. The passage stands virtually alone in its context. Verse 22 is obviously an editorial summary, and one of a number of Johannine notes of itinerary (*cf.* 5: 1, 7: 1, 10: 40, 11: 54). It is structurally and verbally parallel to 2: 12 and appears to be

---

[1] B. W. Bacon, 'After six days: A new clue for gospel critics', *HTR* 8 (1915), 94–121, especially 112 f.; Barrosse, 'Seven days'; Boismard, *Baptême*; J. Jeremias, 'Die Berufung des Nathanael', Ἄγγελος 3 (1928), 2–5; Michel, 'Anfang'; G. Quispel, 'Nathanael und der Menschensohn (Joh 1, 51)', *ZNW* 47 (1956), 281–3.

[2] The only references to the Baptist's association with the Jordan—1: 28, 3: 26, 10: 40—are oblique ones found in Johannine passages; John simply takes that locale for granted.

John's imitation of that partly pre-Johannine verse (see above, pp. 102 f.).[1] Verses 25 ff., while possibly containing a traditional saying, are a Johannine unit,[2] prepared for by 22.

The diction of *v.* 23 is very similar to that of 2: 1 f. (SQ). For ἦν δέ at the opening of a passage in the source *cf.* 4: 46*b*, 5: (2), 5, 11: 1. The third word (καί) is John's only insertion. The parallel to (and obvious independence of) Mk 1: 5 in 23*c* is noteworthy; with respect to Mk 1: 14, the same is true of *v.* 24.[3]

If, as seems likely (see Brown, 151), Aenon is in either Samaria or the northern Jordan valley and it is there (not the Judean region of the Jordan) that according to the source the Baptist points out Jesus, it is quite natural that the next episode after this one (*viz.* 2: 1 ff.) should take place, without explanation, in Galilee.

The place of this fragment in the source suggested here is by no means certain; a case (rather weaker) might be made for it between 1: 7 and 1: 19.[4] But 1: 35 (εἱστήκει κτλ) follows naturally after the imperfects of 3: 23*c*; and 3: 24 might have served to explain the sudden disappearance of the Baptist after *v.* 36: this is his last act before being imprisoned.

1: 35–50. Unlike 1: 19–34, this passage is 'essentially a unity; only minor additions interrupt the course of the narrative'.[5] Dodd (305–12) is undoubtedly right that several pericopes, of various types, have been combined,[6] but it is clear that this combination had already taken place in the pre-Johannine source, since the unity thereby achieved is partly undone in the later (clearly Johannine) redaction. This is evident in the way

---

[1] The assertion (here and in 4: 1) that Jesus himself baptized (corrected by the obviously post-Johannine gloss at 4: 2) appears to be Johannine, used (if not invented) by the evangelist for apologetic purposes *vis-à-vis* latter-day followers of the Baptist.

[2] That there continue to be disciples of the Baptist who do not know who Jesus really is (*vs.* 1: 35) is probably a sign of John's apologetic concern with Baptist disciples in his own time.

[3] Schnackenburg (45, 451), however, thinks it a Johannine parenthesis.

[4] Boismard even holds that it is part of the original opening of the gospel.

[5] Bultmann, 68. It is apparently for this reason that he finds the source beginning only here. But while it is more difficult to analyse 19–34, that section is not therefore from a different source (see above).

[6] He identifies three: the naming of Peter, the call of Philip, the dialogue with Nathanael.

the present text has more or less obscured two distinct but related schemes[1] which originally gave unity to the passage: (1) the chain-reaction of conversion, each new disciple finding another and bringing him to Jesus, and (2) the progression of testimony to Jesus, extending the work of the Baptist in the previous passage to each new disciple.

This account has obvious affinities to the synoptic material and just as obvious differences, a circumstance which is not adequately explained by literary dependence. Details illustrating this will emerge in the ensuing analysis; two broader matters can be noted in advance. First, this passage is plainly equivalent to the synoptics' 'call of the disciples'[2] and is so named by Bultmann (68); yet, with the possible exception of Philip (but see below on 43 b), none of the disciples is called by Jesus, but they rather 'find' him, who takes little initiative in their joining themselves to him.[3] Secondly, the particular disciples named here obviously represent a somewhat different tradition from the synoptic lists, notably in the prominence of Philip, who is just a name in the synoptics, and Nathanael, unknown outside Jn. Dodd (304 f.) notes also the importance of Andrew, who seems to take precedence over his usually more illustrious brother (but see below on 1: 40 a). The contacts of this passage with the list in 21: 2 are obvious (Simon Peter, Nathanael, ἐκ τῶν μαθητῶν αὐτοῦ δύο), and the differences[4] do not suggest either later imitation or synoptic harmonization but rather two glimpses of a unique tradition; neither is meant to give an exhaustive list of Jesus' inner circle.

1: 35. The phrases τῇ ἐπαύριον and πάλιν are John's additions, respectively making of this passage another day in his temporal scheme and referring us to his artificial anticipation of the

---

[1] Seen by Dodd, 302, but understood by him to be Johannine.

[2] Strictly only Mk and Mt; Lk's account (5: 1 ff.) of the miraculous draught of fish is clearly understood by him as serving the same purpose, but the summons is only implicit and the verb καλεῖν (Mk 1: 20, Mt 4: 21) is nowhere used.

[3] This is not John's *Tendenz*—cf. 5: 14 a, 9: 35, where it is Jesus who finds; and 6: 70, 15: 16, where Jesus 'chooses' the disciples (all Johannine passages).

[4] Andrew and Philip only here; Thomas Didymus and the sons of Zebedee only in 21: 2.

present episode in 29. Otherwise there is nothing here to suggest John's hand.[1]–From the standpoint of *Überlieferungsgeschichte*, the 'two disciples' may be the same as those whom the Baptist sends to Jesus in Lk 7: 18 ff. (*cf.* Mt 11: 2 ff.).

1: 36 f. Just as in Mk 1: 9 (and pars.), Jesus' appearance here is sudden and without preparation. The Baptist at last gives direct testimony to Jesus, another in the series of titles ascribed to him in the source. The present instance of *Lamb of God* (36 *b*) is not a contraction of the longer phrase in 29, but rather the pre-Johannine basis for John's creation there (see above). That it is probably understood by John as paschal (Wilkens, but *cf.* Dodd, 270 f.) is evident from John's expansion of it in 29; its original meaning is less certain. It is most likely, though, to have been intended as strictly christological (rather than soterio-logical), like the other confessions in the series (34, 41, 45, 49).[2] It is just possible that at 36 *a* the source read, as in John's imitation at *v.* 29, *seeing Jesus coming to him,* a phrase possibly derived at some earlier stage from an account of Jesus' baptism.[3] Then, since it is obviously out of place in the present context, John replaces it with the vague *seeing Jesus walking.*– While ἀκολουθεῖν (37) could be taken literally (as it is by the following verse), it probably has the technical meaning given it in all the gospels—to become an adherent (Mk 2: 14, *etc.*). The Baptist's disciples thus hear his witness and through him become believers, according to the pattern of 1: 7 *ac.*[4]

1: 38 f. Verse 38 *a* is probably Johannine,[5] for the two disciples' question in 38 *b* ignores that of Jesus.–*Rabbi* as a title is prob-

---

[1] *Versus* Barrett, 150, who sees εἱστήκει and partitive ἐκ as typical of John. As to the former, the one parallel he finds (7: 37) has a different semantic value: here the verb expresses an attitude (*standing*), there an action (*stood up*); and as we shall see (below, p. 210), this use of ἐκ cannot be treated as Johannine. [2] Dodd, *Interpretation*, 230 ff. See further below, p. 230.

[3] See also *v.* 47.

[4] We are not told of actual belief on their part till 2: 11, but their conversion plainly occurs at this point.

[5] ἀκολουθεῖν has a literal meaning here, *vs.* 37, 40, 43. The question τί(να) ζητεῖς(-εῖτε); is Johannine in 4: 27, 20: 15 (but apparently pre-Johannine in 18: 4). Brown, 78, finds a profoundly Johannine meaning in these, Jesus' first words in the gospel.

ably traditional,[1] John supplying the explanatory parenthesis;[2] it appears again several times in SQ contexts (1: 49, ?3: 2, ?4: 31, 6: 5, 9: 2, 11: 8), but may be the product of John's imitation in one or more of these cases.–For *Come and... see* (39*a*) and the theme of compliance with a command of Jesus, both typical of the source, *cf.* respectively 11: 34 and p. 99, above.–μένειν (39*c*) has a special importance for John (Barrett, 150 f.; see above on *v.* 32) but is not used here, as usually by him, to express the idea of indwelling; rather it either bears a technical meaning (like ἀκολουθεῖν implying discipleship) or is entirely literal, as in the question (direct and indirect) ποῦ μένει(ς); of 38*d* and 39*b*. The phrase *that day* (*i.e.* ἡ ἐπαύριον [ἡμέρα] of 35) may be John's addition, but is more likely a gratuitous note from tradition.–The point of 'It was about the tenth hour' (39*d*) for John is not clear; it is best explained, with *that day*, as pre-Johannine. In form it is typical of SQ (2: 6, ?4: 6, 6: 10, 19, 19: 14, 39, 21: 8; *cf.* 4: 52, 5: 5).

1: 40 f. The first stage in the scheme of progressive testimony to Jesus is complete. Now one of the first converts comes to the centre of the stage to carry on the witness. That Andrew is the first named, rather than Peter, is surprising but not unique; Dodd (304 f.) notes a similar prominence given him by Papias. Spitta sees ὁ ἀδελφὸς Σίμωνος Πέτρου as a redactional attempt to harmonize with the usual order; it could be, but it may only reflect the fact that even in this unique tradition Andrew is less well known than Peter and so is identified in terms of the more famous brother.

A good deal hangs on the correct reading for the third word in 41. Several attempts to find a seven-day scheme in 1: 19—2: 11[3] depend on the reading behind *b e* sy[s], presumably πρωΐ. But the attempt is also made without this reading,[4] and in any case it is unsound to go at textual criticism *via* exegesis.[5] Bultmann (and, with more confidence, Wilkens) wonders

[1] *Cf.* Mk 9: 5, 11: 21, 14: 45 par., Mt 26: 25.

[2] See above on 5: 2.

[3] *E.g.* those of Boismard and Barrosse.

[4] Bacon, Barrett.

[5] Furthermore it is hard to see how this reading would give rise to either of the variants πρῶτον or πρῶτος, whereas either of these, made obscure by John's addition of 43*a* (see below), could have given rise to πρωΐ as a guess.

whether πρῶτος is not original (first *Andrew* found his brother...)
and whether the other, now nameless, disciple (who on this
interpretation later found Philip) has not been suppressed by
John. I find this fanciful and unnecessary. Andrew finds *Peter*
first (πρῶτον), then *Philip*.[1] When, due to John's redaction, the
subject of 43 *b* appeared to be Jesus, πρῶτον became meaning-
less and in some MSS was rather lamely changed to πρῶτος,
either as a kind of title (Andrew the first missionary) or to
underline his surprising primacy over Peter.

In this second stage of the spread of witness to Jesus, Andrew
expresses his testimony in the title Μεσσίας[2] (translated by John
for his readers), perhaps meant as a more explicit form of the
Baptist's 'Lamb of God' and 'Son [or Chosen One] of God'.

1: 42. The basis for Andrew's recognition of Jesus (41) was as
unspoken as it had been in the first stage; Peter's response,
correspondingly, is not expressed here but only implied, the
emphasis centring on Jesus' famous remark to Peter. That John
is dependent on a non-synoptic source is clear from the phrases
'son of John' and Κηφᾶς (only here in the gospels—characteristically translated by John).[3]

1: 43 f. The redactional character of 43 *a* is clear: it artificially
makes Jesus[4] the subject of εὑρίσκει (43 *b*), whereas both that
verb's use elsewhere in the passage and its point here show that
it originally applied to Andrew and completed the stage begun
in 40. Thus not only the scheme of days but also the theme of
Jesus' pointed removals to Galilee (*cf.* 4: 3, 43, 6: 1, 7: 1) is an
artificial insertion by John.[5] Originally the locale of the Baptist's

---

[1] If ἴδιον is emphatic, and not a simple possessive, it does not necessarily
support πρῶτος, despite the frequent claim that it does (first Andrew found
his brother, then *X* found his, Philip), which invalidly assumes that a second
pair of brothers is to be found here because of the sons of Zebedee in
Mk 1: 19 f. Rather it probably points toward πρῶτον: Andrew first found
his own brother, then his fellow-townsman.

[2] See further below, on *v.* 45.

[3] But at the same time the parallels to Mt 16: 17 f. are clear.

[4] The suggestion that Andrew or Peter is the intended subject of ἠθέλησεν
in 43 *a*, not Jesus, is pointless. At the same time the position of ὁ 'Ιησοῦς in
the verse as it stands is awkward.

[5] When does Jesus find Philip, before or after (or during) the journey?
Where does Philip bring Nathanael to Jesus?

ministry and of the first disciples' joining themselves to Jesus may have been unspecified (but *cf.* on 3: 23, above). The journey from Bethany to Galilee is John's creation, in any case.

Because Philip is found by Andrew, who has already made his confession of Jesus to Peter, no new title is announced here. The traditional character of the episode, otherwise so unlike anything in the synoptics, is shown by Jesus' command to Philip: ἀκολούθει μοι (*cf.* on 1: 37).–As in 11: 1, the coincidence of ἀπό and ἐκ is surprising; but there is no reason to suppose that John has added either phrase—the gratuitous identification of both Philip's home and that of Andrew and Peter[1] is undoubtedly traditional. The notice seeks to explain Andrew's contact with Philip.

1: 45 f. The third phase of the chain-reaction caused by the Baptist's witness is Philip's witness to Nathanael, who appears here without identification; in 21: 2 he is named as from Cana. This testimony is not exactly in the form of a title, unlike the others—'him of whom Moses in the Law and the prophets have written'. But if the three roles which in the source the Baptist is shown to have rejected for himself (1: 20 f.) are to be attributed to Jesus, two titles are perhaps implied here (the third, Messiah, having already been named): 'the prophet' of whom Moses wrote (Deut. 18: 15) and Elijah of whom the prophets wrote (*e.g.* Mal. 4: 5).[2]–Both the name by which Jesus is called (Jesus ben-Joseph of Nazareth) and Nathanael's snobbery toward Nazareth[3] are probably traditional; they conflict with 4: 44 f. (Johannine) in which Jerusalem is understood to be Jesus' πατρίς. Philip's reply ('Come and see') is typical of the source.

[1] Conflicting on this point with the synoptics, who apparently understand the brothers to live in Capernaum. For *Bethsaida* in the tradition, *cf.* Mk 6: 45, 8: 22, Lk 9: 10, Mt 11: 21 par.

[2] For *prophet*, *cf.* our reconstruction of the source at 6: 14.–The identification with Elijah is less clear, but *cf.* the synoptic transfiguration stories, where Jesus takes the place of Moses and Elijah.–The fact that in 1: 20 χριστός is used, but here (41) Μεσσίας, probably indicates two traditions which were originally (*i.e.* before SQ) quite distinct.

[3] This is similar to the Pharisees' retort to Nicodemus in 7: 52 (Johannine) but by comparison has a popular, non-academic ring. In ch. 7 John has perhaps paraphrased the source here.

1: 47–50. The entire episode involving Nathanael, including the present dialogue with Jesus, probably derives from a single tradition.[1] While it is unknown to the other evangelists, there is no reason to suppose that John has created it. Some[2] have felt that John must have omitted part of the source, since a previous episode under the fig tree is perhaps alluded to. But if, as is quite possible, to see someone *under the fig tree* had a symbolic meaning in the source, such as is often ascribed to John, the source may be intact, sounding cryptic only to us who are not familiar with the symbol.[3]

Just as in *v.* 42, with Peter (and *cf. v.* 36), so here (47) Jesus *sees* Nathanael and identifies him with a descriptive epithet.[4] Whereas the evangelist apparently takes *an Israelite in whom is no guile* to suggest a contrast with Jacob (*cf. v.* 51, his addition),[5] in the source Jesus' words had a religious, not a moral, sense, based on Ps. 32: 2 (Schnackenburg, 315).[6] ἀληθῶς is probably John's insertion (*cf.* 4: 42, 6: 14, 55, 7: 40, 8: 31).

The question πόθεν (48) is sometimes Johannine, but not so here, where it expresses perplexity, as in 6: 5 (see above, p. 57).–The formula ἀπεκρίθη . . . καὶ εἶπεν (48, 50), so common in Jn (where the usual synoptic ἀποκριθεὶς εἶπεν is wanting), is perhaps a characteristic of the evangelist;[7] it is used repeatedly in the dialogues. But it is not unknown outside Jn (Mk 7: 28, Lk 17: 20; *cf.* also Mk 14: 61*b*, *etc.*) and may have been suggested to John by occasional use in the source.

Jesus' display of supernatural insight (*cf.* 5: 6*b*, 11: 11, and see below on 4: 16 ff.), or possibly some deeper meaning related to the phrase *under the fig tree*, inaccessible to us, overcomes Nathanael's scepticism. His double acclamation (49) brings to a climax the series of confessions of Jesus. Each title

---

[1] One which perhaps also included the Cana pericope, 2: 1 ff.—Michel, 16.

[2] *E.g.* M. Dibelius, *From tradition to gospel*, tr. B. L. Woolf (New York, 1935), 117 f.

[3] For various interpretations see Brown, *ad loc.*

[4] In that sense, Andrew and Philip are subordinate to Peter and Nathanael. Their role is to *follow* Jesus (40, 43) and to *find* others and bring them to him (41 f., 43, 45 f.).

[5] *Cf.* Gen. 28: 12 (Jacob's ladder), also 27: 35 (his guile).

[6] *Israelite* only here in John.

[7] So Ruckstuhl, 197 f., following Menoud, *L'évangile de Jean*, 16.

reappears at a pivotal point later in the source—the prelude to the passion (12: 13)[1] and the peroration (20: 31).[2]

Hartke, and now also Bultmann,[3] takes *v.* 50 to be Johannine, along with 51. The device of Jesus' self-quotation and the parallel with 20: 29 (Johannine) might seem to support this. But this leaves unexplained the very clear aporia between 50 and 51, and ignores the *sachlich* inconsistency with 20: 29, where faith on the basis of sight is criticized, whereas here it is encouraged.[4] The verse is a most effective transition to what follows in ch. 2, for self-contained as the account of the conversion of the first disciple is, it is only intended as an introduction to the signs of Jesus. And as soon as the disciples do see *greater things than these*,[5] we are told immediately that they *believe* (2: 11*c*).

In *v.* 51, the sudden shift to 2nd person plural (*cf.* 4: 48, also 3: 11) suggests that the verse is John's addition. This is supported by the phrase *Son of Man*, which appears elsewhere only in the discourses.[6] That it may nevertheless be traditional does not affect this judgment.

With some confidence we can assign the following to the source:

3: 23 (ἦν δὲ |...| Ἰωάννης βαπτίζων ἐν Αἰνὼν ἐγγὺς τοῦ Σαλίμ, ὅτι ὕδατα πολλὰ ἦν ἐκεῖ, καὶ παρεγίνοντο καὶ ἐβαπτίζοντο·) 24 (οὔπω γὰρ ἦν βεβλημένος εἰς τὴν φυλακὴν Ἰωάννης.)

[1] *King of Israel* is possibly John's addition (so Barrett, 155, on grounds of syntax): it is a kind of appendix also in 12: 13 (the only occurrences in Jn), and the source (at least in the trial and death of Jesus) uses *King of the Jews*. But the climactic use of a double title may be typical of the source (*cf.* 20: 31), and the phrase is both known to synoptic tradition (Mk 15: 32 par.) and appropriate here, on the lips of the model Israelite.

[2] See below, p. 198. The clearly pre-Johannine occurrence of the title *Son of God* here, at the end of ch. 1, argues for the reading ἐκλεκτός in *v.* 34, at the start of the series of confessions, so that there is a kind of array in the titles ascribed to Jesus: God's Chosen One, Lamb of God, Rabbi, Messiah, he of whom Moses and the prophets wrote, Son of God, (King of Israel).

[3] *Ergänzungsheft* (1957), supplement to p. 68 of the commentary.

[4] A further difference between the two passages is that here no emphasis is placed on seeing *per se*; Schnackenburg, 317, rightly interprets ὄψη as 'you will experience' (*erfahren*).

[5] It is noteworthy that the greater things are not called *works*, as in 5: 20, 14: 12 (Johannine). [6] For other indications of disjuncture, see Brown, 88 f.

1 : 35 |...| εἰστήκει ὁ Ἰωάννης καὶ ἐκ τῶν μαθητῶν αὐτοῦ δύο,

36 καὶ ἐμβλέψας τῷ Ἰησοῦ [ἐρχομένῳ πρὸς αὐτὸν] λέγει· ἴδε ὁ ἀμνὸς τοῦ θεοῦ.

37 καὶ ἤκουσαν οἱ δύο μαθηταὶ αὐτοῦ λαλοῦντος καὶ ἠκολούθησαν τῷ Ἰησοῦ.

38 |...| οἱ δὲ εἶπαν αὐτῷ· ῥαββί |...|, ποῦ μένεις;

39 λέγει αὐτοῖς· ἔρχεσθε καὶ ὄψεσθε. ἦλθαν οὖν καὶ εἶδαν ποῦ μένει, καὶ παρ' αὐτῷ ἔμειναν (τὴν ἡμέραν ἐκείνην)· ὥρα ἦν ὡς δεκάτη.

40 ἦν Ἀνδρέας ὁ ἀδελφὸς Σίμωνος Πέτρου εἷς ἐκ τῶν δύο τῶν ἀκουσάντων παρὰ Ἰωάννου καὶ ἀκολουθησάντων αὐτῷ·

41 εὑρίσκει οὗτος πρῶτον τὸν ἀδελφὸν τὸν ἴδιον Σίμωνα καὶ λέγει αὐτῷ· εὑρήκαμεν τὸν Μεσσίαν |...|.

42 ἤγαγεν αὐτὸν πρὸς τὸν Ἰησοῦν. ἐμβλέψας αὐτῷ ὁ Ἰησοῦς εἶπεν· σὺ εἶ Σίμων ὁ υἱὸς Ἰωάννου, σὺ κληθήσῃ Κηφᾶς |...|.

43 καὶ εὑρίσκει Φίλιππον. καὶ λέγει αὐτῷ ὁ Ἰησοῦς· ἀκολούθει μοι.

44 ἦν δὲ ὁ Φίλιππος ἀπὸ Βηθσαϊδά, ἐκ τῆς πόλεως Ἀνδρέου καὶ Πέτρου.

45 εὑρίσκει Φίλιππος τὸν Ναθαναὴλ καὶ λέγει αὐτῷ· ὃν ἔγραψεν Μωϋσῆς ἐν τῷ νόμῳ καὶ οἱ προφῆται εὑρήκαμεν, Ἰησοῦν υἱὸν τοῦ Ἰωσὴφ τὸν ἀπὸ Ναζαρέθ.

46 καὶ εἶπεν αὐτῷ Ναθαναήλ· ἐκ Ναζαρὲθ δύναταί τι ἀγαθὸν εἶναι; λέγει αὐτῷ ὁ Φίλιππος· ἔρχου καὶ ἴδε.

47 εἶδεν Ἰησοῦς τὸν Ναθαναὴλ ἐρχόμενον πρὸς αὐτὸν καὶ λέγει περὶ αὐτοῦ· ἴδε |...| Ἰσραηλίτης, ἐν ᾧ δόλος οὐκ ἔστιν.

48 λέγει αὐτῷ Ναθαναήλ· πόθεν με γινώσκεις; ἀπεκρίθη Ἰησοῦς καὶ εἶπεν αὐτῷ· πρὸ τοῦ σε Φίλιππον φωνῆσαι ὄντα ὑπὸ τὴν συκῆν εἶδόν σε.

49 ἀπεκρίθη αὐτῷ Ναθαναήλ· ῥαββί, σὺ εἶ ὁ υἱὸς τοῦ θεοῦ (σὺ βασιλεὺς εἶ τοῦ Ἰσραήλ).

50 ἀπεκρίθη Ἰησοῦς καὶ εἶπεν αὐτῷ· ὅτι εἶπόν σοι ὅτι εἶδόν σε ὑποκάτω τῆς συκῆς, πιστεύεις; μείζω τούτων ὄψῃ.

The scheme of seven (or six) days which appears in 1 : 19—2 : 1, and which we have ascribed to the evangelist's redaction, is sufficiently unclear (*cf.* the differing reconstructions cited by Brown, and especially at *v.* 41) to raise the question whether it is not in fact pre-Johannine and has been partly destroyed by the evangelist. This could be supported by the sevenfold character of the central section of the source (see above, p. 101). But two things argue against this: the artificial way the scheme of days breaks up an otherwise continuous and integral account, and the lack of evidence in the source for any typological interest, of the sort usually found in the seven-day scheme (*i.e.* new creation). The plan of days has clearly been super-imposed by John, however imperfectly, on an earlier whole— in most cases by the insertion of no more than the single phrase *on the next day*.

2. JESUS AND THE SAMARITAN WOMAN
(4: 4–42)[1]

A number of critics have found evidence of more than one literary stratum in this story: it is one of the few passages apart from the sign stories which Bultmann assigns to his SQ. Besides 1: 19 ff., it is the only passage not involving a true miracle where Windisch sees the same elaboration in a series of scenes as we have already noted in chs. 5, 6, 9, 11 and 21. Both Hirsch[2] and Hartke (39–44) consider it part of the *Grundschrift*. Finally Wilkens (135–57) finds in it a pre-Johannine pericope, *i.e.* one lying *behind* the *Grundschrift*, a very unusual judgment for him. There is, then, a strong presumption in favour of the presence of material from the source we have been pursuing.

It is quite obvious that a simple narrative—Jesus' encounter with the woman at Sychar, culminating in a semi-miraculous disclosure to her of his status—has been expanded by the addition of several dialogues on themes which have only incidental ties to the story proper; the closest analogy to this editorial treatment is the interpretive expansion John gives to the Lazarus story, involving Jesus' conversations with another woman, Martha.[3] Further, while unique to Jn, the episode contains substantive parallels with synoptic tradition (Syro-Phoenician woman, woman with the haemorrhage, Lk's

[1] J. Bligh, 'Jesus in Samaria', *HeyJ* 3 (1962), 329–46; J. Bowman, 'Samaritan studies', *BJRL* 40 (1957/8), 298–327.

[2] Who notes (133) that like 5: 1 ff. (Bethzatha) and 9: 1 ff. (Siloam), both SQ, this is a local legend centring around a specific source of water.

[3] For the possibility of a pre-Johannine connection between these two stories, see below, p. 194.

Samaritan episodes) such as we have come to expect in the source.

The dialogues John has introduced are readily identified, each with its own theme: the gift of living water (*vv.* 10–15), true worship (20–4), Jesus' 'food' and the Christian 'harvest' (31–8). When these are removed, a coherent story, with only slight Johannine retouching, remains.

4: 4–9. Verse 4, while now dependent on the Johannine context of *vv.* 1–3, may have had a place in the source (see below). The logical relation (consecutive οὖν) of *v.* 5 to the present notice argues for a pre-Johannine provenance, as does the interest in specific geographical data shown in both verses. – There are several style characteristics of SQ in 6–7 *a*: ἦν δέ, consecutive οὖν (again), the time of day (presumably explaining Jesus' fatigue and thirst), ἐκ of origin, ἀντλεῖν (*cf.* 2: 8 f.).[1] – Dodd (317) sees Jesus' words in 7 *b* (*Give me a drink*) as the typically Johannine initiation of a discourse (*cf.* 3: 3, 5: 17, 6: 26, *etc.*), and it is true that the giving of water is basic to the following Johannine dialogue (10–15). But it is really *v.* 10 (restating 7 *b*) that bears this role; Jesus' question is natural enough, given the preface to the story.

Verse 8 appears to be John's addition, setting the stage for the eventual dialogue between Jesus and the disciples about food (31 ff.);[2] even if the presence of the disciples is implied by the story's context in the source (see below), they fade into the background during this story, as for example in 4: 46 ff.

In *v.* 9 the woman responds to Jesus' request—not by raising the theological question of the nature of water (as in the ensuing dialogue) but with wonder at the source of the petition; already the question of Jesus' identity, the central issue of the story, is implicitly raised. The parenthesis in 9*c*, if it is not a post-Johannine addition (missing in some MSS), is John's explanation for Gentiles.

4: 16–19. If Jesus gave a direct answer to the woman's original question in the source, it has been replaced by *vv.* 10–15.[3] But

---

[1] ἔρχεσθαι with infinitive, only here in Jn.

[2] τροφή only here in Jn, but in the plural it appears to be the evangelist's imitation of ἄρτους in 6: 5.

[3] An illustration of the extraneous nature of this dialogue is its use of both φρέαρ (11 f.) and πηγή (14), while the source uses only the latter (6).

more likely he answers, as here, only by showing himself to her as more than simply *a Jew*, and this he does by displaying his supernatural knowledge of her past life.—The details in this part of the story are unique in the gospels,[1] but the theme of Jesus confronted by a sinful (or otherwise unclean) woman is common enough. Although she does not yet understand who Jesus is, her reaction (19) is appropriate and amounts to an unwitting confession of Jesus.[2]

4: 25–30. The natural implication of the word *prophet* is not a cultic one (as in the ensuing discussion of the true place of worship), but—for a Samaritan at least—the question whether one so described is the Messiah. And mention of the latter's omniscience here (25) alludes not to the preceding dialogue (though John has skilfully made it do so) but to Jesus' display of supernatural knowledge, for he had *proclaimed everything* about the woman.[3] John reintroduces the source, which he interrupted in the midst of the woman's reply to Jesus, by the first four words of *v.* 25; the bilingual note (*who is called Christ*) is probably not John's usual translation of Hebrew for his readers.[4] While ἐγώ εἰμι (26) is a highly important phrase for John (8: 24, 28, 58, 13: 19), it always has for him a theophanic significance (*I AM*), whereas in the source (6: 20, 18: 5), while possibly revelatory in effect, it has, as here, a basically matter-of-fact sense: either 'I am the one in question' (*cf.* Mk 14: 62) or simply 'it is I'. The participial phrase at the end of the verse is probably Johannine (*cf.* 9: 37).

Verse 27 interrupts the story and only prepares for the

[1] In seeking to explain them it would be tempting to find in the woman's past a symbol of the Samaritans, but there is little solid basis for such an explanation—see Schnackenburg and Brown.

[2] For a *prophet's* knowledge of sin, *cf.* Lk 7: 39; for the role as ascribed to Jesus, Mt 21: 11, 46, Lk 7: 16. Schnackenburg (469) is right that there is no indication here of the prophet-like-Moses, but in the source that followed immediately.

[3] While similar to the Johannine theme of Jesus' foreknowledge (*e.g.* 2: 25), it is different in that the knowledge is not private, but involves proclaiming (*cf.* 1: 48).

[4] Unless it should be translated *which means anointed*—*cf.* W. C. van Unnik, 'The purpose of St John's gospel', *StudEv* i (1959), 390, who, however, fails to note how the usage here differs from that in 1: 41, where his point applies. See above on 5: 2 and 21: 2.

Johannine dialogue between Jesus and the disciples (30 ff.).[1] In 28 the woman responds (consecutive οὖν) to Jesus' self-disclosure: leaving her water jar,[2] she goes to spread the news. Her challenge to the townsmen (*Come see. . .* [29a]) is like that to the potential disciples in 1: 39, 46.[3] Her hesitant question in 29b (*Can this be the Christ?*) is probably Johannine even if χριστός in *v.* 25 is not (see above, p. 191 n. 4): but her belief in Jesus' messiahship is at least implied in the words *a man who told me all I ever did* with their reference to 25, and the source can hardly have intended to contrast the woman's faith with that of her fellow townsmen. The latter obey her command without hesitation (30),[4] but John postpones their encounter with Jesus (note the imperfect ἤρχοντο) by the insertion of a scene quite foreign to the source (31-8).[5]

4: 39–42. Here the conclusion of the episode, interrupted at *v.* 30, is taken up again. Verse 39, Johannine on many counts,[6] ignores *v.* 30 and interjects the note of preliminary faith (*cf.* John's redaction in 4: 50–3). Verse 40 first restates 30b and then resumes the story. It perhaps read as follows: (30a) ἐξῆλθον οὖν ἐκ τῆς πόλεως καὶ (40) ἦλθον πρὸς αὐτὸν οἱ Σαμαρῖται · ἠρώτων κτλ. For the notice that Jesus *remained* with them, *cf.* 1: 39.[7] – Verses 41 f. are Johannine on many of the

---

[1] μέντοι is found in Johannine insertions at 20: 5, 21: 4.

[2] *Cf.* 2: 6; she leaves it apparently in her haste—so Θ correctly interprets in adding τρέχουσα.

[3] *Cf.* 11: 34, 43, ?21: 12.

[4] Read perhaps οὖν, with 𝔓⁶⁶ ℵ λ φ *pm.*

[5] ῥαββί in 31 is John's imitation of the source's style, as in 3: 2, 11: 8.

[6] For this use of ἐκ, see above, p. 59 n. 3. With πολλοὶ ἐπίστευσαν, *cf.* 10: 42, 11: 45; with μαρτυρεῖν, *cf.* 1: 7b, 8, 15, 32a, 34a (the verb, as opposed to the noun, is never found in the source but is very frequent in Johannine passages). Belief on the basis of someone's *word* (*cf.* 4: 50b) and the device of quotation are characteristic of John.

[7] W. A. Meeks, 'Galilee and Judea in the fourth gospel', *JBL* 85 (1966), 167, suggests that both these passages, together with 2: 12b, 7: 9, 10: 40, 11: 6, 54 (all Johannine) reflect John's theological use of μένειν. But this is not borne out by J. Heise, *Bleiben: Menein in den johanneischen Schriften* (Hermeneutische Untersuchungen zur Theologie, 8; Tübingen, 1967), 47 ff. In any case, the two passages, which we assign to SQ, show a more specific use of the verb than the others, in which only a vague indication of time, if any, is given (on 11: 6 see below, p. 194). Evidently John has inexactly imitated the source's usage.

same counts as 39. But it is possible that 42 contains an original confession of Jesus on the part of the Samaritans; the textual variation at the end (𝕶 *D* Θ *pl* it add ὁ χριστός) suggests a redactional pleonasm which has been eased by omission.[1] But if so which title is John's addition—*saviour of the world* or *the Christ*? The former has a Johannine ring,[2] and the latter is consistent with the pre-Johannine version of the episode; but Bowman (313) notes that *saviour of the world* is Samaritan usage for the Messiah (*Taheb*), so it may be the pre-Johannine element, John seeking to interpret it by adding ὁ χριστός. Very tentatively we read: καὶ ἔλεγον ὅτι οὗτός ἐστιν ὁ σωτὴρ τοῦ κόσμου.[3]

The result of the foregoing analysis of the source is as follows:

4: 4 ἔδει δὲ αὐτὸν διέρχεσθαι διὰ τῆς Σαμαρείας.

5 ἔρχεται οὖν εἰς πόλιν τῆς Σαμαρείας λεγομένην Σύχαρ, πλησίον τοῦ χωρίου ὃ ἔδωκεν Ἰακὼβ τῷ Ἰωσὴφ τῷ υἱῷ αὐτοῦ·

6 ἦν δὲ ἐκεῖ πηγὴ τοῦ Ἰακώβ. ὁ οὖν Ἰησοῦς κεκοπιακὼς ἐκ τῆς ὁδοιπορίας ἐκαθέζετο οὕτως ἐπὶ τῇ πηγῇ· ὥρα ἦν ὡς ἕκτη.

7 ἔρχεται γυνὴ ἐκ τῆς Σαμαρείας ἀντλῆσαι ὕδωρ. λέγει αὐτῇ ὁ Ἰησοῦς· δός μοι πεῖν.

9 λέγει οὖν αὐτῷ ἡ γυνὴ ἡ Σαμαρῖτις· πῶς σὺ Ἰουδαῖος ὢν παρ' ἐμοῦ πεῖν αἰτεῖς γυναικὸς Σαμαρίτιδος οὔσης;

16 λέγει αὐτῇ· ὕπαγε φώνησον τὸν ἄνδρα σου καὶ ἐλθὲ ἐνθάδε.

17 ἀπεκρίθη ἡ γυνὴ καὶ εἶπεν· οὐκ ἔχω ἄνδρα. λέγει αὐτῇ ὁ Ἰησοῦς· καλῶς εἶπες ὅτι ἄνδρα οὐκ ἔχω.

18 πέντε γὰρ ἄνδρας ἔσχες, καὶ νῦν ὃν ἔχεις οὐκ ἔστιν σου ἀνήρ· τοῦτο ἀληθὲς εἴρηκας.

19 λέγει αὐτῷ ἡ γυνή· κύριε, θεωρῶ ὅτι προφήτης εἶ σύ.

25 |...| οἶδα ὅτι Μεσσίας ἔρχεται, (ὁ λεγόμενος χριστός)· ὅταν ἔλθῃ ἐκεῖνος, ἀναγγελεῖ ἡμῖν ἅπαντα.

26 λέγει αὐτῇ ὁ Ἰησοῦς· ἐγώ εἰμι. |...|

28 ἀφῆκεν οὖν τὴν ὑδρίαν αὐτῆς ἡ γυνὴ καὶ ἀπῆλθεν εἰς τὴν πόλιν, καὶ λέγει τοῖς ἀνθρώποις·

29 δεῦτε ἴδετε ἄνθρωπον ὃς εἶπέν μοι πάντα ἃ ἐποίησα· |...|

30 ἐξῆλθον (οὖν) ἐκ τῆς πόλεως καὶ |...|

---

[1] Why would the quite unnecessary ὁ χριστός be added in transmission?

[2] *Cf.* 1 Jn 4: 14, and John's use of *world* to mean mankind (3: 16, 8: 26, *etc.*).

[3] For the omission of ἀληθῶς, see above on 1: 47.

40 |...| ἦλθον πρὸς αὐτὸν οἱ Σαμαρῖται· ἠρώτων αὐτὸν μεῖναι παρ' αὐτοῖς· καὶ ἔμεινεν ἐκεῖ δύο ἡμέρας. καὶ |...|
42 |...| ἔλεγον |...| ὅτι οὗτός ἐστιν |...| ὁ σωτὴρ τοῦ κόσμου.

It is perhaps impossible to recover the original setting of the pericope, but one or two clues are available to us. Verse 4, if original, suggests that originally the episode took place during a brief journey through Samaria; that there was no account of a Samaritan ministry as such is perhaps supported by the lack of any tradition, even in Lk, of a protracted period of activity there, and *v.* 40 implies that Jesus stayed with the Samaritans only at their importuning. The length of the stay (*two days*) is made curiously explicit in that verse (and reiterated by John in *v.* 43). Now in the Lazarus episode (11: 6) John mentions another arbitrary stay of two days, and although the pre-Johannine version of that story uniquely involves a journey, the actual account of the trip is missing. (We have already noted the connection, yet also the gap, between 11: 15 and 17; the latter only mentions Jesus' arrival.) As we reconstructed the source, that journey was not from trans-Jordan to Bethany, but from Capernaum in Galilee (see above, p. 106). The present passage, in its Johannine context, reports a journey in the opposite direction; but there is nothing in the story itself to indicate this.[1]

It is possible, then, that the episode of the Samaritan woman originally came between 11: 15 and 17. The resulting story-within-a-story would be strikingly parallel to Mk 5: 22–43, where Jesus, on his way to raise someone from (at least apparent) death, stops to deal with a woman of whom he has a kind of supernatural knowledge. When John postponed the first

[1] W. Grundmann, 'Verkündigung und Geschichte in dem Bericht vom Eingang der Geschichte Jesu im Johannes-Evangelium', in *Der historische Jesus und der kerygmatische Christus: Beiträge zum Christusverständnis in Forschung und Verkündigung*, ed. H. Ristow and K. Matthiae (Berlin, 1961), 291, suggests another explanation of the *two days* in 4: 40, *viz.* that the Samaritan episode originally led up to the wedding at Cana, which opens with the words *On the third day*. If so, the story in ch. 4 may have provided the pre-Johannine transition from the conversion of the disciples, in the south, to the first sign, in Galilee. But on good grounds we have assigned the opening phrase in 2: 1 not to the source but to John.

Judean miracle, and what had been the occasion for Jesus' transfer to the south, to the end of the public ministry, he separated out the story of the journey and used it in one of his invented withdrawals to Galilee. But, because the Lazarus story requires a time lapse, he rather lamely asserts (11: 6) that 'Jesus stayed where he was' (*cf.* John's artificial preparation for this in 10: 40–2) and supplies the length of the stay from the original version.[1]

If our suggestion is correct, there is evident in the source a structural parallel with the story of the disciples' conversion:[2] just as Nathanael's confession (1: 49) inaugurates the miraculous ministry in *Galilee* (2: 1–11, 4: 46–54, 21: 1–14, 6: 1–25), so that of the Samaritans (4: 29, 42) leads into the ministry in *Jerusalem* (11: 1–45, 5: 2–9, 9: 1–8). It is interesting, further, that the former episode may also have taken place in Samaria (see above, p. 180).

3. AN UNRECOVERABLE FRAGMENT: PETER'S CONFESSION (6: 67–71)[3]

Most critics recognize a relation between this passage and the synoptic episode at Caesarea Philippi (Mk 8: 27–33 pars.). Barrett (252–4) sees the differences as due to John's deliberate rewriting (*e.g.* Judas, not Peter, is now the devil). Dodd (219–22), on the other hand, finds it impossible to explain some of the variation in this way (*e.g. the holy one of God*,[4] a title which appears nowhere else in Jn), and he ventures to attribute the whole passage (except a few obviously Johannine phrases—68*c*, 71) to a pre-Johannine form of the story.[5] I find reason to believe that John uses a distinctive tradition here,[6] but that it has been considerably rewritten by him. And because it

---

[1] Why Jesus would stop on his way to an ailing friend is perhaps a psychological question we can no more ask of the source than of John; it is noteworthy, however, that in the source, on this hypothesis, the delay was not gratuitous.   [2] We have already noted several parallels as to detail.

[3] Bligh, 'Galilee', 24–6; Brown, *Essays*, 207–12; E. Haenchen, 'Die Komposition von Mk viii 27—ix 1 und Par' [the title as printed incorrectly reads Mk vii], *NovT* 6 (1963), 81–109.

[4] In place of *the Christ*. The alternate readings are all to be explained as assimilations to Mk and Mt.   [5] *Cf.* Haenchen, 106–9.

[6] It is noteworthy that *the twelve* are mentioned; elsewhere in Jn only at 20: 24 (by imitation?).

displays no obvious aporias, we cannot claim to recover a source or even assert that the tradition came to John *via* SQ, though that is far from unlikely. If it did, the question arises as to the original context of the story. There is perhaps more than coincidence in the striking parallel between the structures of Mk 8 and Jn 6: feeding, trouble at sea, demand for a sign, discourse on bread, Peter's confession, prediction of the passion, devil saying.[1] It is possible, therefore, that the pericope was part of a larger block of material in the source, originally following the double sign of 6: 1–25; John has then radically reworked it to produce his discourse on the bread of life. But this is only conjecture, and while noting the possibility that SQ material may be buried here, we must leave the passage out of our reconstruction.

A NOTE ON JN 7: 3 ff.

This exhausts those narrative episodes in Jn where evidence of a source can be found. But there is one other passage, namely 7: 3 ff., which has often been taken to rest on a *Vorlage*.[2] The aporia generally pointed to is the suggestion of Jesus' brothers (*v.* 3) that he has not yet done any signs in Judea, in contradiction of 2: 23, 3: 2, 4: 45, and 5: 1 ff.; on this basis, the passage (along with 4: 45 *a*, which makes the same assumption) is assigned to an earlier strand than those verses. But, as a matter of fact, the saying of the brothers implies that Jesus *has* 'worked' in Judea,[3] since it is taken for granted that he has disciples there. The passage, certainly in its present form, is Johannine[4] and is entirely consistent with the circumstance that although Jesus has believers in Judea (*cf.* 2: 23, 4: 1) he has not 'shown' himself there (as he did at Cana)[5] because he could not, due to 'the Jews'—even a sign done in Jerusalem (5: 1 ff.) is rejected. In *v.* 4 the idea of openness (παρρησία) is Johannine (7: 26,

---

[1] Jeremias, 'Literarkritik', 42. *Cf.* Dodd, 218 f., who however is less willing to find clear-cut parallels here.

[2] See, for example, Bultmann, 217 n. 2. Dodd, 241, wonders if *vv.* 1–2 are traditional, but suspects that they are not.

[3] There is no mention of 'signs'. For 'works' as Johannine, *cf.* on 9: 3 *b*.

[4] So J. Schneider, 'Zur Komposition von Joh 7', *ZNW* 45 (1954), 108–19, esp. 113.

[5] *Cf.* 2: 11 *b* (Johannine); this is the only sign seen as a manifestation of himself by Jesus.

10: 24, 11: 54, 16: 25, 29), as also that of manifestation to *the world* (*cf.* 14: 22); further, the assertion that the brothers are faithless (5), and Jesus' answer about his 'time' (6; *cf.* 2: 4). The episode is based entirely on the occasion of the feast in Jerusalem, and we have seen evidence that the festal scheme in Jn is due to the evangelist. That Jesus' subsequent behaviour is arbitrary and inconsistent (as in 2: 1 ff., 2: 23 f.) is due to the artificiality of this scene (*cf.* also 5: 1, 10: 40–2, 11: 54). John's tradition may have contained reference to Jesus' brothers,[1] but their appearance here (*cf.* 2: 12) is Johannine.

4. THE PERORATION (20: 30 f.)[2]

There remains the question how the source ended, and the answer is not hard to find. The last two verses of ch. 20 are a notorious crux in the extant gospel. On the basis of them ch. 21 is widely held to be a late addition. We have shown methodological reasons for questioning that judgment (above, p. 7 n. 1, and pp. 87 f.), but even if the last chapter is not part of John's original gospel, 20: 30 f. pose a problem. For it is strange to hear of *signs* for the first time since ch. 12,[3] and the connection of the two verses to the preceding episode (doubting Thomas, 20: 24–9) is not entirely smooth. It is true that in a sense the verses provide a fitting conclusion to the Thomas story:[4] Thomas believes only when he has seen, a beatitude is spoken over those who believe without seeing, and the reader (who ostensibly has not seen) is encouraged to believe. But at the same time, there is a certain *sachlich* tension between the two passages, for example, that between the high christology of Thomas' confession (28) and the more primitive messianism in

---

[1] *Cf.* 20: 17; the phrase there, however, may mean Jesus' *disciples*.

[2] L. Vaganay, 'Le finale du quatrième évangile', *RB* 45 (1936), 512–28. Also the bibliography for 21: 1 ff., above, p. 87.

[3] This has been explained by maintaining that John sees the resurrection as a sign, but Schnackenburg ('Traditionsgeschichte', 78 f., citing Rengstorf) is right that for John (unlike SQ; see below, p. 198 n. 4) the resurrection is wholly God's deed. Thus ταῦτα in *v.* 31 must for the evangelist refer not merely to the signs but to Jesus' words as well; it is clear, however, from the inseparable relation of *vv.* 30 and 31, that originally ταῦτα meant *these signs*.

[4] Jeremias, 'Literarkritik', 43 f., believes 30 f. originally ended the story in some source.

31.[1] And the reader is, practically speaking, one who *has* seen (*viz.* the signs as represented in the gospel), and on the basis of that seeing he can be expected to believe—'these are written *in order that you may believe*; he is thus closer to Thomas than to the μακάριοι of *v.* 29, though this can hardly have been John's intent, for he included the Thomas story to deepen the understanding of faith. The two passages are not flatly contradictory, and they have a certain affinity; but they do not stem from the same mode of thought.

This state of affairs can be explained as follows: the source, which John has followed throughout the passion narrative and which he left at *v.* 20, closed with 30 f.[2] If this passion source was part of the longer signs source,[3] the mention of signs in 30 is not so surprising.[4]

In 30–1 *a* there are many indications of the style and thought of SQ;[5] but the last clause (31 *b*), which has the form of an afterthought, disturbing the rhetorical balance of the μὲν...δέ construction, is obviously Johannine in content (*cf.* 1: 12, 10: 10, *etc.*) and almost certainly the evangelist's addition.

The final item in our intermittent résumé of the source is thus:

20: 30 πολλὰ μὲν οὖν καὶ ἄλλα σημεῖα ἐποίησεν ὁ Ἰησοῦς ἐνώπιον τῶν μαθητῶν, ἃ οὐκ ἔστιν γεγραμμένα ἐν τῷ βιβλίῳ τούτῳ.

31 ταῦτα δὲ γέγραπται ἵνα πιστεύητε ὅτι Ἰησοῦς ἐστιν ὁ χριστὸς ὁ υἱὸς τοῦ θεοῦ |...|.

---

[1] *Cf.* Thompson, 'Composition', 40.

[2] So, more or less, Wilkens; *cf.* Bultmann and Hartke, who ascribe the verses to the conclusion of the *signs source* but, except for the present passage, see no evidence of it beyond ch. 12.

[3] We have of course not yet shown this, though we have noted a number of stylistic pointers in that direction; see further below, pt. IV.

[4] That the word σημεῖον does not appear in the passion *Vorlage* only suggests, what is virtually certain, that the latter once had a separate existence. That term belongs to the editorial framework of the source, in any case, of which 20: 30 f. would inevitably be a part. The source undoubtedly regards the resurrection as Jesus' sign *par excellence*, for although he is not here depicted as accomplishing his own resurrection (but *cf.* 2: 19—SQ) his appearing to the disciples (19 f.) is deliberate (*came and stood, showed*).

[5] The construction of 30 *a* is similar to that of 2: 11 *a*, 4: 54 *a*, and 21: 14 *a*; ἐνώπιον only here in Jn (*vs.* John's ἔμπροσθεν: 1: 15, 30, 3: 28, 10: 4, 12: 37). For belief as the result of signs (31), *cf.* 2: 11 *c*, 4: 53 *etc.*; for the titles ascribed to Jesus, *cf.* 1: 49. This is perhaps not the only gospel describing itself as a *book* (30 *b*)—*cf.* Mt 1: 1.

We have called these verses the 'peroration'. So formal a description is perhaps not quite appropriate, yet it serves to point up the *sachlich* parallel with 1: 6 f. (the source's 'exordium'): just as John came that all *might believe*, so these signs are written 'that you *might believe*'.

A NOTE ON JN 12: 37 f.

Faure held that 12: 37 f. was a part of SQ, on the basis of the formula of OT citation in 38, as compared with that in 39 f. Bultmann rightly rejects that criterion (see above on 12: 14) but maintains that the Septuagintal character of the passage quoted in 38 shows it to be from a different hand than that in 40, and he ascribes the verses to SQ, immediately preceding 20: 30 f. Smend, however, has disproved this.[1] Bultmann's other argument—that the unexpected mention of signs, together with the suggestion that men failed to believe in them, is unaccountable if Johannine—is invalid. John frequently summarizes Jesus' activity as that of 'doing (many) signs', apart from any specifically miraculous episode (2: 23, 3: 2, 7: 31, 10: 41, 11: 47, *etc.*), and although many have believed Jesus' signs up till now in the gospel, for John this is the turning point. If the assertion of 12: 37 is strange in Jn, it is even stranger in a source that is purely concerned to show Jesus as winning faith on the basis of signs. The possibility of not believing in signs is one which only John conceives.[2]

5. SAYINGS?

While we have limited ourselves in this study to the gospel's narratives, making no attempt to examine the great body of Jesus' sayings as they appear in the discourses that are so distinctive of the gospel, we have come across a small number of sayings within the narrative. These are mainly of a type closely tied to the narrative, which Bultmann calls 'framed' sayings;[3] and most of them are found in the passion narrative.

---

[1] 'Behandlung', 149 f.

[2] See further Schnackenburg, 'Traditionsgeschichte', 78, for a decisive demonstration of the Johannine character of 37–43.

[3] Review of Noack, 524: *gerahmte Herrenworte*. Beyond this there are only elements of Jesus' conversation (questions, commands), which have no status as sayings in their own right.

There are also a few independent logia.[1] But most of the latter which we have encountered (*e.g.* 1: 51, 2: 4, 4: 48), while in some cases traditional, are Johannine in their present setting and very likely came to the evangelist directly from free oral tradition.[2]

The question whether our source contained sayings that found their way into other parts of the gospel is outside our scope, for the canons governing the source analysis of the narrative material can hardly apply to the discourses. Dodd believes that a number of passages, either short dialogues or sequences of sayings, are almost wholly pre-Johannine, and the question arises whether our source provided the evangelist with any of these. One such possibility is the episode of Peter's confession (see above, sec. 3).[3] But if so, there are now no contextual grounds for recovering them, nor do we have any indication of their original setting.[4]

The search for any additional dominical teaching our source may have contained is therefore vain. And it is entirely possible that it contained none whatever. If it appears strange that a source, particularly a gospel, should be based almost solely on narrative about Jesus, it is hardly more so than the fact that the gospel of Mk is, by the standard of Mt and Lk, deficient in the teaching of Jesus, or, on the other hand, the fact that the source Q seems to have been virtually devoid of narrative. Our source was unusual in any case; it deliberately sought to present Jesus as the Messiah on the basis of his significant acts, and those alone (see below, pt. v).

[1] Notably only the sayings to Peter (1: 42) and Nathanael (1: 47). To these should perhaps be added 1: 50, but it may have had a purely editorial origin, preparing the reader for the signs to follow; that is clearly its function in the source, though an earlier eschatological use is not excluded.

[2] So Bultmann, agreeing with Noack.

[3] Another may be 12: 20–36, the opening of which (*vv.* 20–2) is similar in form and *dramatis personae* to 1: 35 ff. But it is more likely to be John's imitation of the source, providing a setting for the series of independent logia which follow (23 ff.).

[4] Hoskyns, 288 f., holds that 6: 3 ('Jesus went up into the mountain and there sat down with his disciples'—probably SQ) was originally such a setting, as it is in Mt 5: 1 f. (*cf.* Lk 6: 12, 17 ff.); but it is more likely that the expansion Mt gives is peculiar to him. In any case, if teaching originally followed here, it has been dispersed by John irretrievably.

PART FOUR

STYLISTIC TESTS OF THE SOURCE'S PURITY AND INTEGRITY

STYLISTIC TESTS OF THE SOURCE'S PURITY AND INTEGRITY

I. THE METHOD OF SCHWEIZER AND RUCKSTUHL

In 1939 Eduard Schweizer made an important advance in the source analysis of Jn when he devised an objective way to test the stylistic distinctiveness and homogeneity of any hypothetically reconstructed source allegedly underlying the gospel.[1] He was able to do this because of the fact, long recognized, that Jn as a whole, together with the Johannine epistles, has a style unique with respect not merely to the synoptic gospels but to the remainder of the NT. His innovation was the careful selection of thirty-three style characteristics on the basis both of their frequency in Jn and of their infrequency or absence elsewhere in the NT. He reasoned that each of these usages would be characteristic either of the evangelist or of one of his sources (or a later redactor) and that it is therefore possible to compare a putative source with a list of them to see if that source is stylistically distinct from the rest of the gospel. If it proves not to be, the validity of the source as reconstructed is thereby called in question.

Emanuel Hirsch, one of the three critics whose analyses failed to pass Schweizer's test, responded[2] (1) by raising the question whether any source could be entirely distinct in style from the rest of the gospel, since John will consciously or unconsciously have imitated its style in other parts of the gospel; and (2) by noting that some of the characteristics which Schweizer chose, while rare in the NT, are common in late Koine Greek and may reflect not so much a style distinctive of Jn as a linguistic milieu which he and his sources share. Hirsch's caveats are to be heeded as qualifications of the method, if not the vindication of his own theory he supposes them to be.[3] The possibility of imitation must be taken seriously, as subsequent users of the method have not sufficiently done; and it must be asked whether the rest of the NT is always a valid standard by which to

---

[1] *Ego eimi*, 82–112; see at length above, pp. 13 f.
[2] 'Stilkritik'.   [3] So Haenchen, 'Literatur'.

measure the distinctiveness of John's style with respect to his sources. On the latter point, however, it has to be admitted that as one moves behind Jn to a source, the possibility increases that the latter will reflect a Greek more akin to that of the rest of the NT than to later Koine, especially as the date of Jn is pushed back (as in current scholarly opinion) further into the first century.

Shortly after Schweizer's book appeared, some additions to his list were suggested by Jeremias[1] and Menoud,[2] and a few years later a full-scale adaptation of the method was made by Ruckstuhl,[3] who took up most of the suggestions of Jeremias and Menoud, eliminated as invalid several of the original characteristics, and expanded the list with his own additions, to a total of fifty.

As we have noted,[4] Ruckstuhl's extension of the discussion is twofold. Not only does he apply the tests to Bultmann's source analysis, which had appeared after Schweizer's work was done, and claim it to be wholly disproved as a result; but further, examining the seeming lack of clustering of characteristics within the gospel, he maintains that Jn is a 'literary unity', not based on any written sources, and that all source theories are therefore disproved in advance.

With respect to the former, it can be asked what kinds of evidence Ruckstuhl would require to establish the existence of a source. Whereas none of the hypothetical sources Schweizer examines (those of Spitta, Wendt, and Hirsch) is free of more than six (*i.e.* 18%) of the thirty-three characteristics in his list, Bultmann's signs source (SQ) lacks thirty-two (or 64%) of Ruckstuhl's fifty, and his other narrative source (EQ) gives an identical result. If any theory could satisfy him, Bultmann's narrative sources certainly come nearer than those of the earlier critics.

We may reject so sweeping a conclusion as Ruckstuhl's second and major one,[5] and it will not surprise us that a source cannot be recovered simply by looking for relationships among various style characteristics. Schweizer noted that certain passages in Jn, notably the synoptic-like narratives, were

---

[1] 'Literarkritik', 35–41. [2] *L'évangile de Jean*, 16.
[3] *Einheit*, pt. 2. [4] Above, pp. 13 f.
[5] See above, pp. 17 f.

relatively free of the characteristics, but even there, if our analysis is right, the source does not now appear in entirely homogeneous blocks but has been interspersed with John's (sometimes quite minute) additions. Only when the source has been completed, and correctly separated in detail from John's editorial work, can we expect a clear-cut stylistic distinction between the two strata to appear. And conversely, the style characteristics provide a test of the success of that separation.

Other criteria besides those in Ruckstuhl's list could undoubtedly be devised, but in view both of the refinement to which he has brought it and of the radical claims he makes on the basis of it, his method will provide a rigorous enough test of our analysis.

In so far as we have relied on stylistic evidence in our source analysis, the procedure will involve a logical circle. But we have never used such criteria in isolation from other ones, and never by making prior assumptions as to what John's style actually was. And as a check against the possibility of circularity we shall consider (sec. 2, below) whether in fact the source we have distinguished is stylistically colourless ('neutral') as Ruckstuhl insists all hypothetical sources must inevitably appear to be.

How, then, does our source fare when it is checked against Ruckstuhl's list?

Thirty-two (or 64%) of the characteristics are *never found in the source*.[1] They are as follows, in Ruckstuhl's order[2] and with their frequency expressed according to Schweizer's formula:[3]

---

[1] A few exceptions occur in passages (all of them in the account of the last supper) where we have sensed the presence of pre-Johannine fragments, but where John's recasting of traditional material is so thorough as to make source reconstruction impossible: no. 18 (13: 1*b*), no. 25 (13: 37 f.), no. 40 (13: 21, 28; here evidently John has simply doubled the ἀμήν found in the synoptic parallels, in accordance with his unvarying usage).

[2] One of Ruckstuhl's improvements on Schweizer was to arrange the characteristics in three groups of decreasing validity. Thus the first nineteen are considered better as a group than all that follow them; likewise the next twelve (nos. 20–31) better than the last nineteen.

[3] *Viz.* $a+b/x+y$, where a and b represent the number of occurrences in Jn and the Johannine epistles, respectively; x, independent occurrences in the rest of the NT; and y, synoptic parallels to instances in x. (So I interpret Schweizer's ambiguous and overly terse explanation (88); it is apparently understood slightly differently by Menoud, and differently still by Ruckstuhl, but the differences are negligible.) Figures in parentheses include doubtful

3. ἄν = ἐάν: 4(5) / (1).[1]
5. Epexegetic ἵνα: 10(11) + 12 / (1).[2]
7. Inversion of previous sentence ending: 6.[3]
8. ἐμός in 2nd attributive position: 25(27) + 1 / 0.[4]
10. Unusual word separation: 12 / 0.[5]
11. Collective neuter singular: 4(5) / 0.[6]
12. καθώς... καί (without οὕτως): 6 + 2 / 1.[7]
13. οὐ... ἀλλ' ἵνα: 5 + 1 / 1.[8]
14. οὐχ ὅτι... ἀλλ' ὅτι: 2 + 2 / 1.[9]
15. ὥρα ἵνα (ὅτε): 8 / 0.[10]
18. ὥρα with personal pronoun: 6 / 1.[11]
19. παρρησίᾳ : 7 / 1.[12]
20. οὐ μή... εἰς τὸν αἰῶνα: 5(6) / 1.[13]
21. παροιμία: 4 / 0.[14]
22. σκοτία (for σκότος): 8 + 5 / 1 + 1.[15]

cases; '+0' before or after / is omitted; figures in square brackets represent instances in the synoptic gospels only. If any of the instances in Jn are pre-Johannine, they are expressed by a figure following a second /.—Where possible, I have cited in a footnote all the instances of the characteristic in Jn, which Schweizer does not always do, and Ruckstuhl almost never.

The figures cited by Schweizer and Ruckstuhl are based mainly on the concordance of Bruder, mine on J. B. Smith, *Greek–English concordance to the New Testament: A tabular and statistical Greek–English concordance based on the King James Version...* (Scottdale, Pa.; 1955). Smith has the disadvantage of being based on the *Textus Receptus* (in most cases I have been able to correct his figures on the basis of Nestle), but his 'tabular and statistical' format is more useful for present purposes than that of the other concordances or of Morgenthaler's work.

[1] 5: 19, (12: 32), 13: 20, 16: 23, 20: 23.
[2] 3: 19, 4: 34, 6: 29, 39, 40, (50), 9: 30, 15: 8, 13, 16: 19, 17: 3.
[3] 1: 1, 3: 32 f., 8: 15 f., 12: 35, 16: 27 f., 18: 36.
[4] 3: 29, 5: 30, 30, 6: 38, 7: 6, 8: 16, 31, 37, 43, 43, (51), 56, 10: 26, 27, 12: 26, 14: 15, (24), 27, 15: 9, 11, 12, 17: 13, 24, 18: 36, 36, 36, 36.
[5] 4: 39, 5: 20, 7: 12, 38, 44, 10: 32, 11: 15, 12: 11, 18, 37, 17: 5, 19: 20.
[6] 6: 37, 39, (10: 29), 17: 2, 24.
[7] 6: 57, 13: 15, 33, 15: 9, 17: 18, 20: 21.
[8] 1: 8, 9: 3, 11: 52, 13: 18, 14: 30 f.
[9] 6: 26, 12: 6.
[10] 4: 21, 23, 5: 25, 12: 23, 13: 1, 16: 2, 25, 32.
[11] 2: 4, 7: 30, 8: 20, 13: 1, 16: 4, 21.
[12] 7: 13, 26, 10: 24, 11: 14, 54, 16: 25, 18: 20.
[13] 4: 14, 8: (35), 51, 52, 11: 26, 13: 8.
[14] 10: 6, 16: 25, 25, 29.
[15] 1: 5, 5, 6: 17, 8: 12, 12: 35, 35, 46, 20: 1.

23. λαμβάνειν τινά: 5 + 1 / 0.[1]
25. τιθέναι ψυχήν: 8 + 2 / 0.[2]
26. μέντοι: 5 / 3.[3]
27. γύναι (of Jesus' mother): 2 / 0.[4]
28. φανεροῦν with reflexive: 2 / 0.[5]
29. Metaphoric μεταβαίνειν: 2 + 1 / 0.[6]
30. μαρτυρεῖν περί τινος (of a person): 17 + 2 / 0.[7]
31. ἀφ' ἑαυτοῦ: 13 / 1(2).[8]

32. τῇ ἐσχάτῃ ἡμέρᾳ : 7 / 0.[9]
33. οὐ...πώποτε: 4 + 1 / 1.[10]
34. μικρός (of time): 11 / 3 + 1.[11]
36. ἐκ τούτου ('henceforth'): 2 / 0.[12]
40. ἀμὴν ἀμήν: 25 / 0.[13]
41. Metaphoric ὑπάγειν (πορεύεσθαι): 20 / 2 + 1.[14]
44. οὐ...ἐὰν (εἰ) μή: 19 / 16 + 1.[15]
46. εἶναι (γεννηθῆναι) ἐκ: 22 + 26 / 11 + 6.[16]
47. (ἐ)ὰν (μή) τις: 24 + 4 / 19 + 2.[17]

While some of these usages are by their nature appropriate
only to the discourses and so inevitably absent from a narrative
source, some could as well appear in narrative,[18] and a number

[1] 1: 12, 5: 43, 43, 13: 20, 20.
[2] 10: 11, 15, 17, 18, 18, 13: 37, 38, 15: 13.
[3] 4: 27, 7: 13, 12: 42, 20: 5, 21: 4.
[4] 2: 4, 19: 26.   [5] 7: 4, 21: 1.   [6] 5: 24, 13: 1.
[7] 1: 7, 8, 15, 2: 25, 5: 31, 32, 32, 36, 37, 39, 7: 7, 8: 13, 14, 18, 18, 10: 25, 15: 26.
[8] 5: 19, 30, 7: 17, 18, 28, 8: 28, 42, 10: 18, 11: 51, 14: 10, 15: 4, 16: 13, 18: 34.   [9] 6: 39, 40, 44, 54, 7: 37, 11: 24, 12: 48.
[10] 1: 18, 5: 37, 6: 35, 8: 33.
[11] 7: 33, 12: 35, 13: 33, 14: 19, 16: 16, 16, 17, 17, 18, 19, 19.
[12] 6: 66, 19: 12.
[13] 1: 51, 3: 3, 5, 11, 5: 19, 24, 25, 6: 26, 32, 47, 53, 8: 34, 51, 58, 10: 1, 7, 12: 24, 13: 16, 20, 21, 38, 14: 12, 16: 20, 23, 21: 18.
[14] 7: 33, 8: 14, 14, 21, 21, 22, 13: 3, 33, 36b, 14: 2, 3, 4, 12, 28, 28, 16: 5a, 7, 10, 17, 28.
[15] 3: 2, 3, 5, 27, 4: 48, 5: 19, 6: 44, 53, 65, 9: 33, 13: 8, 15: 4, 4, 22, 24, 16: 7, 18: 30, 19: 11, 20: 25.
[16] 1: 13, 3: 5, 6, 6, 8, 31, 8: 23, 23, 23, 23, 44, 47, 47, 15: 19, 19, 17: 14, 14, 16, 16, 18: 36, 36, 37.
[17] 3: 3, 5, 5: 19, 6: 51, 7: 17, 37, 8: 51, 52, 9: 22, 31, 10: 9, 11: 9, 10, 57, 12: 26, 26, 47, 13: 20, 14: 14, 23, 15: 6, 16: 23, 20: 23, 23.
[18] And, in another form, are found in the source: e.g. ἀποθνήσκειν (for τιθέναι ψυχήν), μαρτυρία (cf. no. 30).

in fact occur in SQ *contexts*, but not in the verses we have assigned, on other grounds, to the source.

Before looking at the remaining characteristics, some of which will appear on closer inspection to belong to the above list, we may note that our source appears to be at least as pure as Bultmann's SQ and EQ: in all three cases, as it happens, thirty-two of the characteristics (not the *same* thirty-two in each case) are wholly lacking in the source. In fact, our score is somewhat higher than Bultmann's, on two counts: (1) When the *bulk* of our source compared to his SQ and EQ is taken into account, our figures prove to be better. It is a fact that the longer a source, the greater is the chance that it will show stylistic blurring with the rest of the gospel. Thus, when his two sources are taken together (what in both size and content is roughly equivalent to our source), the number of Ruckstuhl's characteristics not found in the combined source drops to *twenty-four* (or 48%), for some of those missing in one appear in the other, and *vice versa*. (2) If the *quality* of the characteristics, according to Ruckstuhl's ranking, is considered, our source again scores higher than either of Bultmann's. That is, a greater proportion (*viz.* 72%) of the thirty-two we list is found *in the first and second groups* than is the case for his two sources (59 and 66%, respectively).

But these comparisons are inexact, for they are made on a relatively superficial application of the tests to our source. In fact we must adjust the data in two ways. First of all, three of Ruckstuhl's characteristics are *imperfectly defined* and on closer inspection belong to the above list:

38. While the relatively rare word ἑλκύειν (5 / 1) is surprisingly frequent in Jn, it is used there in two ways—literal (dragging a person or a net, drawing a sword) and metaphoric (attracting a person). Only the latter usage occurs in Johannine passages (twice), and it is found nowhere else in the NT.[1] The rest of the instances in Jn are found in the source. Thus there appear to be not one but two usages here, one characteristic of John:

38*a*. Metaphoric ἑλκύειν: 2 / 0[2]

and the other characteristic of the *source*:

---

[1] The variant form, ἕλκειν, occurs twice in the NT, and in both cases in the literal sense.　　[2] 6: 44, 12: 32.

38 *b*. Literal ἑλκύειν: 3 / 1 / 3.¹

39. A similar case is that of ὀψάριον (5 / 0). As we have noted (above, p. 93 n. 2), it appears in the source always in the plural; in Johannine (or post-Johannine) passages, in the collective singular. Thus:

39 *a*. ὀψάριον (collective): 2 / 0.²

39 *b*. ὀψάρια: 3 / 0 / 3.³

Each of these double characteristics must therefore be counted as two;⁴ due to their relative infrequency they are not of great value, but they can hold their own in Ruckstuhl's third rank.

45. In the case of partitive ἐκ (31 + 3 / 26 + 3),⁵ we have a far more telling state of affairs. On the basis of the frequency in the rest of the NT, Ruckstuhl puts this characteristic almost at the end of his list. But the usage is not defined precisely enough by him and Schweizer.

By far the most common use of partitive ἐκ in Jn is that after τις or τινές (fourteen or fifteen times),⁶ πολλοί (seven),⁷ and οὐδείς (four).⁸ This usage appears only once in the synoptics (Lk 11: 15), and *never* in our source. Thus:

45 *a*. τις (πολλοί, οὐδείς) ἐκ: 25(26) / [1] / 0.⁹

Schweizer apparently includes in his instances of partitive ἐκ its use with a noun, usually meaning 'from among'. This is fairly common in the synoptics, and in Jn appears *only* in passages from the source:

45 *b*. Noun + ἐκ ('from among'): 4(6) / [8] / 4(6).¹⁰

¹ 18: 10, 21: 6, 11. For explanation of this formula, see above, p. 205 n. 3.
² 21: 9, 13.   ³ 6: 9, 11, 21: 10.
⁴ As Ruckstuhl frequently does: *cf.* nos. 1 and 2; 3 and 47; 15, 18, and 49; 45 and 46.
⁵ These are Schweizer's figures; it is not clear what they include.
⁶ 6: 64, 7: 25, 44, 48, 48, 9: 16, 11: 37, 46, 49, 12: 20; also to be included are instances where the pronoun is only implied, an especially striking usage: (1: 24), 6: 39, 7: 40, 9: 40, 16: 17.
⁷ 4: 39, 6: 50, 7: 31, 10: 20, 11: 19, 45, 12: 42.
⁸ 7: 19, 16: 5, 17: 12, 18: 9.
⁹ For the instances in Jn, see the preceding three notes. Here, and in what follows, I have not cited any instances in the Johannine epistles. – Thus defined this usage is clearly of much greater validity than its place in Ruckstuhl's list suggests.
¹⁰ 3: 1, 4: 7, 6: (11), 13, 18: 3, (3). The instance in 6: 11 is good if what follows (ὅσον ἤθελον) is to be taken substantively.

To this we might add the use of ἐκ after a noun with a verb of making—three times in Jn, all from the source, once only in the synoptics (Mt 27: 29):

45 c. Noun + ἐκ ('made of'): 3 / [1] / 3.[1]

Finally there is the use of partitive ἐκ with a numeral (εἷς or δύο). Because it is common in the synoptic gospels (at least 15 times), Schweizer has eliminated it. But the distribution of its use in Jn is striking. Of the thirteen or fourteen instances in the gospel, all but two are probably found in the source,[2] and the two Johannine instances (7: 50, 20: 24) are both in passages which patently imitate the language of the source (at 3: 1, 6: 70 f., respectively). Thus we may enumerate, but because of the slight blurring it shows, not add it to the present list:

45 d. εἷς (δύο) ἐκ: 13(14) / [15+] / 11(12).

The list of usages where no blurring occurs as between strata may therefore be extended from thirty-two to thirty-nine (by the addition of nos. 38 a, 38 b, 39 a, 39 b, 45 a, 45 b, 45 c; most of these are pre-Johannine characteristics which John does not imitate). The proportion to the total is then 39:54 (the latter figure representing Ruckstuhl's fifty plus our additions: 38 b, 39 b, 45 b, 45 c). But this ratio must be altered in a second way, since some of the remaining characteristics appear to be *invalid*.

In five cases, all but one of them in Ruckstuhl's third (*i.e.* least valid) category, while the frequency of the characteristic in Jn is clearly out of proportion to the gospel's length in comparison with the rest of the NT, the usage is found often enough outside the Johannine writings to account for a few instances in the source:

17. The independent (*i.e.* non-attributive) use of singular ἐκεῖνος ('he' or 'she')—44 + 6 / 11 / (4)—is only very briefly defined by Schweizer and Ruckstuhl, so that it is not clear exactly what it includes, or what are the 'resumptive' (*wiederaufnehmend*) instances excluded. In any case, I find at most four instances in the source.[3] In view of the occurrences in the rest of the NT and the ease with which this usage could simply be

---

[1] 2: 15, 9: 6, 19: 2.

[2] 1: 35, 40, 6: 8, 70, 71, 12: 2, (4), 13: 21, 18: 17, 25, 26, 21: 2. In two of these instances (18: 17, 25—*cf.* Lk 22: 58) εἷς only implied. The expression εἷς τις ἐκ (11: 49) is unique in the NT; does it represent John's combination of his usage with that of his source?

[3] 4: 25, 18: 17, 25, 20: 16.

inserted by John into pre-Johannine material, these instances are hardly significant.

37. πάλιν + δεύτερος: 2 / 2 / (1). The instances in Jn are hardly enough, in view of the two other NT occurrences, to identify this as a Johannine characteristic. Ruckstuhl's rule of multiplying all instances in Jn by 8.5, due to the gospel's size relative to the rest of the NT, is invalid when a usage occurs only once or twice. It is to be noted, in any case, that the instance in the source (4: 54) is doubtful.

42. πιστεύειν εἰς: 36 + 3 / 8(9) / 1(2).[1]

48. ἐντεῦθεν: 5 / 6 / 3.[2]

50. πιάζειν: 8 / 4 / 2.[3]

A sixth invalid characteristic is:

49. ὥρα ἐν ᾗ : 3 / 0 / 1.[4] It is surely no more than accident that this usage does not appear again in the NT, for the analogous expression is found with καιρός, χρόνος, and ἡμέρα. While ὥρα is especially common in Jn (see above, nos. 15 and 18), it is common enough in the NT, and if the usage ὥρα ἵνα (ὅτε) is taken to be idiomatic of John, this phrase, which is the only other way of expressing the by no means unusual phrase 'the hour when', can hardly be also.

With the omission of these six characteristics, the ratio can thus now be corrected to 39: 48. This means that no less than 81% of the valid characteristics occur in Jn without blurring, that is, either wholly in Johannine passages (as in most cases) or wholly in the source.

Such a result is hardly negligible. It is all the more striking in view of the fact that the blurring of the remaining nine characteristics is in every case explicable as the result of John's having either (a) imitated or (b) redacted the source.

(a) Although John's style is largely his own, he would not have been immune to occasionally imitating, whether consciously or not, the idioms of the source which he made the nucleus of his own gospel and which clearly influenced him in a fundamental way. It is likely, then, in those cases where most of

---

[1] 2: 11, (11: 45).

[2] 2: 16, 14: 31, 19: 18; in the latter verse, the word appears twice, but the double use ('on either side') comprises a single idiom.

[3] 21: 3, 10. It is perhaps significant that here the word means 'catch' (of fish; cf. Rev. 19: 20), but in the Johannine instances always 'arrest'.

[4] 4: 52.

the instances of a characteristic are found in the source, with only one or two appearing in Johannine passages, that the usage is pre-Johannine in origin.

(*b*) It is evident from our source analysis that, apart from adding great blocks of supplementary material, John redacted his source chiefly by interjecting brief comments into it. Occasionally this results in a radically altered, even rearranged, passage, but seldom did he actually reword the material before him (ch. 13 being the only notable exception). Most often the insertions he makes are whole verses or self-contained phrases, and in the nature of things only insertions of this size would have been evident in the course of the source analysis. But it is entirely possible that he has also added single words or part phrases, typical of his own style, in the course of his redaction, where he can do so without doing violence to the source. It is noteworthy, then, in every one of those remaining characteristics where imitation does not seem likely, that the usage in question could have been introduced simply by a brief insertion.

The characteristics which belong in these two categories are as follows:

1. τότε οὖν: 4 / 0 / 2.[1] This is only a special case of the following characteristic. Like the single word οὖν it is readily inserted,[2] and it appears in the source in both cases at a seam.

2. οὖν-*historicum*: 146 / 8 / 24(30). There are two problems here: the wide textual variation in Jn as to parataxis and the difficulty in identifying historical (*vs.* consecutive) uses of οὖν. I cite Ruckstuhl's figures for the gospel as a whole, but do not find quite so many occurrences. Smith, *Concordance*, gives 130 instances where (according to KJV) the particle is translated neither 'therefore' nor 'so', but even in some of these it is clearly not used historically.[3] In any case, the usage appears at least twenty-four times in the source, usually at a seam.[4] The ease with which it could have been inserted by John in the process of adapting material from his source is obvious.

4. Ἱεροσόλυμα with article: 3(4) / 0 / 2(3).[5] In Johannine

---

[1] 19: 1, 16.   [2] τότε by itself does not appear in the source.
[3] At least the following: 1: 21, 25, 4: 5, 28, 6: 62, 11: 41, 47, 53, 13: 14, 18: 3, 12, 16, 19: 29.
[4] 2: 18, ?4: 9, 6: 5, 11, 14, (67), 11: 17, 20, 32, 12: 1, 2, 3, 7, (13: 27), 18: 10, 11, 17, (19), 27, 28, 40, 19: 23, (40), 20: 10, 11, 19, 20, 30, 21: (5), 7.
[5] 5: 2, 11: 18; possibly also 11: 19 before John's alteration.

passages the anarthrous noun appears eight or nine times, and only at 2: 23 (and possibly 10: 22) with the article, presumably in imitation of the source.

6. Asyndeton: 39 / 5 / 15(16). Here there is even greater textual variation than in no. 2 (above); of the fifteen or so cases I find in the source (using Nestle),[1] more than half are textually uncertain, though the tendency of scribes is probably to add rather than remove a conjunction. If this usage is characteristic of John, he may have imposed it on his source by *omitting* pre-Johannine particles. On the other hand, given the frequency of asyndeton in passages from the source, it may be a pre-Johannine trait which he has imitated.

9. Noun used as attributive: 8(10) / [1] / 1.[2] Since data are not available outside Jn except for the synoptics, one instance in the source is perhaps not out of the question. But John can simply have inserted the second noun in 18: 17.

16. ἀπεκρίθη καὶ εἶπεν (λέγει): 30 / [2(3)] / 5. Here also there is considerable variation among the MSS.[3] Proceeding nevertheless on the basis of Nestle's text, I find five instances of the full phrase in the source.[4] The evangelist has either inserted it there[5] or possibly, in view of the phrase's occasional appearance in the synoptics, found it in the source and himself widely imitated it elsewhere.

24. Σίμων Πέτρος: 17 / 2(3) / 9(10).[6] This usage, in place of Πέτρος alone, is easily imitated; on the other hand, Σίμων could readily be John's insertion.

35. ἀνθρακιά: 2 / 0 / 1. This is hardly a valid criterion: the

---

[1] 1: 40, 41, 42, 45, 47, 4: 6*c*, 7, 30, 11: 44, 44, 19: 29, 20: 18, 21: 3, 3, 3, (12).

[2] 18: 17. The usage is possibly found also in 18: 1, but being in the genitive case there, the second noun is probably a genitive in its own right: *the brook of the Kidron* [*Valley*]. The Johannine instances are: 2: 23, 6: 4, 27, 7: 2, 8: 44, 11: 13, 13: 1, (14: 26, 15: 26).

[3] Almost half of the instances in Nestle's text lack the second verb, or give the participial form, in some MSS; on the other hand, of forty-six occurrences of ἀπεκρίθη alone, more than half have the parallel verb in some MSS.

[4] 1: 48, 50, 2: 18, 19, 4: 17.

[5] As is not the case in the synoptic usage (ἀποκριθεὶς εἶπεν [λέγει]), the single phrase can be changed into the double one simply by the addition of a second indicative.

[6] 1: 40, 6: 8, (68), 18: 10, 15, 20: 2, 21: 2, 3, 7*b*, 11.

word (or rather the thing) is inherently unusual. If not co-incidence, the instance in 21: 9 may be an imitation, by John or a later editor, of the source at 18: 18.

43. μετὰ τοῦτο: 4 / 1 / (2).[1] Like μετὰ ταῦτα this usage may be a Johannine insertion (see above, on 6: 1). On the other hand, it is not unique to Jn, and so may have been imitated by him in 11: 7, 11.

This concludes Ruckstuhl's list of characteristics. There is some question whether those Johannine usages which could readily have been inserted into pre-Johannine passages (as many could not) can be considered valid characteristics, for such minor retouching is entirely to be expected. And it is not in the least surprising that some of the characteristics which appear to have a pre-Johannine origin have been adopted by John into his own style. What is striking is not that there is blurring of style, but that there is so little of it.

Far from demolishing our reconstruction, then, the stylistic tests would seem in the main to have verified it, and to suggest that while it may contain errors of detail,[2] as reconstructed it is relatively pure.

2. THE SOURCE'S STYLE

By its nature a method such as that of Schweizer and Ruckstuhl will tend to identify Johannine characteristics rather than pre-Johannine ones. What, then, can we say about the style of the source? Is it stylistically 'neutral' as Ruckstuhl holds it must be? If not, does its style pervade the whole of the source we have reconstructed?

In the first place, it is not surprising, in view of the source's relation to synoptic tradition, that its style is at points far closer to the other gospels than is John's. Thus, a number of words, very common in the NT, particularly in the synoptics, and rare in Jn are found there *only in the source*:

ἕτερος: 1 / 101 / 1—19: 37.

---

[1] (2: 12, 19: 28).

[2] The tests, in fact, can be used to make minor corrections in the source. Those characteristics which seem clearly to have been inserted by John (*viz.* τότε οὖν, οὖν-*historicum*) can be removed from the source, and others where insertion is possible (nos. 9, 16, 24, 43) treated as doubtful.

ἐνώπιον:¹ 1 / 96 / 1—20: 30.
ἄρχεσθαι ποιεῖν τι: 1 / 77 / 1—13: 5.
ὑπό with accusative: 1 / 46 / 1—1: 48.
ἰσχύειν: 1 / 28 / 1—21: 6.
σύν: 3 / 127 / 3[4]—[11: 33], 12: 2, 18: 1, 21: 3.
ἕκαστος: 3 / 82 / 3—6: 7, 16: 32b, 19: 23.
εὐθέως:² 3 / 77 / 3—5: 9, 6: 21, 18: 27.
Adverbial πρῶτον:³ 3 / [24] / 3—1: 41, 2: 10, 18: 13.

The source is more akin to synoptic style than Johannine in many other ways as well, for example:

Infrequency of the word 'Ιουδαῖος: 71 / [11 + 5] / 4(5)—18: (12), 33, 39, 19: 3, 19.

Frequency of the genitive absolute.⁴

Absence of the expression λέγειν πρός τινα.⁵

Given the kinship of the source to the synoptics, then, and its size,⁶ it is all the more striking that lists of words and usages characteristic of the source can be drawn up.

There are first of all a few words which are lacking or rare in the NT apart from Jn and which are there confined wholly to the source:

κολυμβήθρα: 3 / 0 / 3—5: 2, 7, 9: 7.
ὑδρία: 3 / 0 / 3—2: 6, 7, 4: 28.
Μεσσίας: 2 / 0 / 2—1: 41, 4: 25.
κῆπος: 3 / 1 / 3—18: 1, 26, 19: 41.
ῥάπισμα: 2 / 1 / 2—18: 22, 19: 3.
ἀπό ('off', of distance): 2 / 1 / 2—11: 18, 21: 8.
πρός with dative: 4 / 3 / 4—18: 16, 20: 11, 12, 12.

¹ ἔμπροσθεν is found five times in Jn, always Johannine (note especially 12: 37, in contrast to 20: 30), and possibly once in the source (1: 27), where, however, it has a quite different meaning (*prior*).

² *Versus* εὐθύς, three times in Jn, always Johannine.

³ With the article, the adverb is found only in Jn (three times), in every case in Johannine passages.

⁴ Of the sixteen or so occurrences in Jn, more than half stand in the source, a frequency typical of the synoptics (139 times in all) but atypical of the rest of Jn (which by my estimate is roughly four times as long as the source). For a list of occurrences, see Schweizer, 98 n. 120.

⁵ Unknown to Mk and Mt, though frequent in Lk. None of the eleven instances in Jn occurs in the source, where λέγειν with the dative is very common.   ⁶ See above, n. 4.

κραυγάζειν:[1] 6 / 3 / 5(6)—11: 43, 12: 13, 18: 40, 19: 6, ? 12, 15.[2]

To these we can add those terms in Ruckstuhl's list which we have attributed to the source:

4. Ἱεροσόλυμα with article: 3(4) / 0 / 2(3).
38b. ἑλκύειν (lit.): 3 / 1 / 3.
39b. ὀψάρια: 3 / 0 / 3.
45c. Noun + ἐκ ('made of'): 3 / [1] / 3.
50. πιάζειν ('catch'): 2 / 1 / 2.

Some of the lexical terms in these lists are open to the criticism of being fortuitous—found in the source only by virtue of the subject matter peculiar to it. It is noteworthy, however, that all of them appear in more than one context in the source. In any case, it is perhaps more appropriate to look for expressions (phrases and syntactic idioms) which, while not always peculiar to the source in the NT, are characteristic of it and are largely if not wholly absent from the rest of Jn:[3]

(a) Introductory or resumptive ἦν (δέ) (τις): 11 / 7 + 2[4] / 10— 2: 6, 3: 1, 4: 6, 46, 5: 5, 6: 10, 11: 1, 38, *12: 20*, 19: 41, 21: 2.

(b) Parenthetical or explanatory ἦν (δέ): 11: 2, 18, 18: 10, 13, *14*, 28, 40, 19: 14, 19, 23.[5]

(c) ὡς with numeral: 8 / 10 / 7(8)—1: 39, 4: 6, 6: 10, 19, 11: 18, 19: 14, (39), 21: 8.

(d) Singular verb with double subject (often αὐτὸς καὶ...): 1: 35, 45, 2: 2, 12, 4: *12*, 53, 18: 1b, 15, etc.

(e) οὖν after a command: 1: 39, ?4: 30, 6: 10, (13), 9: 7, 11: 41, 21: 6.[6]

(f) εἷς (δύο) ἐκ: 12(13) / [15+] / 10(11) [= 45d, above].

(g) Noun + ἐκ ('from among'): 4(6) / [8] / 4(6) [= 45b, above].

---

[1] Versus κράζειν, four times in Jn, always Johannine.

[2] To this list should probably be added ἀντλεῖν: 4 / 0 / 2—2: 8, 4: 7 (imitated by John in 2: 9, 4: 15, respectively).

[3] Johannine instances are cited in *italics*.

[4] Not included here are instances of καὶ ἦν and ἦν with participle, both quite frequent in the synoptic gospels; cf. 3: 23 (SQ).

[5] John uses a similar construction five times, always of a Jewish holiday: 5: 9, 6: 4, 7: 2, 9: 14, 11: 55.

[6] And, in general, excessive use of consecutive οὖν.

(*h*) ῥαββί(-ουνί) addressed to Jesus: 9 / 5 + 1 / 4(5)—1: 38, 49, *3: 2, 26, 4: 31*, (6: 25), 9: 2, *11: 8*, 20: 16.

(*i*) 'Come and see': 1: 39, 46, 4: 29, 11: 34.

(*j*) ἔχειν with expression of time: 4 / 0 / 3—5: 5, 6, *8: 57*, 11: 17; *cf.* κομψότερον ἔσχεν (4: 52).[1]

(*k*) ὄνομα αὐτῷ: 3 / 5(7) / 3—1: 6, 3: 1, 18: 10.

This list could doubtless be extended, but enough has been said to answer any charge that our source is stylistically 'colourless'. A far more important consequence of the lists we have drawn up, however, is their implication for the source's *integrity*. We have held in abeyance until now the question whether all the pre-Johannine material uncovered belonged to a single source, particularly whether the signs source ended with a passion narrative. It is not possible, of course, to prove the stylistic unity of any document, and we cannot be sure that at every point where we have found a *Vorlage* we are in touch with a single source. But it is clear from even a quick perusal of the characteristics we have listed above that they are not confined to one part of the source, nor is it possible to group them into two or more substrata. On closer inspection it appears that, with one exception,[2] every pericope in the source contains at least one instance of the usages characteristic of the source. This fact is all the more startling when it is recalled how different the original milieu of the passion account, for example, must have been from that of the signs stories, or what a diversity of form-critical backgrounds the various miracles display. What all this means is that we have uncovered, however inexactly in detail, a pre-Johannine stratum which had already a distinctive *literary* character imposed upon it.[3]

[1] Two Johannine instances (9: 21, 23) are reminiscent of the source.

[2] Namely 1: 19–34. It may be that its presence in the source is thereby called in question. But it should be noted that it is one of the shortest of the source's pericopes (the equivalent of twelve lines in Nestle, more than half of *vv.* 19–34 being Johannine additions), and also that its connection with what originally preceded (1: 6 f.) and followed (35–50), both passages showing characteristics of the source, is very clear.–The pre-Johannine fragments 11: 47*a*, 53*b* also lack any of the characteristics, but given their bulk (two and a half lines in Nestle) this is hardly surprising.

[3] Bultmann's distinction between SQ and the other narrative sources which he lumps together as EQ, is understandably cautious, but it is probably based on Faure's contention that chs. 1–12 have a different style

(and thus a different source underlying them) than chs. 13–20. Schweizer (100) disproved this by identifying a style common to both halves of the gospel, and Smend earlier questioned whether the formula for OT citations that on the whole distinguishes the first twelve chapters was due to a different source, suggesting instead that the change that occurs at 12: 37 is a function of John's theological schema. On the basis of our reconstruction, we can see that in fact John derived both of his principal citation formulae from the source (contrast ?1: 23 and 12: 14, on one hand, with 19: 24, 28, 36, on the other), which thus displays just the variety in this regard found in the synoptics.

PART FIVE
THE CHARACTER OF THE SOURCE

THE CHARACTER OF THE SOURCE

What over-all appraisal can be made of our source, hypo-thetical and perhaps incomplete as it may be?

First of all we can say that it was a *gospel*. The question what constitutes a gospel is a difficult one, yet in the case of the synoptics it is probably correct to say that their sources, as usually defined, differ from them precisely in that they are not strictly gospels.[1] By contrast, it would be hard to find a definition of the *Gattung* gospel that included Jn and the synoptics but excluded our source.[2] It begins, like the canonical gospels, with an account of the *Baptist* as a prelude to the *ministry of Jesus*. That ministry, carried on in the presence of *disciples*, involves the *miraculous deeds* of Jesus in *Galilee and Judea*, seen as the works of the *Messiah*. Above all it culminates in the story of Jesus' *death and resurrection*. All of this is presented as gospel, that is as kerygma to be *believed*, fulfilling the *scriptures*. Where it is deficient, by comparison with the canonical gospels (even Mark's), is in the teaching of Jesus; to this extent it is a rudi-mentary gospel, but a gospel nevertheless.[3] And it influenced

---

[1] This is not true of *Ur-Markus* or Proto-Luke, if such existed; our source appears to be a *Grundevangelium* very much like those sometimes postulated for Mk and Lk.—See the following note, on Köster.

[2] F. F. Bruce, 'When is a gospel not a gospel?', *BJRL* 45 (1963), 319–39, has stated five criteria, over against some of which our source is probably deficient, but they are based on a particular interpretation of Christian salvation (one explicitly identifying the Pauline view of grace). If SQ altogether lacks a scheme of salvation, such as that found in Jn, so also does Mk.—H. Köster, 'One Jesus and four primitive gospels', *HTR* 61 (1968), 203–47, criticizes the making of too sharp a distinction between the canonical gospels on the one hand and both their sources and the apocryphal 'gospels' on the other. He is right in doing so, but I take it he would allow to stand the classic definition of a gospel in the strict sense (proclamation of Jesus as crucified and risen Lord). As we have reconstructed SQ, with its inclusion of a passion narrative, and in contrast to earlier discussion of a signs source (see Köster, 230–2), it is clearly a gospel in the *narrower* sense.

[3] The tradition of the teaching of Jesus (*i.e.* the continuation of his proclamation of the Kingdom) is not strictly essential to the church's proclamation *about* Jesus. While it could be put to work in the service of that kerygma, it apparently had a separate existence from 'the gospel', as is clear both from Paul's letters and the existence of Q, and its inclusion in

John as to both the shape and content of his gospel, every bit as much as Mk (*vs.* Q) influenced Matthew and Luke.

That the source is more than a random collection of materials about Jesus is evident not only from its selectiveness (20: 31) but especially from its *literary structure*. Each episode is connected to what precedes and follows by a carefully conceived itinerary of Jesus. At the centre is the stylized series of seven miracles. These divide into two groups, four in Galilee and three in Judea. Introducing each group is a narrative (set in Samaria?) in which an unlikely person (sceptical Nathanael, the Samaritan woman) encounters Jesus and, in the course of a conversation with him, believes. What precedes the ministry of signs is patterned also: the three denials by the Baptist,[1] the chain-reaction of witness. If the passion narrative is not so evidently structured, that is only because it is the most traditional and extensive of the units from which the source is made. But it begins, as does the series of signs, with a double confession of Jesus (1: 49, 12: 13; *cf.* 20: 31), and it may not be accidental that the Jerusalem period (*i.e.* the last three signs together with the passion) begins and ends with accounts of resurrection (of Lazarus and of Jesus, respectively), accounts which appear to be in contrast to each other.[2] Finally the source opens and closes with balanced, two-sentence editorial units (1: 6 f., 20: 30 f.).[3] While not all of these structural elements are necessarily deliberate on the author's part, they show the source to be a far from haphazard document.

the gospel form is in one sense a *tour de force*. See J. M. Robinson, 'The problem of history in Mark, reconsidered', *Union Seminary Quarterly Review* 20 (1964/5), 135–8. – *That* Jesus taught was apparently asserted in the source (18: 20), in accordance with his role as Mosaic prophet (see below), but presumably there was no interest in the content of that teaching. It is his deeds (including the act of teaching), not his words, that are presented as kerygmatic.

[1] Balancing, perhaps, the three denials of Peter at the end of the gospel.

[2] So Trudinger, 'Lazarus Motif', 30, noting how the details of the duration of death, the moving of the stone, and the graveclothes differ in the two stories. This is markedly distinct from John's desire to make the Lazarus story *prefigure* the resurrection of Jesus.

[3] Other structural details could perhaps be cited, *e.g.* the fact that the Galilean group of signs begins with a wine- and ends with a bread-miracle (Schnackenburg, 53). Also that it is separated from the Judean group by a christophany as a kind of coda (6: 16 ff.).

Was the source written or oral, and did John only quote it from memory? The former question involves a distinction which was presumably of far less moment in the ancient world than it is today. Nevertheless it is clear from 20: 30 f. that SQ was 'written' and referred to itself as a 'book'. And because John's reproduction of it is evidently more faithful and detailed than Matthew's and Luke's use of Mk, we can probably say that John had the source before him when he wrote.

I. ORIGIN AND PURPOSE

If the question of provenance is difficult in the case of an extant gospel, it is more so for our hypothetical one. Nevertheless it is a safe assertion that the source sprang from a *Jewish-Christian* milieu. This judgment is made first of all on the basis of its linguistic character. Its quite unstilted Greek may suggest that it is not a translation of a Semitic original, but in any case its author and audience are no less Jewish for being Greek-speaking. They seem in fact to have been bilingual: the text is interspersed with (i) Aramaic words which the author (unlike John) felt it unnecessary to translate;[1] (ii) Greek words to which the *Semitic* equivalent is added;[2] and (iii) certain words used interchangeably in Greek and Aramaic.[3]

The Jewishness of the source is borne out also by the lack of concern with either the Gentile question or polemic against Torah. While this can be argued only from silence, in the latter case it is noteworthy that when John wishes, even in his unhistorical way, to take up the Sabbath question, he cannot find it in his source but must quite artificially introduce it at points where the source breaks off (5: 9b, 9: 14).

Similarly, there is no deliberate use of the OT, such as one finds either in the Gentile gospels of Mk and Lk or in Mt's

---

[1] In addition to the many place-names which are peculiar simply to the source's tradition, note the striking use of Μεσσίας (only here in NT) and Κηφᾶς (elsewhere only in Paul). – All of the 'explanations for Gentile readers', interspersed throughout the gospel, are Johannine.

[2] On the use of Ἑβραϊστί, see above on 5: 2. When both Greek and Semitic names are given, the Greek is usually given first (*e.g.* 19: 13, 17), with which contrast John's regular use and Mk 15: 22. An exception may be personal names (4: 25, 21: 2).

[3] *E.g.* Μεσσίας/χριστός, ῥαββ[ουν]ί/κύριος/διδάσκαλος.

elaborately Jewish proof-texting; rather the Jewish scriptures are simply taken for granted (*cf.* 4: 5 f.). The exception is of course the passion account, but there an apologetic motive is at work (see below).

To place the *background* of the source precisely in the development of first-century Christian thought is probably impossible, but we may perhaps find an analogy in the situation Paul faced in 2 Cor. 10–13, where he opposes 'pseudo-apostles' (11: 13) who relied on (their own?) 'signs and wonders and mighty works', which Paul was forced to emulate (12: 12; *cf.* 1 Cor. 12: 9 f., also Mk 13: 22, Mt 7: 22). These have been identified as non-gnostic Hellenist-Jewish Christians who presented the deeds of Jesus as those of a θεῖος ἀνήρ (*cf.* Acts 2: 22) and as faith-healers strove to achieve union with him through imitation. The suggestion is made that the miracle tradition in Mk and Jn stems from such a school of thought.[1] Paul's incidental polemic in 1 Cor. against the Jews who 'seek signs' (1: 22), if it applies to Jewish *Christians*, may slightly reinforce this picture, for it seems to have nothing to do with the deviation Paul attacks in 1 Cor. generally[2] but applies instead simply to those whose interpretation of the miracles of Jesus is mistaken. While both these hints are voiced to the church in Corinth, the incipient heresy they allude to has no necessary attachment to that place.[3] And if John saw a danger of this sort in his own church, it would partially explain his desire to reinterpret the data its gospel contained.

As to the question of the source's *place of origin*, it can be

---

[1] H. Köster, 'Häretiker im Urchristentum', *RGG*, 3rd ed. III (1959), 17–21; D. Georgi, *Die Gegner des Paulus im 2. Korintherbrief: Studien zur religiösen Propaganda in der Spätantike* (Neukirchen–Vluyn, 1964), esp. 282–92; J. M. Robinson, 'Kerygma and history', 135–41; also *Kerygma und historischer Jesus* (2nd ed.; Zürich, 1967), 68–71.–The element of *imitation* does not fit our source very well, for unlike the synoptics it shows no interest in faith as a component of healing (rather only in that which *results* from the miracles), and there is no suggestion that Jesus' miracles are meant to be repeated. See further below, p. 229 n. 1.

[2] In fact, J. M. Robinson, 'Basic shifts in German theology', *Interpretation* 16 (1962), 82–6, considers traditions like those in Q, which contains the strongest polemic *against* signs in the synoptics, a source of the Corinthian heresy.

[3] The 'super-apostles' of 2 Cor. 11–12 seem to be interlopers, and the 'Jews' of 1 Cor. 1 could have been encountered by Paul anywhere.

pointed out that the evidence which suggests to some a Syrian rather than an Asian provenance for the gospel as a whole[1] belongs largely to the source. There obviously are close contacts with Palestinian tradition. But whatever its roots, the Greek-speaking community which used the source as a gospel could have existed in almost any part of the Hellenistic world.

Even less can be said of the source's *date*. Depending on that given to Jn and judgment as to the character (whether 'primitive' or 'developed') of the tradition embodied in the source (see below, sec. 2), a date either before or after the Jewish War is possible. If there are contacts with a movement contemporary with Paul (see above), they would perhaps argue for the earlier period. And there may be indications of a date earlier than 70 in 5: 2 (note the present tenses) and the form of 2: 19.[2] But these point only to a relatively early origin of the tradition in question, and say nothing as to the date of their inclusion either in the source or the extant gospel. Similarly the relative lack of dominical sayings, the apparent independence of any of the synoptics in their finished form (see below), and the utter absence of eschatology (see sec. 3) are undoubtedly functions of the source's historical setting, but do not help us much in identifying it.

We are on firmer ground as to the *intent* of the source, for in 20: 30 f. (*cf*. 1: 7*c*) the author states his purpose explicitly. The gospel is a missionary tract with a single end, to show (presumably to the potential Jewish convert) that Jesus is the Messiah. The suggestion of missionary terminology in 4: 53 is consonant with this end, as is the exemplary way the witnesses to most of the signs 'believe in him'. It is, among other things, this unifying purpose that differentiates the source from a mere collection of stories. (The question how the various contents of the source serve this end is taken up in sec. 3, below.)

---

[1] *Cf*. Lightfoot, *Commentary*, 5 f., following T. W. Manson.

[2] W. Gericke, 'Zur Entstehung des Johannes-Evangeliums', *TL* 90 (1965), 810 f. In the latter case he points out how the temple saying differs from its synoptic counterparts, where the form is not conditional ('Destroy this temple and I will...') but predictive ('I will destroy this temple and...'). On the other hand, as we have seen, the saying probably has a symbolic meaning already in the source, pointing to the resurrection; is this primitive or developed?

2. RELATION TO THE SYNOPTIC GOSPELS
AND HISTORICAL VALUE

Enough has been said, in the course of pts. I–III, to indicate in detail how close our source, unique as it is, stands to the synoptic tradition. And in pt. IV we saw that its linguistic style is both very similar to that of the synoptics and lacking in the notable departures from the synoptic diction found in the Johannine strata. In fact, one might loosely define the source as the body of synoptic and synoptic-like material in the fourth gospel, for the only extensive contact John had with synoptic tradition appears to have been through the source.

It seems to me quite unlikely that the author of the source knew any of the synoptics in their canonical form. The extensive evidence which discourages the theory of John's direct dependence on one or more of them applies equally well to him. It is instead a case of parallel traditions. Whether the source had literary contact with any of the synoptic *sources* it would be impossible to say; there is some evidence of close contact with the material peculiar to Lk, but not necessarily in a literary form.

The 'synoptic problem' is still an open one. There is increasing evidence of a complex and quite fluid oral tradition existing alongside the literary deposits which that tradition produced from time to time. If our reconstruction has any validity, it may contribute to this question both by solving the heretofore paralysing issue of John's dependence on the synoptics and by isolating (in the form of the source) another distinct form of that tradition.[1]

At the outset we chose to leave aside all questions of historicity in isolating the pre-Johannine stratum in the gospel, since so much Johannine research has been distorted by the failure to insist that such a concern has its legitimate place only after the literary task is complete. But now that the analysis has been made, it is valid to raise the question. Does John's tradition,

---

[1] Synoptic studies have too long been isolated from the data to be found in Jn, and the reappearance recently of synopses which present that data, yet do not seek to harmonize it, is a necessary and welcome development. – For a comparison of the *miracle* stories in the source with their synoptic counterparts, see Fuller, 90–2; also Brown, *Essays*, 168–91.

specifically that contained in his major narrative source, embody early or accurate data for the historian, especially since it appears to be independent of the synoptics as we have them?

Issues beyond the scope of this study are involved in the answer one gives to this question. And while an early date for the source is not impossible, it is by no means certain, nor would it necessarily indicate historical reliability. The source provides, as we saw, new raw material for the historian, and material the more useful for being distinguished from an editorial framework (that of John) which is later and more developed; nevertheless it does not provide us with a short cut through the laborious methods and tentative results of form criticism. Each element of tradition must be examined separately, apart from the question of the date of its literary appearance.

At a few points in the analysis we concluded that a story in the source represented a more primitive form than one or more of its parallels in the synoptics. But on the whole the source shows a relatively developed form of the tradition. This is evident both in its novelistic features and in the heightening of miracle which it displays (cf. on 4: 47, 6: 7, 21, etc.). While we could only guess as to the milieu which gave rise to the source (see above, sec. 1), the possibility that it grew out of a somewhat derived theological climate suggests that, however early it may be in date, it does not represent an unadulterated strain of tradition about Jesus. This is shown in its lack of apparent contact with the teachings of Jesus, and in particular in its seeming ignorance of the (probably dominical) polemic against those who seek signs (Mk 8: 11 f. pars.). Not only are the miracles taken by the author as *proofs* of Jesus' messiahship, but Jesus is represented as voluntarily performing (ποιεῖν) the signs.[1] The outlook of the author is thus apparently separated

---

[1] The few points at which Jesus goes through the motions of refusing to work a sign (2: 4, 4: 48, 7: 6–8) are John's additions. – It might be argued that the tradition of Jesus' refusal to work signs is not early after all but, on the contrary, a late reaction against just such interest in the miracles as is represented by SQ. All of the other evidence takes the form of such a reaction (both Paul and John; cf. also the rejection of miracle-working in Q's version of the temptations—so Robinson, 'Kerygma and history', 140), and none of it makes use of the synoptic logion. But it would be hard to argue that the form of the logion ('this generation') is anything but early.

from that of Jesus in this respect and no doubt in others. With this rather derivative attitude toward the miracles goes a naive view of what in modern terms may be called the relation of an event to its interpretation;[1] the miracles are taken simply as facts, and the possibility (as raised by John in 12: 37 ff.) of their not being seen as demonstrations of Jesus' nature is apparently never faced.

The detailed and fairly reliable knowledge of Palestinian geography shown by the source probably argues for a close connection with the Palestinian church, but does not necessarily demonstrate its historical reliability for the time of Jesus. As is the case with all the gospels, the passion narrative is perhaps freest of the *Tendenz* of the source, but while the tradition it contains is undoubtedly distinct in many details from the synoptic tradition, it is not clear to what extent it is more primitive or reliable.

The reconstruction of the source, then, provides a new, or rather a better focused, corpus of data with which the historian can deal—no negligible contribution—but it is too soon to say in what ways it will contribute to our knowledge of the historical Jesus whose deeds it claims to recount.

3. THEOLOGY

The source, as its conclusion tells us, is frankly and simply *christological*. In contrast to almost ever other early Christian document we possess, its message is not that a new age has dawned, not that salvation is made available in Jesus, not that suffering and sin and death are now destroyed, not that the Spirit is bestowed on men. Unlike the contemporary Jewish apocalyptic it does not even claim that such eschatological happenings are imminent.[2] It affirms simply 'that Jesus is the Christ, the son of God'. He alone possesses the Spirit (1: 33). His miracles are recounted simply as legitimating signs of his messianic status.[3] Even the healings are christological, not soteriological or eschatological. In so far as they impinge

---

[1] Unlike the evangelist, who is profoundly aware of this question.

[2] *Cf.* on 1: 50, p. 200 n. 1 above.

[3] For the question *how* the miracles are a legitimation of Jesus' messiahship, see below.

personally on the reader, they do so only as affording paradigms for belief in Jesus on the basis of signs.[1] The eschatological element so evident in many of the synoptic healings—especially the victory over the demons represented by Jesus' exorcisms— is wholly lacking; it is the power of Jesus as the Messiah, not the cosmic consequences of his appearance, that is everywhere focused on.[2] And there is no suggestion that either of the two resurrection accounts (those of Lazarus and of Jesus) is seen as a conquering of death.

Certainly the whole of the prelude to the signs—the accounts of the Baptist and the conversion of the disciples—is concerned with only one thing, that Jesus is the Messiah. In the case of the passion narrative this emphasis is not so obvious, for un- doubtedly that account got its basic formulation before the author employed it; yet even there it is easy to see how he could find (or insert) in it a fundamentally christological sense, for in virtually every one of the sayings of Jesus contained in it (and only here in the source do we find real sayings) Jesus calls attention to himself.[3] Whereas the synoptic accounts of the passion contain other teaching, only sayings of Jesus explicitly about himself are found here.

The question what led our author to join the passion narrative to his account of the deeds of Jesus, while an important one, since he may have been the first to do so, is probably not fully answerable. Nevertheless it is likely that his motive was an apologetic one, in two senses: his version of the passion account still, as it always had, sought to *justify* the fact that a crucified criminal is held to be Messiah, but at the same time it sought also to *proclaim* that messiahship. It is significant that all of the OT citations in the source are found in the passion narrative,[4]

---

[1] Unlike many of the synoptic healings, there is no suggestion that faith is an ingredient of the healings and so is to be regarded as in itself a virtue. For SQ Jesus is not a faith-healer in the strict sense; it is by his power alone that he performs the miracles. Faith is solely a consequence of the miracles he does.

[2] It is perhaps significant that Jn lacks the term ἐπιτιμᾶν, so important in the exorcisms of the synoptic tradition and probably expressing there the subduing of the power of evil. See H. C. Kee, 'The terminology of Mark's exorcism stories', *NTS* 14 (1967/8), 232–46.

[3] Note the first personal pronoun in every case: 2: 16, 19, 12: 7, ?8, 27, 13: 13, 18, 21, 38, 18: 11, 20, 19: 28, 20: 17.

[4] With the possible exception of 1: 23, which in any case has a plainly christological purpose.

and that the usual formula of citation is 'in order that the scripture might be fulfilled': as the fulfilment of prophecy the crucifixion is both necessary to and the confirmation of Jesus' status. In the long run, the death of Jesus is seen almost as another of his own deeds, for beyond the general suggestion of divine necessity, nowhere is it depicted as God's act—the prodigies of the synoptic accounts (darkness, temple veil rending, earthquake) are missing. At the least Jesus' death is seen as the necessary prelude to his greatest sign, that of the resurrection (*cf.* 20: 30 f.).[1]

The number and variety of the various *titles* ascribed to Jesus suggest that a systematic correlation of them is no more worked out in the source than in Mk. They all have a Semitic background and a generally christological intent—Messiah/Christ, Son of God, Lamb of God, Rabbi/Lord/Teacher, Prophet,[2] God's Chosen One, 'King of the Jews', ?King of Israel, ?Saviour of the World, (Elijah).[3] Undoubtedly the title which is fundamental to all the others is Messiah (20: 31; *cf.* 1: 41, 4: 25, 29); it is this role which the signs are held to demonstrate.

But the question then arises on what basis they do so, for there is surprisingly little direct evidence that the Jewish Messiah was expected to be a worker of miracles.[4] Why do the *signs* prove him to be Messiah? A possible answer is the suggestion that the middle element in the syllogism—Jesus did signs, therefore Jesus is the Messiah—is the assumption that Jesus is the (quasi-messianic) Prophet-like-Moses (*cf.* 4: 19, 6: 14), who as the antitype of Moses would perform a series of wonders. But the identification specifically with Moses is not fully established; the source's OT typology seems to have a more general reference, involving allusions also to figures like Elijah, Elisha, perhaps even Joseph.[5] The kinds of miracles Jesus performs in

---

[1] Nowhere does the source suggest that God raised Jesus or even that he was raised; rather he *must rise* (20: 9). Twice Jesus is subject of the verb ἐγείρειν (elsewhere in the NT only God): he announces that he *will raise* [his body] (2: 19) and we are told that he *raised* Lazarus (12: 1).

[2] *Cf.* 'of whom Moses wrote'. See further below.

[3] 'Of whom the prophets wrote'? See below.

[4] I owe this observation and elements of the following discussion to Prof. J. Louis Martyn.

[5] On the importance of these various figures to the source's picture of Jesus, see below. In the case of Joseph, see above, pt. 1, sec. 1 (on 2: 5).

the source conform exactly to those done by many of the heroes of the OT: healings, raisings, miracles involving food...and no exorcisms.[1] It is these earlier wonder-workers, in the loose sense types of the Messiah, who perhaps provide the key to the source's understanding of the relation between Jesus' miracles and his status. They apparently were regarded among certain Hellenistic Jews as θεῖοι ἄνδρες[2] and so, to one seeking to demonstrate Jesus' messiahship to such Jews, may have suggested applying to him the character of wonder-worker. The tradition of his miracles is older, of course, but there is a difference here from the significance still given them in the synoptics. In the source they are not primarily indices of Jesus as saviour (healing, exorcizing, dealing with hunger, danger, death) but rather demonstrations of his authority.[3]

At the same time, however, they are not sheer prodigies for their own sake; the legendary element is controlled by comparison, for example, with [Mk] 16: 17 f. Thus, although the concept of θεῖος ἀνήρ is useful in attempting to understand the background of the source, it is only a hypothesis, and it must be stressed that for the source Jesus is no mere thaumaturge, only one among many θεῖοι ἄνδρες. He is rather the unique Messiah of Israel. The variety of titles applied to him in no way argues against this. There is in fact an almost exaggerated preoccupation with the *fact* of his messiahship, at the expense of spelling out its nature. The miracles are christological chiefly in this bare sense. On the other hand, they are not mere wonders, to be sure, but signs, pointing beyond themselves to their author.[4]

[1] Prof. Morton Smith has pointed out the absence of OT parallels to the synoptic exorcisms.　　　　　[2] Georgi, *Gegner*, 148.

[3] For this reason, therefore, we find the *Luxuswunder* of 2: 1–11, to use Bauer's phrase (cited by Dinkler, 'Kana-Wunder', 53).

[4] They are of course not signs in the sense that they have the kind of symbolic meaning John gives them (see Schnackenburg, 'Traditionsgeschichte', 65). For this reason it has been suggested that this distinction—between the pre-Johannine and Johannine uses of σημεῖον—can most effectively be made clear by using different words to translate the term, *miracle* for the source and *sign* only for John. There is a good deal to commend such a device, for the source comes nearer than John to viewing the σημεῖα as miraculous deeds pure and simple. But the word *miracle* today has meanings that are not applicable to the source, particularly the elements of *wonder* and the *preternatural*. In the former case, it is noteworthy that fear and amazement, so prominent in the synoptics as responses to Jesus' miracles,

Because of the OT basis for the picture given of Jesus, he always has the quality of *prophet*, most notably in his characteristic performance of the miracle by means of a *command*.[1] Here the parallel is strongest to the Elijah/Elisha tradition. Nowhere is Jesus explicitly identified with either of those earlier prophets, but that the identification is intended is evident in several ways: the Baptist's denial that he is Elijah, implying that Jesus in fact is; the phrase 'of whom the prophets wrote', which probably has at least Mal. 4: 5 in mind; and the parallels in the source both to the diction of 1 and 2 Kings (Jn 4: 50, 6: 9, 9: 7) and to the particular miracles done by Elijah and Elisha (esp. Jn 6 and 11).

Parallels to Moses, while not wholly lacking (*e.g.* with 6: 5, *cf.* Num. 11: 13), are not so clear. Attempts to find exact counterparts in the seven miracles to the ten Egyptian signs done by Moses in Exodus, in so far as they are valid, seem to apply to the evangelist, not his source.[2] The same is true of the related indications of paschal elements in the gospel.[3] If the Johannine date for the crucifixion stems from the source, it had there no soteriological meaning, apparently, but only a christo-

are almost wholly absent from SQ (only 6: 19). While the crowd may ask a question suggesting wonder (4: 29, 6: 25, 9: 8), it is their eventual belief that is ultimately emphasized. Only John adds the detail of explicit amazement (5: 20, 7: 21; *cf.* 4: 48). Similarly the element of the preternatural is a modern concept. To most moderns a deed such as those Jesus is shown doing in the source suggests either the inexplicable or at most the occult; to the ancient, it is an indication of the divine, in short a *sign*. We thus retain this word as appropriate to the source within its own frame of reference.

[1] *Cf.* Schulz, 'Kana', 93 f. For this reason, perhaps, the use of *touch* as a thaumaturgic device, found more than fourteen times in the synoptics, is noticeably absent (except indirectly in 9: 6)—*cf.* ?20: 17. This omission (if it is made by the author of the source and not at an earlier stage in the tradition) obviously does not stem from any avoidance of the thaumaturgic, for such elements remain, but probably in order to show that it is the word, not the action, of Jesus which in the end accomplishes the miracle.

[2] *Cf.* esp. R. H. Smith, 'Exodus typology in the fourth gospel', *JBL* 81 (1962), 329–42; also J. J. Enz, 'The book of Exodus as a literary type for the gospel of John', *JBL* 76 (1957), 208–15.

[3] Wilkens, *passim*; G. Ziener, 'Weisheitsbuch und Johannesevangelium', *Bib* 38 (1957), 396–418, and 39 (1958), 37–60; also 'Johannesevangelium und urchristliche Passafeier', *BZ* n.s. 2 (1958), 267–74. The explicit parallel between the feeding of the multitude and the sign of the manna is Johannine as well: Borgen, 'John 6'; also E. J. Kilmartin, 'Liturgical influence on John 6', *CBQ* 22 (1960), 183–91. See above, p. 61 n. 2.

logical one. Even the phrase 'Lamb of God', while capable of bearing a paschal meaning, does not necessarily do so,[1] and there is no evidence that it did for the author.

By comparison with John, the author of the source took little interest in such questions as the nature and origin of faith.[2] The Baptist bears witness, men hear, and they immediately follow Jesus (1: 37; cf. 1: 7c).[3] Others see Jesus' deeds and believe;[4] for still others simply to read of the signs is to see them (20: 31).[5] Yet faith is not simply to believe *that* Jesus is a wonder-worker; it is to believe that as wonder-worker he is the Messiah, and so to believe *in* him (2: 11, 11: 45), that is, to become a believer (4: 53).

In so far as the identification of the Messiah may have eschatological overtones, the source can be said to have concerned itself with the question of the turn of the age, but in no other sense. Besides its wholly missionary emphasis on the christological question, there appears to be in the source little theological interest—Spirit,[6] church, sacraments, ethics, the ideas of salvation,[7] forgiveness,[8] grace, and sanctification, find either no place in it or only passing mention. In this regard, it

---

[1] Dodd, 269–71 (*cf. Interpretation*, 230–8) argues convincingly that the phrase is messianic in meaning.

[2] See above, p. 229 n. 1. It is the evangelist who is responsible for passages like 4: 48, 6: 26, 20: 24–9.

[3] For this reason, apparently, Jesus is not shown as *calling* the first disciples, as in the synoptics; rather, on hearing of him they *find* him.

[4] Dinkler, 'Kana-Wunder', 49, is right that in Jn (*i.e.* the source) the emphasis is not on the moment of the miracle *per se*, as in the synoptics, but on the effect it has on the witnesses. – It is perhaps not accidental that in the Zechariah *testimonium* in 12: 14 f. the element of the Messiah's meekness is missing; there is no paradox or hiddenness in Jesus' messiahship. Even the foot-washing scene lacks emphasis on the anomaly of Jesus' action; rather his status is reaffirmed—'You call me Teacher and Lord'.

[5] And, as that verse shows, it is necessary to know only a selection of them. There is no interest in SQ in the multitude of Jesus' signs (*vs.* Robinson, 'Kerygma and history', 137 f.); the passages where that is emphasized are all Johannine (7: 31, 11: 47, 12: 37).

[6] That Jesus (alone) has the Spirit only affirms his status.

[7] The title 'Saviour of the World' (4: 42), if pre-Johannine, is found significantly on the lips of Samaritans, for whom it is equivalent to *Taheb* and so simply messianic (see above, p. 193).

[8] Even when Jesus is dealing with a notorious sinner, the Samaritan woman, it is not a matter of forgiving her, but of revealing himself to her. *Cf.* also ?5: 14b.

must have been unique in first-century Christian literature. Undoubtedly both author and reader would have been confronted with many other theological issues; but as a textbook for potential Jewish converts[1] the Gospel of Signs sought to prove one thing, and one thing only: that Jesus was the Messiah in whom men should believe.

[1] That John may have had a similar purpose (among others) is not excluded by this characterization of the source—on the contrary; *cf.* Robinson, 'Destination'.

APPENDIX

THE TEXT OF THE SOURCE

In the following, words or phrases which are not certainly to be assigned to the source are enclosed in parentheses ( ), conjectural or uncertain readings in square brackets [ ], and passages whose position in the source is uncertain in double brackets ⟦ ⟧. Points at which John has made insertions into the text of the source are indicated as follows: |...|.

Introduction

Exordium

1 ⁶Ἐγένετο ἄνθρωπος, ἀπεσταλμένος παρὰ θεοῦ, ὄνομα αὐτῷ Ἰωάννης· ⁷οὗτος ἦλθεν εἰς μαρτυρίαν, |...| ἵνα πάντες πιστεύσωσιν δι' αὐτοῦ. |...|

The Baptist's testimony

¹⁹Καὶ αὕτη ἐστὶν ἡ μαρτυρία τοῦ Ἰωάννου, ὅτε ἀπέστειλαν πρὸς αὐτὸν |...| ἱερεῖς καὶ Λευῖτα[ι] ἵνα ἐρωτήσωσιν αὐτόν· σὺ τίς εἶ; ²⁰|...| οὐκ ἠρνήσατο, καὶ ὡμολόγησεν ὅτι ἐγὼ οὐκ εἰμὶ ὁ χριστός. ²¹καὶ ἠρώτησαν αὐτόν· τί οὖν; Ἠλίας εἶ σύ; καὶ λέγει· οὐκ εἰμί. ὁ προφήτης εἶ σύ; καὶ ἀπεκρίθη· οὔ. |...| (²³ἐγὼ φωνὴ βοῶντος ἐν τῇ ἐρήμῳ· εὐθύνατε τὴν ὁδὸν κυρίου, καθὼς εἶπεν Ἠσαΐας ὁ προφήτης.) |...| ²⁶ἐγὼ βαπτίζω ἐν ὕδατι· |...| ²⁷ὁ ὀπίσω μου ἐρχόμενος, (ὃς ἔμπροσθέν μου γέγονεν,) οὗ οὐκ εἰμὶ ἐγὼ ἄξιος ἵνα λύσω αὐτοῦ τὸν ἱμάντα τοῦ ὑποδήματος, |...| ⟦³³οὗτός ἐστιν ὁ βαπτίζων ἐν πνεύματι ἁγίῳ.⟧ ³²τεθέαμαι τὸ πνεῦμα καταβαῖνον ὡς περιστερὰν ἐξ οὐρανοῦ, καὶ ἔμεινεν ἐπ' αὐτόν. ³⁴|...| οὗτός ἐστιν ὁ [ἐκλεκτὸς] τοῦ θεοῦ.

The conversion of the first disciples

3 ⟦²³ᵛἩν δὲ |...| Ἰωάννης βαπτίζων ἐν Αἰνὼν ἐγγὺς τοῦ Σαλίμ, ὅτι
1 ὕδατα πολλὰ ἦν ἐκεῖ, καὶ παρεγίνοντο καὶ ἐβαπτίζοντο· ²⁴οὔπω γὰρ ἦν βεβλημένος εἰς τὴν φυλακὴν Ἰωάννης.⟧ ³⁵|...| εἱστήκει ὁ Ἰωάννης καὶ ἐκ τῶν μαθητῶν αὐτοῦ δύο, ³⁶καὶ ἐμβλέψας τῷ Ἰησοῦ [ἐρχομένῳ πρὸς αὐτὸν] λέγει· ἴδε ὁ ἀμνὸς τοῦ θεοῦ. ³⁷καὶ ἤκουσαν οἱ δύο μαθηταὶ αὐτοῦ λαλοῦντος καὶ ἠκολούθησαν τῷ

Ἰησοῦ. ³⁸|...| οἱ δὲ εἶπαν αὐτῷ· ῥαββί |...|, ποῦ μένεις; ³⁹λέγει
αὐτοῖς· ἔρχεσθε καὶ ὄψεσθε. ἦλθαν οὖν καὶ εἶδαν ποῦ μένει, καὶ παρ'
αὐτῷ ἔμειναν (τὴν ἡμέραν ἐκείνην)· ὥρα ἦν ὡς δεκάτη. ⁴⁰ἦν
Ἀνδρέας ὁ ἀδελφὸς (Σίμωνος) Πέτρου εἶς ἐκ τῶν δύο τῶν ἀκουσάντων παρὰ Ἰωάννου καὶ ἀκολουθησάντων αὐτῷ· ⁴¹εὑρίσκει οὗτος
πρῶτον τὸν ἀδελφὸν τὸν ἴδιον Σίμωνα καὶ λέγει αὐτῷ· εὑρήκαμεν
τὸν [Μεσσίαν |...|. ⁴²ἤγαγεν αὐτὸν πρὸς τὸν Ἰησοῦν. ἐμβλέψας
αὐτῷ ὁ Ἰησοῦς εἶπεν· σὺ εἶ Σίμων ὁ υἱὸς Ἰωάννου, σὺ κληθήσῃ
Κηφᾶς |...|. ⁴³καὶ εὑρίσκει Φίλιππον. καὶ λέγει αὐτῷ ὁ Ἰησοῦς·
ἀκολούθει μοι. ⁴⁴ἦν δὲ ὁ Φίλιππος ἀπὸ Βηθσαϊδά, ἐκ τῆς πόλεως
Ἀνδρέου καὶ Πέτρου. ⁴⁵εὑρίσκει Φίλιππος τὸν Ναθαναὴλ καὶ
λέγει αὐτῷ· ὃν ἔγραψεν [Μωϋσῆς ἐν τῷ νόμῳ καὶ οἱ προφῆται
εὑρήκαμεν, Ἰησοῦν υἱὸν τοῦ Ἰωσὴφ τὸν ἀπὸ Ναζαρέθ. ⁴⁶καὶ εἶπεν
αὐτῷ Ναθαναήλ· ἐκ Ναζαρὲθ δύναταί τι ἀγαθὸν εἶναι; λέγει
αὐτῷ ὁ Φίλιππος· ἔρχου καὶ ἴδε. ⁴⁷εἶδεν Ἰησοῦς τὸν Ναθαναὴλ
ἐρχόμενον πρὸς αὐτὸν καὶ λέγει περὶ αὐτοῦ· ἴδε |...| Ἰσραηλίτης,
ἐν ᾧ δόλος οὐκ ἔστιν. ⁴⁸λέγει αὐτῷ Ναθαναήλ· πόθεν με γινώσκεις;
ἀπεκρίθη Ἰησοῦς (καὶ εἶπεν) αὐτῷ· πρὸ τοῦ σε Φίλιππον
φωνῆσαι ὄντα ὑπὸ τὴν συκῆν εἶδόν σε. ⁴⁹ἀπεκρίθη αὐτῷ Ναθα-
ναήλ· ῥαββί, σὺ εἶ ὁ υἱὸς τοῦ θεοῦ (σὺ βασιλεὺς εἶ τοῦ Ἰσραήλ).
⁵⁰ἀπεκρίθη Ἰησοῦς (καὶ εἶπεν) αὐτῷ· ὅτι εἶπόν σοι ὅτι εἶδόν σε
ὑποκάτω τῆς συκῆς, πιστεύεις; μείζω τούτων ὄψῃ. |...|

The Signs of Jesus

1. Water changed into wine

2 ¹Καὶ |...| γάμος ἐγένετο ἐν Κανὰ (τῆς Γαλιλαίας καὶ ἦν ἡ μήτηρ
τοῦ Ἰησοῦ ἐκεῖ). ²ἐκλήθη δὲ καὶ ὁ Ἰησοῦς καὶ οἱ μαθηταὶ αὐτοῦ
εἰς τὸν γάμον. ³καὶ [οἶνον οὐκ εἶχον, ὅτι συνετελέσθη ὁ οἶνος τοῦ
γάμου· εἶτα] λέγει ἡ μήτηρ τοῦ Ἰησοῦ |...| ⁵τοῖς διακόνοις· ὅ τι
ἂν λέγῃ ὑμῖν, ποιήσατε. ⁶ἦσαν δὲ ἐκεῖ λίθιναι ὑδρίαι ἓξ |...|
κείμεναι, χωροῦσαι ἀνὰ μετρητὰς δύο ἢ τρεῖς. ⁷λέγει αὐτοῖς ὁ
Ἰησοῦς· γεμίσατε τὰς ὑδρίας ὕδατος. καὶ ἐγέμισαν αὐτὰς ἕως ἄνω.
⁸καὶ λέγει αὐτοῖς· ἀντλήσατε νῦν καὶ φέρετε τῷ ἀρχιτρικλίνῳ. οἱ
δὲ ἤνεγκαν. ⁹ὡς δὲ ἐγεύσατο ὁ ἀρχιτρίκλινος, τὸ ὕδωρ οἶνο[ς]
γεγενημένον. |...| φωνεῖ τὸν νυμφίον (ὁ ἀρχιτρίκλινος) ¹⁰καὶ
λέγει αὐτῷ· πᾶς ἄνθρωπος πρῶτον τὸν καλὸν οἶνον τίθησιν, καὶ
ὅταν μεθυσθῶσιν τὸν ἐλάσσω· σὺ τετήρηκας τὸν καλὸν οἶνον ἕως
ἄρτι. ¹¹[τοῦτο πρῶτον ἐποίησεν σημεῖον] ὁ Ἰησοῦς |...| καὶ
ἐπίστευσαν εἰς αὐτὸν οἱ μαθηταὶ αὐτοῦ.

2. A nobleman's son healed

2

4

¹²ᵃ(Μετὰ τοῦτο) κατέβη[-βαινεν] εἰς Καφαρναοὺμ αὐτὸς |...| καὶ οἱ μαθηταὶ αὐτοῦ. |...| ⁴⁶ᵇ[ἦν δέ] τις βασιλικὸς οὗ ὁ υἱὸς ἠσθένει ἐν Καφαρναούμ· ⁴⁷οὗτος ἀκούσας ὅτι 'Ιησοῦς [ἔρχεται] |...| ἀπῆλθεν πρὸς αὐτὸν καὶ |...| ⁴⁹λέγει |...|· κύριε, κατάβηθι πρὶν ἀποθανεῖν τὸ παιδίον μου. ⁵⁰λέγει αὐτῷ ὁ 'Ιησοῦς· πορεύου, ὁ υἱός σου ζῇ. |...| καὶ ἐπορεύετο, [καὶ ἰάθη ὁ παῖς ἐκείνῃ τῇ ὥρᾳ]. ⁵¹ἤδη δὲ αὐτοῦ καταβαίνοντος οἱ δοῦλοι ὑπήντησαν αὐτῷ (καὶ [ἀπ/ἀν-]ἤγγειλαν) λέγοντες ὅτι ὁ παῖς αὐτοῦ ζῇ. ⁵²ἐπύθετο οὖν τὴν ὥραν παρ' αὐτῶν ἐν ᾗ κομψότερον ἔσχεν· εἶπαν οὖν αὐτῷ ὅτι ἐχθὲς ὥραν ἑβδόμην ἀφῆκεν αὐτὸν ὁ πυρετός. ⁵³|...| καὶ ἐπίστευ-σεν αὐτὸς καὶ ἡ οἰκία αὐτοῦ ὅλη. ⁵⁴τοῦτο (πάλιν) δεύτερον [ἐποίησεν σημεῖον] ὁ 'Ιησοῦς |...|.

3. A miraculous draught of fish

21

²ᵀΗσαν ὁμοῦ (Σίμων) Πέτρος καὶ Θωμᾶς (ὁ λεγόμενος Δίδυμος) καὶ Ναθαναὴλ ὁ ἀπὸ Κανᾶ (τῆς Γαλιλαίας) καὶ οἱ τοῦ Ζεβεδαίου καὶ ἄλλοι ἐκ τῶν μαθητῶν αὐτοῦ δύο. ³λέγει αὐτοῖς (Σίμων) Πέτρος· ὑπάγω ἁλιεύειν. λέγουσιν αὐτῷ· ἐρχόμεθα καὶ ἡμεῖς σὺν σοί. ἐξῆλθον καὶ ἐνέβησαν εἰς τὸ πλοῖον, καὶ ἐν ἐκείνῃ τῇ νυκτὶ ἐπίασαν οὐδέν. ⁴πρωΐας δὲ ἤδη γινομένης ἔστη 'Ιησοῦς εἰς τὸν αἰγιαλόν. |...| (⁵λέγει |...| αὐτοῖς 'Ιησοῦς· παιδία, μή τι προσφάγιον ἔχετε; ἀπεκρίθησαν αὐτῷ· οὔ.) ⁶ὁ δὲ εἶπεν αὐτοῖς· βάλετε εἰς τὰ δεξιὰ μέρη τοῦ πλοίου τὸ δίκτυον, καὶ εὑρήσετε. ἔβαλον οὖν, καὶ οὐκέτι αὐτὸ ἑλκύσαι ἴσχυον ἀπὸ τοῦ πλήθους τῶν ἰχθύων. ⁷|...| (Σίμων οὖν) Πέτρος |...| τὸν ἐπενδύτην διεζώσατο, (ἦν γὰρ γυμνός,) καὶ ἔβαλεν ἑαυτὸν εἰς τὴν θάλασσαν· |...| ⁸ᵇοὐ γὰρ ἦσαν μακρὰν ἀπὸ τῆς γῆς ἀλλὰ ὡς ἀπὸ πηχῶν διακοσίων. |...| ¹⁰λέγει αὐτοῖς ὁ 'Ιησοῦς· ἐνέγκατε ἀπὸ τῶν ὀψαρίων ὧν ἐπιάσατε νῦν. ¹¹ἀνέβη (οὖν Σίμων) Πέτρος καὶ εἵλκυσεν τὸ δίκτυον εἰς τὴν γῆν μεστὸν ἰχθύων μεγάλων ἑκατὸν πεντήκοντα τριῶν· καὶ τοσούτων ὄντων οὐκ ἐσχίσθη τὸ δίκτυον. ¹²(λέγει αὐτοῖς ὁ 'Ιησοῦς· δεῦτε ἀριστήσατε.) |...| ¹⁴τοῦτο (ἤδη) τρίτον [ἐποίησεν σημεῖον] 'Ιησοῦς |...|.

4. The multitude fed

6

¹|...| 'Απῆλθεν ὁ 'Ιησοῦς πέραν τῆς θαλάσσης τῆς Γαλιλαίας |...|. ²ἠκολούθει δὲ αὐτῷ ὄχλος πολύς |...|. ³ἀνῆλθεν δὲ εἰς τὸ ὄρος 'Ιησοῦς, καὶ ἐκεῖ ἐκάθητο μετὰ τῶν μαθητῶν αὐτοῦ. |...|

⁵ἐπάρας |...| τοὺς ὀφθαλμοὺς ὁ Ἰησοῦς καὶ θεασάμενος ὅτι πολὺς ὄχλος ἔρχεται πρὸς αὐτόν, λέγει [τοῖς μαθηταῖς αὐτοῦ]· πόθεν ἀγοράσωμεν ἄρτους ἵνα φάγωσιν οὗτοι; |...| ⁷ἀπεκρίθη[σαν] αὐτῷ |...| διακοσίων δηναρίων ἄρτοι οὐκ ἀρκοῦσιν αὐτοῖς, ἵνα ἕκαστος βραχύ τι λάβῃ. ⁸λέγει αὐτῷ εἷς ἐκ τῶν μαθητῶν αὐτοῦ, Ἀνδρέας ὁ ἀδελφὸς (Σίμωνος) Πέτρου· ⁹ἔστιν παιδάριον ὧδε ὃς ἔχει πέντε ἄρτους κριθίνους καὶ δύο ὀψάρια· ἀλλὰ ταῦτα τί ἐστιν εἰς τοσούτους; ¹⁰εἶπεν ὁ Ἰησοῦς· ποιήσατε τοὺς ἀνθρώπους ἀναπεσεῖν. ἦν δὲ χόρτος πολὺς ἐν τῷ τόπῳ. ἀνέπεσαν οὖν οἱ ἄνδρες τὸν ἀριθμὸν ὡς πεντακισχίλιοι. ¹¹ἔλαβεν |...| τοὺς ἄρτους ὁ Ἰησοῦς καὶ εὐχαριστήσας διέδωκεν τοῖς ἀνακειμένοις, ὁμοίως καὶ ἐκ τῶν ὀψαρίων ὅσον ἤθελον. (**Either**¹²ὡς δὲ ἐνεπλήσθησαν, λέγει τοῖς μαθηταῖς αὐτοῦ· συναγάγετε τὰ περισσεύσαντα κλάσματα |...|· ¹³ᵃσυνήγαγον οὖν, **or** [καὶ ἔφαγον (πάντες) καὶ ἐχορτάσθησαν,]) ¹³ᵇκαὶ ἐγέμισαν δώδεκα κοφίνους κλασμάτων ἐκ τῶν πέντε ἄρτων τῶν κριθίνων ἃ ἐπερίσσευσαν τοῖς βεβρωκόσιν. ¹⁴[τοῦτο τέταρτον ἐποίησεν σημεῖον ὁ Ἰησοῦς καὶ] οἱ |...| ἄνθρωποι |...| ἔλεγον ὅτι οὗτός ἐστιν |...| ὁ προφήτης |...|.

Interlude: walking on water and a miraculous landing

¹⁵ᵇ[Καὶ ἀποταξάμενος αὐτοῖς ἀπῆλθεν ὁ Ἰησοῦς] εἰς τὸ ὄρος αὐτὸς μόνος. ¹⁶ὡς δὲ ὀψία ἐγένετο, κατέβησαν οἱ μαθηταὶ αὐτοῦ ἐπὶ τὴν θάλασσαν, ¹⁷καὶ ἐμβάντες εἰς πλοῖον ἤρχοντο πέραν τῆς θαλάσσης εἰς Καφαρναούμ. |...| ¹⁸ἥ τε θάλασσα ἀνέμου μεγάλου πνέοντος διηγείρετο. ¹⁹ἐληλακότες οὖν ὡς σταδίους εἴκοσι πέντε ἢ τριάκοντα θεωροῦσιν τὸν Ἰησοῦν περιπατοῦντα ἐπὶ τῆς θαλάσσης καὶ ἐγγὺς τοῦ πλοίου γινόμενον, καὶ ἐφοβήθησαν. ²⁰ὁ δὲ λέγει αὐτοῖς· ἐγώ εἰμι· μὴ φοβεῖσθε. ²¹ἤθελον οὖν λαβεῖν αὐτὸν εἰς τὸ πλοῖον, καὶ εὐθέως ἐγένετο τὸ πλοῖον ἐπὶ τῆς γῆς εἰς ἣν ὑπῆγον. (²²|...| ὁ ὄχλος ὁ ἑστηκὼς πέραν τῆς θαλάσσης [ἰδὼν] ὅτι πλοιάριον ἄλλο οὐκ ἦν ἐκεῖ |...| καὶ ὅτι οὐ συνεισῆλθεν τοῖς μαθηταῖς αὐτοῦ ὁ Ἰησοῦς εἰς τὸ πλοῖον |...| ²⁵καὶ εὑρόντες αὐτὸν πέραν τῆς θαλάσσης εἶπον αὐτῷ· ῥαββί, πότε ὧδε γέγονας;) |...| (The source may have continued here with material which is now buried in the rest of ch. 6, notably in the episode with Peter in 6: 67 ff.)

5. A dead man raised; a Samaritan woman

11 ¹ᵀΗν δέ τις ἀσθενῶν, Λάζαρος ἀπὸ Βηθανίας, ἐκ τῆς κώμης Μαρίας καὶ Μάρθας τῆς ἀδελφῆς αὐτῆς. ²ἦν δὲ Μαριὰμ ἡ ἀλείψασα

τὸν κύριον μύρῳ καὶ ἐκμάξασα τοὺς πόδας αὐτοῦ ταῖς θριξὶν
αὐτῆς, ἧς ὁ ἀδελφὸς Λάζαρος ἠσθένει. ³ἀπέστειλαν οὖν αἱ
ἀδελφαὶ πρὸς αὐτὸν λέγουσαι· κύριε, ἴδε ὃν φιλεῖς ἀσθενεῖ.
⁴ἀκούσας δὲ ὁ Ἰησοῦς |...| ⁷λέγει τοῖς μαθηταῖς· |...| ¹¹Λάζαρος
ὁ φίλος ἡμῶν κεκοίμηται |...| ¹⁵ἀλλὰ ἄγωμεν πρὸς αὐτόν.
|...|

4 ⟦⁴Ἔδει δὲ αὐτὸν διέρχεσθαι διὰ τῆς Σαμαρείας. ⁵ἔρχεται οὖν εἰς
πόλιν τῆς Σαμαρείας λεγομένην Σύχαρ, πλησίον τοῦ χωρίου ὃ
ἔδωκεν Ἰακὼβ τῷ Ἰωσὴφ τῷ υἱῷ αὐτοῦ· ⁶ἦν δὲ ἐκεῖ πηγὴ τοῦ
Ἰακώβ. ὁ οὖν Ἰησοῦς κεκοπιακὼς ἐκ τῆς ὁδοιπορίας ἐκαθέζετο
οὕτως ἐπὶ τῇ πηγῇ· ὥρα ἦν ὡς ἕκτη. ⁷ἔρχεται γυνὴ ἐκ τῆς
Σαμαρείας ἀντλῆσαι ὕδωρ. λέγει αὐτῇ ὁ Ἰησοῦς· δός μοι πεῖν.
|...| ⁹λέγει |...| αὐτῷ ἡ γυνὴ ἡ Σαμαρῖτις· πῶς σὺ Ἰουδαῖος ὢν
παρ' ἐμοῦ πεῖν αἰτεῖς γυναικὸς Σαμαρίτιδος οὔσης; |...| ¹⁶λέγει
αὐτῇ· ὕπαγε φώνησον τὸν ἄνδρα σου καὶ ἐλθὲ ἐνθάδε. ¹⁷ἀπεκρίθη
ἡ γυνὴ (καὶ εἶπεν)· οὐκ ἔχω ἄνδρα. λέγει αὐτῇ ὁ Ἰησοῦς· καλῶς
εἶπες ὅτι ἄνδρα οὐκ ἔχω. ¹⁸πέντε γὰρ ἄνδρας ἔσχες, καὶ νῦν ὃν
ἔχεις οὐκ ἔστιν σου ἀνήρ· τοῦτο ἀληθὲς εἴρηκας. ¹⁹λέγει αὐτῷ ἡ
γυνή· κύριε, θεωρῶ ὅτι προφήτης εἶ σύ. |...| ²⁵οἶδα ὅτι Μεσσίας
ἔρχεται, (ὁ λεγόμενος χριστός)· ὅταν ἔλθῃ ἐκεῖνος, ἀναγγελεῖ ἡμῖν
ἅπαντα.²⁶ λέγει αὐτῇ ὁ Ἰησοῦς· ἐγώ εἰμι. |...| ²⁸ἀφῆκεν οὖν τὴν
ὑδρίαν αὐτῆς ἡ γυνὴ καὶ ἀπῆλθεν εἰς τὴν πόλιν, καὶ λέγει τοῖς
ἀνθρώποις· ²⁹δεῦτε ἴδετε ἄνθρωπον ὃς εἶπέν μοι πάντα ἃ ἐποίησα·
|...| ³⁰ἐξῆλθον (οὖν) ἐκ τῆς πόλεως καὶ |...| ⁴⁰ἦλθον πρὸς
αὐτὸν οἱ Σαμαρῖται· ἠρώτων αὐτὸν μεῖναι παρ' αὐτοῖς· καὶ
ἔμεινεν ἐκεῖ δύο ἡμέρας. (⁴²καὶ |...| ἔλεγον |...| ὅτι οὗτός ἐστιν
|...| ὁ σωτὴρ τοῦ κόσμου.)⟧

II ¹⁷Ἐλθὼν |...| ὁ Ἰησοῦς εὖρεν αὐτὸν τέσσαρας ἤδη ἡμέρας ἔχοντα
ἐν τῷ μνημείῳ. ¹⁸ἦν δὲ Βηθανία ἐγγὺς τῶν Ἱεροσολύμων ὡς ἀπὸ
σταδίων δεκαπέντε. ¹⁹πολλοὶ δὲ (ἐκ τῶν Ἱεροσολύμων) ἐληλύθεισαν πρὸς τὴν Μάρθαν καὶ Μαριάμ, ἵνα παραμυθήσωνται αὐτὰς
περὶ τοῦ ἀδελφοῦ. ²⁰ἡ |...| Μάρθα ὡς ἤκουσεν ὅτι Ἰησοῦς
[ἤκει], ὑπήντησεν αὐτῷ· Μαριὰμ δὲ ἐν τῷ οἴκῳ ἐκαθέζετο. |...|
²⁸καὶ |...| ἀπῆλθεν καὶ ἐφώνησεν Μαριὰμ τὴν ἀδελφὴν αὐτῆς
|...| εἰποῦσα· ὁ διδάσκαλος πάρεστιν καὶ φωνεῖ σε. |...| ³²ἡ
|...| Μαριὰμ ὡς ἦλθεν ὅπου ἦν Ἰησοῦς, ἰδοῦσα αὐτὸν ἔπεσεν
αὐτοῦ πρὸς τοὺς πόδας |...|. ³³Ἰησοῦς οὖν ὡς εἶδεν αὐτὴν
κλαίουσαν καὶ τοὺς σὺν |...| αὐτῇ |...| κλαίοντας, ἐνεβριμήσατο
τῷ πνεύματι καὶ ἐτάραξεν ἑαυτόν, ³⁴καὶ εἶπεν· ποῦ τεθείκατε
αὐτόν; λέγουσιν αὐτῷ· κύριε, ἔρχου καὶ ἴδε. |...| ³⁸Ἰησοῦς οὖν

|...| ἔρχεται εἰς τὸ μνημεῖον· ἦν δὲ σπήλαιον, καὶ λίθος ἐπέκειτο ἐπ' αὐτῷ. ³⁹λέγει ὁ Ἰησοῦς· ἄρατε τὸν λίθον. |...| ⁴¹ἦραν οὖν τὸν λίθον. ὁ δὲ Ἰησοῦς ἦρεν τοὺς ὀφθαλμοὺς ἄνω |...| ⁴³καὶ |...| φωνῇ μεγάλῃ ἐκραύγασεν· Λάζαρε, δεῦρο ἔξω. ⁴⁴ἐξῆλθεν ὁ τεθνηκὼς δεδεμένος τοὺς πόδας καὶ τὰς χεῖρας κειρίαις, καὶ ἡ ὄψις αὐτοῦ σουδαρίῳ περιεδέδετο. λέγει αὐτοῖς ὁ Ἰησοῦς· λύσατε αὐτὸν καὶ ἄφετε αὐτὸν ὑπάγειν. ⁴⁵[τοῦτο πέμπτον ἐποίησεν σημεῖον ὁ Ἰησοῦς καὶ] |...| οἱ ἐλθόντες πρὸς τὴν Μαριὰμ καὶ θεασάμενοι ὃ ἐποίησεν ἐπίστευσαν εἰς αὐτόν. |...|

6. A man blind from birth healed

9   ¹Καὶ παράγων εἶδεν ἄνθρωπον τυφλὸν ἐκ γενετῆς. ²καὶ ἠρώτησαν αὐτὸν οἱ μαθηταὶ αὐτοῦ λέγοντες· ῥαββί, τίς ἥμαρτεν, οὗτος ἢ οἱ γονεῖς αὐτοῦ, ἵνα τυφλὸς γεννηθῇ; (³ᵃἀπεκρίθη Ἰησοῦς· οὔτε οὗτος ἥμαρτεν οὔτε οἱ γονεῖς αὐτοῦ.) |...| ⁶(ταῦτα εἰπὼν) ἔπτυσεν χαμαὶ καὶ ἐποίησεν πηλὸν ἐκ τοῦ πτύσματος, καὶ ἐπέθηκεν αὐτοῦ τὸν πηλὸν ἐπὶ τοὺς ὀφθαλμούς, ⁷καὶ εἶπεν αὐτῷ· ὕπαγε νίψαι εἰς τὴν κολυμβήθραν τοῦ Σιλωάμ |...|. ἀπῆλθεν οὖν καὶ ἐνίψατο, καὶ ἦλθεν βλέπων. [τοῦτο ἕκτον ἐποίησεν σημεῖον ὁ Ἰησοῦς.] (⁸οἱ οὖν γείτονες καὶ οἱ θεωροῦντες αὐτὸν τὸ πρότερον, ὅτι προσαίτης ἦν, ἔλεγον· οὐχ οὗτός ἐστιν ὁ καθήμενος καὶ προσαιτῶν;) |...|

7. A thirty-eight-year illness healed

5   ²Ἔστιν δὲ ἐν τοῖς Ἱεροσολύμοις ἐπὶ τῇ προβατικῇ κολυμβήθρα, ἡ ἐπιλεγομένη Ἑβραϊστὶ Βηθζαθά, πέντε στοὰς ἔχουσα. ³ἐν ταύταις κατέκειτο πλῆθος τῶν ἀσθενούντων, τυφλῶν, χωλῶν, ξηρῶν. ⁵ἦν δέ τις ἄνθρωπος ἐκεῖ τριάκοντα καὶ ὀκτὼ ἔτη ἔχων ἐν τῇ ἀσθενείᾳ αὐτοῦ· ⁶τοῦτον ἰδὼν ὁ Ἰησοῦς κατακείμενον, καὶ γνοὺς ὅτι πολὺν ἤδη χρόνον ἔχει, λέγει αὐτῷ· θέλεις ὑγιὴς γενέσθαι; ⁷ἀπεκρίθη αὐτῷ ὁ ἀσθενῶν· κύριε, ἄνθρωπον οὐκ ἔχω, ἵνα ὅταν ταραχθῇ τὸ ὕδωρ βάλῃ με εἰς τὴν κολυμβήθραν· ἐν ᾧ δὲ ἔρχομαι ἐγώ, ἄλλος πρὸ ἐμοῦ καταβαίνει. ⁸λέγει αὐτῷ ὁ Ἰησοῦς· ἔγειρε ἆρον τὸν κράβατόν σου καὶ περιπάτει. ⁹καὶ εὐθέως ἐγένετο ὑγιὴς ὁ ἄνθρωπος, καὶ ἦρεν τὸν κράβατον αὐτοῦ καὶ περιεπάτει. |...| (¹⁴καὶ [ὁ Ἰησοῦς] εἶπεν αὐτῷ· |...| μηκέτι ἁμάρτανε, ἵνα μὴ χεῖρόν σοί τι γένηται.) [τοῦτο ἕβδομον (or ἔσχατον) ἐποίησεν σημεῖον ὁ Ἰησοῦς.]

The Death and Resurrection of Jesus

The cleansing of the Temple and death plot

2 ¹⁴Καὶ εὗρεν ἐν τῷ ἱερῷ τοὺς πωλοῦντας βόας καὶ πρόβατα καὶ περιστερὰς καὶ τοὺς κερματιστὰς καθημένους, ¹⁵καὶ ποιήσας φραγέλλιον ἐκ σχοινίων πάντας ἐξέβαλεν ἐκ τοῦ ἱεροῦ, τά τε πρόβατα καὶ τοὺς βόας, καὶ τῶν κολλυβιστῶν ἐξέχεεν τὰ κέρματα καὶ τὰς τραπέζας ἀνέτρεψεν, ¹⁶καὶ τοῖς τὰς περιστερὰς πωλοῦσιν εἶπεν· ἄρατε ταῦτα ἐντεῦθεν, μὴ ποιεῖτε τὸν οἶκον τοῦ πατρός μου οἶκον ἐμπορίου. |...| ¹⁸ἀπεκρίθησαν |...| [οἱ ἀρχιερεῖς καὶ οἱ Φαρισαῖοι] (καὶ εἶπαν) αὐτῷ· τί σημεῖον δεικνύεις ἡμῖν, ὅτι ταῦτα ποιεῖς; ¹⁹ἀπεκρίθη Ἰησοῦς (καὶ εἶπεν) αὐτοῖς· λύσατε τὸν ναὸν **11** τοῦτον, καὶ ἐν τρισὶν ἡμέραις ἐγερῶ αὐτόν. |...| ⁴⁷ᵃσυνήγαγον οὖν οἱ ἀρχιερεῖς καὶ οἱ Φαρισαῖοι συνέδριον. |...| ⁵³ἀπ' ἐκείνης οὖν τῆς ἡμέρας ἐβουλεύσαντο ἵνα ἀποκτείνωσιν αὐτόν. |...|

The anointing at Bethany

12 ¹ʽΟ |...| Ἰησοῦς πρὸ ἓξ ἡμερῶν τοῦ πάσχα ἦλθεν εἰς Βηθανίαν, ὅπου ἦν Λάζαρος, (ὁ τεθνηκὼς) ὃν ἤγειρεν ἐκ νεκρῶν Ἰησοῦς. ²ἐποίησαν |...| αὐτῷ δεῖπνον ἐκεῖ, καὶ ἡ Μάρθα διηκόνει, ὁ δὲ Λάζαρος εἷς ἦν ἐκ τῶν ἀνακειμένων σὺν αὐτῷ· ³ἡ |...| Μαριὰμ λαβοῦσα λίτραν μύρου νάρδου πιστικῆς πολυτίμου ἤλειψεν τοὺς πόδας τοῦ Ἰησοῦ καὶ ἐξέμαξεν ταῖς θριξὶν αὐτῆς τοὺς πόδας αὐτοῦ· ἡ δὲ οἰκία ἐπληρώθη ἐκ τῆς ὀσμῆς τοῦ μύρου. ⁴λέγει δὲ Ἰούδας ὁ Ἰσκαριώτης εἷς (ἐκ) τῶν μαθητῶν αὐτοῦ (ὁ μέλλων αὐτὸν παραδιδόναι)· ⁵διὰ τί τοῦτο τὸ μύρον οὐκ ἐπράθη τριακοσίων δηναρίων καὶ ἐδόθη πτωχοῖς; |...| ⁷εἶπεν |...| ὁ Ἰησοῦς· ἄφες αὐτήν, ἵνα εἰς τὴν ἡμέραν τοῦ ἐνταφιασμοῦ μου τηρήσῃ αὐτό· (⁸τοὺς πτωχοὺς γὰρ πάντοτε ἔχετε μεθ' ἑαυτῶν, ἐμὲ δὲ οὐ πάντοτε ἔχετε.)

The triumphal entry

¹²(Τῇ ἐπαύριον) ὄχλος πολύς |...|, ἀκούσαντες ὅτι ἔρχεται Ἰησοῦς (εἰς Ἱεροσόλυμα), ¹³ἔλαβον τὰ βαΐα τῶν φοινίκων καὶ ἐξῆλθον εἰς ὑπάντησιν αὐτῷ, καὶ ἐκραύγαζον· ὡσαννά, εὐλογημένος ὁ ἐρχόμενος ἐν ὀνόματι κυρίου (καὶ ὁ βασιλεὺς τοῦ Ἰσραήλ). ¹⁴εὑρὼν δὲ ὁ Ἰησοῦς ὀνάριον ἐκάθισεν ἐπ' αὐτό, καθώς ἐστιν γεγραμμένον· ¹⁵μὴ φοβοῦ, θυγάτηρ Σιών· ἰδοὺ ὁ βασιλεύς σου ἔρχεται, καθήμενος ἐπὶ πῶλον ὄνου. |...|

The Last Supper

(Fragments of the source's account are probably to be found in the following passages: 12:27; 13: (1 *b*), 2*a*, 4–5, 12–14, 18*b*, 21*b*, 26–7, 37–8; 14: 31*b*; 16: 32*b*.)

The arrest

18 ¹|...| Ἰησοῦς ἐξῆλθεν σὺν τοῖς μαθηταῖς αὐτοῦ πέραν τοῦ χειμάρρου τοῦ Κεδρών, ὅπου ἦν κῆπος, εἰς ὃν εἰσῆλθεν αὐτὸς καὶ οἱ μαθηταὶ αὐτοῦ. ²ᾔδει δὲ καὶ Ἰούδας ὁ παραδιδοὺς αὐτὸν τὸν τόπον, ὅτι πολλάκις συνήχθη Ἰησοῦς ἐκεῖ μετὰ τῶν μαθητῶν αὐτοῦ. ³ὁ οὖν Ἰούδας λαβὼν τὴν σπεῖραν καὶ ἐκ τῶν ἀρχιερέων καὶ ἐκ τῶν Φαρισαίων ὑπηρέτας ἔρχεται ἐκεῖ μετὰ φανῶν καὶ λαμπάδων καὶ ὅπλων. ⁴Ἰησοῦς οὖν |...| ἐξῆλθεν καὶ λέγει αὐτοῖς· τίνα ζητεῖτε; ⁵ ἀπεκρίθησαν αὐτῷ· Ἰησοῦν τὸν Ναζωραῖον. λέγει αὐτοῖς· ἐγώ εἰμι. |...| ¹⁰(Σίμων) |...| Πέτρος ἔχων μάχαιραν εἵλκυσεν αὐτὴν καὶ ἔπαισεν τὸν τοῦ ἀρχιερέως δοῦλον καὶ ἀπέκοψεν αὐτοῦ τὸ ὠτάριον τὸ δεξιόν· ἦν δὲ ὄνομα τῷ δούλῳ Μάλχος.¹¹ εἶπεν |...| ὁ Ἰησοῦς τῷ Πέτρῳ· βάλε τὴν μάχαιραν εἰς τὴν θήκην· τὸ ποτήριον ὃ δέδωκέν μοι ὁ πατήρ, οὐ μὴ πίω αὐτό; ¹²ἡ οὖν σπεῖρα καὶ χιλίαρχος καὶ οἱ ὑπηρέται (τῶν Ἰουδαίων) συνέλαβον τὸν Ἰησοῦν καὶ ἔδησαν αὐτόν·

Jesus in the high priest's house

¹³καὶ ἤγαγον πρὸς Ἄνναν πρῶτον· ἦν γὰρ πενθερὸς τοῦ Καϊάφα, ὃς ἦν ἀρχιερεὺς τοῦ ἐνιαυτοῦ ἐκείνου. |...| [[²⁴ἀπέστειλεν οὖν αὐτὸν ὁ Ἄννας δεδεμένον πρὸς Καϊάφαν |...|.]] ¹⁵ἠκολούθει δὲ τῷ Ἰησοῦ (Σίμων) Πέτρος καὶ ἄλλος μαθητής. ὁ δὲ μαθητὴς ἐκεῖνος ἦν γνωστὸς τῷ ἀρχιερεῖ, καὶ συνεισῆλθεν τῷ Ἰησοῦ εἰς τὴν αὐλὴν τοῦ ἀρχιερέως, ¹⁶ᵃὁ δὲ Πέτρος εἱστήκει πρὸς τῇ θύρᾳ ἔξω. |...| ¹⁹(ὁ |...| ἀρχιερεὺς ἠρώτησεν τὸν Ἰησοῦν περὶ τῶν μαθητῶν αὐτοῦ καὶ περὶ τῆς διδαχῆς αὐτοῦ). ²⁰ἀπεκρίθη αὐτῷ Ἰησοῦς· |...| ἐγὼ πάντοτε ἐδίδαξα ἐν συναγωγῇ καὶ ἐν τῷ ἱερῷ |...|. ²¹(τί με ἐρωτᾷς; ἐρώτησον τοὺς ἀκηκοότας τί ἐλάλησα αὐτοῖς·) |...| ²²ταῦτα δὲ αὐτοῦ εἰπόντος εἷς παρεστηκὼς τῶν ὑπηρετῶν ἔδωκεν ῥάπισμα τῷ Ἰησοῦ εἰπών· οὕτως ἀποκρίνη τῷ ἀρχιερεῖ; ²³ἀπεκρίθη αὐτῷ Ἰησοῦς· εἰ κακῶς ἐλάλησα, μαρτύρησον περὶ τοῦ κακοῦ· εἰ δὲ καλῶς, τί με δέρεις; |...| [[¹⁶ᵇἐξῆλθεν οὖν ὁ μαθητὴς ὁ ἄλλος ὁ γνωστὸς τοῦ ἀρχιερέως καὶ εἶπεν τῇ θυρωρῷ, καὶ εἰσή-

γαγεν τὸν Πέτρον. ¹⁷λέγει |...| τῷ Πέτρῳ ἡ παιδίσκη (ἡ θυρω-
ρός)· μὴ καὶ σὺ ἐκ τῶν μαθητῶν εἶ τοῦ ἀνθρώπου τούτου; λέγει
ἐκεῖνος· οὐκ εἰμί. ¹⁸εἰστήκεισαν δὲ οἱ δοῦλοι καὶ οἱ ὑπηρέται
ἀνθρακιὰν πεποιηκότες, ὅτι ψῦχος ἦν, καὶ ἐθερμαίνοντο· ἦν δὲ
καὶ ὁ Πέτρος μετ᾽ αὐτῶν ἑστὼς καὶ θερμαινόμενος.] ²⁵ᵇεἶπον
οὖν αὐτῷ· μὴ καὶ σὺ ἐκ τῶν μαθητῶν αὐτοῦ εἶ; ἠρνήσατο
ἐκεῖνος καὶ εἶπεν· οὐκ εἰμί. ²⁶λέγει εἷς ἐκ τῶν δούλων τοῦ ἀρχιερέως, συγγενὴς ὢν οὗ ἀπέκοψεν Πέτρος τὸ ὠτίον· οὐκ ἐγώ σε
εἶδον ἐν τῷ κήπῳ μετ᾽ αὐτοῦ; ²⁷πάλιν |...| ἠρνήσατο Πέτρος, καὶ
εὐθέως ἀλέκτωρ ἐφώνησεν. ²⁸ἄγουσιν |...| τὸν Ἰησοῦν ἀπὸ τοῦ
Καϊαφᾶ εἰς τὸ πραιτώριον·

The trial before Pilate

ἦν δὲ πρωΐ· (καὶ αὐτοὶ οὐκ εἰσῆλθον εἰς τὸ πραιτώριον, ἵνα μὴ
μιανθῶσιν |...|.) |...| ³³ὁ Πιλᾶτος |...| ἐφώνησεν τὸν Ἰησοῦν
καὶ εἶπεν αὐτῷ· σὺ εἶ ὁ βασιλεὺς τῶν Ἰουδαίων; |...| ³⁷ἀπεκρίθη
ὁ Ἰησοῦς· σὺ λέγεις |...|. ³⁸ᶜκαὶ λέγει αὐτοῖς· ἐγὼ οὐδεμίαν
εὑρίσκω ἐν αὐτῷ αἰτίαν. [¹⁵ἐκραύγασαν οὖν ἐκεῖνοι· ἆρον ἆρον,
σταύρωσον αὐτόν. λέγει αὐτοῖς ὁ Πιλᾶτος·] ³⁹ἔστιν δὲ συνήθεια
ὑμῖν ἵνα ἕνα ἀπολύσω ὑμῖν ἐν τῷ πάσχα· βούλεσθε οὖν ἀπολύσω
ὑμῖν τὸν βασιλέα τῶν Ἰουδαίων; ⁴⁰ἐκραύγασαν |...| πάλιν
λέγοντες· μὴ τοῦτον, ἀλλὰ τὸν Βαραββᾶν. ἦν δὲ ὁ Βαραββᾶς
λῃστής. [ὁ δὲ Πιλᾶτος πάλιν εἶπεν αὐτοῖς· τί οὖν ποιήσω τὸν
Ἰησοῦν;] |...| ⁶οἱ ἀρχιερεῖς καὶ οἱ ὑπηρέται ἐκραύγασαν
λέγοντες· σταύρωσον σταύρωσον. λέγει αὐτοῖς ὁ Πιλᾶτος·
λάβετε αὐτὸν ὑμεῖς καὶ σταυρώσατε· ἐγὼ γὰρ οὐχ εὑρίσκω ἐν
αὐτῷ αἰτίαν. |...| (¹²ὁ Πιλᾶτος ἐζήτει ἀπολῦσαι αὐτόν· οἱ δὲ
|...| ἐκραύγασαν λέγοντες· ἐὰν τοῦτον ἀπολύσῃς, οὐκ εἶ φίλος
τοῦ Καίσαρος· πᾶς ὁ βασιλέα ἑαυτὸν ποιῶν ἀντιλέγει τῷ Καί-
σαρι.) ¹³ὁ οὖν Πιλᾶτος ἀκούσας τῶν λόγων τούτων ἤγαγεν ἔξω
τὸν Ἰησοῦν, καὶ ἐκάθισεν ἐπὶ βήματος εἰς τόπον λεγόμενον
Λιθόστρωτον, Ἑβραϊστὶ δὲ Γαββαθᾶ. ¹⁴ᵃἦν δὲ παρασκευή |...|,
ὥρα ἦν ὡς ἕκτη. [¹|...| ἔλαβεν ὁ Πιλᾶτος τὸν Ἰησοῦν καὶ ἐμαστίγω-
σεν. ²καὶ οἱ στρατιῶται πλέξαντες στέφανον ἐξ ἀκανθῶν ἐπέθηκαν
αὐτοῦ τῇ κεφαλῇ, καὶ ἱμάτιον πορφυροῦν περιέβαλον αὐτόν, ³καὶ
ἤρχοντο πρὸς αὐτὸν καὶ ἔλεγον· χαῖρε ὁ βασιλεὺς τῶν Ἰουδαίων·
καὶ ἐδίδοσαν αὐτῷ ῥαπίσματα.] |...| ¹⁶ |...| παρέδωκεν αὐτὸν
αὐτοῖς ἵνα σταυρωθῇ.

19
18

19

243   16-2

The crucifixion and burial

παρέλαβον οὖν τὸν Ἰησοῦν· ¹⁷καὶ βαστάζων ἑαυτῷ τὸν σταυρὸν ἐξῆλθεν εἰς τὸν λεγόμενον κρανίου τόπον, ὃ λέγεται Ἑβραϊστὶ Γολγοθά, ¹⁸ὅπου αὐτὸν ἐσταύρωσαν, καὶ μετ' αὐτοῦ ἄλλους δύο ἐντεῦθεν καὶ ἐντεῦθεν, μέσον δὲ τὸν Ἰησοῦν. ¹⁹ἔγραψεν δὲ καὶ τίτλον ὁ Πιλᾶτος καὶ ἔθηκεν ἐπὶ τοῦ σταυροῦ· ἦν δὲ γεγραμμένον· ΙΗΣΟΥΣ Ο ΝΑΖΩΡΑΙΟΣ Ο ΒΑΣΙΛΕΥΣ ΤΩΝ ΙΟΥΔΑΙΩΝ. |...| (²⁰ᵇκαὶ ἦν γεγραμμένον Ἑβραϊστί, Ῥωμαϊστί, Ἑλληνιστί.) |...| ²³οἱ |...| στρατιῶται |...| ἔλαβον τὰ ἱμάτια αὐτοῦ καὶ ἐποίησαν τέσσερα μέρη, ἑκάστῳ στρατιώτῃ μέρος, καὶ τὸν χιτῶνα. ἦν δὲ ὁ χιτὼν ἄρραφος, ἐκ τῶν ἄνωθεν ὑφαντὸς δι' ὅλου. ²⁴εἶπαν οὖν πρὸς ἀλλήλους· μὴ σχίσωμεν αὐτόν, ἀλλὰ λάχωμεν περὶ αὐτοῦ τίνος ἔσται· ἵνα ἡ γραφὴ πληρωθῇ· διεμερίσαντο τὰ ἱμάτιά μου ἑαυτοῖς καὶ ἐπὶ τὸν ἱματισμόν μου ἔβαλον κλῆρον. |...| ²⁸(μετὰ τοῦτο) |...| ἵνα τελειωθῇ ἡ γραφή, λέγει· διψῶ. ²⁹σκεῦος ἔκειτο ὄξους μεστόν· σπόγγον οὖν μεστὸν τοῦ ὄξους [ὑσσῷ] περιθέντες προσήνεγκαν αὐτοῦ τῷ στόματι. |...| ³⁰ᵇκαὶ κλίνας τὴν κεφαλὴν παρέδωκεν τὸ πνεῦμα. ⟦²⁵εἱστήκεισαν δὲ παρὰ τῷ σταυρῷ τοῦ Ἰησοῦ ἡ μήτηρ αὐτοῦ καὶ ἡ ἀδελφὴ τῆς μητρὸς αὐτοῦ, Μαρία ἡ τοῦ Κλωπᾶ καὶ Μαρία ἡ Μαγδαληνή.⟧ ³¹|...| ἐπεὶ παρασκευὴ ἦν, ἵνα μὴ μείνῃ ἐπὶ τοῦ σταυροῦ τὰ σώματα ἐν τῷ σαββάτῳ, |...| ἠρώτησαν τὸν Πιλᾶτον ἵνα κατεαγῶσιν αὐτῶν τὰ σκέλη καὶ ἀρθῶσιν. ³²ἦλθον οὖν οἱ στρατιῶται, καὶ τοῦ μὲν πρώτου κατέαξαν τὰ σκέλη καὶ τοῦ ἄλλου τοῦ συσταυρωθέντος αὐτῷ· ³³ἐπὶ δὲ τὸν Ἰησοῦν ἐλθόντες (ὡς εἶδον ἤδη αὐτὸν τεθνηκότα) οὐ κατέαξαν αὐτοῦ τὰ σκέλη, ³⁴ᵃἀλλ' εἷς τῶν στρατιωτῶν λόγχῃ αὐτοῦ τὴν πλευρὰν ἔνυξεν. |...| ³⁶ἐγένετο γὰρ ταῦτα ἵνα ἡ γραφὴ πληρωθῇ· ὀστοῦν οὐ συντριβήσεται αὐτοῦ. ³⁷καὶ πάλιν ἑτέρα γραφὴ λέγει· ὄψονται εἰς ὃν ἐξεκέντησαν. ³⁸(μετὰ δὲ ταῦτα) ἠρώτησεν τὸν Πιλᾶτον Ἰωσὴφ ἀπὸ Ἁριμαθαίας, ὢν μαθητὴς τοῦ Ἰησοῦ |...|, ἵνα ἄρῃ τὸ σῶμα τοῦ Ἰησοῦ· καὶ ἐπέτρεψεν ὁ
3 Πιλᾶτος. ἦλθ[ο]ν οὖν καὶ ἦρ[α]ν τὸ σῶμα αὐτοῦ. (⟦¹ἦν δὲ
19 ἄνθρωπος ἐκ τῶν Φαρισαίων, Νικόδημος ὄνομα αὐτῷ.⟧ ³⁹ἦλθεν δὲ καὶ Νικόδημος |...| φέρων μίγμα σμύρνης καὶ ἀλόης ὡς λίτρας ἑκατόν. ⁴⁰ἔλαβον |...| τὸ σῶμα τοῦ Ἰησοῦ) καὶ ἔδησαν αὐτὸ ὀθονίοις (μετὰ τῶν ἀρωμάτων) |...|. ⁴¹ἦν δὲ ἐν τῷ τόπῳ ὅπου ἐσταυρώθη κῆπος, καὶ ἐν τῷ κήπῳ μνημεῖον καινόν, ἐν ᾧ οὐδέπω οὐδεὶς ἦν τεθειμένος· ⁴²ἐκεῖ οὖν διὰ τὴν παρασκευήν |...|, ὅτι ἐγγὺς ἦν τὸ μνημεῖον, ἔθηκαν τὸν Ἰησοῦν.

The resurrection

20 ¹Τῇ δὲ μιᾷ τῶν σαββάτων Μαρία ἡ Μαγδαληνὴ ἔρχεται πρωῒ
|...| εἰς τὸ μνημεῖον, καὶ βλέπει τὸν λίθον ἠρμένον ἐκ τοῦ μνη-
μείου. ²τρέχει οὖν καὶ ἔρχεται πρὸς (Σίμωνα) Πέτρον |...| καὶ
λέγει αὐτ[ῷ]· ἦραν τὸν κύριον ἐκ τοῦ μνημείου, καὶ οὐκ οἴδαμεν
ποῦ ἔθηκαν αὐτόν. ³ἐξῆλθεν οὖν ὁ Πέτρος |...| καὶ ἤρχοντο εἰς τὸ
μνημεῖον. |...| ⁵καὶ παρακύψας βλέπει κείμενα τὰ ὀθόνια |...|
⁷καὶ τὸ σουδάριον, ὃ ἦν ἐπὶ τῆς κεφαλῆς αὐτοῦ, οὐ μετὰ τῶν
ὀθονίων κείμενον ἀλλὰ χωρὶς ἐντετυλιγμένον εἰς ἕνα τόπον. ⁸|...|
καὶ [ἐθαύμασεν] |...|· ⁹οὐδέπω γὰρ ᾔδεισαν τὴν γραφήν, ὅτι δεῖ
αὐτὸν ἐκ νεκρῶν ἀναστῆναι. ¹⁰ἀπῆλθ[ε]ν |...| πάλιν πρὸς
αὐτ[ὸν ὁ Πέτρος]. ¹¹Μαρία δὲ εἰστήκει πρὸς τῷ μνημείῳ |...|
κλαίουσα. ὡς |...| ἔκλαιεν, παρέκυψεν εἰς τὸ μνημεῖον, ¹²καὶ
θεωρεῖ δύο ἀγγέλους ἐν λευκοῖς καθεζομένους, ἕνα πρὸς τῇ κεφαλῇ
καὶ ἕνα πρὸς τοῖς ποσίν, ὅπου ἔκειτο τὸ σῶμα τοῦ Ἰησοῦ. |...|
¹⁴ἐστράφη εἰς τὰ ὀπίσω, καὶ θεωρεῖ τὸν Ἰησοῦν ἑστῶτα |...|.
¹⁶λέγει αὐτῇ Ἰησοῦς· Μαριάμ. |...| ἐκείνη λέγει αὐτῷ Ἑβραϊστί·
ῥαββουνί |...|. ¹⁷λέγει αὐτῇ Ἰησοῦς· (μή μου ἅπτου) |...|·
πορεύου (δὲ) πρὸς τοὺς ἀδελφούς μου καὶ εἰπὲ αὐτοῖς. |...|
¹⁸ἔρχεται Μαριὰμ ἡ Μαγδαληνὴ ἀγγέλλουσα τοῖς μαθηταῖς ὅτι
ἑώρακα τὸν κύριον |...|, [ἀλλ᾽ ἠπίστησαν]. ¹⁹οὔσης |...| ὀψίας
|...| καὶ τῶν θυρῶν κεκλεισμένων ὅπου ἦσαν οἱ μαθηταί |...|,
ἦλθεν ὁ Ἰησοῦς καὶ ἔστη εἰς τὸ μέσον, καὶ (λέγει αὐτοῖς· εἰρήνη
ὑμῖν. ²⁰καὶ τοῦτο εἰπὼν) ἔδειξεν καὶ τὰς χεῖρας καὶ τὴν πλευρὰν
αὐτοῖς. ἐχάρησαν (οὖν) οἱ μαθηταὶ ἰδόντες τὸν κύριον.

Peroration

³⁰Πολλὰ μὲν |...| καὶ ἄλλα σημεῖα ἐποίησεν ὁ Ἰησοῦς ἐνώπιον
τῶν μαθητῶν, ἃ οὐκ ἔστιν γεγραμμένα ἐν τῷ βιβλίῳ τούτῳ·
³¹ταῦτα δὲ γέγραπται ἵνα πιστεύητε ὅτι Ἰησοῦς ἐστιν ὁ χριστὸς
ὁ υἱὸς τοῦ θεοῦ |...|.

BIBLIOGRAPHY

For works cited by author only, see the List of Abbreviations (pp. xi–xii) and the bibliography, if any, at the beginning of the section in question. Reference works used are cited only in the List of Abbreviations.

BACON, B. W. *The fourth gospel in research and debate.* New York, 1910.
'After six days: A new clue for gospel critics', *HTR* 8 (1915), 94–121.
'Sources and method of the fourth evangelist', *HJ* 25 (1926/7), 115–30.
The gospel of the Hellenists. Ed. C. H. Kraeling. New York, 1933.
BAILEY, J. A. *The traditions common to the gospels of Luke and John.* (Supplements to *NovT*, 7.) Leiden, 1963.
BALMFORTH, H. 'The structure of the fourth gospel', *StudEv* II (1964), 25–33.
BARRETT, C. K. 'The Old Testament in the fourth gospel', *JTS* 48 (1947/8), 155–69.
'The Lamb of God', *NTS* 1 (1954/5), 210–18.
The gospel according to St John: An introduction with commentary and notes on the Greek text. London, 1955.
Review of Wilkens, *Entstehungsgeschichte,* in *TL* 84 (1959), 828–9.
BARROSSE, T. 'The seven days of the new creation in St John's gospel', *CBQ* 21 (1959), 507–16.
BAUER, W. *Das Johannesevangelium.* 3rd ed. (Handbuch zum Neuen Testament, 6.) Tübingen, 1933.
A Greek–English lexicon of the New Testament and other early Christian literature. Tr. and ed. W. F. Arndt and F. W. Gingrich. Chicago, 1957.
BAUR, F. C. *Kritische Untersuchungen über die kanonischen Evangelien, ihr Verhältnis zu einander, ihren Charakter und Ursprung.* Tübingen, 1847.
BEHM, J. 'Der gegenwärtige Stand der Erforschung des Johannesevangeliums', *TL* 73 (1948), 21–30.
BENOIT, P. 'Marie-Madeleine et les disciples au tombeau selon Joh 20,1–18', in *Judentum, Urchristentum, Kirche* (Jeremias Festschrift; ed. W. Eltester; *Beihefte zur ZNW,* 26; Berlin, 1960), 141–52.
BEVAN, E. 'Note on Mark i 41 and John xi 33, 38', *JTS* 33 (1932), 186–8.

BLACK, M. *An Aramaic approach to the gospels and Acts.* Oxford, 1946.

BLANK, J. 'Die Verhandlung vor Pilatus Joh 18,28–19,16 im Lichte johanneischer Theologie', *BZ* n.s. 3 (1959), 60–81.

BLIGH, J. 'Jesus in Samaria', *HeyJ* 3 (1962), 329–46.

'Jesus in Jerusalem', *ibid.* 4 (1963), 115–34.

'Jesus in Galilee', *ibid.* 5 (1964), 3–26.

BOISMARD, M.-É. 'Le chapitre 21 de saint Jean: Essai de critique littéraire', *RB* 54 (1947), 473–501.

'Problèmes de critique textuelle concernant le quatrième évangile', *RB* 60 (1953), 347–71.

Du baptême à Cana (Jean 1: 19–2: 11). (Lectio Divina, 18.) Paris, 1956.

St John's prologue. Tr. Carisbrooke Dominicans. London, 1957.

et al. L'évangile de Jean: Études et problèmes. (Recherches Bibliques, 3.) Bruges, 1958.

'Saint Luc et la rédaction du quatrième évangile (Jn 4. 46–54)', *RB* 69 (1962), 185–211.

'Les traditions johanniques concernant le Baptiste', *RB* 70 (1963), 5–42.

'Le lavement des pieds (Joh xiii,1–17)', *RB* 71 (1964), 5–24.

Review of Schnackenburg and Brown, *RB* 74 (1967), 581–5.

BONNER, C. 'Traces of thaumaturgic technique in the miracles', *HTR* 20 (1927), 171–81.

BORGEN, P. 'John and the synoptics in the passion narrative', *NTS* 5 (1958/9), 246–59.

'Observations on the midrashic character of John 6', *ZNW* 54 (1963), 232–40.

BOUSSET, W. 'Ist das vierte Evangelium eine literarische Einheit?', *TR* 12 (1909), 1–12, 39–64.

'Johannesevangelium', *RGG*, 1st ed. III (1912), 608–36.

BOWMAN, J. 'Samaritan studies', *BJRL* 40 (1957/8), 298–327.

BRAUN, F.-M. 'Quatre "signes" johanniques de l'unité chrétienne', *NTS* 9 (1962/3), 147–55.

BROWN, R. E. *New Testament essays.* Milwaukee, 1965.

The gospel according to John (i–xii). (Anchor Bible, 29.) Garden City, 1966.

BRUCE, F. F. 'When is a gospel not a gospel?', *BJRL* 45 (1963), 319–39.

BRUN, L. *Die Auferstehung Christi in der urchristlichen Überlieferung.* Oslo, 1925.

BULTMANN, R. 'Das Johannesevangelium in der neuesten Forschung', *CW* 41 (1927), 502–11.

'Hirsch's Auslegung des Johannesevangeliums', *EvTh* 4 (1937), 115–42.

BULTMANN, R. Review of Noack, *Tradition*, in *TL* 80 (1955), 521–6.
Das Evangelium des Johannes. 16th ed. with Ergänzungsheft.
(Meyers Kommentar.) Göttingen, 1959.
'Johannesevangelium', *RGG*, 3rd ed. III (1959), 840–50.
The history of the synoptic tradition. Tr. J. Marsh. Oxford, 1963.
BUSE, I. 'John v. 8 and Johannine–Marcan relationships', *NTS* 1 (1954/5), 134–6.
'St John and the Marcan passion narrative', *NTS* 4 (1957/8), 215–19.
'St John and "The first synoptic pericope"', *NovT* 3 (1959), 57–61.
'St John and the passion narratives of St Matthew and St Luke', *NTS* 7 (1960/1), 65–76.
CASEY, R. P. 'Professor Goodenough and the fourth gospel', *JBL* 64 (1945), 535–42.
CASSIAN, Bishop (S. Bésobrasoff). 'John xxi', *NTS* 3 (1956/7), 132–6.
COLWELL, E. C. *John defends the gospel.* Chicago, 1936.
CULLMANN, O. *The christology of the New Testament.* Tr. S. C. Guthrie and C. A. M. Hall. Philadelphia, 1959.
DAUBE, D. *The New Testament and Rabbinic Judaism.* (Jordan Lectures 1952.) London, 1956.
DELFF, H. *Das vierte Evangelium, ein authentischer Bericht über Jesus von Nazareth, wiederhergestellt, übersetzt und erklärt.* Husum, 1890.
DERRETT, J. D. M. 'Fresh light on St Luke xvi: II. Dives and Lazarus and the preceding sayings', *NTS* 7 (1960/1), 364–80.
'Water into wine', *BZ* n.s. 7 (1963), 80–97.
'The anointing at Bethany', *StudEv* II (1964), 174–82.
DIBELIUS, M. *Die urchristliche Überlieferung von Johannes dem Täufer.* (*FRLANT*, 15.) Göttingen, 1911.
'Johannesevangelium', *RGG*, 2nd ed. III (1929), 349–63.
From tradition to gospel. Tr. B. L. Woolf. New York, 1935.
Review of Bultmann, *TL* 67 (1942), 257–63.
'Die alttestamentlichen Motive in der Leidensgeschichte des Petrus- und des Johannes-evangeliums', in *Botschaft und Geschichte*, I (Tübingen, 1953), 221–47.
DILLON, R. J. 'Wisdom tradition and sacramental retrospect in the Cana account (Jn 2, 1–11)', *CBQ* 24 (1962), 268–96.
DINKLER, E. 'Das Kana-Wunder (Joh. 2,1–12)', in *Fragen der wissenschaftlichen Erforschung der Heiligen Schrift: Sonderdruck aus dem Protokoll der Landessynode der evg. Kirche im Rheinland Jan. 1962*, 47–61.
DODD, C. H. *The interpretation of the fourth gospel.* Cambridge, 1953.
'The appearances of the risen Christ: An essay in form-criticism

of the gospels', in *Studies in the gospels: Essays in memory of R. H. Lightfoot*, ed. D. E. Nineham (Oxford, 1957), 9–35.

'The prophecy of Caiaphas', in *Neotestamentica et Patristica* (Cullmann Festschrift; ed. W. C. van Unnik; Supplements to *NovT*, 6; Leiden, 1962), 134–43.

Historical tradition in the fourth gospel. Cambridge, 1963.

DUNKERLEY, R. 'Lazarus', *NTS* 5 (1958/9), 321–7.

EISSFELDT, O. *The Old Testament: An introduction...* Tr. P. R. Ackroyd. New York and Evanston, 1965.

ELTESTER, W. 'Der Logos und sein Prophet, Fragen zur heutigen Erklärung des johanneischen Prologs', in *Apophoreta* (Haenchen Festschrift; ed. W. Eltester and F. H. Kettler; Berlin, 1964), 109–34.

EMERTON, J. A. 'The hundred and fifty-three fishes in John xxi. 11', *JTS* n.s. 9 (1958), 86–9.

ENZ, J. J. 'The book of Exodus as a literary type for the gospel of John', *JBL* 76 (1957), 208–15.

EPPSTEIN, V. 'The historicity of the gospel account of the cleansing of the temple', *ZNW* 55 (1964), 42–58.

FAURE, A. 'Die alttestamentlichen Zitate im vierten Evangelium und die Quellenscheidungshypothese', *ZNW* 21 (1922), 99–121.

FEUILLET, A. *Études johanniques*. (Museum Lessianum, Section biblique, 4.) Paris/Bruges, 1962.

FREED, E. D. 'The entry into Jerusalem in the gospel of John', *JBL* 80 (1961), 329–38.

'Variations in the language and thought of John', *ZNW* 55 (1964), 167–97.

Old Testament quotations in the gospel of John. (Supplements to *NovT*, 11.) Leiden, 1965.

FULLER, R. H. *Interpreting the miracles*. Philadelphia, 1963.

GÄRTNER, B. *John 6 and the Jewish Passover*. (Coniectanea Neotestamentica, 17.) Lund/Copenhagen, 1959.

GARDNER-SMITH, P. *Saint John and the synoptic gospels*. Cambridge, 1938.

'St John's knowledge of Matthew', *JTS* n.s. 4 (1953), 31–5.

GARVIE, A. E. *The beloved disciple: Studies of the fourth gospel*. New York, 1922.

GEORGI, D. *Die Gegner des Paulus im 2. Korintherbrief: Studien zur religiösen Propaganda in der Spätantike*. Neukirchen–Vluyn, 1964.

GERICKE, W. 'Zur Entstehung des Johannes-Evangeliums', *TL* 90 (1965), 807–20.

GLASSON, T. F. 'John the Baptist in the fourth gospel', *ET* 67 (1955/6), 245–6.

DE GOEDT, M. 'Un schème de révélation dans le quatrième évangile', *NTS* 8 (1961/2), 142–50.

GOGUEL, M. *Les sources du récit johannique de la passion.* Paris, 1910. *Introduction au Nouveau Testament.* II: *Le quatrième évangile.* Paris, 1923.

GOODENOUGH, E. R. 'John a primitive gospel', *JBL* 64 (1945), 145–82.

GOODWIN, C. 'How did John treat his sources?', *JBL* 73 (1954), 61–75.

GRANT, F. C. 'Was the author of John dependent upon the gospel of Luke?', *JBL* 56 (1937), 285–307.

GRANT, R. M. '"One hundred fifty-three large fishes" (John 21. 11)', *HTR* 42 (1949), 273–5.

GREEN, H. C. 'The composition of St John's prologue', *ET* 66 (1954/5), 291–4.

GROBEL, K. '"He that cometh after me"', *JBL* 60 (1941), 397–401.

GROSSOUW, W. K. 'A note on John xiii 1–3', *NovT* 8 (1966), 124–31.

GRUNDMANN, W. 'Die Apostel zwischen Jerusalem und Antiochia', *ZNW* 39 (1940), 110–37.
Zeugnis und Gestalt des Johannesevangeliums: Eine Studie zur denkerischen und gestalterischen Leistung des vierten Evangelisten. Stuttgart, 1961.
'Verkündigung und Geschichte in dem Bericht vom Eingang der Geschichte Jesu im Johannes-Evangelium', in *Der historische Jesus und der kerygmatische Christus: Beiträge zum Christusverständnis in Forschung und Verkündigung* (ed. H. Ristow and K. Matthiae; Berlin, 1961), 289–309.

HAENCHEN, E. 'Aus der Literatur zum Johannesevangelium 1929–56', *TR* n.s. 23 (1955), 295–335.
'Johanneische Probleme', *ZTK* 56 (1959), 19–54.
'Jesus vor Pilatus (Joh 18,23–19,15): Zur Methode der Auslegung', *TL* 85 (1960), 93–102.
'Die Komposition von Mk vii [viii] 27—ix 1 und Par', *NovT* 6 (1963), 81–109.
'Probleme des johanneischen "Prologs"', in *Gott und Mensch: Gesammelte Aufsätze* (Tübingen, 1965), 114–43 [= *ZTK* 60 (1963), 305–34].

HARTKE, W. *Vier urchristliche Parteien und ihre Vereinigung zur apostolischen Kirche.* I: *Johannes und die Synoptiker.* Berlin, 1961.

HARTMANN, G. 'Die Vorlage der Osterberichte in Joh 20', *ZNW* 55 (1964), 197–220.

HEISE, J. *Bleiben: Menein in den johanneischen Schriften.* (Hermeneutische Untersuchungen zur Theologie, 8.) Tübingen, 1967.

HEITMÜLLER, W. 'Zur Johannes-Tradition', *ZNW* 15 (1914), 189–209.

HIRSCH, E. *Studien zum vierten Evangelium.* (Beiträge zur historischen Theologie, 4.) Tübingen, 1936.

'Stilkritik und Literaranalyse im vierten Evangelium', *ZNW* 43 (1950/1), 129–43.

HOSKYNS, E. C. *The fourth gospel.* Ed. F. N. Davey, 2nd ed. rev. London, 1947.

HOWARD, W. F. *The fourth gospel in recent criticism and interpretation.* London, 1931. (4th ed. rev. C. K. Barrett, London, 1955.)

HOWTON, J. ' "Son of God" in the fourth gospel', *NTS* 10 (1963/4), 227–37.

VAN IERSEL, B. M. F. 'Tradition und Redaktion in Joh I 19–36', *NovT* 5 (1962/3), 245–67.

JEREMIAS, J. 'Die Berufung des Nathanael', Ἄγγελος 3 (1928), 2–5.

'Johanneische Literarkritik', *TB* 20 (1941), 33–46.

Die Wiederentdeckung von Bethesda, Johannes 5,2. (*FRLANT* n.s. 41.) Göttingen, 1949.

The parables of Jesus. Tr. S. H. Hooke. New York, 1955.

'The copper scroll from Qumran', *ET* 71 (1959/60), 227 f.

'The revealing word', in *The central message of the New Testament* (New York, 1965), 71–90.

JOHNSTON, E. D. 'The Johannine version of the feeding of the five thousand: An independent tradition?', *NTS* 8 (1961/2), 151–4.

KÄSEMANN, E. Review of Bultmann, in *VF* 3 (1942–6), 182–201.

'Aufbau und Anliegen des johanneischen Prologs', in *Libertas Christiana* (Delekat Festschrift; ed. W. Matthias; München, 1957), 75–99.

KEE, H. C. 'The terminology of Mark's exorcism stories', *NTS* 14 (1967/8), 232–46.

KILMARTIN, E. J. 'Liturgical influence on John 6', *CBQ* 22 (1960), 183–91.

KNACKSTEDT, J. 'Die beiden Brotvermehrungen im Evangelium', *NTS* 10 (1963/4), 309–35.

KÖSTER, H. *Synoptische Überlieferung bei den apostolischen Vätern.* Berlin, 1957.

'Häretiker im Urchristentum', *RGG*, 3rd ed. III (1959), 17–21.

'One Jesus and four primitive gospels', *HTR* 61 (1968), 203–47.

KRAFFT, E. 'Die Personen des Johannesevangeliums', *EvTh* 16 (1956), 18–32.

KÜMMEL, W. G. *Introduction to the New Testament.* Tr. A. J. Mattill, jr. 14th rev. ed. ('Founded by Paul Feine and Johannes Behm.') Nashville–New York, 1966.

LAGRANGE, M.-J. *Évangile selon saint Jean.* 3rd ed. Paris, 1927.

LEANEY, A. R. C. 'The resurrection narratives in Luke (xxiv. 12–53)', *NTS* 2 (1955/6), 110–14.

LEE, E. K. 'St Mark and the fourth gospel', *NTS* 3 (1956/7), 50–8.

LEGAULT, A. 'An application of the form-critique method to the anointings in Galilee (Lk 7, 36–50) and Bethany (Mt 26, 6–13; Mk 14, 3–9; Jn 12, 1–8)', *CBQ* 16 (1954), 131–45.

LÉON-DUFOUR, X. 'Passion', II, 1: 'Le récit selon S. Jean', in *Dictionnaire de la Bible, Supplément*, VI (Paris, 1957–60), 1438–44.

LIGHTFOOT, R. H. 'The narrative of St John 21', in *Locality and doctrine in the gospels* (New York–London, [1937]), 101–5.

'The cleansing of the temple in St John's gospel', in *The gospel message of St Mark* (Oxford, 1950), 70–9.

St John's gospel: A commentary. Ed. C. F. Evans. Oxford, 1956.

LINDARS, B. 'The composition of John xx', *NTS* 7 (1960/1), 142–7.

LOHMEYER, E. 'Über Aufbau und Gliederung des vierten Evangeliums', *ZNW* 27 (1928), 11–36.

MARTIN, J. P. 'History and eschatology in the Lazarus narrative, John 11. 1–44', *SJT* 17 (1964), 332–43.

MARTIN, V. *Papyrus Bodmer II: Évangile de Jean, Chap 1–14*. (Bibliotheca Bodmeriana, 5.) Cologny–Genève, 1956.

MASSON, C. 'Le prologue du quatrième évangile', *RThPh* 28 (1940), 297–311.

MEEKS, W. A. 'Galilee and Judea in the fourth gospel', *JBL* 85 (1966), 159–69.

MENDNER, S. 'Johanneische Literarkritik', *TZ* 8 (1952), 418–34.

'Die Tempelreinigung', *ZNW* 47 (1956), 93–112.

'Zum Problem "Johannes und die Synoptiker"', *NTS* 4 (1957/8), 282–307.

'Nikodemus', *JBL* 77 (1958), 293–323.

MENOUD, P.-H. *L'évangile de Jean d'après les recherches récentes*. Neuchâtel–Paris, 1943; 2nd ed. 1947.

'Les études johanniques de Bultmann à Barrett', in Boismard *et al. L'évangile de Jean*, 11–40.

MERLIER, O. *Le quatrième évangile*. II: *Généralités: La question johannique*. Athènes, 1961.

MEYER, P. W. 'The eschatology of the fourth gospel: A study in early Christian reinterpretation.' Unpublished ThD dissertation, Union Theological Seminary. New York, 1955.

MICHAELIS, W. *Einleitung in das Neue Testament*. 2nd ed. Bern, 1954.

MICHEL, O. 'Der Anfang der Zeichen Jesu', in *Die Leibhaftigkeit des Wortes* (Köberle Festgabe; ed. O. Michel and U. Mann; Hamburg, 1958), 15–22.

'Ein johanneischer Osterbericht', in *Studien zum Neuen Testament und zur Patristik* (Klostermann Festschrift; Texte und Untersuchungen, 77; Berlin, 1961), 35–42.

MOFFATT, J. *Introduction to the literature of the New Testament.* New York, 1911.

MOLLAT, D. 'La guérison de l'aveugle-né', *BVC* 23 (1958), 22–31. *L'évangile de Saint Jean.* 2nd ed. (Bible de Jérusalem.) Paris, 1960.

MORRIS, L. 'Synoptic themes illuminated by the fourth gospel', *StudEv* II (1964), 73–84.

NOACK, B. *Zur johanneischen Tradition: Beiträge zur Kritik an der literarkritischen Analyse des vierten Evangeliums.* København, 1954.

OSTY, E. 'Les points de contact entre le récit de la passion dans saint Luc et dans saint Jean', in *Mélanges Jules Lebreton*, I (Recherches de science religieuse, 39; Paris, 1951), 146–54.

QUISPEL, G. 'Nathanael und der Menschensohn (Joh 1,51)', *ZNW* 47 (1956), 281–3.

VON RAD, G. *Genesis: A commentary.* Tr. J. H. Marks. London, 1961.

RAMSEY, A. M. 'The narratives of the passion', *StudEv* II (1964), 122–34.

RICHARDSON, A. *The miracle-stories of the gospels.* 2nd ed. London, 1942.

RIDDERBOS, H. N. 'The structure and scope of the prologue to the gospel of John', *NovT* 8 (1966), 180–201.

ROBINSON, J. A. T. 'Elijah, John, and Jesus: An essay in detection', *NTS* 4 (1957/8), 263–81.
'The destination and purpose of St John's gospel', *NTS* 6 (1959/60), 117–31.
'The significance of the foot-washing', in *Neotestamentica et Patristica* (Cullmann Festschrift; ed. W. C. van Unnik; Supplements to *NovT*, 6; Leiden, 1962), 144–7.
'The relation of the prologue to the gospel of St John', *NTS* 9 (1962/3), 120–9.

ROBINSON, J. M. 'Recent research in the fourth gospel', *JBL* 78 (1959), 242–52.
'Basic shifts in German theology', *Interpretation* 16 (1962), 76–97.
'The problem of history in Mark, reconsidered', *Union Seminary Quarterly Review* 20 (1964/5), 131–47.
'Kerygma and history in the New Testament', in *The Bible in modern scholarship: Papers read at the 100th meeting of the Society of Biblical Literature—December 28–30, 1964* (ed. J. P. Hyatt; Nashville, 1965), 114–50.
Kerygma und historischer Jesus. 2nd ed. Zürich, 1967.

RUCKSTUHL, E. *Die literarische Einheit des Johannesevangeliums: Der gegenwärtige Stand der einschlägigen Forschungen.* (Studia Friburgensia n.s. 3.) Freiburg in der Schweiz, 1951.

SAHLIN, H. 'Zwei Abschnitte aus Joh 1 rekonstruiert', *ZNW* 51 (1960), 64–9.

SANDERS, J. N. '"Those whom Jesus loved" (John xi. 5)', *NTS* 1 (1954/5), 29–41.

SCHMIDT, K. L. 'Der johanneische Charakter der Erzählung vom Hochzeitswunder in Kana', in *Harnack-Ehrung: Beiträge zur Kirchengeschichte*... (Leipzig, 1921), 32–43.

SCHNACKENBURG, R. *Das erste Wunder Jesu (Joh 2, 1–11).* Freiburg i. B. 1951.

'Logos-Hymnus und johanneischer Prolog', *BZ* n.s. 1 (1957), 69–109.

'Zur Traditionsgeschichte von Joh 4, 46–54', *BZ* n.s. 8 (1964), 58–88.

Das Johannesevangelium. 1: Einleitung und Kommentar zu Kap. 1–4. (Herders Theologischer Kommentar zum Neuen Testament, IV.) Freiburg, 1965.

SCHNEIDER, J. 'Zur Komposition von Joh 7', *ZNW* 45 (1954), 108–19.

'Zur Komposition von Joh 18,12–27', *ZNW* 48 (1957), 111–19.

SCHULZ, A. 'Das Wunder zu Kana im Lichte des Alten Testaments', *BZ* 16 (1922), 93–6.

SCHULZ, S. *Untersuchungen zur Menschensohn-Christologie im Johannesevangelium: Zugleich ein Beitrag zur Methodengeschichte der Auslegung des 4. Evangeliums.* Göttingen, 1957.

'Die Komposition des Johannesprologs und die Zusammensetzung des 4. Evangeliums', in *Stud Ev* 1 (1959), 350–62.

SCHWARTZ, E. 'Aporien im vierten Evangelium', in *Nachrichten von der Königlichen Gesellschaft der Wissenschaften zu Göttingen: Philologisch-historische Klasse* (1907), 342–72; (1908), 115–88, 497–650.

'Johannes und Kerinthos', *ZNW* 15 (1914), 210–19.

SCHWEIZER, E. *Ego eimi...: Die religionsgeschichtliche Herkunft und theologische Bedeutung der johanneischen Bildreden, zugleich ein Beitrag zur Quellenfrage des vierten Evangeliums.* (*FRLANT* n.s. 38.) Göttingen, 1939; 2nd ed. 1965.

'Die Heilung des Königlichen, Joh 4,46–54', *EvTh* 11 (1951/2), 64–71.

'Das johanneische Zeugnis vom Herrenmahl', *EvTh* 12 (1952/3), 341–63.

SEITZ, O. J. F. 'Gospel prologues: A common pattern?', *JBL* 83 (1964), 262–8.

SMEND, F. 'Die Behandlung alttestamentlicher Zitate als Ausgangspunkt der Quellenscheidung im 4. Evangelium', *ZNW* 24 (1925), 147–50.

SMITH, C. W. F. 'Tabernacles in the fourth gospel and Mark', *NTS* 9 (1962/3), 130–46.

SMITH, D. M. 'John 12: 12 f. and the question of John's use of the synoptics', *JBL* 82 (1963), 58–64.

'The sources of the gospel of John: An assessment of the present state of the problem', *NTS* 10 (1963/4), 336–51.

The composition and order of the fourth gospel: Bultmann's literary theory. New Haven and London, 1965.

SMITH, J. B. *Greek–English concordance to the New Testament: A tabular and statistical Greek–English concordance based on the King James Version.* . . Scottdale, Pa., 1955.

SMITH, R. H. 'Exodus typology in the fourth gospel', *JBL* 81 (1962), 329–42.

SMITMANS, A. *Das Weinwunder von Kana: Die Auslegung von Jo 2, 1–11 bei den Vätern und heute.* (Beiträge zur Geschichte der biblischen Exegese, 6.) Tübingen, 1966.

SOLTAU, G. C. W. *Das vierte Evangelium in seiner Entstehungsgeschichte dargelegt.* Heidelberg, 1916.

SPARKS, H. F. D. 'St John's knowledge of Matthew: The evidence of John 13. 16 and 15. 20', *JTS* n.s. 3 (1952), 58–61.

SPITTA, F. *Das Johannes-Evangelium als Quelle der Geschichte Jesu.* Göttingen, 1910.

STENDAHL, K. *The school of St Matthew and its uses of the Old Testament.* Uppsala, 1954.

STRACHAN, R. H. 'Spitta on John xxi', *Exp* 4 (1912), 363–9, 554–61.

'Is the fourth gospel a literary unity?', *ET* 27 (1916), 22–6, 232–7, 280–2, 330–3.

STREETER, B. H. *The four gospels: A study of origins.* . . New York, 1925.

TAYLOR, V. *The formation of the gospel tradition.* London, 1933.

TEEPLE, H. M. *The Mosaic eschatological prophet.* (*JBL* Monograph Series, 10.) Philadelphia, 1957.

'Methodology in source analysis of the fourth gospel', *JBL* 81 (1962), 279–86.

TEMPLE, S. 'The two traditions of the last supper, betrayal, and arrest', *NTS* 7 (1960/1), 77–85.

'The two signs in the fourth gospel', *JBL* 81 (1962), 169–74.

TENNEY, M. C. 'The footnotes of John's gospel', *Bibliotheca Sacra* 117 (1960), 350–64.

THOMPSON, J. M. 'Is John xxi an appendix?', *Exp* 10 (1915), 139–47.

'The structure of the fourth gospel', *Exp* 10 (1915), 512–26.

THOMPSON, J. M. 'The composition of the fourth gospel', *Exp* 11 (1916), 34–46.

'Some editorial elements in the fourth gospel', *Exp* 14 (1917), 214–31.

TRUDINGER, P. 'A "Lazarus motif" in primitive Christian preaching?', *Andover Newton Quarterly* 7 (1966/7), 29–32.

VAN UNNIK, W. C. 'The purpose of St John's gospel', in *StudEv* 1 (1959), 382–411.

VAGANAY, L. 'Le finale du quatrième évangile', *RB* 45 (1936), 512–28.

VIRGULIN, S. 'Recent discussion of the title, "Lamb of God"', *Scripture* 13 (1961), 74–80.

WELLHAUSEN, J. *Erweiterungen und Änderungen im vierten Evangelium.* Berlin, 1907.

Das Evangelium Johannis. Berlin, 1908.

WENDT, H. H. *The gospel according to St John: An inquiry into its genesis and historical value.* Tr. E. Lummis. New York, 1902. (Original German edition, 1900.)

Die Schichten im vierten Evangelium. Göttingen, 1911.

WIEAND, D. J. 'John v. 2 and the pool of Bethesda', *NTS* 12 (1965/6), 392–404.

WILKENS, W. *Die Entstehungsgeschichte des vierten Evangeliums.* Zollikon, 1958.

'Die Erweckung des Lazarus', *TZ* 15 (1959), 22–39.

'Evangelist und Tradition im Johannesevangelium', *TZ* 16 (1960), 81–90.

WILLIAMS, F. E. 'Fourth gospel and synoptic tradition: Two Johannine passages', *JBL* 86 (1967), 311–19.

WILSON, R. McL. Review of Köster, *Überlieferung*, in *NTS* 5 (1958/9), 144–6.

WINDISCH, H. 'Der johanneische Erzählungsstil', in ΕΥΧΑΡΙΣ-ΤΗΡΙΟΝ (Gunkel Festschrift; ed. H. Schmidt; *FRLANT* n.s. 19 [1923], pt. 2), 174–213.

Johannes und die Synoptiker: Wollte der vierte Evangelist die älteren Evangelien ergänzen oder ersetzen? (Untersuchungen zum Neuen Testament, 12.) Leipzig, 1926.

WINK, W. *John the Baptist in the gospel tradition* (Society for New Testament Studies Monograph Series, 7.) Cambridge, 1968.

WINTER, P. *On the trial of Jesus.* (Studia Judaica, 1.) Berlin, 1961.

ZAHN, T. *Einleitung in das Neue Testament.* 2nd ed. Leipzig, 1900.

ZIENER, G. 'Weisheitsbuch und Johannesevangelium', *Bib* 38 (1957), 396–418, and 39 (1958), 37–60.

'Johannesevangelium und urchristliche Passafeier', *BZ* n.s. 2 (1958), 263–74.

I. INDEX OF PASSAGES CITED

A. OLD TESTAMENT AND APOCRYPHA

John (cont.)

13: 1–3	156
13: 1	32 n., 130 n., 149 n., 206 nn., 207 n., 213 n.
13: 1b	**157**, 205 n.
13: 3	115, 130 n., 207 n.
13: 4f.	92 n., 155, **157**
13: 5	215
13: 6–11	156
13: 8	206 n., 207 n.
13: 11	58
13: 12–15	156
13: 13	229 n.
13: 14	212 n.
13: 15	206 n.
13: 16f.	156
13: 16	207 n.
13: 18	71, 138 n., 206 n., 229 n.
13: 18b	**157**
13: 19	191
13: 20	156, 206 n., 207 nn.
13: 21	82, 205 n., 207 n., 210 n., 229 n.
13: 21b	**157**
13: 23	77, 135 n.
13: 24	43 n.
13: 26f.	**157**
13: 27	212 n.
13: 28	205 n.
13: 29	151
13: 30	52
13: 32f.	123
13: 32	52
13: 33	206 n., 207 nn.
13: 36b	207 n.
13: 37f.	**157**, 205 n.
13: 37	207 n.
13: 38	121, 207 nn., 229 n.
14–17	**157f.**
14: 1	82, 148
14: 2	207 n.
14: 3	152, 207 n.
14: 4	207 n.
14: 5	79, 132, 142 n.
14: 8	132
14: 10	207 n.
14: 12	187 n., 207 nn.
14: 14	207 n.
14: 15	206 n.
14: 16b	141
14: 19	207 n.
14: 22	197
14: 23	207 n.

14: 24	206 n.
14: 26	213 n.
14: 27	82, 141 n., 206 n.
14: 28	207 n.
14: 30	206 n.
14: 31	71, 211 n.
14: 31b	**157**
15: 4	207 nn.
15: 6	207 n.
15: 8	206 n.
15: 9	206 nn.
15: 11	206 n.
15: 12	206 n.
15: 13	206 n., 207 n.
15: 16	181 n.
15: 18	176
15: 19	207 n.
15: 22	207 n.
15: 24	207 n.
15: 25	71, 123 n.
15: 26	207 n., 213 n.
16: 2	206 n.
16: 4	206 n.
16: 5	209 n.
16: 7	207 nn.
16: 10	207 n.
16: 13	207 n.
16: 16–19	43
16: 16	207 n.
16: 17	207 nn., 209 n.
16: 18	207 n.
16: 19	206 n., 207 n.
16: 20	207 n.
16: 21	206 n.
16: 22	141
16: 23	94, 206 n., 207 nn.
16: 25	79 n., 197, 206 nn.
16: 27f.	206 n.
16: 27	58
16: 28	79 n., 207 n.
16: 29	197, 206 n.
16: 32	206 n.
16: 32b	**157**, 215
17: 1	37 n., 57
17: 2	206 n.
17: 3	206 n.
17: 5	37 n., 206 n.
17: 6	37, 89
17: 12	138 n., 209 n.
17: 13	206 n.
17: 14	207 n.
17: 15	41 n.
17: 16	207 n.

C. OTHER ANCIENT WRITINGS

II. INDEX OF GREEK WORDS AND PHRASES

271

III. INDEX OF AUTHORS

Aland, K., 135 n.

Bacon, B. W., 1 n., 3 n., 9, 179 n., 183 n.
Bailey, J. A., 9 n., 47 n., 95 n., 157
Balmforth, H., 9 n.
Barosse, T., 167 n., 179 n., 183 n.
Barrett, C. K., xi, 1 n., 7 n., 9 n., 10 n., 12 n., 36 n., 50 n., 54, 55 n., 56, 57, 59, 62, 67, 68, 76, 81 n., 88 n., 92 n., 105 n., 115, 123 n., 129 n., 151 n., 175 n., 182 n., 183, 195
Bauer, W., xi, 30, 32 n., 50, 51, 57 n., 62 n., 71, 75, 76, 80, 89, 91, 125 n., 171 n., 172, 177 n., 231 n.
Baur, F. C., 9
Behm, J., 1 n., 3 n.
Benoit, P., 131 n., 134 n., 135 n., 138 n.
Bevan, E., 82 n.
Blank, J., 122 n., 125
Bligh, J., 48 n., 55 n., 56 n., 189 n., 195 n.
Boismard, M.-É., 4 n., 9 n., 10 n., 29 n., 31 n., 38 n., 39 n., 46, 47, 58 n., 64 n., 87 n., 88 n., 155 n., 162 n., 167, 168, 170 n., 179 n., 180 n., 183 n.
Borgen, P., 9 n., 11 n., 113 n., 172 n., 232 n.
Bousset, W., 1 n.
Bowman, J., 189 n., 193
Braun, F.-M., 59 n., 87 n.
Brown, R. E., xi, 2 n., 6 n., 9 n., 32 n., 39 n., 49 n., 50 n., 52 n., 55 n., 57 n., 62 n., 67, 69 n., 81, 102 n., 106 n., 145 n., 157 n., 162 n., 163, 167 n., 169, 170 n., 171 n., 172 n., 174, 176 n., 177 n., 178 n., 186 n., 188, 191 n., 195 n.
Bruce, F. F., 221 n.
Brun, L., 87 n.
Bultmann, R., xi, 1 n., 6 n., 9 n., 13, 14 n., 16, 18 n., 20, 21 n., 22 n., 23 n., 24, 25, 29 n., 30, 32 n., 33, 35, 36, 37, 39, 40, 44f., 49 n., 50, 51, 52, 54 n., 55 n., 57, 58, 60, 62, 64, 65, 66, 67, 68, 69, 70 n., 71f., 73 n., 77, 78 n., 80 n., 84, 89, 91, 92, 93 n., 94,

95, 97, 101 n., 105 n., 106 n., 108, 109, 115, 122 n., 123, 129, 142, 156 n., 161, 167, 173, 174, 180 n., 183, 187, 189, 196 n., 198 n., 199, 200 n., 204, 208, 217 n.
Buse, I., 9 n., 10 n., 113 n., 167 n.

Casey, R. P., 9 n.
Cassian, Bishop (S. Bésobrasoff), 87 n.
Colwell, E. C., 9
Cullman, O., 61 n.

Daube, D., 10 n., 132 n., 149 n.
Delff, H., 1 n.
Derrett, J. D. M., 29 n., 85, 149 n.
Dibelius, M., 1 n., 45, 113 n., 119 n., 134 n., 140 n., 186
Dillon, R. J., 29 n.
Dinkler, E., 29 n., 32 n., 233 n.
Dodd, C. H., xi, 1 n., 9 n., 11 n., 14 n., 29 n., 30 n., 32 n., 34 n., 36 n., 37 n., 45, 47 n., 51, 54 n., 56 n., 57, 59, 60, 62 n., 63, 66, 70 n., 71, 72, 73, 74, 85, 87 n., 92, 101 n., 104 n., 113 n., 114, 115, 118 n., 119, 122 n., 123, 129, 130 n., 134 n., 142, 144 n., 145, 147 n., 149 n., 152, 155, 157, 170, 172 n., 174, 175 n., 176 n., 181 n., 182, 183, 195, 196 n., 200, 233 n.
Dunkerley, R., 74 n.

Eissfeldt, O., 15 n.
Eltester, W., 162 n., 163, 164, 166 n., 175
Emerton, J. A., 94 n.
Eppstein, V., 144 n.

Faure, A., 1 n., 23f., 25, 33
Feuillet, A., 29 n., 31 n., 36 n., 38 n., 94 n.
Freed, E. D., 2 n., 9 n., 13 n., 152 n., 154 n., 172 n.
Fuller, R. H., xi, 24 n., 32 n., 37 n., 48 n., 52 n., 81 n., 108, 147

Gärtner, B., 55 n.
Gardner-Smith,., P 9, 10 n.

273

INDEX OF AUTHORS